The Perfect Name For Your Baby

LORETO TODD is Visiting Professor at the University of Ulster and has lectured worldwide. Educated in Northern Ireland and Leeds, she has degrees in English and Linguistics. She has written more than thirty books, including *Words Apart: A Dictionary of Northern Ireland English* and *The Language of Irish Literature*, as well as the bestselling *Celtic Names For Children* and has edited and contributed to a wide range of journals.

The Perfect Name for Your Baby

Loreto Todd

THE O'BRIEN PRESS
DUBLIN

First published 2008 by The O'Brien Press Ltd,
12 Terenure Road East, Rathgar, Dublin 6, Ireland
Tel. +353 1 4923333; Fax. +353 1 4922777
email: books@obrien.ie
website: www.obrien.ie

ISBN: 978-1-84717-008-8

British Library Cataloguing-in-Publication Data
Todd, Loreto
The perfect name for your baby : over 2,500 names from
around the world : history, meaning, significance
1. Names, Personal - Dictionaries
I. Title
929.4'4

1 2 3 4 5 6 7 8 9 10
08 09 10 11 12

Cover Design: Anú Design
Cover photograph: Getty Images
Editing, typesetting, layout, design: The O'Brien Press Ltd
Printed and bound in the UK by J.H. Haynes & Co Ltd, Sparkford

INTRODUCTION

As soon as your baby is born – and even during the pregnancy – people will want to know, 'What are you calling her/him?' And the reaction to the choice is, like the naming itself, very much a matter of personal taste or experience. You are unlikely to choose a name that belonged to your least favourite relative or is so obscure that the unfortunate child will have to spend their life explaining it. On the other hand, you may want your baby to have a name that will stand out from the crowd. But, and this is the really important thing to remember in the naming process, although *you* have the privilege of naming the baby, it is the infant, blissfully unaware of your choice and unable to have any say in the matter, who will have to carry this name for the rest of his or her days.

Throughout recorded history, people have named their gods, the places where they lived and the individuals who have been significant to them. As soon as human beings developed speech, they gave names to everything that touched their lives: their environment, their food, and the people with whom they came into contact. The *Book of Genesis* gives an early account of naming:

And Adam gave names to all cattle, and to the fowl of the air, and to every beast of the field. Genesis, 2:19-20

There are, literally, hundreds of thousands of names that parents can choose from for their children. Often, children's names have been inspired by the environment – Anamitra, 'the sun', or Arundhati, 'star', Alan, 'rock', Aurora, 'dawn', or Leo, 'lion'; jewels give us Beryl and Jade; from colours we get Bianca, 'white', and Bruno, 'brown'. Sometimes parents choose qualities that they would like to see reflected in their children, such as Agnes, which comes from a Greek adjective meaning 'pure, holy', or 'Casimir' meaning 'bringer of peace' or Felix, 'lucky, happy, fortunate'. Most frequent of all, perhaps, are biblical names, from Abigail to Zara or Adlai to Zachary. Two of the most widely used biblical names throughout the world are Mary and Joseph, names that have been extremely popular in Europe for at least 1500 years.

It might seem a simpler option to follow the example of boxer George Foreman, who has named each of his five sons George, but wouldn't life be so boring, not to mention confusing, without the rich diversity of names that set us apart one from the other?

Over the last twenty years, a number of trends can be seen in the naming of children. One is the incredible popularity of monosyllabic names such as Ben, Fred, Jack, Jake, Joe, Sam for boys. A second is the vogue for a small set of names, including Aaron, Amy, Chloe, Conor, Emma, Ethan, James, Lucy, Luke, Maria, Matthew. A third is the increased popularity of African, Native American and Islamic names. Since 2001, Mohammed, for example, has been between numbers 20 and 26 in the top 100 names in Britain and other variants such as Mohammad also appear in the top 100.

As one set of names becomes popular, another set fades. Michael was in the top ten names for boys in the United States for fifty years in the twentieth century but is currently less in vogue. However, just as today's icicle can be tomorrow's hot water, names that may not seem trendy today may be the height of fashion in the next decade.

The names I have selected for this book come from a wide diversity of cultures. Some will be familiar to you, but you may not have known their origins or significance. Some are internationally popular, occurring in many variants around the world. Others are very localized. Some have historical resonance. Some belonged to famous people – you will find their names in the 'Notable Namesakes' panels. And of course there are the exotics – names whose creation may be uncertain but that simply sound beautiful.

Whatever name you choose for your baby, I hope that it will accompany them in joy, good health and a long life.

Loreto Todd

GIRLS' NAMES

A

ABBEY, ABBIE, ABBY were originally abbreviated forms of *Abigail* but are widely used as names in their own right. Ultimately, they come from Hebrew and may mean 'rejoicing by the father', 'father's joy and exaltation'. One of King David's wives was called *Abigail*.

ABIGAIL is a Hebrew name. It belonged to the wife of Nabal who is described in 1 Samuel 25:3 as *a woman of good understanding, and of a beautiful countenance*. It was popular in the 17th and 18th centuries and seems to be enjoying a 21st-century resurgence. Like many Hebrew names, its precise meaning is uncertain but it relates to the joy and pleasure that a father takes in his new daughter. It has a range of derivatives, including *Abbee, Abbi, Abbs, Abby, Gail, Gale* and *Gayle*.

ABENE (pronounced 'a + bay + nay') is a Ghanaian name meaning 'born on the second day of the week'. An English

equivalent would be *Tuesday*, the name of a 20th-century Hollywood actress, Tuesday Weld, who starred opposite Elvis Presley in *Wild in the Country*.

ABENI (pronounced 'a + bay + nee') sounds like the previous name and it, too, is African. This time, it comes from Nigeria and is a favourite Yoruba name for a longed-for daughter. It means 'we longed for you'.

ABIRA (pronounced 'a + beer + a') is a Hebrew name meaning 'strong'. It is one of the many names by which parents indicate their hopes for a child in the choice they make. *Abira* is easy to pronounce and that can be useful if a person travels.

ADA, ADAH may be an abbreviated form of *Adelaide* or *Adèle* or it may be a modified spelling of the Hebrew name that is more frequently spelt *Adah*. The form *Ada* can be traced back fourteen centuries to a French abbess. If the abbess was using a European name, then it is likely to have been a variant of *adal*, 'noble', also found in *Adolf*, from *adal*, 'noble' + *wolf*, 'wolf'. If she was using a biblical form, then it comes from a Hebrew name meaning 'adornment, embellishment'. Esau's wife was called *Adah* and Lord Byron's daughter was *Ada*.

ADARYN, ADERYN

Welsh names have always been appealing because of their musicality and their meanings. *Aderyn* means 'bird' and, like *Columba* and *Paloma*, suggests that the child will be a free spirit, soaring above difficulties.

ADELA

ADELA is either a reduced form of *Adelaide* or a latinised version of *Adèle*. It comes from a Germanic adjective *adal*, meaning 'noble'.

ADELAIDE

ADELAIDE Many of us associate this name with the Australian city, but it is much older than that. It is a blend of two Germanic elements *adal*, 'noble' and *heid* 'sort, nature', and suggests a nobility of mind and spirit. An early 10th century *Adelaide* was the daughter of King

Rudolph II of Burgundy and wife of the Holy Roman Emperor, the most important ruler in Europe at the time. It was also the name of Queen Adelaide, the wife of William IV of England. The Australian city took its name as a tribute to her in 1836.

ADELAJDA (pronounced 'a + del + eye + da') is an East European form of *Adelaide*.

ADELE, ADÈLE Although these forms are French, the root of the name is the Germanic adjective *adal*, 'noble'. It has been the name of at least one saint and two princesses. William the Conqueror's daughter was called *Adèle*. SEE Edel

ADELINA, ADELINE Both forms are derived from *Adèle* and mean 'noble little one'. They were popular in the 19th and early 20th centuries and there is an American song about 'Sweet Adeline':

> *Sweet Adeline, my Adeline,*
> *At night, dear heart, for you I pine.*
> *In all my dreams*

Your fair face beams.
You're the flower of my heart,
Sweet Adeline.

ADEOLA (pronounced 'a + day + ola') Some African names have become popular in Europe, partly because of African immigration, but also because the names are visually attractive and have meanings that fit into all cultures. *Adeola* , pronounced like 'add' + 'ey' + 'ola', is a Yoruba name implying 'crown of life, princess', a fitting name for any longed-for daughter.

ADERYN SEE Adaryn

ADIBA This Arabic given name means 'cultured, 'refined'. It is unusual but easy to pronounce, making it a possible choice for any family.

ADILA, ADILAH Like *Adiba*, these names are Arabic in origin and mean 'honest, sincere'. They could also be used as a modification of *Adela*, 'noble one'.

ADITI In Hindu mythology, *Aditi* was the mother of all the gods and so worthy of the 'boundless' respect that her name implies. *Aditi* has a prestigious origin and could be shortened to *Adi*.

ADRIANA is a female form of *Adrian*, a name originally derived from the Italian town of Hadria. One well-known *Adriana* appears in Shakespeare's play *The Comedy of Errors*, where she is a loving but feisty wife. Indeed, she is a feminist centuries before her time! When her sister, Luciana, suggests that a wife's duty is to obey her husband, who is her lord and master, Adriana insists that:

There's none but asses will be
bridled so.
(Act 2, Scene 1, line 14)

ADRIENNE is the French female equivalent of *Adrian*. Originally, the name meant 'person from Hadria, in northern Italy'. The town gave its name to the Adriatic Sea, and the Roman Emperor Hadrianus built a wall in the north of England (Hadrian's Wall) in the second century to stop the Scots invading!

AELA is occasionally used as a modified spelling of *Isla*. SEE Isla

AFRICA Place names are often used for girls' names in particular. We find it in *Dakota*, *Kerry* and *Roma*, for example. There was a queen in the Isle of Man in the 12th century called *Africa*. It is not possible, at this stage, to be certain whether she was called after the continent or whether it was a modified form of a Celtic name.

AFTON This is a place name meaning 'settlement by the river', and will probably always be associated with the beautiful song written by Robbie Burns, probably for Mary Campbell:

Flow gently, sweet Afton, among thy green braes,
Flow gently, I'll sing thee a song in thy praise,
My Mary's asleep by thy murmuring stream,
Flow gently, sweet Afton, disturb not her dreams.

Afton is an easy-to-pronounce, gentle name that has become popular in the recent past.

AGATHA comes from a Greek adjective *agathos*, meaning 'honourable, decent, good, virtuous'. Its use in Europe dates back to the 3rd century, when a young Sicilian girl was martyred for her faith. Her feast day was celebrated in February. The novelist Agatha Christie helped to popularise the name in the 20th century. The most widely used variants are *Agathe*, *Aggie* and *Aggy*. The reduced forms *Ags* has been recorded in Australia.

AGNES comes from a Greek adjective *hagnos*, 'pure, holy'. It was the name of an early 4th-century virgin martyr in Rome and, because of its similarity to Latin *agnus*, 'lamb', St Agnes has always been associated with a lamb. It has been popular throughout Europe and appears in such forms as *Agnèce*, *Agnetha*, *Agnethe*, *Inez* and *Nessa* as well as sharing *Aggie* with *Agatha*. *Agnetha* became popular in the 1980s partly as a result of the success of ABBA, whose name was an acronym for *Agnetha*, *Bjorn*, *Benny* and *Anni-Frid*.

AIKO (pronounced 'a + ee + ko') is a Japanese name meaning 'beloved child'. The name is popular in Japan and has recently become more fashionable because of the popularity of the singer-songwriter Aiko Yanai.

AILEEN is an Irish form of *Helen* and an alternative of *Eileen*. Forms of *Helen* occur in many variants worldwide. One of the most comprehensive studies of the myths and legends of the Navaho people in America was written by Aileen O'Bryan. SEE Helen

AILSA is probably of Germanic origin, meaning 'cheerful', but it may also come from Scotland's Ailsa Crag, where it may mean 'island'. Often, when people leave a place, they recreate its well-loved aspects. This may include naming a new place after the old, as in New York and New Zealand, or calling a child after a county, such as Kerry, or after a town, or part of one, as in Roma and Chelsea.

ÁINE (pronounced 'awe + the 'nia' of 'Sonia') Although Áine is regularly used as an Irish form of Anne, it can also have the Gaelic meaning of 'pleasure, agility and melody'.

AINSLEE, AINSLEY, AINSLIE These variants possibly originated in Scotland and may mean 'single poem' or 'one valley'. It also occurs as a surname.

AISHA This name is popular throughout the Islamic world and means 'alive, vibrant'. It is an acknowledgement of the joy of a living child and an appreciation of the fact that one's memory depends largely on one's children. It is usually pronounced like 'a' + 'ee' + 'sha'.

AISLING (pronounced 'ash + ling' or 'ash + lin' or, on occasions, 'ash + leen') appears in a variety of spellings, including *Aislin, Aislinn, Ashling and Ashleen*. It is a Gaelic name meaning 'vision, dream'. It is often given to a longed-for daughter, especially if the other children are boys.

ALANA, ALANNA(H) has two possible sources. It can be a female form of *Alan*, possibly meaning 'rock' or 'cheerful, resourceful'. It can also be a modified spelling of the Gaelic word for 'child', *leanbh* (pronounced 'lan + a' or 'lan + ev') a word that has overtones of 'darling child'.

ALBINKA (pronounced 'al + been + ka') is a Polish name that may come from one of the many Latin place names *Alba*, 'white, fair'. (The Irish name for Scotland is also *Alba* but, although the first English martyr was called *Albanus*, it is unlikely that this fact has influenced Polish parents.)

ALDONA is also a Polish name, meaning 'with the wisdom of age'. It fits in with a contemporary taste for such names as *Iona*, *Rona* and *Winona*.

ALBERTA is a female form of *Albert*, which is a combination of two Germanic elements, *adal*, 'noble' and *beorht*, 'bright, light, splendid'. The male form was extremely popular throughout the 19th-century British Empire because it was the name of Queen Victoria's husband. The name *Alberta* was given to a Canadian province in 1905. It was called after the borough of St. Albert, near Edmonton, which had been named after its founder, Father Albert Lacombe. Many expatriate Canadian *Albertas* are called after the province.

ALEGRIA is a well-liked Spanish name meaning 'cheerfulness, happiness', and it could prove a popular choice for parents who may, for example, want to honour an *Alice*, while giving their daughter an unusual alternative. *Allegra*, also meaning 'cheerfulness', is beginning to be more widely used in English-speaking communities.

ALEXA is one of several names based on the Greek verb *alexein*, 'to defend', and so it can be interpreted as 'defender, helper'. *Alexa* was originally an abbreviated form of *Alexandra* but it is now used as a name in its own right. It is popular among East Europeans because of the honour paid in the Orthodox Church to the 5th-century Saint Alexis.

ALEXANDRA was the name of the wife of King Edward VII of England and her position encouraged a growth in its popularity at the beginning of the 20th century. *Alexandra* is, of course, a female form of *Alexander*, which means 'defender of mankind'. The most famous bearer of this name was Alexander the Great of Macedonia (356-323 BC) who died at the age of thirty-three, but not before he had conquered most of the known world. There are many female forms of *Alexander* and that is only to be expected, perhaps, in that the original Greek compound, *alexein*, 'to defend' and *andros*, 'mankind', was originally a title of the Greek Goddess, Hera.

ALEXIS was originally a boy's name, like *Evelyn*, *Hilary* and *Vivien*, but it is now used almost

exclusively for girls in the English-speaking world. It comes from Greek *alexein*, 'to defend'. Its use in Polish communities is linked to respect for a 5th-century saint, also called Alexius.

ALFREDA is usually chosen by parents to honour an *Alfred*, but there was an 8th-century English saint called *Alfreda*. Her name may be a blend of *ælf*, 'fairy, elf', and *ræd*, 'counsel, advice', or of *athol*, 'noble', and *fleda*, 'beauty'. We cannot be certain because her name appears in at least six different versions. She was the daughter of King Offa of Mercia, in the English midlands, who built 'Offa's Dyke' as a means of limiting Welsh forays into his kingdom.

ALICE Few parents who select this name for their child realise that, like *Adelaide*, it comes from a Germanic name, *Adalheidis*, meaning 'noble kind, noble nature'. The Normans took the name to the British Isles, where it was popular in several forms, including *Alicia*, *Alyce*, *Alys* and *Elise*. It enjoyed a wave of popularity in the 19th century, partly because it was a favourite with the royal family and partly because of Lewis Carroll's *Alice's Adventures in Wonderland* (1865) and its sequel, *Through the Looking Glass* (1872). Its popularity faded in the mid-20th century but it became re-established as a favourite in the last decade of the 20th century.

ALICIA SEE Alice

ALIENA (pronounced 'ali + yen + a') This created name was first used by Shakespeare in *As You Like It*. Celia, the Duke's daughter, adopts it when she leaves the court to accompany her banished cousin, Rosalind, in her journey through the Forest of Arden. The name suggests 'a person in exile', 'one living in a strange land'.

ALIMA is an Arabic name for a daughter. It means 'musically gifted'.

ALISHA is an Indian name that looks and sounds like a form of *Alicia*. It means 'protected' and could function as an alternative to *Alice*.

ALINA This is sometimes used as an alternative spelling of *Alana*, and sometimes as a variant of *Lena*. SEE Alana, Lena

ALISON is a Norman diminutive of *Alice* and so means 'noble nature'. It was an extremely popular name in the 14th and 15th centuries but almost died out in England, although it continued to be in style in Scotland. It is currently experiencing a new wave of popularity. SEE Alice

ALLEGRA SEE Alegria

ALMA It is not often that children are called after battles. To the best of my knowledge, there are no *Waterloos* or *Trafalgars*, although Trafalgar is a possible contender. The Crimean War of the mid-19th century gave the English language the phrase 'the lady with the lamp' for Florence Nightingale, 'balaclava' for a woollen cover for the head and neck, and *Alma* for daughters, in celebration of an 1854 victory, when the

Anglo-French forces defeated the Russians at the battle of the river Alma, in Crimea. *Alma* can also be from Latin, meaning 'generous, loving, nourishing', and Lord Byron wrote poetry in celebration of Egyptian dancing girls called *almas*.

ALTHEA In Greek mythology, Althea was given a fiery torch when her son, Meleager, was born. She was advised that the child's life was linked to the life of the fire. As long as she preserved it, her son would live. Althea tended the flame assiduously until her son was twenty, but then Meleager slew Althea's brothers and she destroyed the torch in anger, causing her son's death. It is not certain what the name means although it may be related to *aletheia*, 'truth'.

ALVERA is a feminine form of the Old English name, *Ælf*, 'elf, fairy, supernatural being' + *here*, 'army'. It is also a variant of the Spanish name *Alvara*, 'totally reliable'.

ALYSIA SEE Alice

AMA African children are often given 'day names', commemorating the day on which they are born. This one means 'born the day before the Sabbath, Saturday'. *Ama* can also be in honour of a parent's mother. In many languages, the word for 'mother' includes the syllable 'ma'.

AMALA has two sources and two meanings. In Arabic it implies 'hope' and in Sanskrit it suggests 'pure'.

AMANDA This name comes from the Latin verb *amare*, 'to love', and means 'worthy of being loved'. It came into being in the 17th century and was possibly influenced by Shakespeare's *Miranda*, a character in *The Tempest*. A popular abbreviated form is *Mandy*.

AMARA This can be an alternative form of *Amala*. The 'l' and 'r' are closely related in many languages. English 'Harry' has been reduced to 'Hal' and 'Terry' to 'Tel' and, in Holland, the

Amstel River runs through Amsterdam. *Amara* can also be from Greek and mean 'everlastingly beautiful'. SEE Amala

AMBER comes from an Arabic word, *anbar*, meaning 'ambergris', a substance frequently used in perfume. *Amber* now refers to the resin that is used in jewellery. Although it does not come from the same root as *ambrosios*, 'immortal', it is sufficiently similar in sound and so a child named *Amber* may be thought of as an eternal jewel.

AMELIA It seems likely that *Amelia* is a blend of two names, Germanic *Amalia*, meaning 'industrious', and Latin *Emelia*, 'rival'. It has been a name in its own right since the 18th century. One of the most famous bearers of this name was Amelia Earhart (1897-1937), who was a pioneer aviator. She became the first woman to fly across the Atlantic in 1928. In 1932, she flew the same journey solo and established a new transatlantic record of 13 hours and 30 minutes. In 1937, Amelia set out with a navigator to fly around the world. They flew successfully from the USA to South America, to Africa, Asia and Australia. On one of the last legs of the journey, from Papua New Guinea, contact with the plane was lost.

AMIRA is a well-loved Arabic name, meaning 'princess'. It is occasionally spelt *Ameera* to reflect the pronunciation. It is a title of honour and is the female equivalent of Arabic *amir*, 'leader, prince, military commander'. This word has been written *emir* in English since 1625.

AMY looks very modern but it has an extremely long history. It comes from the Latin verb *amare*, 'to love', and means 'beloved, loved one'. The mother-in-law of Aeneas, who escaped the Trojan War and is reputed to be the founder of Rome, had a form of this name. The modern English usage almost certainly comes from *Aimée*, which is from the French form of the Latin verb.

ANASTASIA The Greek root of this name is *anastasis*, 'resurrection'. The earliest use of the name can be traced to a 4th-century saint who was martyred in Sirmium, Dalmatia, in the Balkans. This saint is unique in the Roman calendar in that she is specially remembered in the second mass of Christmas Day because she was reputed to have died on December 25. Although the Sirmium link accounts for her popularity in Eastern Europe, the name became popular in Western Europe because of the story of Anastasia, a daughter of the last Czar of Russia. His family was assassinated by the Bolsheviks in 1918, but rumours suggested that one of the daughters, Anastasia, survived. A woman claiming to be Anastasia turned up in Germany in 1920. Many people believed that she was, indeed, the Russian princess. A film of her story, starring Ingrid Bergman and Yul Brynner, was made in 1956 and a fantasy animation version with Meg Ryan's voice as Anastasia's was released in 1997. The name has given rise to *Stacey*.

ANASTAZJA This is a Polish form of *Anastasia*. SEE Anastasia

ANDREA is a feminine form of *Andrew*, the name of the apostle who was the brother of Simon Peter and who was probably executed for his beliefs while preaching in Asia Minor. It is likely that *Andrew* is derived from Greek *andr-*, 'man, warrior' and so a feminine equivalent would be 'womanly, having all the qualities appropriate to a woman, such as gentleness, courage, loyalty, devotion to family'. SEE Andrew

ANGELA has been popular in the English-speaking world since the 18th century although the name goes back to ancient Greek, where it meant 'messenger' and, more particularly, 'messenger of the gods'. The Greek noun, latinised as *angelus*, was a translation of Hebrew *malak*, meaning 'God's messenger'.

ANGELICA is the name of a

herb that was called both *herba angelica* and *root of the Holy Ghost*. It has been cultivated in England since the 16th century because of its reputed value against poison and plague. It is not unusual for a child to be named after a herb or plant. Apart from *Angelica*, we have, for example, *Rosemary* and *Basil*. Many parents who call their daughter *Angelica* think of it as a variant of *Angela*.

ANGELINA is a diminutive form of *Angela*. SEE Angela

ANGHARAD This Welsh name has been popular since the Middle Ages, when Angharad of the Golden Hand featured in the *Mabinogion*. It is pronounced 'an + harrad'. It is like *Amy* in meaning 'beloved, greatly loved' although it may also imply 'without reproach'. Whichever meaning one prefers, this is a popular choice for a daughter.

ANIA is one of the many forms of *Anne*. It is particularly popular among Eastern Europeans. SEE Anne

ANIELA This is a Polish form of *Angela*. SEE Angela

ANITA was originally Spanish and meant 'little Anne, little graceful one'. It is widely used in English-speaking communities. SEE Anne

ANJALI (pronounced 'an + ja + lee') is a Hindu form of *angel*. Although it retains its meaning of 'messenger', it also carries the connotation of 'with godlike qualities'. SEE Angela

ANKA is a diminutive form of *Anne* that is particularly popular with Polish parents. SEE Anne

ANN Until Victorian times, *Ann* was more widespread in England than *Anne*, which was more popular on the continent. The form with 'e' has almost completely ousted *Ann*, except in blends such as *Mary-Ann* or *Sarah-Ann*, although even here, the *Anne* form is more popular. SEE Anne

ANNA For most people, *Anna* is a Latin form of the Hebrew name which is closer to *Hannah*

and means 'gracious'. Like *Ann*, *Anna* is currently less widely used than *Anne*, except in such blends as *Anna-Maria* or *Anna-Lucia*. SEE Anne

ANNABEL Like *Christabel*, *Mirabel* and *Isabel*, this name has become more popular in the recent past. It has two possible origins. It may be a combination of *Anne* 'gracious' + French *belle*, 'beautiful', or a form of an older name *Amabel(le)* meaning 'loved' + 'beautiful'. Whatever its exact origin, the name is popular and may be reduced to either *Anna* or *Bel/Bella*. SEE Belle

ANNE has been a popular name throughout Europe for almost two thousand years and its Hebrew source, *Hannah*, was widely used for centuries before that. The Hebrew name means 'gracious, graceful' and its early Christian popularity was due to the belief that it was the name of the Blessed Virgin Mary's mother. Anne occurs in a variety of forms including *Áine*, *Ana*, *Aña*, *Ann*, *Anna*, *Annette*, *Annie*, *Annika*, *Annike*, *Anita*, *Anya*, *Enya*, *Hanna*, *Hannah*, *Nan*, *Nana*, *Nancy*, *Nanette* and *Nanetta*, as well as in such compounds as *Anne-Marie* and *Mary-Anne*. It has been used for princesses, saints, film stars and people of every rank and class. It is usually written *Anne* in Germany but pronounced closer to *Anna*.

ANNEKE/ANNIKA/ ANNIKE These forms are popular in Holland and Scandinavia and are diminutive forms of *Anne*. SEE Anne

ANNETTE started as a French form meaning 'little, gracious one' but it has been popular outside France for centuries. SEE Anne

ANNIE is a pet form of *Anne* and was exceptionally popular during the 1990s. SEE Anne

ANTHEA Flower names for girls have been popular in all ages and in all cultures. *Anthea* is Greek in origin and comes from *antheios*, 'flowery, like a flower'. (It has the same origin as 'anther', the part of the plant containing the pollen.) One of the attractions of *Anthea* is that it gives a girl scope to call herself *Anne* and *Thea* as well as the full form. Often *Thea* is a reduced form of *Dorothea*, 'gift of God', but it works equally well for *Anthea*. SEE Anne, Dorothea

ANTOINETTE is a French feminine form of *Antoine*, more usually *Anthony* in English and *Anton* in Germany. All the variants come from the Latin *Antonius*, which is an extremely

NAMES FROM FLOWERS AND PLANTS
Dahlia, Daisy
Erica, Heather (mean the same)
Holly, Hyacinth
Iris, Ivy
Jacek (means Hyacinth, very popular in Polish communities)
Jasmine, Jonquil
Laurel, Lily
Pansy, Peaches, Poppy, Primrose
Viola, Violet

old Italian family name. Its meaning is uncertain but it may mean 'without equal'. It has also sometimes been associated with Greek *antheios*, 'like a flower', but this seems unlikely. One of the best-known holders of this name was Marie-Antoinette, the 18th-century Queen of France.

ANTONIA This is a female form of Latin *Antonius* and, unlike *Anthony*, which introduced an 'h' into the spelling, *Antonia* is closer to the Latin original. Like *Antoinette*, it has given rise to the popular abbreviations *Toni*, *Tony* and it has also generated *Tonia*, which is also sometimes used as a variant of *Tania*. SEE Tania

ANTONINA is a diminutive of *Antonia*. SEE Antonia

AOBH (pronounced 'eve' or can rhyme with 'save') is an Irish name meaning 'beauty'. It is sometimes used as an equivalent of *Eve*. SEE Eve

ANYA is a form of *Anna* used mostly in Eastern Europe but becoming popular throughout the English-speaking world. SEE Anne

AOIFE (pronounced 'ee + fa') is a traditional Irish name that is probably related to *aoibh*, 'exceptional beauty'. It started to become popular in Ireland in the 1960s and has increased in popularity each decade since then. It is often equated with *Eva* because of the pronunciation but the similarity is fortuitous.

APHRA With this name, we are in uncertain territory but there are a few claims that we can make. First, it may be related to *Afra*, a name that was used in Roman times to refer to a North African woman. Second, it came to be used of a woman with a dark complexion or dark hair and is thus similar in implication to Ireland's *Ciara*. Thirdly, it may refer to a place mentioned in the *Book of Micah*, Chapter 1, verse 10:

> *Declare ye it not at Gath; weep ye not at all; in the house of Aphrah, roll thyself in the dust.*

Fourthly, it is sometimes related to Aphrodite who was the Greek equivalent of Venus and whose name means 'born of the foam of the sea'. Aphra Behn (1640-89) was the first woman in England to make her living as a professional writer. She was a highly successful dramatist and wrote an early novel dealing with Surinam and the slave trade. She was buried in Westminster Abbey.

APRIL is one of three months frequently used as girls' names, the other two being *May* and *June*. These three months represent Nature at its most promising and this may account for their popularity. *August* has, more recently, joined the group of months used as given names. *April* probably comes from a Latin verb *aperire*, 'to open'. April was the first month of the old Roman calendar and so it 'opened' the year. The French equivalent *Avril* has also been widely used although its popularity may not depend entirely on its reference to the month. SEE Avril

ARABELLA like many

long-established names, has several possible origins. It may be a blend of Greek *Ara*, a goddess, and *bella*, 'beautiful'. It may also come from Latin *ora*, 'pray' + the ending *–bilis*, 'able to', and would thus mean 'able to be prayed to' or, less prosaically, 'adorable'. The *Bel(la)* ending is also found in *Annabel(la)* and *Christabel(la)*. *Arabella* was, for centuries, more popular in Scotland than in other parts of the world and was the given name of royalty, including Arabella Stuart, niece of Mary Queen of Scots.

ARETA/ARETHA may come from either a Greek or an Arabic source, but in both traditions it means 'virtuous'. It was made popular by Aretha Franklin, the so-called 'Queen of Soul', whose records have been popular since the late 1960s. The form without 'h' is sometimes shortened to *Reta*.

ARIA comes from Italian and is the same word as 'air'. Like *Carmen*, 'song', it has been used as a name for a girl who is as beautiful as a melody.

ARIDNA/ARIADNE owes its origin to Greek mythology. The name means 'very holy one, blessed one' and, although it does not look it, it is related to *Agnes*. Ariadne was the daughter of King Minos of Crete. She saved the life of Theseus, who was able to escape from a maze because of the ball of thread she gave him. The form ending in 'a' is more typical of Spain and Poland. *Arianna* is an Italian version of the name, whereas *Arienne* is most likely to occur in France. SEE Agnes

ARIELLA is occasionally used as a female form of *Ariel*, a Hebrew name meaning 'lion of God'. It can also be derived from Arabic *aryel*, 'gazelle'. Ariel is also a spirit character in Shakespeare's *The Tempest*. He is capable of producing such beautiful music that no one can resist it. One of the moons of Uranus is called *Ariel*.

ARINA is a Russian form of *Irene*. SEE Irene

ARISU is a Japanese form of *Alice*. SEE Alice

ARLENE It is uncertain where this name developed or what it means, although the likelihood is that it is Celtic and means 'binding promise'. It has many variants, including *Arleen*, *Arlina*, *Arline* and *Arlyn*. It has been suggested that contemporary *Arlene* is a creation based on such names as *Charlene* and *Marlene*.

ARLETTA/ARLETTE This name has sometimes been described as a pet form of *Arlene* and, although that possibility cannot be ruled out, it has another likely source. The Normans used the name to mean 'little eagle' and it became popular because it was the name of William the Conqueror's mother.

ARTEMESIA/ ARTEMISIA is a variant of *Artemis*, the name of the Greek goddess of the moon and hunting and of safe childbirth. (The Roman equivalent is *Diana*.) It

probably comes from a Greek adjective meaning 'safe'. A variant of the name, *Artemisia*, is an aromatic plant. The 4th-century Artemesia built a mausoleum in honour of her dead husband. The mausoleum was one of the seven wonders of the ancient world and was even more famous in its day as a symbol of undying love than the Taj Mahal is today.

ARUNDHATI (pronounced 'a + roon + da + tee') is a widely used Hindi name for a star. It has a long history and may come ultimately from a Sanskrit word meaning 'unbound, unrestricted'.

ASHIRA is a Hebrew name meaning 'blessed'. It is the feminine form of *Asher*, the son of the Patriarch, Jacob. It has been suggested, too, that *Ashira* was a Middle Eastern goddess whose name may have meant 'sea-walker'. The link with the sea associates her with both Aphrodite and Venus. SEE Aphra

ASHLEIGH/ASHLEY This was originally a surname meaning

'clearing where the ash trees were' or 'ash wood' and it became first a boy's name and then a girl's. It is one of the very few names that is still used as much for boys as girls. In Ireland, it is sometimes used as a variant of *Aisling*.

ASIA can be a place name, in which case it comes from a very old word possibly meaning 'east'. Children of migrant parents often name their children after their place of origin. We find this tendency in names as disparate as *Brittany*, *India* and *Jordan*. *Asia* is also a Polish pet form of *Joanna* meaning 'God is gracious'.

ASTRA is one of the many names meaning 'star' or 'starlike'. It comes from Greek and has the same root as 'astronomy'.

ASTRID is one of several Scandinavian names that became popular in the 20th century. It comes from combining two Norse elements *ans*, 'god', and *fríðr* 'beautiful'. Because of its similarity to *Astra*, it is also sometimes linked to 'star'.

ATALYA is more popular in Spanish-speaking communities but it has spread into English-speaking communities in parts of the United States. It means 'protector, custodian' and suggests that the child will preserve and honour her heritage.

ATARA is one of the hundreds of Hebrew-inspired names in the language. This one means 'crown' and implies that the child is the jewel in the family, a mark of honour and achievement.

ATHENA is the name of the Greek goddess to whom the city of Athens was dedicated. She was the daughter of Zeus and was linked to the owl, the symbol of wisdom. The meaning of her name is uncertain but it is believed to be a combination of an adjective meaning 'sharp' and a noun suggesting 'praise, admiration'.

AUDREY is an Old English name meaning 'noble strength'. It has been the name of a 6th-century saint, a character in

Shakespeare's *As You Like It* and an influential 20th-century film icon, Audrey Hepburn.

NAMES THAT MEAN PRINCESS

Adeola (Yoruba)
Amira (Arabic)
Elmira (Arabic)
Orfhlaith/Orla (Irish)
Sara(h) (Hebrew)

AUGUSTA is a feminine form of Latin *Augustus*, meaning 'great, auspicious', a name that probably owes its origin to the verb *augere*, 'to increase, magnify'. It is a strong, noble name, quite a lot for a little girl to live up to.

AUGUSTINA is a popular diminutive variant of *Augusta* and suggests less solemnity. It also allows for the abbreviation *Tina*.

AUNE is a Finnish form of *Agnes*. SEE Agnes

AURELIA This ancient Latin name comes from the adjective *aureus*, 'golden'. It could be

selected for a golden-haired little girl. It has the abbreviated form *Aura*, which is a Greek word meaning 'gentle breeze' and has the modern meaning of an emanation that surrounds an individual and which mystics believe contains the essence or 'soul' of an individual.

AURORA was the Roman goddess of the morning and the word translates directly as 'dawn'. It has overtones of 'golden dawn' and is an alternative to the popular *Dawn*. SEE Dawn

AVA was given a boost in second half of the 20th century by the popularity of the film star Ava Gardner. It is likely that the name is a modified form of Hebrew *Eve*, meaning 'breath', but it has a number of alternative etymologies. It may come from a Persian name meaning 'water' or from Latin *avis*, 'bird'. Wherever it comes from, it has been used in Europe since the 9th century, when it was recorded as the name of a saintly abbess. SEE Eve, Havah

AVELINE is probably a French diminutive of the Hebrew name *Aviva*, meaning 'springtime', although the first syllable may be from an old Germanic noun, *eofor*, 'boar', and the name would thus suggest strength, courage and determination. It is also possible that it has been influenced by Latin *avis*, 'bird, free spirit'. SEE Ava, Aviva, Avril

AVIVA is a beautiful Hebrew name meaning 'spring' and suggesting 'optimism and hope'. It is growing in popularity and may sometimes be considered a variant of *Eva*. If an abbreviation of this name is required, a parent or child may use *Viv*.

AVRIL For most people, *Avril* is the French form of the fourth month and so is equivalent to *April*. Like most names, however, this one has hidden depths. It has a history that goes back long before the 11th-century Norman Conquest and is a form of *eofor*, 'boar' + *hild*, 'battle'. This meaning may not seem appropriate to a baby girl but it suggests courage, strength and

endurance, qualities that most parents would find appealing.

AWENA comes from a Welsh word for 'poetry' and the meaning links the name with *Aria* and *Carmen*. SEE Carmen

AYAKA is a Japanese name meaning 'colourful flower'. Flowers have long been associated with girls. We have scores of them from many cultures and may think of *Daisy*, *Hyacinth*, *Lily*, *Rose* and *Violet*.

AYLEN could be an alternative to *Aileen*, which comes ultimately from *Helen*. *Aylen* is a Native American name meaning 'happiness'. It is moving into mainstream American English because of its meaning and as a method of preserving the culture of the original Americans. SEE Aileen, Helen

AZARIA is one of the names with 'Z' that are currently popular. This one has an ancient pedigree. It is from Hebrew and means 'God has been my helper'. It was originally a man's name. In fact, it was the Hebrew equivalent of *Abednego*, who was thrown into the fiery furnace in Babylon but survived the ordeal. It is sometimes abbreviated to *Zara*.

NOTABLE NAMESAKES
Agnetha Fältskog (b.1950) member of Swedish group ABBA; Anne Frank (1929-1945) Jewish Holocaust victim famous for her Diary; Aretha Franklin (b.1942) American soul singer; Arundhati Roy (b.1961) Booker prizewinning Indian novelist; Ava Gardner (1922-90) film actress and inspiration for Frank Sinatra's song 'I am a fool to want you'.

B

BABETTE is an abbreviation of *Barbara*, 'foreign, unfamiliar'. SEE Barbara

BABS is a popular abbreviation of *Barbara*, 'foreign, unfamiliar'. SEE Barbara

BAHIYA (pronounced 'ba + he + ya') is from an Arabic adjective meaning 'beautiful'. Many Arab names for girls have three syllables and end in 'a'. *Bahiya* fits into the same category as *Basima*, *Fatima* and *Ayisha*.

BAKOA is a Ghanaian name that means 'first child' and implies great joy that the family will continue.

BAI is a Chinese name meaning 'white'. It tends to be pronounced with two syllables, as in 'ba + ee'.

BAIBÍN (pronounced 'bab + een') is an Irish pet form of *Barbara*. SEE Barbara

BÁIRBRE (pronounced 'bawr + bra') is an Irish form of *Barbara*. SEE Barbara

BAPTISTA is widely used in southern European communities. The name comes from a Greek verb meaning 'immerse, wash, bathe'. It has taken on the Christian meaning of 'the symbolic act of initiating one as a Christian'. *Baptista* means 'the baptised girl' and it occurs in such variants as *Baptiste, Batista* and *Battista*.

BARBARA comes from a Greek adjective *barbaros*, 'foreign'. The name has been popular throughout Europe largely due to the legend of St Barbara. She was, according to one version of the story, a beautiful girl who wanted to dedicate her life to Christ. Her father had her imprisoned and murdered, but he was then killed by a lightning strike. Barbara is the patron saint of architects, geologists and stonemasons. The form *Barbra* has been popularised by the singer and actress Barbra Streisand.

BASIMA comes from an Arabic word meaning 'smiling, cheerful'.

BATHSHEBA This Hebrew name means 'daughter of the oath'. (Hebrew names beginning with *Bar* mean 'son of' and those

beginning with *Bat* mean 'daughter of'.) It is not widely chosen as a given name but it is well known because the biblical *Bathsheba* was the wife of David and the mother of Solomon, as well as being exceptionally beautiful.

BEATA (pronounced 'bay + a + ta'or 'bee + a + ta') comes from Latin *beata*, 'blessed'. It is widely used in Catholic countries and is sometimes modified to *Beatie* or *Beaty*.

BEATRICE/BEATRIX This name started life as *Viatrix*, 'one making a journey through life', and it was widely used in the early Christian church. It was often associated with 'Beata', the Latin word for 'blessed', as in 'Beata Viatrix', and the two words were blended into *Beatrix* or *Beatrice*. There was a 4th-century martyr called *Beatrice*. The name, with the 'x' ending has been used by European royalty and was chosen by the parents of Beatrix Potter (1866-1943), the author and illustrator, creator of such characters as Peter Rabbit and Jemima Puddleduck, who first designed children-sized books for children.

BECKY is an abbreviated form of *Rebecca*. SEE Rebecca

BEDELIA There are conflicting views about the origins of *Bedelia*. It has been suggested that it is a modified form of Irish *Bríd*, a name that is linked with fire and light and probably means 'vigour, vitality, virtue'. It is also possible that *Bedelia* is a blend of *Bríd* and *Celia*, meaning 'heavenly', or of *Bríd* and *Delia*, a name of the goddess Aphrodite. If we link the three names together, then *Bedelia* implies heavenly beauty and virtue.

BELA is occasionally used as an alternative spelling for *Bella*, 'the beautiful one'. It also occurs in Serbia and means 'white'.

BELINDA This well-liked girl's name was first recorded in a play by John Vanbrugh in 1697 (*The Provoked Wife*), and was used again in 1712 by the poet

Alexander Pope in *The Rape of the Lock*. Its meaning is uncertain. It may be a blend of *Bella* and *Linda* and would thus mean 'beautiful shield' or a blend of *Bella* and *Lucinda*, suggesting 'beauty and light'.

BELITA is a Spanish diminutive meaning 'beautiful little one'. SEE Bella

BELLA For many parents, *Bella* is an abbreviation of *Isabella*, which is an Italian form of *Isabel*, which comes ultimately from *Elizabeth*, 'God is my oath'. *Bella* is also an Italian adjective meaning 'beautiful' and it is thus a name in its own right. The French equivalent *Belle* also occurs.

BENEDICTA is a female form of *Benedict* which comes from two sources, although both derive from Latin *Benedictus*, meaning 'blessed, well spoken'. The first comes from the Hail Mary where Our Lady is addressed in Latin as *Benedicta tu in mulieribus*, 'Blessed are you among women'. The second is from Saint Benedict, who was an Italian monk and founder of the Benedictines. The name has been selected by sixteen popes. Alternative variants are *Benedetta* and *Benedikta*.

BENITA is found in most Spanish-speaking communities. It is a diminutive and means 'blessed little girl'. SEE Benedicta

BENOITE (pronounced 'ben + wat') is a French diminutive form of *Benedicta*. SEE Benedicta

BERENICE is from Greek *Pherenike* meaning 'the bringer of victory'. One of Alexander the Great's generals was called Ptolemy. When Alexander died, Ptolemy declared himself king of Egypt, and his descendants ruled Egypt for almost 300 years until Cleopatra committed suicide in 30 BC. The Ptolemy dynasty frequently used this name for their daughters. The form *Bernice* is now slightly more widespread than *Berenice*. *Bernie* is occasionally used as an abbreviation.

BERNADETTE is a feminine diminutive of *Bernard*, which is a

Germanic name meaning 'brave bear'. St Bernard was a French monk who died in AD1081. He founded hospices for travellers crossing the Alps. *Bernadette* became world famous after 1858, when a young French girl, Bernadette Soubirous, experienced a series of visions of Our Lady in Lourdes in southwest France, now a major place of Christian pilgrimage. SEE Bernard

BERNADINE is, like *Bernadette*, a female diminutive of *Bernard* and so means 'brave little bear'. SEE Bernard

BERNICE is a contracted form of *Berenice* but widely used as a full name in its own right. SEE Berenice

BERTHA is a Germanic name, based on the same word that has given us modern 'bright'. It has been used in Europe for well over 1000 years but was given a new lease of life in the 19th century when it became extremely popular in Germany. According to German legend, *Bertha* is a benign character who tiptoes into rooms where babies are crying and gently rocks them to sleep.

BERYL is one of a number of jewels that became popular as girls' names. They include *Amber*, *Emerald*, *Jade*, *Pearl* and *Ruby*. The implication of all of them is that the child is more beautiful and more precious than any jewel. The name is found in Indian, Arabic and European traditions. Although it has the theoretic appeal of other gems, its use may have declined because the gemstone is no longer widely known. In many traditions, the gemstone is associated with good luck.

BESS is one of the numerous abbreviated forms of *Elizabeth*, which comes originally from Hebrew and means 'dedicated to God' or 'my God is abundance'. It became widely used during the reign of Elizabeth 1 (1558-1603). She was often referred to as 'Good Queen Bess'. An earlier holder of the name was Bess of Hardwick, who supervised the building of Hardwick Hall in Derbyshire. Like many women, she wanted a lot of light in her house and insisted on so much glass that her home was described as 'Hardwick Hall – more glass than wall'. SEE Elizabeth

BETH is an abbreviated form of *Elizabeth* and indicates a devotion and dedication to God. The name became extremely popular in the 19th and 20th centuries, due in part to the character of Beth March in Louisa M. Alcott's book *Little Women*. SEE Elizabeth

BETHAN is a relatively modern name. It may be a blend of *Beth* and *Ann* and would thus imply dedication to God and receiving God's favour. It may also be an abbreviated form of *Bethany*, which is the name of a town close to Jerusalem. The word *beth* can occur in both Arabic and Hebrew with the meaning of 'house, settlement'. SEE Anne, Elizabeth

BETHANY In the New Testament, the town of Bethany

is mentioned by all four evangelists. It seems to mean 'house of dates', presumably because dates were grown in the area. Jesus spent some time in Bethany before going to Jerusalem where he was crucified.

BETSY is another of the numerous abbreviated forms of *Elizabeth*, which comes originally from Hebrew and means 'dedicated to God' or 'my God is abundance'. *Betsy* seems to be a cross between *Betty* and *Bess* or a pet form of the name based on such rhymes as 'itsy bitsy'. One of the best-known characters in literature is Betsy Trotwood, the aunt of David Copperfield in the novel by Charles Dickens. SEE Elizabeth

BETTE is an abbreviated form of *Elizabeth*, which comes from Hebrew and means either 'dedicated to God' or 'my God is abundance'. The film stars Bette Davis and Bette Midler have created a fashion for this particular variant. It is sometimes pronounced like *Bet* and other

times like *Betty*. SEE Elizabeth

BETTY It seems very likely that in the 16th and early 17th centuries, many people pronounced *Elizabeth* as if it ended in *Bet*. This ending gave rise to *Betty* and helped in the formation of *Betsy*. It is a widespread custom among English-speaking people to use '-ie/-y' as affectionate diminutives. Many names have such endings and we even do it with *doggie* and *pussy*. SEE Elizabeth

BEULAH (pronounced 'byoo + la') In the Old Testament prophecies, *Beulah* is the name given to Zion when it is totally at one with God. In the *Book of Isaiah*, Chapter 62: 4 says:

> *Thou shalt no more be termed Forsaken; neither shall thy land any more be termed Desolate; but thou shalt be called Hephzibah, and thy land Beulah, for the Lord delighteth in thee, and thy land shall be married.*

Beulah means 'married' so this is an example of wordplay. The

name *Beulah* was thought
by many in the 17th century
to apply to 'heaven' and this
is when it began to be used as a
girl's name.

BEVERLEY/BEVERLY is a

place name in Yorkshire that
comes from Old English *beofor*,
'beaver' + *leac*, 'river, stream'. It
was used first as a surname, then
as a male name but recently it
has become almost exclusively
female in usage. This is
particularly true of *Beverly*.

BHAVANI/BHAVYA These

Indian names have been used to
refer to the goddess Parvati, and
the parents who select them are
making a wish that their
daughter may be as beautiful and
as cherished as a goddess.

BIANCA is an Italian name

meaning 'white, pure'.
Shakespeare uses *Bianca* for
female characters in plays with
an Italian setting. The name is in
no way limited to Italy now but
occurs in all parts of the
English-speaking world. A variant
form, *Blanca*, is also used.

BIBIANA occurs as a Spanish

and Italian form of *Viviana* or
Vivian, and means 'lively'. Saint
Bibiana (Viviana, Vivian, Vibiana)
was a 4th-century Roman virgin
and martyr. SEE Vivian.

BIDDIE/BIDDY is a reduced

form of Bridget. In the late 19th
and early 20th centuries, there
were so many maids and
housekeepers with this name
that *Biddy* became a generic
name for this type of female
worker. In Eugene O'Neill's 1953
play *More Stately Mansions*, Act 2,
Scene 3, had the line:

*A mother of children, our Irish
biddy nurse girl and house servant.*
SEE Bridget

BILLIE used to be regarded as a

boy's name, an abbreviated
version of *William*. In the late
20th century, a group of male
diminutives started to be used
almost exclusively for girls. They
include *Billie* and *Charlie*. The
meaning implies 'protection'. SEE
Wilhelmina, William

BINA is one of those names

that can be used in Africa with

the meaning of 'dance', in India
with the meaning of 'musical
instrument' and in English as a
reduced form of *Sabina*. SEE
Sabina

BLAINE is a Celtic name that
is growing in popularity. It seems
likely that it comes from Gaelic
bléan, 'arrow, hollow', or it may
imply 'whiteness, fairness'. It is
also possible that it is one of the
many names in a variety of
languages that begin with 'Bl'
and relate to flowers, for
example, *Blodwyn*, 'white flower',
from Welsh, *Blossom* from English
or *Blume* from German.

BLANCHE is derived from a
French adjective meaning 'white,
fair'. The name implies both
'beautiful' and 'pure'. The name
is frequently found in the
southern states of America but it
has been popular since the
Middle Ages. Other variants are
Bianca and, less frequently,
Blanca.

BLODWYN is Welsh and
means 'white flower'. It has
various spellings, including

Blodwen and *Blodwin*. The
choice of Welsh names by
Welsh parents spread in the
second half of the 20th century
and many non-Welsh people
were attracted to the names and
to the long history behind them.

BO comes from an old
Scandinavian verb *bua*, 'to live',
and suggests 'lively, animated'. It
has found considerable
popularity outside Scandinavia.
The name also occurs in Asia. In
India, it can refer to the fig tree
that is sacred to Buddhists and in
Sri Lanka it suggests the 'tree of
knowledge', similar to but not
identical with the tree in the
Garden of Eden. In Chinese, it
means 'wave' and suggests the
vitality and the beauty of the sea.

BOBBIE/BOBBY This name
used to be male but it is now
regularly used for girls. It may be
considered a name in its own
right with the meaning of 'bright
fame' or it may be a friendly
diminutive of *Roberta*. Two other
variants, *Bobette* and *Bobina* occur.
SEE Roberta

37

BODGANA is a Polish name that means 'gift of God'. Because of its meaning, it is the equivalent of *Dorothy* and *Theodora*.

BONITA is a 20th-century name and seems to have been created from Spanish *bonito*, 'good, pretty'. It is easily pronounced worldwide and linked to all languages that are related to Latin, where *bonus* is 'good'.

BONNIE can be an abbreviated form of *Bonita* but it has a much longer history than *Bonita*. It has been used as an adjective in Scots for at least four centuries. The Scots borrowed it from French *bon* and it means 'pretty, attractive'. Robbie Burns used the adjective in his song, 'The Banks o' Doon':

Ye banks and braes o' bonnie Doon,
How can ye bloom sae fresh and
fair?

The speaker in the song is traditionally regarded as a lovely young woman who has lost her beloved. She cannot understand how nature can appear so beautiful when she is so sad.

Bonnie Parker was the female partner in the infamous bank-robbing duo, Bonnie and Clyde.

BRANCA is a Portuguese equivalent of *Blanche*. SEE Blanche

BRANNA is one of several names that may include the Celtic element *bran*, 'raven', or the Scandinavian noun *brand*, 'flaming torch'. In Celtic society, the raven was not simply a black bird of the crow family, but was symbolic of the life of the spirit. *Branna* may also be a surname, more usually written *Brannagh*. This name is also Celtic and originally meant 'Welsh person' or 'non-Anglo-Saxon'. SEE Brenda

BRANWEN is a Welsh name that incorporates the Celtic *bran*, 'raven' + the element that also occurs as the first syllable in *Guinevere*, an adjective that can mean 'fair, beautiful'. SEE Bronwen

BRENDA is often regarded as a female equivalent of *Brendan*. But, whereas *Brendan* occurs in writings that are over 1000 years old, *Brenda* is much later and seems to occur mainly in Scotland. It may well be derived from Celtic *bran*, 'raven' + *dubh*, 'dark, black', or from Scandinavian *brand*, 'fiery torch', or from a combination of the two. It is certainly found throughout the world today.

BRENNA is likely to be a variant of *Branna* or *Brenda*. SEE Brenda

BRIANA is occasionally used as a variant of *Brenna*, but it is normally given as a female equivalent of *Brian*. *Brian* is such an old name that its origins are uncertain. The name may be related to a Celtic adjective meaning 'noble, virtuous' or to a noun meaning 'hill, eminence' and thus implying 'eminent'. The name was used by Breton settlers who arrived in England at the time of the Norman Conquest, 1066. SEE Brian

BRIANNE is an alternative female equivalent of *Brian*. SEE Brian, Briana

BRÍD (pronounced 'breedge'/'breed') is a modern Irish spelling of an older form, usually written *Brighid*. This name has given rise to numerous variants including *Bride*, *Bridie*, *Biddie*, *Bids* and *Bridget*. There was a Saint Bridget (c. 450-525) of Kildare whose fame spread throughout Europe and generated versions of her name in virtually all European languages. St Bridget's fame partly rested on the fact that her legends became interwoven with those of the Celtic Goddess *Bríd*, whose name seems to have meant 'the exalted one'. It may, in addition, include *brigh*, meaning 'power, strength, virtue'.

BRIDGET is an anglicised form of *Bríd*, the goddess of fire, poetry and wisdom. This name was borne by two important saints: a patron saint of Ireland, who is buried with St Patrick and St Colmcille, and Saint Bridget of Sweden (also known as Birgitta) who founded an order of nuns in the 14th century. SEE Bríd

BRIGETTE is a modern equivalent of *Bríd*. It looks French but is probably a blend of *Bridget* and the French ending *–ette*, as in *Georgette*. SEE Bríd

BRIGID This is a variant spelling of the older Irish form *Brighid*. SEE Bríd

BRIGITTE This form is found in both France and Germany. In France, the 'g' is pronounced like 'j' in French *je*, 'I'. In Germany, the first syllable rhymes with 'dig' and the final 'e' sounds like 'a'. SEE Bríd

BRIONY is like *Daisy, Ivy, Rose* and *Violet* in being derived from flowers and shrubs. The Latin name is *bryonia* and a variety of this climbing plant was once called Our Lady's Seal. The form *Bryony* is equally popular.

BRITA can be an abbreviated form of *Brigitta* or of *Brittany*. SEE Bríd, Brittany

BRITNEY is a popular name derived from Brittany in north-west France. (The French

name is *Bretagne*.) The name comes ultimately from Latin *Brittones*, 'people from the British Isles'. They fled from England and Wales in the 5th and 6th centuries to escape the Anglo-Saxon invasion. The people who fled spoke a Celtic language that is closely related to Welsh.

BRITT like *Brita*, has been used as a variant of both *Bridget* and *Brittany*. SEE Bríd

BRITTANY is a more widely used form of *Britney*. It is sometimes spelt with one 't'. SEE Britney

BRÓNA/BRÓNAGH

(rhymes with 'phone + a') is an Irish name related to *brón*, 'sorrow'. It is sometimes given to a girl as a token of devotion to Our Lady of Dolours. *Bróna* is a meaning equivalent of *Dolores*. SEE Dolores

BRONWEN There are at least six different spellings for this Welsh name. It is sometimes spelt with 'a' as in *Branwen*, sometimes with a 'g' as in

Brongwen; and sometimes with a 'y' as in *Brangwyn*. The name probably derives from *bron*, 'breast' + *gwen*, 'fair, beautiful'. Although *Brangwen* is treated as an alternative spelling, it is possible that it is a different name, in that *bran* is a Celtic noun meaning 'raven' but symbolising the world of the spirit. *Brangwen* could thus be an appropriate choice for a dark-haired child.

BROOK/BROOKE Film
stars often inspire fans and there were many stars in the last half of the 20ᵗʰ century who had names such as *Brook* or *River*. Brook is from an Old English noun *broc* that originally meant 'moor, bog, fen' but developed the meaning of a small stream.

BRYGID is a variant of *Brigid*.
The letter 'y' was regularly used for 'i' in Elizabethan English and many modern parents have renewed that practice.

BRYNA is sometimes used as a
female form of *Brian* and thus means 'eminence, height'. It

might also be considered a variant of *Brenna*. SEE Brenda

BRYONY is a variant spelling
of *Briony*. SEE Briony

NOTABLE NAMESAKES
Barbara Cartland (1901-2000) English socialite and author of 657 popular romances; Beatrix Potter (1866-1943) writer, artist and botanist, best known for her children's books which were published in child-sized formats and dealt with characters such as Squirrel Nutkin and Mr Tod; Bernadette Soubirous (1844-79) visionary from Lourdes and canonised in 1933; Bette Midler (b.1945) singer, actress and comedienne. Her record 'Wind beneath my Wings' was nominated record of the year in 1989.

C

CADENZA is an Italian name meaning 'cadence, falling in music'. It ties this name in with others such as *Carmen* ('song, poem') that relate to poetry and music and suggest 'grace and beauty'. SEE Carmen

CAITLIN is one of the many Irish names that have become popular worldwide. This one comes ultimately from *Catheline*, an old French form of *Catherine*, which may mean 'pure' or may be the name of a goddess associated with enchantment. Outside Ireland this name is pronounced like 'Kate + lin' and this pronunciation is also filtering into Irish use. The Irish form *Caitlín* is often pronounced like 'kotch + leen'. SEE Catherine

CAITRIONA (pronounced 'cat + ree + on+ a') is an Irish form of *Catherine*. SEE Catherine

CALA is an Arabic name meaning 'fortress, castle'. It is pronounced with equal stresses on both syllables and the first syllable rhymes with 'gal' and not 'Gail'. It can also be used as a reduced form of *Calandra*, 'lark', or *Calantha*, 'beautiful flower'. SEE Calandra and Calantha

CALANDRA Girls, rather than boys, tend to be called after birds, such as *Merle*, 'blackbird', and flowers, such as *Daisy. Calandra* is from Greek and means 'lark', a bird that is renowned for the height it soars in order to sing its early morning song.

CALANTHA/CALANTHE

This Greek name comes from *kalos*, 'beautiful' + *anthos*, 'flower', and is thus a name that any little girl would enjoy having. The flower referred to is a type of orchid that is both striking and rare. *Callie* and *Cali* can be used as abbreviations.

CALIDA is most frequently found in Spanish-speaking communities. It means 'warm and loving' and may have the abbreviations *Cal* and *Ida*, which rhymes with 'seed + a' and not 'sighed + a'.

CALISTA/CALLISTA In Greek mythology, Callisto was a nymph who was so beautiful that Zeus, the king of the gods, fell in love with her. (In Greek, *kalos* is 'beautiful'.) Unfortunately, Hera, the wife of Zeus, was unwilling to tolerate a rival. Callisto was transformed into a bear, but Zeus placed her in the sky as a star in the constellation Ursa Major, 'Great Bear'. Many Greek female names end in 'o' but, as 'o' often indicates a male name in European languages, the spelling of *Callisto* is often changed so that it ends in 'a'. It gained renewed popularity through the actress, Calista Flockhart, who played the title character of *Ally McBeal* (1997-2002).

CALLEY/CALLI/CALLIE/ CALLY are used as abbreviated forms of a variety of names beginning with 'Cal'. SEE Calandra, Calantha, Calista, Calliope

CALLIOPE comes from Greek and means 'beautiful voice'. Calliope was the ninth muse in Greek mythology and was thought to be the inspiration for eloquence and heroic poetry. The name has been applied by metaphorical extension to a musical instrument and to a humming-bird. The name is sometimes abbreviated to *Calli*.

CAMILLA is a name with a history that goes back thousands of years. Its meaning is uncertain, but it comes from *Camillus*, which is an old, noble Roman family. It suggests 'noble' and also 'courageous'. According to Virgil, the Roman poet who wrote the *Aeneid*, Camilla was a warrior queen who led her army into war. In this respect, she resembles the Celtic queen Boudicca.

CANDACE/CANDICE is the name of many Ethiopian queens, one of whom is mentioned in the Acts of the Apostles. Her name was spelt *Candice*. It is not possible to be certain of its exact meaning but it has been linked to Latin *canditia*, 'whiteness', although that does not seem totally appropriate for an African queen.

Any parent who chooses this name will know that it represents beauty, culture and wealth. *Candy* is occasionally used as an abbreviated form of *Candice*.

CANDIDA became popular with people who were impressed by Voltaire's novel, *Candide* (1759). The name comes from the Latin adjective *candidus*, 'white, shining, pure, innocent'. It gave rise to the English adjective *candid*, meaning 'straightforward, sincere'. *Candy* is used as an abbreviation.

CANDY has an extremely illustrious pedigree, possibly shedding light on our human fondness for sweets. A form of the phrase 'sugar candy' appears in French, Italian, Portuguese and Spanish. Although they appear as early as the 14th century, Europeans borrowed the phrase from Arabic *qandah*, and that seems to have been borrowed from Sanskrit *khanda*, 'pieces of crystalline sugar'. The given name *Candy* seems to have started life as an endearment,

like 'Honey' or 'Sweetie', but it is now used in its own right as well as being an abbreviation of both *Candice* and *Candida*.

CARA is used in Italian and in the Celtic languages to mean 'beloved, friend'. Its meaning and its ease of pronunciation make this a popular choice.

CARI can be an abbreviation of several names such as *Caroline*, but it can also come directly from Turkish and mean 'moving with the grace and beauty of water'. SEE Carlotta, Caroline

CARLA is a feminine form of *Carl*, which is a German form of *Charles* and means 'man'. It is sometimes used as an abbreviation of *Carlotta*. SEE Charlotte

CARLOTTA is the Italian form of *Charlotte*, which is related to *Carl* but has a diminutive ending. SEE Charlotte

CARMEL is from Mount Carmel in north western Israel. The Carmelite Order of friars was formed during the Crusades and the female order was founded 300 years later in 1452. The meaning of *Carmel* is not absolutely certain but scholars suggest that it implies 'God's vineyard'. The name has become increasingly popular since the 16th century due, in part, to the fame of such Carmelite saints as Teresa of Avila and John of the Cross. SEE Carmen

CARMELA is the Spanish, Portuguese and Italian form of *Carmel*. SEE Carmel

CARMELITA means 'little vineyard of God' and is a popular form in Spain. SEE Carmel

CARMEN is the Latin for 'song, poem' but, coincidentally, it is also a Spanish form of *Carmel*. Most people will link the name to Bizet's opera *Carmen* (1875) and to its Gypsy heroine, and many more will think of the modern version, *Carmen Jones*, where Bizet's music is set to African American English. Queen Elisabeth of Romania (1843-1916) wrote poetry under the pseudonym *Carmen Sylva*. SEE Carmel

CARO is a recent popular abbreviation, usually of *Caroline*, although it can be used for any similar given name, including *Carlotta*.

CAROL, like *Hilary*, *Jocelyn* and *Vivien*, was originally a name for a boy and was based on *Carolus*, a Latin form of *Charles*. From the 19th century, however, it has been used almost exclusively for girls. It comes from a Germanic word that has also given us English *churl*, which was originally the male equivalent of 'wife' but which could mean 'ordinary man'. It is impossible not to link *Carol* also with the word for a religious popular hymn, especially in the phrase 'Christmas carol'. This word originally meant a 'ring dance' that was probably accompanied by a song and may be related to *choral*. *Carole* used to be equally popular but the final 'e' is less widely used now.

CAROLINE/CAROLYN It is not easy to explain why certain names suddenly become popular. Sometimes the link is with a star,

45

a member of a royal family or a politician. For a mixture of reasons, *Caroline* has been fashionable since the 1960s. This popularity has been aided, no doubt, by Princess Caroline of Monaco and Caroline Kennedy, daughter of President Kennedy. The name is a diminutive of *Carol* and it also appears frequently as *Carolyn*. The 'lyn' ending may be due to the increased use of 'y' in names (in *Bryanne*, for example), but it may also have been influenced by names such as *Evelyn*. There is a tendency to pronounce *Caroline* to rhyme with 'wine' and *Carolyn* with 'win'. SEE Carol

CARON may be linked to *cara*, 'beloved, friend', or it may be a reduced form of Welsh *Caronwen*. It is also likely that some families choose it as a variant of *Karen*, a Scandinavian form of Catherine, meaning 'pure'. SEE Caronwen and Catherine

CARONWEN/CARONWYN is a Welsh name combining elements which mean 'beloved' and 'fair'. To call a child the equivalent of 'beautiful and well-loved' is a gift that many little girls will appreciate.

CARYN may be another example of the use of 'y' in girls' names, and so this one may be a form of *Caron* or *Karen*. SEE Caron and Karen

CASEY has been used as a spoken form of the initials K.C., and as a given name based on a surname. The Irish surname means 'vigilant in war'. *Casey* is now almost exclusively female and may, in some cases, be an abbreviated form of *Cassandra*. SEE Cassandra

CASSANDRA has become increasingly popular since the end of the 20th century and is now almost as fashionable as it was in the Middle Ages. In Greek mythology, *Cassandra* was the beautiful young daughter of King Priam of Troy. Apollo fell in love with her and gave her the gift of prophecy. When she did not return his adulation, Apollo was angry. He could not take away the first gift so he gave her a second gift: although her prophecies were always accurate, no one would believe her! The meaning of *Cassandra* is unclear but it now symbolises psychic ability. *Cass* and *Cassie* are popular abbreviations.

CATE is a modern abbreviation of *Catherine*. It is equivalent to *Kate*. SEE Catherine

CATERINA is an Italian form of one of the most widely used names in the world. SEE Catherine

CATHERINE or, occasionally, *Catharine*, are versions of the Greek name *Aikaterine*. It is possible that this Greek name is related to *Hecate*, the goddess of magic, whose name means 'the distant one'. Because of the Greek adjective, *katharos*, 'pure', this name has for almost two millennia symbolised 'purity'. There are many famous *Catherines* who could act as role models for children. St Catherine of Alexandria is said to have been martyred on a spiked wheel for her faith in AD 307. (The spinning Catherine Wheel firework

is named after her.) A less spiritual bearer of the name was Catherine the Great of Russia (1729-96). This name has given rise to at least twenty variants, some beginning with 'K'. The most widespread are *Caitriona*, *Catalina*, *Caitlin*, *Catharina*, *Cathleen*, *Catriona* and abbreviations such as *Cate* and *Cathie*.

CATRIONA tends to be a Scottish variant of *Catherine*. It occurs in this spelling in Ireland, too, although the form *Caitriona* used to be preferred. This form of *Catherine* was popularised by Robert Louis Stephenson, whose novel sequel to *Kidnapped* was entitled *Catriona*.

CECILIA is a female form of *Cecil* and both names derive from an ancient Roman family called *Caecilius*, which related to a nickname *Caecus*, 'blind'. St Cecilia was a martyr in either the 2nd or 3rd century and is the patron saint of music. The name occurs in a variety of forms, including *Cecily*, *Celia* and the pet forms *Celi* and *Sissy*.

CECILY is an English form of *Cecilia* and possibly related to one of the most important families in English history, the Cecils. William Cecil (1520-98), for example, was Elizabeth I's Secretary of State and Lord High Treasurer. He was among her most trusted advisors and ran an efficient spy network for her.

CELANDINE The Greek noun from which this name comes has two meanings, 'swallow' and 'yellow flower'. The two were linked because it was believed that the arrival of the swallows heralded the blossoming of the flower and their departure coincided with the withering of the plant.

CELESTE was originally a French name suggesting 'heavenly'. It comes ultimately from Latin *caelum*, 'sky, heavens'. The diminutive *Celestina* is also growing in popularity. There have been five popes called *Celestin*, the male equivalent of this name.

CELIA can come from two sources. It can be a form of an old Roman family name, *Caelius*, which probably comes from a nickname based on *caelum*, 'sky, heavens'. It can also be a reduced form of *Cecilia*. Shakespeare was the first writer to use the name *Celia*. He gave it to a feisty, generous, attractive character in *As You Like It*. SEE Cecilia

CELIE can be a reduced form of *Celia* and *Cecilia* and thus mean 'heavenly', or it can be an abbreviation of *Selena*, a name that related to the moon. SEE Celia and Selena

CELINA is usually an alternative spelling of *Selena* but it could mean 'little Celia'. SEE Selena

CERI is usually considered a Welsh name and it can certainly come from Welsh *caru*, 'to love' and mean 'beloved'. It has also been used as an alternative spelling of *Kerry*, which may come from County Kerry. Since *Ceri* does not seem to occur in early records, it is possible that it is a reduced form of *Ceridwen*. SEE Ceridwen and Kerry

CERIDWEN

(pronounced 'care + id + win') is clearly Welsh and is occasionally spelt *Ceiridwen*. It is the name of a Welsh mythological goddess of poetic inspiration. It seems to be composed of two words, *cerdd*, 'poetry' and *gwen*, 'fair, beautiful'. It is a poetic name and richly deserves its recent popularity.

CHANDRA

('ch' as in 'chant') is a widely-used Hindi name that comes from Sanskrit, where it refers to the moon and is thus approximately equivalent to *Diana* and *Selena*. One of the most powerful Hindu goddesses, *Diva*, was sometimes known as *Chandra*. One of the great warrior emperors of India, Chandragupta Maurya (325-297BC) has the goddess's name incorporated into his own.

CHANTAL/CHANTALE

('ch' pronounced 'sh') is a French name that owes its origin to *Chantal*, a town in central France. Although most parents link the name to French *chanter*, 'to sing', it seems more likely that it comes from an old noun *cantal*, 'boulder, large stone'. The name is also occasionally spelt *Chantelle* but this is more likely to occur outside France.

CHARITA

is an Indian name that means 'good, excellent'. It is often chosen because it can be substituted for *Charity*, 'benevolent', which continues to be a popular choice among parents who like to give their children names that reflect the qualities they would like their children to possess.

CHARITY

is the English equivalent of Latin *caritas*, 'unselfish love'. Puritans, from the late 16th century, began the tradition of calling children after virtues. (There are a few examples from the Middle Ages but they are not widespread.) *Charity* is still extremely popular in Africa, but is less popular in English-speaking communities than *Faith*, *Hope* or *Prudence*.

CHARLEEN/ CHARLENE

may well come from an anglicisation of French *Charline*, a feminine form of *Charles*, thus meaning 'person'. The 'een' ending may have been influenced by *Eileen* or *Kathleen*, and the 'ene' ending reflects a 20th-century fondness for names such as *Jolene* and *Marlene*.

CHARLOTTE

illustrates the movement of names from one group to another. It is a female form of *Charlot*, a pet form of *Charles*. *Charles* is a French form of a Germanic name that originally meant 'man'. It is thus similar in meaning to *Adam*. *Charlotte* became fashionable in England in the 18th century because it was the name of George III's wife. It was so popular that it was given to the paddle steamer, *Charlotte Dundas*, which was the first vessel to use steam propulsion for a commercial venture. *Charlotte* has several popular abbreviations. *Lottie* was a favourite in the past, but *Charley* and *Charlie* are currently much more widely used and *Charo* seems to be coming in.

CHARMAINE

was the title of a song that was popular in the 1960s and the song both reflected and generated an interest in the name. It may be a modified form of *Charmian*, a Greek name meaning 'delight', or it may be a blend of any of the 'Char-' names with the ending of *Germaine* or *Lorraine*. SEE Charmian

CHARMIAN

appears as the name of one of Cleopatra's handmaidens in Shakespeare's *Antony and Cleopatra*. The name comes from Greek *kharma*, 'delight'. This name is currently less popular than *Charmaine* but it could easily become a favourite.

CHELSEA

is spelt in a variety of ways, including *Chelsey*, *Chelsie* and *Chelsy*. The name is an example of a place name being transferred to a girl. The part of London from which the name derives is recorded from the 8th century and meant 'landing place for chalk or limestone'. *Chelsea* sounds like a diminutive such as *Mollie* or *Teri*.

CHERIE/CHERRY comes from the French endearment meaning 'darling, my dear'. It is normally pronounced with the stress on the second syllable but there has been a tendency recently to pronounce it like 'cherry' and some parents prefer this spelling. Girls have often been called after flowers and shrubs such as *Rose* and *Holly*. *Cherry* would fit into this category. The French pronunciation of *Cherie* begins with the sound 'sh' and this has helped the spread of *Sherry* as an alternative spelling. SEE Sherry

CHERYL is a modern creation. It is pronounced 'Sher + ill' and it may be from French *cher*, 'dear', or it may be modelled on *Beryl*, 'a green gemstone'. Whatever its origins, it has become fashionable.

CHIKA is for parents who are interested in giving their child a Japanese name. This one means 'wisdom, sound judgement'. The name is pronounced to rhyme with 'cheek + a', rather than 'chick + a', although if one likes the underlying link with 'chick' as a term of endearment, then that is a bonus.

CHIKAKO Many Japanese names end in 'ko', meaning 'child'. This one means 'child of wisdom' and it rhymes with 'cheek + ack + o'. There is equal stress on each syllable.

CHINATSU means 'a thousand summers' in Japanese and, as one might expect, this is a popular name for a little girl who brings eternal summer into a family.

CHIQUITA (pronounced 'chee + keeta') is a popular Spanish name meaning 'little one'.

CHLOE (pronounced 'klow + 'ee') is an anglicised form of Greek *Khloe*. It is not certain what this name means, although it may be related to the Greek word for 'green', a very suitable choice for ecologically friendly parents. This name was used to refer to the Greek corn Goddess Demeter.

CHO is pronounced like 'cho', not 'sho' or 'ko'. It is a Japanese name meaning 'butterfly'. Parents who choose this name may be attracted to Puccini's music, although they would undoubtedly prefer their child not to have the same experiences as *Madame Butterfly*.

CHRISTABEL It seems probable that Samuel Taylor Coleridge (1772-1834) coined this name for his poem of that name:

*The lovely lady, Christabel
Whom her father loves so well,
What makes her in the wood so late,
A furlong from the castle gate?*

It is probably a blend of *Christine* and *Isabel* and it would thus mean 'beautiful follower of Christ'.

CHRISTIANA is one of the many names related to *Christian* and meaning 'follower of Christ'. *Christiana* is a female form of Latin *Christianus*. For those who want to trace the meaning further, the Greek noun *Khristos* is a translation of the Hebrew title *Messiah*, meaning 'the Anointed One'. There are many widely-used abbreviations, including *Chris*, *Chrissie* and *C(h)rissy*.

CHRISTINA/CHRISTINE is a simplified form of Latin *Christiana*. Until recently, Christina was the most widely occurring form of the many variants linked to *Christianus*. Now, it seems as if *Christine*, which was the usual French form, is becoming more popular.

CIARA/KEIRA (pronounced 'key + erra') is from the Irish word *ciar*, 'dark, dark brown'. Its variants are Ciarra, Keera, Keira and Kiera.

CILLA has become a name in its own right, although it was originally a shortened form of *Priscilla*, which is a feminine diminutive form of the Roman family name, *Priscus*. The Latin form was originally a nickname meaning 'ancient, original'. Some parents use *Cilla* as the equivalent of the scilla, a flower that resembles a lily. SEE Priscilla

CINDY has been popular for almost fifty years. It was often used as an abbreviation of *Cynthia* and it may also have been influenced by *Lucinda* and by *Cinderella*. *Cynthia* is connected with 'the moon', *Lucinda* with 'light' and *Cinderella* is the title of a well-loved fairy tale. SEE Cynthia and Lucinda

CLAIRE was introduced into the British Isles by the Normans. It is a French name that comes directly from Latin *clarus*, which had a wide range of meanings including 'bright, clear, famous, illustrious'. This spelling was superseded in English by *Clara* but the French spelling is again dominant. A few parents like the Italian version, *Chiara*, and it is a pretty alternative.

CLARA For centuries, *Clara* and *Clare* were the favoured form of the name in the English-speaking world. They come from Latin *clarus*, 'bright, clear, illustrious'. Occasionally, 'bel' or 'bell' was added to *Clara*, producing *Clarabel* and *Clarabella*, both meaning 'famous and beautiful'.

CLARE is less widely used than previously but it is a simple, straightforward spelling of the name. One of the most interesting holders of this name was St Clare of Assisi (1194-1253). She was a friend of St Francis of Assisi and she founded the Poor Clare Order of nuns. St Clare might appeal to most children in her role as patron saint of television! SEE Clara

CLARICE is a French name that has had some popularity since the Middle Ages. It comes from Latin *Claritia*, 'fame'. The ending tends to be pronounced like 'iss', although some parents prefer to keep a more French-sounding pronunciation and say 'ees'.

CLARISSA is a latinate spelling of *Clarice*. It gained considerable popularity after the publication of Samuel Richardson's long epistolary novel, *Clarissa*, which was published in 1748. Clarissa was a beautiful young woman who made the mistake of trusting herself to an untrustworthy man. It is hard to estimate the popular appeal of this novel except to say that its impact could be compared to the Harry Potter phenomenon – but for adults. SEE Clara

CLAUDETTE is a French female form of *Claude*, a name that was popularised in France in the 7th century by St Claude of Besançon, and then by the painter Claude Lorraine (1600-82), whose works were commended for their atmospheric use of light. *Claudette* comes from the name of an old Roman family, *Claudius*, and this is almost certainly derived from a nickname *Claudus*, meaning 'lame'.

CLAUDIA is a female form of the Latin name *Claudius*. Its use is considerably more widespread than *Claudette* in the English-speaking world. SEE Claudette

CLAUDINE gained popularity in the 20th century because it was the name of a heroine in several novels by Colette. It is a feminine form of *Claude*. SEE Claudette

CLEMENTINE is the most frequently used form of Latin *clemens*, 'merciful'. Other variants, including *Clemence*, *Clemency* and *Clementina*, occur but a popular song has guaranteed the enduring appeal of *Clementine*:

Oh my darling, oh my darling, oh my darling, Clementine!
Thou art lost and gone forever, dreadful sorry Clementine.

Generally, the last syllable is pronounced to rhyme with 'mine'.

CLEO is a shortened form of *Cleopatra*, a name that will always be linked to the last Ptolemaic queen of Egypt. Cleopatra (69-30 BC) ruled Egypt from 47 BC. For a while, she was the mistress of Julius Caesar, to whom she bore a son. Her love for Mark Antony is immortalised in Shakespeare's *Antony and Cleopatra*, where she is described:

Age cannot wither her, nor custom stale
Her infinite variety.

(Act 2, Scene 3)

Cleopatra was Greek. She was descended from one of Alexander the Great's generals, Ptolemy. Her name combines *kleos*, 'glory' and *patra*, 'father', and it was widely used by the females in Ptolemy's line.

CLIO is sometimes equated with *Cleo* but, although they are both Greek, and although their names may both come from *kleos*, 'glory', their origins are different. *Clio* was the Muse of History. In Greek mythology, there were nine sister goddesses, all children of Zeus, who were thought to inspire learning and the arts. They were known as 'Muses'. It has been suggested that *Clio*'s name may come from *kleiein*, 'to celebrate'.

CLODA/CLODAGH

(pronounced 'clo + da') This Irish name may come from the name of a Tipperary river or it may be an Irish form of Latin *Claudia*. SEE Claudette

CODY is, like *Jodi*, a 20th-century addition to the inventory of girls' names. Its origin is uncertain, but it is likely that it comes from the surname *Coady* or *Cody*. It may be linked to an Old English word meaning a 'bag or pillow' or it may come from Irish and mean 'helpful'. The name was immortalised by Buffalo Bill Cody (1846–1917) who was renowned as a sharp shooter. His show travelled the world.

COLEEN/COLLEEN is from an Irish noun *cailín* meaning 'girl'. It became popular as a given name in Australia and the USA, rather than in Ireland.

COLETTE is almost certainly an abbreviated form of *Nicolette*, a female form of *Nicholas*, meaning 'victory to the people'. In the Middle Ages, *Col* was a popular abbreviation of *Nicholas* and it gave rise to *Colin* and, later, to *Colette*. The famous French novelist Colette (1873-1954) gave extra impetus to an already popular name.

COMFORT is an example of the Puritan tendency to give daughters names that reflected virtues. It is extremely popular in Africa. It comes from French and means 'encouragement, aid, support'.

CONNIE is an abbreviation of *Constance* and is probably more popular than the full name. SEE Constance

CONSTANCE probably comes from Latin *constans*, 'constant, resolute, reliable'. It is, like *Comfort* or *Charity*, a name that attracted certain parents because of its moral meaning.

CONSUELA is a popular Spanish name with the meaning of 'consolation'. It is often seen as an attribute of Our Lady and so has been used as an alternative to Maria or as a compound name, for example, *Maria Consuela*.

CORA does not appear in print before the 19th century. It may be an anglicisation of Greek *Kore*, 'maiden', a name that would parallel *Coleen*. Its ease of pronunciation means that it can be used in different cultural contexts. The blend of *Cora + Belle*, *Corabelle*, is found

in the United States.

CORAL is one of a set of names drawn from precious stones. Many of them, including *Coral*, became popular in the 20th century. Coral is a substance found in warm seas. It is often pink or red and is found in coral reefs that have developed over millennia.

CORDELIA seems to have been invented by Shakespeare as the name of the virtuous, loving daughter of King Lear. It is possible that it is a blend of Latin *cor*, 'heart' + *Delia*, 'one from the island of Delos'. SEE Delia

CORELLA is a modern blend of *Cora*, 'maiden' + *Ella*, 'stranger'. SEE Cora and Ella

CORETTA is likely to be a diminutive form of *Cora*. The 'etta' ending is found in many names, including *Jacquetta* and *Loretta*. Coretta Scott King (1927-2006) was the wife of the assassinated civil rights activist Martin Luther King. SEE Cora

**CORINA/CORINNA/
CORINNE** These names are
all variants of *Cora* and probably
mean 'little maiden'. *Corinne* is
French but perhaps the most
popular variant of all. SEE Cora

CORNELIA is a female form
of *Cornelius*, which was the name
of an old Roman family. The
exact meaning of the name is
uncertain but it is likely to be
linked to Latin *cornu*, 'a horn'.
The existence of *Cornelia* may
have suggested Shakespeare's
creation of *Cordelia*.

COSIMA is an Italian name,
usually considered to be the
female form of *Cosmo*, which
comes from Greek *kosmos* and
means 'beautiful order, universe'.
It was given a degree of
popularity by Cosima Liszt
(1837-1930), the daughter of
Franz Lizst.

COURTNEY is taken from an
Old French surname that was
based on a town called *Courtenay*,
'Curtis's domain', and *Curtis*
could mean 'courteous'. Some
people have suggested that

Courtney is a nickname
based on *court*, 'short' +
nez, 'nose'.

CRESSIDA was a Trojan
princess. Her story is told in
Shakespeare's play *Troilus and
Cressida*. The name seems to
come from Greek *khrysos*, 'gold',
and so the name implies 'golden
one'.

CRYSTAL comes from Greek
krystallos, 'ice', but it has been
applied to a mineral that is
transparent, like ice. It is one of a
set of names from minerals and
gemstones that have become
popular since the 19th century.
The name was sometimes used
in Scotland as a pet form of
Christopher, but this usage no
longer occurs.

CYNTHIA comes from the
Greek *Kynthia*, a name applied to
the goddess Artemis. The name
means 'one from Kynthos' and
Kynthos is a mountain on the
island of Delos. Artemis was the
daughter of Zeus and she has
been identified with Selene, the
goddess of the moon. SEE Diana

NOTABLE NAMESAKES

Catherine the Great of Russia (1729-96) ruled Russia for thirty-four years after the death of her husband, Peter III, and made Russia the strongest power in Eastern Europe; Caroline Grimaldi of Monaco (b.1957), the eldest child of Prince Rainier and the actress Grace Kelly; Cherie Blair (b.1954), English barrister and judge and wife of Tony Blair, British Prime Minister from 1997-2007; Colleen McCullough (b.1937) scientist and writer, especially renowned for her novels *Tim*, which launched Mel Gibson's acting career, and *The Thorn Birds* (1987), which is reputed to have had the largest television audience in the BBC's history; Courtney Cox (b.1964) American actress best known for her role as Monica Geller in *Friends* (1994-2004).

D

DACEY (pronounced 'day + see') is occasionally used as a female equivalent of *Desmond*, a Gaelic name from *déise*, meaning 'southerner'.

DAGMAR is a Scandinavian name made up of *dagr*, 'day' + *mær*, 'maiden', thus suggesting 'girl's day'. It has become popular in German-speaking communities, especially among people who are interested in Scandinavian mythology.

DAHLIA is one of the many flower names adopted by parents for their children. The dahlia was named in honour of the Swedish botanist who introduced the plant to Europe in 1789. It is occasionally equated with *Delia*, 'oracle', but the names are distinct.

DAI (rhymes with 'high') is a Japanese name meaning 'great'. It is often given as a second name to daughters.

DAINA is a Lithuanian name meaning 'song'. It is often pronounced 'da + ee + na' and sounds a little like *Dinah*, a Hebrew name meaning 'vindicated'.

DAISY The Old English word *dægesege*, meaning 'day's eye' refers to a common grassland flower that has a yellow centre and white petals. It is often taken to symbolise the coming of spring and it is the same flower that is represented in French by *marguerite*. *Daisy* was popular in Victorian times and regained that popularity in the last decade of the 20th century. It is one of a set of flower names that have been used for girls.

DAIYU (pronounced 'die + you') This name comes from China and means 'black jade', a mineral that is both beautiful and precious.

DAKOTA Most of the little girls called *Dakota* take their name from the city of Dakota in the United States. The town's name is a Native American word taken from the Sioux and meaning 'allies, friends'.

DALLAS began to be used as a girl's name in the 1980s, possibly as a result of the popular soap opera of the same name that ran from 1978 until 1991. Dallas is a city in Texas and it comes from an English surname that also gave rise to Dalhousie. It means 'dweller in the house in the valley'. There is a current vogue of giving daughters place names that is found also in *Dakota*.

DAMARA is an anglicised form of *Damaris*, a Greek name that probably means 'calf'. In the 21st century, it may seem strange to give a child the name of an animal, but if all animal names are avoided, then we lose such possibilities as *Rachel*, 'ewe', *Rebecca*, possibly 'heifer' and *Una*, 'lamb'. SEE Damaris

DAMARIS People who are familiar with the Acts of the Apostles will remember that *Damaris* is the name of a woman whom St Paul converted to Christianity. It is probably the same name as *damalis*, 'calf'. The 'l' and the 'r' are interchangeable in many languages. In English, for example, *Del* is sometimes used as an abbreviation of *Derek*.

DAMHNAIT/DAMHNAT /DAVNET (pronounced 'dav + nat'/'dav + net') This Irish name is usually equated with *Dymphna*, although it seems probable that there were two saints involved, both Irish, but one lived in Monaghan and the other in Belgium. *Damhnait*'s name seems to come from *damh*, 'poet', and it seems likely that she had the powers of a bishop in the convent she established at Tydavnet, 'Damhnait's house'. Her staff is in the National Museum of Ireland, and that is probably the safest place for it! When Damhnait was alive, her staff, *Bachall Dhamhnait*, was used to test whether or not someone was telling the truth. If anyone held the staff and lied, their mouth would be twisted permanently. SEE *Dymphna*

DANA can have a variety of origins. It can mean 'female from Denmark'; it can be an abbreviation of *Danielle*, 'God is my judge'; and it can be the name of the Celtic goddess from whom the *Tuatha de Danaan*, 'People of Dana', take their name. The name was popularised by *Dana*, aka Rosemary Scallon (b. 1951), who won the Eurovision Song Contest for Ireland in 1970.

DANIELLE is a popular French female form of *Daniel*, 'God is my judge'. There is also a form *Daniella* but that is not as widely used. *Dani* and *Danni* are used as abbreviations.

DANUTA is a Polish name whose meaning is debated. It may mean 'judge' and could be an alternative to *Portia*, or it may mean 'fawn, young deer'. In this case, it would be a female equivalent of Irish *Oisín*.

DAPHNE This is one of a large set of flower and plant names that many parents select for their daughters. *Daphne* comes from Greek and means 'laurel'. The foliage of the tree is an emblem of victory and we even have the word in 'poet laureate'. In Greek mythology, the god Apollo chased the nymph Daphne, who was anxious to avoid his advances. She could not outrun him so her father changed her into a laurel just as Apollo caught her.

DARA is a Hebrew name that gained some popularity in the 20th century. It means 'compassion' and that is certainly an attractive attribute to wish on any child.

DARCIA/DARCY/DARCEY

The Norman surname *d'Arcy*, meaning 'from Arcy', has been used as a given name for both girls and boys. In Ireland, it is sometimes a form of *Dorsey*, 'little dark one'. A modern bearer of the name is ballerina Darcey Bussell CBE (b.1969), formerly Principal Dancer with The Royal Ballet.

DARIA is a Persian name, the female equivalent of *Darius* (c. 550-486BC). He was one of the most famous rulers of the period and is known as *Darius the Great*. He built a network of roads throughout the kingdom and joined the River Nile to the Red Sea by means of a canal. It is not absolutely certain what his name means, but it has been suggested that it implies wealth and power.

DARLENE This is one of many names coined in the 20th century and ending in '-een', '-ene' or '-ine'. They were particularly widespread in Australia, where they were influenced by such names as *Eileen* and *Kathleen*. *Darlene* could be regarded as a form of 'darling'. It has also been used as a female form of *Daryl*.

DAVINA This name made its first written appearance in Scotland and is usually regarded as a female form of *David*, 'beloved'. This is certainly possible, as *David* has always been popular in Scotland. It is also possible that it is an anglicised form of *Damhnait*, little poet'.

Parents who like the name may choose their own favourite meaning or decide to combine the two. SEE Damhnait

DAWN is the English word for 'daybreak'. It is not certain where the English word comes from, but it may have been influenced by the Old English phrase *at dagan*, 'by day'. The dawn is a time of new beginnings and fresh hope and is thus extremely appropriate for a child. It is also possible that it is linked to the 'morning star'.

DAYNA is an alternative spelling of *Dana*, stressing the pronunciation that rhymes the first syllable with 'Dane' rather than with 'dan'. It is possible that some parents use it as a variant of Hebrew *Dinah*. SEE Dana

DAYO The Yoruba name, *Dayo*, meaning 'joy has arrived', is used for both girls and boys, especially when the parents have waited a long time for the joy of having a child.

DEBORA/DEBORAH/ DEBRA/DEVORA/ DEVRA is one of the best-loved Hebrew names for girls. The form with 'v' is rarely used outside Jewish circles. The name means 'bee', which is associated with industry, co-operation and honey. In the Old Testament, *Deborah* is the name of a female prophet. The spelling with 'h' is still the most common. It parallels the use of 'h' in such Hebrew names as *Sarah* and *Jeremiah*, but it is not pronounced in English and so has increasingly been dropped. There are several widely used abbreviations, including *Debbie*, *Debby*, *Debi* and *Debs*.

DEE can be used as an abbreviation for any name beginning with 'D' but it is most frequently used for *Deena*, *Deirdre* and *Diana*. SEE Diana and Dinah

DEIRDRE (pronounced 'dear + dreh', 'dare + dree'/'dear + dree')It is uncertain what this ancient Irish name means, although it may be related to *deireadh*, 'end, finish'. Due mainly

to the writings of W B Yeats
(1865-1939) and J M Synge
(1871-1909), Deirdre's story is
known throughout the world.
Deirdre, the most beautiful woman
in Ireland, is destined to be the
wife of the king, *Conchubhar.*
Deirdre, however, falls in love with
Naoise and they run away to
Scotland. They are persuaded to
return to Ulster, where Naoise is
murdered. *Deirdre* is given to the
man who killed Naoise but, as she
is being driven to his house, she
throws herself from the chariot
and is united with Naoise in
death. *Deirdre's* name is linked
with 'sorrow' because of J M
Synge's play, *Deirdre of the Sorrows.*
In this play, Deirdre's old nurse
sums up the tragedy:

> *Deirdre is dead, and Naoise is
> dead; and if the oaks and the stars
> could die for sorrow, it's a dark sky
> and a naked earth we'd have this
> night…*

There is no single spelling of this
name. It also occurs as *Deidre* and
Deirdriú.

DELFINE This is an
increasingly popular spelling of
Delphine, 'woman from Delphi',

one of the most important
religious centres in Greece
and the ancient world. SEE
Delphine

DELIA is another name for
Artemis, the moon goddess, who
was born on the island of Delos.
Delia was popularised in Ireland
by Delia Murphy (1902-71), the
ballad singer who reintroduced
Irish people to songs that had
rarely before been heard on
records or on the radio. It is now
associated with the celebrity
cook, Delia Smith.

DELILAH Delilah is a Hebrew
name meaning 'delicate'. In spite
of its mellifluous sound, *Delilah*
has never been widely used
mainly because she has been
portrayed as the betrayer of
Samson. In the *Book of Judges,* she
tells the Philistines that
Samson's strength resides in his
uncut hair and they are able to
capture him and cut his hair.

DELLA The history of *Della* is
unclear, although we know that it
only began to be recorded in the
last quarter of the 19th century. It

may be a simplified form of *Delia*, 'moon goddess', or of *Delilah*, 'delicate', or of *Adela*, 'noble'. It may also, of course, be a coinage based on *Bella* or *Ella*.

DELPHINE At first sight, *Delphine* is an example of a flower name for a daughter. The *delphinium* is an attractive flower sometimes known as 'larkspur'. In fact, both the flower and the child's name take their origin from Latin *Delphina*, 'woman from Delphi'. This is not just another place name, however, in that Delphi was one of the most significant centres of religious worship in the Greek world. It was particularly associated with the Delphic Oracle where people often were provided with answers that were seemingly ambiguous.

DEMETRIA like *Demi*, is a form of *Demeter*, the corn goddess in Greek mythology. Her name is likely to come from the combination of *de*, 'earth' + *meter*, 'mother', and she was the original earth mother. *Demeter*

was the sister of Zeus and the mother of *Persephone*, who was stolen from her mother and made queen of the Underworld.

DENA is one of the many spellings of Hebrew *Dinah*, 'judgement, vindicated'. Some parents use it as a female equivalent of *Dean*, 'valley' or 'deacon'.

DENISE was originally the French female form of *Denis*, 'godlike', but it is now used worldwide. It is usually pronounced like 'de knees' but there is a growing tendency to pronounce it like 'de + niece' and indeed to spell it *Deniece*.

DESDEMONA This is the name of the brave, generous, loving heroine of *Othello*. Shakespeare's is the first recorded use of *Desdemona* and he seems to have adopted it from Greek *dysdaimon*, 'ill-fated, unlucky'. If Ben Jonson was right about Shakespeare knowing 'little Latin and less Greek', then he may have created the name by blending *Desmond*, 'from the south', with *Mona*, 'noble'.

DEVA is an anglicised form of Sanskrit *devi*, meaning 'goddess'. Among Indian families, *Devi* and *Devika*, 'little goddess', are more usual.

DEVONA Devon is an old Celtic name meaning 'dark water, dark river'. *Devon* has been used as a surname since the 13th century but *Devona* seems to date from the middle of the 20th century, when there was a growth of interest in Celtic traditions. *Devona* fits into the language well and parallels names such as *Rhona*.

DEVORA is an approximation to the Hebrew name which is more frequently realised as *Deborah*, 'bee'. SEE Deborah

DIANA In Roman mythology, *Diana* was a goddess of hunting and the moon. She is, thus, the Roman equivalent of Greek *Artemis*. The meaning of the name is debated, but it is derived from Greek *Dionysus* and is related to Latin *deus*, 'god'. A statue of Artemis was venerated

at Ephesus. Her temple, which is often called the Temple of Diana, was rebuilt in 356BC, and was regarded as one of the Seven Wonders of the ancient world. *Diana* was not popular among early Christians because of its link with pagan worship. In Chapter 18 of the *Acts of the Apostles*, Paul and Barnabas received a hostile time in Ephesus when some people objected to their preaching:

> And when they heard these sayings, they were full of wrath, and cried out saying: 'Great is Diana of the Ephesians.'

DIANE/DIANNE *Diane* is the French form of the goddess of hunting and the moon and it was, until recently, more popular throughout Europe than *Diana*. Some parents have suggested that their choice of this name comes from Greek *dianoetikos*, 'relating to thought'. SEE Diana

DIDO In the Greek tradition, many female names end in 'o', including *Clio* and *Hero*. According to Virgil's *Aeneid*, *Dido*

was the queen of Carthage. She fell in love with Aeneas when he escaped from Troy and, although he vowed to stay with her, he left her and went on to found Rome. *Dido*, whose name seems to mean 'virgin' in Phoenician, was heartbroken and could not live without Aeneas.

DILYS is a Welsh word, meaning 'genuine'. It began to be used in the 19th century and its popularity was helped because of its similarity to *Phyllis*, 'foliage'.

DINAH is a Hebrew name meaning 'vindicated'. The *Book of Genesis* tells us that she was the daughter of the patriarch *Jacob*. *Dinah* has given rise to many variants, including *Deena*, *Dena* and *Dina*.

DIONE/DIONNE is from Greek *Dionysius*, 'godlike', and is related to *Diana*. *Dione* is often regarded as the female equivalent of *Dion*. In Greek mythology, *Dione* was the consort of Zeus and the mother of Aphrodite. The name is pronounced in two ways, 'dee + on' or 'dee + own'. SEE Diana

DOLI/DOLLY

It is strange how often the same sounding name can occur in distinct cultures and that is the case here. *Doli* is a Native American favourite. It comes from a Navaho word meaning 'bluebird' and the bluebird symbolises happiness. *Dolly* was originally a pet form of *Dorothy*, 'gift of God'. Just as *Mary* gave rise to *Molly* and *Sarah* to *Sally*, *Dorothy* gave rise to *Doll* and *Dolly*. Now, *Dolly* is used for several names, including *Dolores* and *Doris*. Singer/songwriter/actress Dolly Parton is the most successful female country music artist in history.

DOLORES used to be limited to Spanish-speaking communities but it is now found throughout the world. It comes from *Maria de los Dolores*, which is usually translated into English as 'Our Lady of Sorrows'. The name is often given to a child as an alternative to *Mary*. Occasionally, the English form of the word, *Dolours*, is used as a girl's name but this usage is less widespread.

DOMINICA is the female form of Latin of *dominicus*, 'belonging to the Lord'. It is not as widely used as the French equivalent, *Dominique*. Both names tend to be linked to respect for St Dominic (c.1170-1221), who founded the Dominican Order.

DONATA is the female equivalent of *Donatus*, the name of a 9th-century Irish saint. It may also be seen as derived from the Latin verb *donare*, 'to give', with *Donata* implying 'gift of God'.

DONGMEI (pronounced 'dong + may') is sometimes written as two words. It is a popular Chinese name, meaning 'winter plum' and suggesting pleasure in a winter baby.

DONNA is a 20th-century name, possibly taken from Italian *donna*, 'lady', or possibly a female form of *Don*, 'ruler of the world'. Although a relatively recent addition to the inventory of girls' names, it is popular and travels easily. No one has any difficulty pronouncing *Donna* and that is an important consideration in a century where travel, especially by the young, is the norm.

DORA Until the 19th century, *Dora* was an abbreviation for *Isadora*, 'gift of the god Isis', or *Theodora*, 'gift of God', but it has been a name in its own right since Charles Dickens used it in *David Copperfield* (1850). The name is often associated with nurses because of the nurse's cap that was tied under the chin. It was called a 'Sister Dora' in honour of Dorothy (Dora) Pattison (1832-78), who was one of the earliest nurses.

DORCAS has a number of very positive associations. It comes from Greek *dorkas*, meaning 'a doe' or 'a gazelle'. In Chapter 9, Verse 36, of the *Acts of the Apostles*, *Dorcas* is given as a Greek equivalent of the Hebrew name *Tabitha*:

Now there was at Joppa a certain

disciple named Tabitha, which by interpretation is called Dorcas. This woman was full of good works and alms deeds which she did.

DOREEN/DORENE/DORINE
This name is a derivative of *Dora* and means 'little gift of God'. The spelling *Doreen* is the most widespread but the other variants also occur. SEE Dora

DORIS
is a Greek name meaning 'Dorian female'. The Dorians were members of a Greek tribe. They are thought to have settled in Greece around 1100BC. They later colonised Sicily and parts of southern Italy. *Doris* was a sea goddess and it is likely that the name is ultimately linked to *doron*, 'gift'.

DOROATA
is a widely used Polish equivalent of *Dorothy*, 'gift of God'. SEE Dorothea

DOROTHEA
is really the reverse of *Theodora*. It comes from Greek *doron*, 'gift' + *theos*, 'god', and means 'gift of God'. *Dorothy* was the usual form in

English until the late 19th century, when *Dorothea* became popular. Both are often given in honour of St Dorothy, who died in the early 4th century. On her way to be executed, a young man, *Theophilus*, is said to have mocked her, asking her to send him some fruit from the paradise she thought she was going to. After her death, an angel appeared to *Theophilus* with a basket containing three apples and three roses.

DRUSILLA
is a Latin name based on the Roman family name *Drusus*. It is believed to be a Gaulish name and the meaning is uncertain. The sister of the Emperor Caligula was called *Drusilla*.

DULCIE
This comes from the Latin adjective *dulcis*, 'sweet, pleasant'. It was quite widely used in the wake of the 1066 Norman Conquest in the forms *Dulcia*, *Duce* and *Douce*. (The loss of 'l' before a consonant was not uncommon. It is also found in 'calm' and 'talk'.) Interest in the name died out for almost 500

years but it began to be used again in the 19th century. The first syllable rhymes with 'gull' and not 'pull'.

DYMPHNA/DYMPNA

Ireland produced more than its fair share of saints during the first millennium and, because they were not overly interested in such temporal things as names, it is not always easy to separate one from the other. It seems highly probable that St Dymphna of Ghent is not the same woman as St Damhnait of Monaghan, although they lived around the same time and their names are supposedly from the same source, *damh*, 'poet'. St Dymphna, like many early Irish saints, travelled to Europe to establish a convent. She looked after the mentally ill and is their patron saint. The two spellings of the name are about equally popular. The first syllable of one is pronounced to rhyme with 'nymph', while the first syllable of *Dympna* rhymes with 'limp'.

E

EARTHA/ERTHA is not used widely but it was made famous by the singer, *Eartha Kitt* (b.1928), many of whose songs were popular worldwide.

Her name comes from Old English *eorþe*, 'the earth'.

There was a Cornish saint called *Ertha* and her name may mean 'strong faith'.

ECHO According to Greek mythology, *Echo* was a nymph who liked to talk. She offended *Hera*, the wife and sister of the supreme god, Zeus. Her punishment meant that she could only repeat what someone else said. *Echo* fell in love with *Narcissus*, but he rejected her and she faded away until only her voice was left. Her name is related to a Greek word meaning 'sound'.

EDANA is occasionally used as an anglicised form of *Eithne*, which may mean 'the kernel of the nut' or fire. SEE Eithne

EDEL is probably a variant of Adele, 'noble'. Irish Edels are usually called after Edel Quinn (1907-1944) who is honoured as Ireland's '20th century apostle to Africa'. SEE Adele

EDEN is one of the many place names that have been taken over as girls' names. It comes from Hebrew and means 'pleasure, delight'.

EDITH This Old English name comes from *ead*, 'prosperity' + *gyð*, 'battle'. The name has remained popular for over a thousand years. St Edith lived in the second half of the 10th century. She was a princess but entered a convent so as to dedicate her life to God. Considering its Old English origin, it is interesting to note that the name is popular in both France and Poland.

EDNA Although this name is more popular in England than in Ireland, it is likely that it is a variant of *Eithne*, 'the kernel of the nut', or 'fire'. It has been suggested that it may be a form of Hebrew *ednah*, 'pleasure, delight'. This is possible and would make *Edna* a variant of *Eden*. SEE Eden and Eithne

EIBHLIN is an Irish name that may have its roots in Gaelic, Hebrew or Greek, or all three. It may be related to *aoibhinn*, 'radiance'; it may be a modified form of *Evelyn*, which is based on Hebrew and means 'to breathe' or 'to live'; or it may be a form of Greek *Helen*, 'like the sun'. *Eibhlin* is sometimes pronounced like 'I've + lean' and sometimes like 'I've + lin'. SEE Eve

EDWINA has only been used since the 19th century. It is a female form of *Edwin* and comes from Old English *ead*, 'prosperity' + *wine*, 'friend', and probably means 'prosperity's friend'.

EDYTA is a popular Polish form of *Edith*. SEE Edith

EHAWEE (pronounced 'ey + ha + wee') Native American parents and parents who are interested in Sioux culture have used this onomatopoeic name. It means 'laughing maiden' in Sioux.

EILEEN It seems probable that *Eileen* is an anglicised spelling of Irish *Eibhlin*, 'radiance'. It is seen as quintessentially Irish, possibly because of its '-een' ending but, in fact, it was one of the most popular girls' names in England in the years between World Wars I and II. SEE Eibhlin

EIREEN This modern coinage is probably a blend of *Eileen*, 'radiance' + *Irene*, 'peace'. It is also possible that it is a variant of Welsh *Eirwin*, 'beautiful snow'. In Greek mythology, *Eirene* was the goddess of peace.

EITHNE (pronounced 'eth + na' where the 'a' is unstressed) is a traditional Irish name which may come from *eithne*, 'nut kernel', or it may be a female form of *Aodh* and so mean 'fire'. There are many stories about Irish Eithnes. According to a pre-Christian story, *Eithne* was the daughter of King Balor. He locked his daughter in a tower because it had been prophesied that he would be killed by a grandson. *Eithne* was made pregnant, however, by *Cian*, who managed to get into the tower dressed as a woman. *Eithne* had triplets but her three sons were cast into the sea by Balor. One of them, *Lugh*, was saved and killed

Balor when he grew up.

There is also a 5th-century St Eithne, who was a princess. She was converted by St Patrick and died shortly after being baptised.

EKATERINA is an Eastern European form of *Catherine*, 'pure' or 'like a goddess'. SEE Catherine

ELAINE is one of several versions of *Helen*, 'like the sun', that has become a name in its own right. It was popular among the Normans. In the Arthurian legends, *Elaine* falls irretrievably in love with *Lancelot*, but her love is unrequited and she dies of a broken heart. It is possible that the Celtic character on whom the Arthurian *Elaine* is based gets her name from a Welsh word, *elain*, meaning 'fawn'.

ELEANOR is an Old French form of an even older name, *Alienor*, which may come from Greek *Helen*, 'ray of sunshine', or it may be from a lost Germanic name, possibly meaning 'stranger'. A number of powerful women have borne this name.

One of the most interesting was Eleanor of Acquitaine (c.1122-1204). She was married to Louis VII of France from 1137 to 1152. In 1152, she met the future Henry II (1133-89) and, although eleven years his senior, they fell in love and got married after *Eleanor* got an annulment. They had ten children, including Richard the Lionheart. Between 1190 and 1194, *Eleanor* acted as regent for her son while he was on a Crusade in the Holy Land. *Eleanor* has many variants, the most popular being: *Eleanora*, *Eleanore*, *Eleonora*, *Eleonore*, *Elinor*, *Elinora* and *Elinore*. The names *Lenore* and *Leonora* are derivatives.

ELECTRA In Greek mythology, *Electra* was the daughter of Agamemnon and Clytemnestra. When her father was murdered, possibly by her mother and her mother's lover, *Electra* persuaded her brother to kill Clytemnestra and her lover. Her name is probably related to the Greek word, *elektron*, 'amber'.

ELFREDA is an Old English

name that is related to *Alfred*, 'fairy counsel'. *Elfreda* comes from *ælf*, 'fairy, elf, supernatural being' + *þryð*, 'strength', and suggests 'supernatural support', or in Christian terms 'guardian angel'.

ELICIA is occasionally used as a form of *Alicia*, 'noble nature'. SEE Alicia

ELISA is an abbreviated form of *Elizabeth*, 'God is my oath'. The use of 's' rather than 'z' is from the form of Elizabeth that was used in the *King James Bible* of 1611. SEE Elisabeth

ELISABETH The Hebrew form of this name was *Elisheba/Elisheva*, 'my God is my oath'. In spite of the fact that one of the most successful monarchs in English history was named *Elizabeth*, with a 'z', the translators of the *King James Bible* of 1611 preferred the form *Elisabeth*. This is also the preferred spelling in most European languages. SEE Elizabeth

ELISE is an abbreviated French

form of *Elizabeth*. It rhymes with 'sees', not 'cease'.

ELISSA It is possible that *Elissa* is used as a pet form of *Elizabeth*, but it was also another name of Queen Dido of Carthage. SEE Dido

ELIZABETH comes from Hebrew *Elisheva*, meaning 'my God is my oath' or perhaps 'my God is more than enough'. The '-th' ending may have been influenced by 'Sabbath'. It has been one of the most widely used names in Christendom for the last 2000 years. In the New Testament this is the name of the mother of John the Baptist. It was also the name of the 13th-century Saint Elizabeth (1207-31), who was a daughter of King Andrew II of Hungary. She was happily married but when her husband died, she became a Franciscan nun and lived in poverty. *Elizabeth* has given rise to a wide variety of pet forms, including *Bess, Bessie, Bet, Beth, Betina, Bette, Bettina, Betty, Elisa, Elise, Eliza, Elsa, Elsabie, Elsbeth, Elsie, Elspeth, Isabel, Isabella, Libby,*

Lisa, *Lise*, *Lisbeth*, *Liz*, *Liza*, *Lizbeth* and *Lizzy*.

Forms of Elizabeth

Variant	Where Found
Elizabet	Scandinavia, Finland
Elisabeta	Romania
Elisabete	Portugal
Elisabetta	Italy
Elisavet	Greece
Elisaveta	Bulgaria
Elixabete	Basque country
Elizaveta	Russia
Elzbieta	Poland
Isabel(la)	Spain
Iseabéal	Ireland
Eilís	Ireland
Iseabeul	Scotland

ELKE can have two different origins. It can be a diminutive of *Adelaide*, 'noble nature', found in the Netherlands. It can also be a feminine form of the Hebrew name *Elkana*, meaning 'God has obtained'.

ELKIE means 'little Ella', 'foreign one' or 'little Helen', meaning 'ray of sunshine'. SEE Ellen

ELLA Over the last twenty-five years, *Ella* has become one of the most popular names in the English-speaking world. Its appeal is obvious. It is short, easy to pronounce and is not fixed to any one place or time. For many parents, it is a modern form of *Ellen*, but for some it is a variant of *Eleanor* or one of the many Germanic names that originally began with *Ali*, 'foreign'.

ELLEN was originally a variant of *Helen*, 'ray of sunshine'. In the Middle Ages, the initial 'h' was sometimes dropped. It was also sometimes added where it did not originally occur, as with *Hester* for *Esther*, although Esther's Hebrew name was *Hadassah*, 'myrtle'. The Welsh name *Elen* comes from the Welsh word for 'nymph', although it can also be a form of *Helen*. SEE Helen

ELMA is occasionally used as a variant of *Alma*, 'nourishing, kind'. It is also used as a pet form of *Fidelma*. SEE Alma

ELMIRA This is a variant of the Arabic name *Almira*, which comes

from *amiri*, meaning 'princess'.
SEE Almira

ELOISE (pronounced 'elo +
wees') was, until recently, found
mainly in France, but in the last
fifty years it has gained
worldwide use. It comes from an
Old French form, *Héloïse*, and,
although its precise meaning is
uncertain, it is probably related
to Greek *Helios*, 'sun'. Eloise was
the wife of the French theologian
Peter Abelard (1079-1142). She
became an abbess after her
husband was castrated by her
uncle, Canon Fulbert.

ELRICA may be considered a
Germanic female equivalent of
Donald, in that it may mean 'ruler
of all'. It is also possible that it
means 'foreign ruler'.

ELSA was originally a German
pet form of *Elisabeth*, 'my God is
my oath' but it is now used
widely as an independent name.

ELSIE is found mainly in
Scotland and Ireland. Originally,
it was probably a pet form of
Elisabeth, especially in the form
Elspeth. SEE Elisabeth

ELSPETH is a Scottish
form of *Elisabeth*, 'my God
is my oath'. SEE Elisabeth

ELUNED is an increasingly
popular Welsh name that is
probably derived from *eilun*,
'image, god'.

ELVA is very probably a
Germanic name related to Old
English *ælf*, 'elf, supernatural
being'. It is sometimes used as a
pet form of *Elfreda*. SEE Alfreda

ELVIRA is a Spanish name of
Germanic origin. It is probably a
combination of *ali*, 'foreign' +
wer, 'true'. It was widely used in
the Middle Ages and began to be
popular again in the early 20th
century. *Elwira* is the Polish
form.

ELZBIETA is the Polish form of
Elizabeth, 'my God is my oath'.
SEE Elisabeth

EMELDA is a form of *Imelda*, a
Spanish name of Germanic
origin. It probably comes from
erman, 'great' + *hild*, 'battle' or
'warrior'. SEE Hilda and Imelda

EMER (pronounced 'ee + mer' or 'aimer') is a popular Irish name. It possibly comes from *eimh*, 'swift'. *Emer* was the wife of the Ulster champion *Cuchulain* and possessed the six gifts that go to make the perfect woman. These are: beauty, chastity, wisdom, a lovely voice, the knowledge of how and when to speak, and the ability to produce superb needlework!

EMERALD is a precious stone that is sometimes used as a girl's name. It came into English from Old French *esmeraude*, which is a form of Latin *smaragdus*. It is usually bright green in colour and is the birthstone for people born in May. Traditionally, the emerald is said to make the wearer of the jewel love the person who gave her/him the stone. SEE Esmeralda

EMI (pronounced 'Amy') is a Japanese name coming from *e*, 'blessed' + *mi*, 'beauty', and meaning 'blessed with beauty'. It is related to *Emiko*, 'blessed child'.

EMILY is related to *Amelia*. They both come from the Latin family name *Æmilius*, 'rival'. It has become one of the top twenty names in the English-speaking world. Emily Brontë (1818-48) wrote what many believe to be one of the greatest novels of all time, *Wuthering Heights*. SEE Amelia

EMMA Although *Emma* is not related to *Emily*, it too has been extremely popular since the 1960s. It was introduced by the Normans and is a reduced form of a Germanic name such as *Ermintrude*. *Ermin* means 'complete' or 'universal'. *Emma* is the title of one of Jane Austen's most popular novels.

EMMANUELLE This is a French feminine form of *Emmanuel*, 'God is with us'.

ENA is one of the anglicisations of the Irish name *Eithne*, 'nut kernel' or 'flame'. It is also sometimes used as a pet form of names than end in '-ena'. SEE Eithne

ENID is a Welsh name that was given wide-reaching circulation by Enid Blyton (1897-1968), who was one of the world's most widely read authors of children's fiction. In the Arthurian Cycle, *Enid* was the virtuous, long-suffering wife of Geraint. Her name is derived from *enaid*, 'soul, life'.

ENIOLA (pronounced 'any + o + la') is a Yoruba name meaning 'wealthy one'. It is not only in Nigeria that parents would want their children to have a life of comfort.

ENYA (pronounced 'ayn + ia') is a form of *Eithne*. It is the stage name of Eithne Ní Bhraonáin (b. 1961). She is one of Ireland's best-known musicians and performers but her fame is not limited to Ireland. In 2006 she was the twelfth biggest-selling female artist in the world. SEE Anne and Eithne

ERICA It seems probable that *Erica* was first used in the 18th century as a feminine form of *Eric*, 'eternal ruler'. This Germanic name is made up of two elements, *ei*, 'forever' + *rikr*, 'ruler, power'. It was carried to the British Isles by the Danes in the form of *Eirikr*. *Erica* is also, however, the Latin word for 'heather' so parents have a choice of etymologies.

ERIN is based on *Éire*, the Irish word for 'Ireland'. In the mid 20th century, it was a popular name for daughters of people with Irish connections. It was further popularised by Julia Roberts in the film *Erin Brockovich*, about a woman who, despite having no formal legal education, was instrumental in constructing a case against the Pacific Gas and Electricity Company of California in 1993. The case was settled for $33 million, the largest settlement ever paid in a direct action lawsuit in US history. Thomas Campbell (1777-1844) used *Erin go bragh*, 'Ireland forever', as the refrain of one of his poems. Campbell was a Glaswegian.

GIRLS

ERMA is occasionally used as a variant of *Irma*. Both are Germanic in origin and are the result of shortening such names as *Ermintrude*. *Irmen*, the section of the name that gave *Erma* and *Emma*, means 'complete, universal'. SEE Ermintrude

ERMINTRUDE It is possible that this once famous Germanic name would be unknown today if it had not occurred as the name of a main character in *The Magic Roundabout*, a children's TV programme that ran from 1965 to 1977. *Ermintrude* comes from *ermen*, 'complete' + *traut*, 'beloved', and it was popular among the Normans.

ERNESTA/ERNESTINE These feminine forms of *Ernest*, 'seriousness', are occasionally used by families who want to pay respect to a father, grandfather or godfather called *Ernest*.

ESHA is used by Indian communities worldwide. It comes from a Sanskrit word meaning 'desire'.

ESHE is a Swahili name meaning 'life'. It is, like many given names, a wish for the child.

ESMÉ is occasionally used as an abbreviation of Spanish *Esmeralda*, 'emerald', but it is, in fact, a French name based on an Old French verb *esmer*, 'to esteem, to value'. It means 'esteemed, valued'.

ESMERALDA For parents who want a mouth-filling name, *Esmeralda*, the Spanish form of 'emerald', fits the bill. Victor-Marie Hugo (1802-85) immortalised the name in his novel *Notre Dame de Paris* in 1831. In the 1939 film version, *The Hunchback of Notre Dame*, the part of the Gypsy girl *Esmeralda*, who was loved by Quasimodo, was played by a very young Maureen O'Hara.

ESTELLA/ESTELLE Both these names owe their origin to the Old French name for 'star', which came from Latin *stella*.

ESTHER It is always interesting to see how names change and how our favourites

78

may not be exactly what we thought. *Esther* is assumed by many to be a Hebrew name, but it is almost certainly Persian and may be a Farsi equivalent of Hebrew *Hadassah*, meaning 'myrtle'. In the Old Testament, *Hadassah/Esther* was a captive in Persia, probably in the reign of Xerxes I (c.519-456BC) although he is referred to as King Ahasuerus in the *Book of Esther*. He asked for all the beautiful young virgins to be brought to him and he was so pleased by Esther that she was made his queen. She used her position to save the Israelites, who were in captivity, from persecution. *Esther* is usually pronounced like 'ester'.

ETAIN (pronounced 'ey + tawn'/'ee + tawn'/'ey + tane'/'ee + tane') is one of the most beautiful and memorable characters in Irish mythology. Her name is likely to be linked to *ét*, an Old Irish word for 'jealousy'. This is very appropriate, because she arouses the jealousy of Fuamnach, Midir's wife, when Midir decides

that he wants to marry *Etain*! Fuamnach uses her magical powers to change *Etain* into a pool of water, then into a worm and finally into a fly that is tossed and buffeted by winds for seven years! Eventually the fly is swallowed by a pregnant woman and *Etain* is reborn.

ETHEL This is an abbreviation of a number of Germanic names, such as *Ethelburga*, 'noble stronghold', or *Ethelgifu*, 'noble gift'. In Old English, *æðel* was the word for 'noble'. The full names have lost out to the abbreviation in that all the long names, including *Etheldreda*, who was a 7th-century princess and saint, have disappeared, but *Ethel* survives.

ETHNA is a modern spelling of *Eithne*, 'nut kernel' or 'flame'. SEE Eithne

ETTA like *Ethel*, is a pet form that has gained the status of a full name. It has been taken from such names as *Loretta*, *Violetta* or *Yvetta*. *Etta* is actually a diminutive and means 'little'.

EUGENIA is a female form of *Eugene*. It comes from Greek *eugenes*, meaning 'well-born'. Napoleon III (1808-73), who was the nephew of Napoleon Bonaparte, had a wife whose name was Doña Maria *Eugenia* Ignacia Augustina de Palafox y Kirkpatrick (1826-1920). She was the first real person to have an asteroid called after her. Eugenia was discovered in 1857 and it is famous for having its own moon orbiting it.

EUNICE is the latinised equivalent of the Greek name, *Eunike*, 'great victory'. The 'Nike' brand of sportswear is taken from the Greek word, *nike*, meaning 'victory'.

EURYDICE (pronounced 'your + id +issay') Most people know this name even if it is not frequently used outside the Greek community. It comes from the Greek name *Eurydike*, from *eurys*, 'wide' + *dike*, 'justice'. In Greek mythology, she was the wife of *Orpheus*, who was a wonderful musician. When *Eurydice* died from a snakebite, Orpheus used his musical skill to win her back from the Underworld. He was instructed not to look back as she followed him from Hades, but Orpheus could not contain his desire to see *Eurydice* again. He looked back and saw his wife returning to Hades.

EUSTACIA (pronounced 'yew + stay + sha') This is a female form of *Eustace*, 'good grapes' or 'of good standing'. The name was popularised by the novelist, Thomas Hardy (1840-1928). In *The Return of the Native* (1878), Eustacia Vye returns to Egdon Heath in Wessex to live with her grandfather. From the moment she returns, she looks for a means of escape and, in Victorian times, that meant finding the right husband!

EVA is often used as a form of *Eve*, 'breath, life'. It is the Latin form of the name. SEE Eve

EVANGELINE is from Greek

eu, 'good' + *angelion*, 'news, message'. It is from the same root as 'evangelist'.

EVE According to the Old Testament, *Eve* is the mother of all human beings. Her Hebrew name, *Chavvah*, is closer in sound to *Havah* than to *Eve*. It suggests 'to breathe' and 'to live' and she is closely linked in the Bible story to her son, *Abel*, whose name also probably means 'to breathe'. According to the *Book of Genesis*, *Eve* is tempted by the serpent and eats the forbidden fruit, which she then shares with *Adam*. Their disobedience causes their expulsion from the Garden of Eden.

EVELYN has the sort of history that we often find associated with favourite names. The Normans had a name *Aveline*, whose meaning is unclear but it has been linked to Latin *avis*, 'bird'. It gave rise to a surname, *Eveling*. This in turn gave rise to the male name *Evelyn*, which has now become a favourite girl's name. Others believe that *Evelyn* is a pet form of *Eve*. SEE Aveline

EVITA This is a Spanish diminutive form of *Eva*. It was the affectionate name that the Argentine people gave to Eva Peron (1919-52), the wife of the President Juan Domingo Peron.

EVONNE This spelling is occasionally used for *Yvonne*, 'yew'. SEE Yvonne

EWA (pronounced 'ey + va') is a popular Polish form of Eve. SEE Eve

NOTABLE NAMESAKES
Edel Quinn (1907-44) Irish lay missionary who worked tirelessly for the poor in Ireland and Africa; Edith Piaf (1915-63) one of France's best-known singers, especially famous for tragic ballads often reflecting her own life; Elizabeth Barrett Browning (1806-61) Victorian poet who supported the abolition of slavery. She eloped with another poet,

Robert Browning;
Eunice Kennedy Shriver
(b.1921) sister of the late
John F Kennedy and founder
of the Special Olympics. She
is the only living woman
whose portrait appears on a
US coin; Eva Peron
(1919-52) as the wife of Juan
Peron, the President of
Argentina, she worked to
help the poor. Andrew
Lloyd Webber's musical
Evita commemorates her
life.

F

FABIA is a female form of the
Latin name *Fabius*, which is
derived from *faba*, 'bean'. The
meaning may not seem attractive
to modern parents but, in a
society where beans played a
large role in the cuisine, it had
increased relevance.

FABIANA is a female form of

Fabian, 'bean'. It is popular in
Spanish communities, where it is
given in honour of a 3rd-century
Pope Fabian.

FAITH is sometimes defined as
'divine virtue by which we desire
and firmly expect that God will
give us eternal life and the means
to attain it'. It became popular
with Puritans in the 1600s and
has remained a favourite ever
since. St Faith was martyred for
her Christian beliefs during the
reign of Diocletian.

FALLON comes from an Irish
surname which is derived from
fallamhan, 'leader'. It began to be
popular in the late 20th century,
possibly as a result of the soap
opera, *Dynasty*.

FARAH/FARRAH is usually
derived from the surname
Farrah, which owes its origin to
the Old French noun, *ferreor*,
'worker in iron or metal'. The
trade was important to the
Normans and the surname has
existed since the 13th century. It
may also owe some of its use to
an Arabic name, *Fariha*, 'happy'.

FATIMA is an Arabic name, probably meaning 'to abstain'. It was the name of the Prophet Muhammad's youngest daughter (c. AD 606-632). She is especially revered by Shi'ite Muslims because they claim descent from her. *Fatima* was also the name of Bluebeard's last wife. It is the name of a village in Portugal where, in 1917, three children reported seeing visions of Our Lady. Fatima is one of the most visited Marian shrines in the world and has helped to popularise the name of one of the visionaries, *Jacinta*, as a girl's name in Christian countries.

FAUSTA is relatively common among Spaniards and Italians and one can understand why. It comes from Latin *Faustus*, meaning 'happy, lucky'. The name is less common in English-speaking communities. This may be because of the play, *Doctor Faustus*, written by Christopher Marlowe (1564-93). The real Johann Faust (c.1488-1541) was a German scholar and necromancer. It was believed that he sold his soul to

the devil. *Faustina*, meaning 'lucky little one' is growing in popularity.

FAY/FAYE This is from Old French and may be from *fei*, 'faith', or *fei*, 'fairy, supernatural being'. It does not seem to have been used as a given name before the 19th century but it has been popular ever since. In Arthurian legend, Morgan le Fay was Arthur's half-sister. According to one account, she is one of the women who take Arthur to Avalon so that he will not die of his wounds.

FELICIA is from Latin and is the female equivalent of *Felix*, 'lucky'. The name is extremely popular in Africa.

FELICITY is related to *Felicia*. It comes from Latin *felicitatem*, 'happiness, luck'. It is the English form of *Felicitas*, the name of a saint who died in Carthage in AD 203. *Felicitas* was in prison with St Perpetua, who wrote an account of their imprisonment and trial. The account goes up to the day before the Games when the Christians were killed by animals and gladiators.

FENELLA It is not always realised that this is a form of the Irish name *Fionnuala*, 'fair shoulders'. SEE: Fionnuala

FERN is one of the many names of plants that parents choose for a daughter. This one comes from Old English *fearn*, 'fern', but it only began to be popular in the 20th century. It emerged at a time when a lot of parents turned to nature for inspiration, choosing *Brooke, Summer, River* and even *Valley*. As early as AD 800, there was a belief that ferns were lucky plants and that wearing a piece of fern transferred that luck to the wearer. The spelling *Ferne* is sometimes used.

FERNANDA is a popular choice among the Spanish and Portuguese and may mean 'prepared to travel' or 'prepared for peace'. The diminutive *Fernandina* is also occasionally used.

FIDELA comes from Latin *fidelis* and means 'faithful one'. Many children who have this name in Cuba have been named after Fidel Castro. The name is not limited to Cuba, however. It has been selected by parents who like the meaning and prefer the Latin form to *Faith*.

FIDELIA also comes from Latin *fidelis*, meaning 'faithful'. It is preferred by some parents to *Fidela*, possibly because its ending is similar to *Cordelia* and *Ophelia*.

FIDELMA seems to be more popular in Ireland than elsewhere. It probably owes its origin to Latin *fidelis*, 'faithful', although it may also owe something to *feidhle*, 'constancy', or *fidchell*, an ancient board game similar to chess. Saint Fidelma (occasionally also spelt *Fedelma*) was a 5th-century saint who was baptised by St Patrick. She was the daughter of the High King and the sister of St Eithne.

FIFI Although this name is no longer widely used as a given name, its form reminds us of how much a pet name can vary from its source. *Fifi* is a French pet form of *Josephine*, a Hebrew name meaning 'God will add'. *Fifi* comes from a doubling of the '-phi-' portion of the name. SEE Josephine

FILIPA The Spanish, unlike the English, have systematically simplified their spelling system so as to reflect pronunciation more closely. This is the same name as *Philippa*, 'lover of horses'. The diminutive form, *Filipina*, also occurs regularly. SEE Philippa

FINOLA is a form of Irish *Fionnghuala*, 'beautiful/fair shoulders'. SEE Fionnghuala

FIONA is a Latinate form of the Gaelic adjective *fionn*, 'white, fair, beautiful'. It was more popular in Scotland than elsewhere in the 19th century but it has become an extremely popular choice. The Welsh form *Ffion* has also increased in popularity.

FIONNGHUALA/ FIONNUALA

(pronounced 'fyon + oo + ala'/'fin + oo + ala') This is a traditional Gaelic name, going back the best part of 2000 years and probably a lot longer than that. It is a blend of *fionn*, 'fair, white' + *gualainn*, 'shoulder'. It was the name of one of the loveliest characters in Irish mythology, the daughter of King Lir. She and her three brothers, *Aedh*, *Conn* and *Fiachra* were transformed into swans by their stepmother, *Aoife*. Their story is referred to in Thomas Moore's song, 'Silent, O Moyle':

Silent, O Moyle, be the roar of thy water,
Break not, ye breezes, your chain of repose,
While mournfully weeping, Lir's lonely daughter
Tells to the night-star her tale of woes.

FLAVIA comes from an old Roman family name that was based on the word *flavus*, 'golden-aired'. The 'Flavian' dynasty lasted from AD 69 to 96 and included the Emperor

85

Vespasian and his two sons, Titus and Domitian.

Several early saints bore the name of *Flavia*.

FLEUR is the French word for 'flower' and this name was popularised throughout the English-speaking world by the novelist John Galsworthy (1867-1933). One of the heroines of his popular set of novels, *The Forsyte Saga*, was called *Fleur*. Very occasionally, the diminutive form, *Fleurette*, also occurs.

FLORA In Roman mythology, *Flora* was the goddess of flowers and plants. Her name comes from *flos*, 'flower'. Flora MacDonald (1722-90) was a Scottish heroine. When Bonnie Prince Charlie – Charles Edward Stuart (1720-88), the Young Pretender – was defeated at the Battle of Culloden (1746), she helped him to escape to the island of Skye, dressed as her maid.

FLORENCE Originally, *Florence* was a man's name coming from *florens*, 'blossoming,

blooming'. The Latin name of the city known in Italian as *Firenze* was *Florentia* and several parents have taken the name directly from the city, which was a leading axis of the Italian Renaissance. Florence Nightingale (1820-1910) was so admired for her work during the Crimean War that thousands of girls were called after her. The abbreviated forms of *Florence* include *Flo*, *Flor*, *Florrie*, *Florry* and *Flossie*, and the variants *Florencia* and *Florenza* are also found.

FRANCES This is the feminine form of *Francis*, 'French man'. It has been used for almost 800 years in honour of St Francis of Assisi (1182-1226) and its use has been augmented by devotion to St Francis Xavier (1506-52). *Francesca* is the Italian form and it, too, is extremely popular. *Françoise* occurs widely in France and the Polish form, *Franciszka*, is a popular choice in Poland. The abbreviated form *Frankie* is probably more widely used today for girls than boys, and JD Salinger (b. 1919) popularised

Franny in his novel *Franny and Zooey* (1961).

FREDA/FRIEDA This name started life as an abbreviation of names such as *Ethelfreda*, 'noble peace', but only the abbreviation has survived. It means 'peace', so one can understand its attraction for parents. *Freda* is often regarded as a female form of *Frederick* but, although they both incorporate the Germanic word for 'peace', the female name is as old as the male. The spelling *Frieda* has been carried over from German, where the name has continued to be popular.

FREDERICA/FREDERIKE/ FRÉDÉRIQUE These names are all female forms of *Frederic(k)*, 'peaceful rule/power'. The first has been Latinised, the second is German and the third is French. Often, *Freddie* occurs as an abbreviation.

FREIYA/FREYA/FREYJA (pronounced 'fray + ya') In Scandinavian mythology, *Freiya* was the goddess of love and of the night. She had a brother god,

called *Frey*, who looked after the sun and rain and who was linked to fertility. It seems probable that both names come from Old Norse *freo*, 'seed', and *frior*, 'fertility'.

NOTABLE NAMESAKES
Fanny Blankers-Koen (1918-2004) Dutch athlete who won four gold medals at the London Olympics in 1948; Florence Nightingale (1820-1910) became known as 'The Lady with the Lamp' because of her pioneering work in nursing during the Crimean War; Dame Freya Stark (1893-1993) writer, explorer and linguist, often travelling alone in the Arabian deserts; Fay Wray (1907-2004) Canadian actress best known for playing in *King Kong* (1933).

G

GABRIELLA/GABRIELLE

These are the Italian and the French female forms of the Hebrew name *Gabriel*, 'man of God'. They are both abbreviated to *Gabby*, *Gabi*, *Gay* and *Gaye*. The first syllable of both names is sometimes pronounced to rhyme with 'fab' and sometimes with 'babe'.

GAEL is sometimes a spelling variant of *Gail*, 'parent of exaltation'. Recently, however, it has been used by Celts because the name means 'Irish, or Scottish Celt'. The name also occurs in the United States, possibly due to the influence of *Clan na Gael*, 'family of the Irish'. This was an Irish American revolutionary organisation that was set up in 1867 to help promote Irish independence. SEE Abigail

GAIA (rhymes with 'my + a') It seems likely that this name, which was rarely used before

> **NAMES FROM JEWELS AND GEMSTONES**
> Amber
> Beryl
> Emerald
> Coral
> Crystal
> Garnet
> Jade
> Opal
> Pearl
> Ruby
> Sapphire

1969, will become increasingly popular as we try to protect the planet. In Greek mythology, it was the name of the goddess of the Earth. In 1969, James Lovelock (b.1919) put forward the hypothesis that the earth, which he called *Gaia*, is a vast self-regulating organism.

GAIL was originally an abbreviated form of *Abigail*, 'parent of exaltation', but it is now regularly used as a given name. The variants *Gael*, *Gale* and *Gayle* are also found. SEE Abigail

GALINA is a Russian form of *Helen*, 'ray of sunlight'. Galina Vasilyevna Amelkina (b.1954) came to prominence as a cosmonaut and scientist. SEE Helen

GANDHALI is used mainly by Indian families. The name means 'attractive, sweet scent'.

GARNET is one of several jewels that parents have chosen for their children's names. *Garnet* may come from Latin *grana*, 'cochineal', or from Old French *pome garnette*, 'pomegranate', because the seeds were often a deep red colour.

GAYNOR comes indirectly from Welsh. It is an anglicised form of *Guinevere*, 'fair and smooth'. SEE Guinevere

GEMMA is an Italian name meaning 'gem, jewel'. It was popularised in the 20th century by St Gemma Galgani (1878-1903). She was born in Camigliano, Italy, and showed signs of sanctity in her response to her poor health. In 1899, she began to display the stigmata. Every Thursday evening, the bleeding from her hands, feet and side would start, and it would end on Saturday. She died of tuberculosis and was canonised in 1940.

GENA is occasionally used as an abbreviated form of *Georgina*, 'farmer', *Eugenia*, 'nobly born', or of *Regina*, 'queen'. It is regularly seen as the female form of *Gene*, the popular abbreviation of *Eugene*. SEE Eugenia and Regina

GENEVIEVE is a French form of a Celtic name that may mean 'fair people'. St Genevieve (d. AD 500) is the patron saint of Paris. She was dedicated to God at an early age and was renowned for her penances and sanctity. Her prayers were credited with turning Attila and his troops away from attacking Paris, but when Paris was subsequently attacked by Childeric, she managed to carry a boatload of grain to the starving.

GEORGETTE/GEORGIA/ GEORGINA These are all female forms of *George*, 'farmer', and they have all been popular at different times and with different communities. *Georgette* is a French diminutive. It was popularised by Georgette Heyer (1902-74) who wrote widely read historical novels. *Georgia* is sometimes used in honour of the State of Georgia in the United States. It was named after George II (1683-1760). *Georgina* was extremely popular in Victorian times and is resurgent at the moment. They are all abbreviated to *Georgie* or *Georgy*.

GERALDINE is derived from *Gerald*, 'strong spear'. It did not come into existence until the 16th century but it has remained a popular choice ever since. The Latinate form, *Geraldina*, is less widely used but also occurs. They are both abbreviated to *Geri* and *Gerri*.

GERDA In Norse mythology, *Gerda* was a fertility goddess and her name seems to be related to *gjorðr*, 'the earth'. In English, the name is usually pronounced like 'gird + a', but occasionally

parents attempt to reflect the Scandinavian pronunciation and say what sounds like 'hair + da'.

GERMAINE is a French name that is related to *Germanus*, possibly 'German' or 'closely related'. When the early Christians used it, they probably meant 'brother in Christ'. *Germaine* can be interpreted as 'sister in Christ'. St Germaine (c. 1579-1601) was canonised in 1867 and her canonisation led to an expansion in the use of the name.

GERTRUD/GERTRUDE is a Germanic name composed of the elements *gar*, 'spear' + *traut*, 'beloved'. (Often, 'spear' was used to represent 'warrior'.) St Gertrude (c. 626-64) was born into a noble family. Indeed, she was the great-aunt of Charlemagne, the Holy Roman Emperor (742-814). She and her mother both entered the convent of Nivelles when her father died and she was renowned for her piety. She is often depicted with a mouse because it was said that when she was absorbed in prayer, a mouse could have run up her staff and she would not have noticed! The usual abbreviations are *Gertie*, *Trudie* and *Trudy*.

GHISLAIN/GHISLAINE

(pronounced 'giz + lane'/'jiz + lane') This French name has only become popular in the last fifty years. Its origins are obscure but it seems to be related to *Giselle*, 'pledge, promise'. SEE Giselle

GILA/GILAH ('g' as in

'garden') is a Hebrew name, probably meaning 'joy, delight'. It is occasionally used as a female form of *Giles*, 'kid', or as an alternative of *Gillian*.

GILLIAN is derived from *Julian*

and was once used as an alternative spelling of the male name. *Gillian* was used in the 16th century to mean 'young girl', possibly suggesting how popular the name was. It derives ultimately from the Roman family name *Julius*, which may be related to Latin *julus*, 'catkin', or may mean 'child of Jove'.

GINA is frequently an

abbreviated form of *Georgina*, 'little female farmer'. SEE Georgette

GINETTE is more popular

in the southern hemisphere than in the north. It can be a modified spelling of the French diminutive *Jeannette*, 'God is gracious'. SEE Jeannette

GISELE/GISELLE ('g' as in

'gendarme') is a French name of Germanic origin. It is a derivation of *gisil*, 'pledge'. *Gizela* is a Polish form. The name was popularised in Europe by the romantic French ballet *Giselle*, which was first performed in Paris in 1841. It is the only ballet from the Romantic era to be performed regularly and in full on the modern stage.

GLADYS/GWLADYS is a

Welsh name that may be a form of Latin *Claudia*, from the nickname *claudus*, 'lame'. It was widely popular in the early 20th century especially in families with Welsh connections. Part of its appeal to parents was a belief that it was related to the wild iris, the gladiolus.

GLENDA is a Welsh name involving two adjectives, *glan*, 'clean, pure' + *da*, 'good'. It can thus be interpreted as 'good and pure'. It is found throughout the world and is no longer associated primarily with Welsh families.

GLENYS/GLYNIS These names may, in fact, be quite distinct but they are often thought to be variants. They come from Welsh *glyn*, 'valley', and can therefore be considered a Welsh female variant of *Glen* and *Glyn*.

GLORIA is a Latin word meaning 'glory'. It is sometimes used as a summary of *Gloria in excelsis deo*, 'Glory be to God in the highest', a prayer that occurs in the Mass. The name is popular in the Caribbean and in Latin America. *Gloriana*, 'glorious one', also occurs but much less frequently. It was coined by Edmund Spenser (c. 1552-99) to honour Queen Elizabeth I in his poem *The Faerie Queene*. Benjamin Britten's opera *Gloriana* was composed in honour of the coronation of Elizabeth II in 1952.

GOLDA/GOLDIE These names come from both Yiddish and German *gold*, 'gold', and they are most frequently found in Jewish communities. Golda Meir (1898-1978) was Prime Minister of Israel and, partly as a result of her popularity, the name has become more widely used.

GRACE is an English form of Latin *gratia*, which in Christian terms means 'the free and unmerited favour of God'. The Puritans of the 17th century used the name widely, and it was used as a mark of honour to Grace Darling (1815-42). She was the daughter of the lighthouse keeper on the Farne Islands. On an exceptionally wild night in September 1838, she and her father rowed through a storm to rescue survivors of the *Forfarshire*.

GRAINNE/GRÁINNE (pronounced 'graw + nye') The meaning of this Irish name is uncertain but it is likely to be linked to *grádh*, 'love', and to imply 'beloved'. In Irish mythology, *Gráinne* is one of several strong women who refuse to be married off to a man they do not love. *Gráinne* is due to marry the aged Fionn Mac Cumhail, but runs off with Fionn's nephew, *Diarmaid*. The old king's curse is that the lovers may never sleep two consecutive nights in the one bed. *Gráinne* remains one of the most popular names in Ireland and in families with Irish connections.

GRETA is an abbreviated form of Swedish *Margareta*, 'pearl'. It was almost entirely due to the fame and reputation of the film actress Greta Garbo (1905-90) that *Greta* became popular worldwide. If anything, the name increased in popularity after 1941 when Greta Garbo gave up films and lived as a recluse.

GRETCHEN is a German abbreviated diminutive of *Margaret*, 'pearl'. Johann Goethe (1749-1832) immortalised the name in *Faust* (1808). It is the name of a young innocent girl who was seduced by Faust.

GRISELDA is a Germanic name, probably coming from *gris*, 'grey' + *hild*, 'battle'. *Griselda* is the heroine of the *Clerk's Tale* by Geoffrey Chaucer (c.1340-1400). In spite of rejection by her husband, she remains patient, loyal and loving and eventually is rewarded by regaining his love. An abbreviated form, *Zelda*, is probably more widespread now than the full name.

GUINEVERE is one of the best known names in mythological traditions. It is based on an old Welsh name, *Gwenhwyfar*, 'fair + smooth'. In the Arthurian Cycle, *Guinevere* is the wife of King Arthur but, like many Celtic heroines, including *Gráinne*, she falls in love with another man, in this case, Lancelot. Part of Guinevere's tragedy is that she loves Arthur and yet, unintentionally, brings about his downfall. *Jennifer* is the Cornish form of the name.

GWEN can be a name in its own right, coming from Welsh

GIRLS

gwen, 'fair, white, holy'. It can also be an abbreviation of *Gwendolen*, 'fair ring'. St David, the patron saint of Wales, had an aunt, also a saint, called *Gwen*.

GWENDOLEN/ GWENDOLIN/ GWENDOLINE/ GWENDOLYN

These are all variants of a Welsh name made up of the elements *gwen*, 'fair, white, holy' + *dolen*, 'ring, bow'. It is not certain what the 'holy ring' or 'bow' refers to, but it may be a reference to the 'rainbow' that was a sign of peace between God and humanity after the Deluge. The name has a range of abbreviations including *Gwen*, *Gwenda* and *Wendy*, although *Wendy* can mean 'friend'. SEE Wendy

GWYNAETH/GWYNETH

is a Welsh name meaning 'prosperity, good luck'. The first variant is mainly used in Wales, with *Gwyneth* being the preferred form for most English speakers.

NOTABLE NAMESAKES
Gabriela Sabatini (b.1970) Argentinian tennis professional who won the women's singles title at the US Open in 1990, the women's doubles title at Wimbledon in 1988, and a silver medal at the 1988 Olympic Games; Germaine Greer (b.1939) Australian scholar and feminist, best known, perhaps, for her pioneering book, *The Female Eunuch* in 1970; Golda Meir (1898-1978) American who became the fourth Prime Minister of Israel; Gladys Aylward (1902-70) English missionary to China. Her life story was filmed in *The Inn of the Sixth Happiness* in 1958.

H

HALCYON comes from Greek *alcyon*, 'kingfisher'. In Greek folklore, the kingfisher bred during the winter solstice, December 21-22, and made a nest on the sea. The bird was thought to have magical powers to keep the sea and the wind calm so that its nest was not disturbed. The expression 'halcyon days' began to be used to refer to a period of peace and calm. The name began to be used for daughters in the early 20th century.

HALEY/HAILEY/HAYLEY

These variants all come from places called in Old English *heg*, 'hay' + *leah*, 'clearing'. The place name became a surname in the 14th century and a given name for girls in the 20th century.

HALIMA (pronounced 'hal + eema') is an Arabic name meaning 'kind, generous, benevolent'.

HALLEY/HALLIE/HALLE

These variants come from a surname that has been in existence since the 13th century. It is derived from *heall*, 'hall, manor' + *leah*, 'clearing'. It is possible that parents who choose this name have been interested in 'Halley's Comet', a comet that becomes visible every seventy-six years. Its first recorded sighting was in 240BC, and it was last seen in 1985-86. It takes its name from the astronomer Edmond Halley (1656-1742), who calculated correctly that the comet would appear in 1758-59. The Halley Comet features on the Bayeux tapestry that depicts William the Conqueror's victory at Hastings in 1066.

HANA is a Japanese name that can mean both 'flower' and 'favourite'. A modified variant, *Hanako*, means 'flower child' or 'favourite child'. Since *Hana* is pronounced like *Hannah*, it can be used as an alternative to the Hebrew name.

HANNA/HANNAH

This Hebrew name means 'graciousness'. It comes from the Hebrew verb *hannan*, 'to be gracious'. It has given rise to *Ann*, *Anna*, *Anne* and to variants in virtually every language in the world. *Hannah* is nearer in pronunciation to the original Hebrew, but the forms without 'h' were preferred until the 17th century, when the form *Hannah* was taken up by Puritans. There are five women named *Anna/Hannah* in the Bible. It is the name of the mother of the prophet *Samuel*; it is the name of the wife and the mother of *Tobias*; St Luke uses it as the name of the aged prophetess who spends most of her time in the Temple; and finally, it is the name of the mother of the Blessed Virgin Mary. SEE Anna

HARMONY

like *Halcyon*, is a name chosen by parents who are making a wish that their child's life may be as serene as her chosen name. The name comes from Greek and means 'concord of sounds in music'.

HARUKO

is a popular Japanese name for a child born in the spring. It means 'spring child' or 'sunny child'.

HARRIET

is a female diminutive form of *Harry*, 'home power'. It seems to have been used only since the 17th century but has become more popular than the older forms *Henrietta* and *Henriette*. SEE Henrietta

HAYLEY

is a more widespread form of *Haley*, 'hay clearing'. SEE Haley

HAZEL

is one of the many flower and plant names chosen by parents for their children. This one comes from Old English *hæsel*, 'hazel, a bush or small tree with edible nuts'. The name began to be used in the 19th century and was extremely popular in the early part of the 20th century.

HEATHER

It seems probable that this name comes from Old English *hæð*, 'heath, uncultivated, uninhabited land'. The word *heather*, 'erica, ling', does not appear in records before the 18th century. It began to be used as a girl's name in the 19th century, somewhat later than its Latin equivalent, *Erica*.

HEBE In Greek mythology, *Hebe* was the daughter of Zeus and the cupbearer of the gods. She represents youthful beauty. Her name comes from *hebos*, 'young', and is often pronounced like 'eve and 'hee + bee'.

HEIDI is a Swiss abbreviation of *Adelheid*, 'noble kind'. In 1881, Johanna Spyri internationalised the name in her children's classic, *Heidi*. This tells the story of a child who is brought up in idyllic alpine conditions. When she is taken to the city, she pines until she returns to her beloved mountains. SEE Adelaide

HELEN/HELENA One of the most perennially popular names for the best part of three thousand years. In Greek mythology, it was the name of the daughter of Zeus and Leda, but it is probably best known as the name of the wife of Menelaus. Her abduction by

Paris caused the ten-year Trojan War. It is likely that *Helen's* name is actually pre-Greek but it is certainly linked to Greek *helios*, 'sun', and may suggest 'ray of sunshine'. The name occurs in a variety of forms, including *Aileen*, *Elaine*, *Elena*, *Ellen*, *Galina*, *Helena*, *Ileana* and *Ilena*. The name was given Christian recognition by the mother of Constantine the Great (c.274-337). He was the Roman Emperor who made Christianity the state religion. St Helena (c.248-c.330) is reputed to have found Christ's cross in AD 326. Traditionally, *Helena* was pronounced with the stress on the second syllable, which rhymes with 'seen'. Recently, there has been a tendency to stress the first syllable and pronounce the name like *Helen* with an attached 'a'.

HELGA This is a Scandinavian name, from Old Norse *heilagr*, meaning 'holy'. It is related to the English word 'hale' and it seems likely that in pre-Christian communities *heilagr* meant 'free from injury'. SEE Olga

HELOISE (pronounced 'el + Louise') This is the same name as *Eloise*, which seems to be linked to Greek *helios*, 'sun'. Like *Hannah* and *Hester*, the name can occur with or without an initial 'h'. In both English and French an initial 'h' is sometimes silent, as in *hour*, or sometimes dropped, so that *Askins* and *Haskins* are now regarded as distinct surnames. The French form of the name is *Héloïse*. *Héloïse* (1098-1164) was a pupil of Peter Abelard (1079-1142), one of the most renowned philosophers of the age. They had an affair, which resulted in the birth of a son. Although they got married, *Héloïse*'s uncle had Abelard castrated. He entered a monastery and she became an abbess.

HENRIETTA/HENRIETTE

Henrietta is a latinised form of French *Henriette*, 'little home power'. The 'etta' form is more widely used than the French original.

HERA is one of the many names taken from Greek mythology. *Hera* was the wife and sister of Zeus. Her name comes from Greek *hera*, 'lady'. One of Hera's titles was 'Queen of Heaven'. She is to be distinguished from another Greek character called *Hero*, whose name seems to have the same origin. *Hero* was a priestess dedicated to the goddess Aphrodite. Each night her lover, Leander, swam across to visit her. One night he was drowned. *Hero* was inconsolable and threw herself into the sea.

HERMIONE (pronounced 'her + my + ony') was the daughter of Helen of Troy and her Greek husband, Menelaus. The name is derived from *Hermes*, the son of Zeus and the messenger of the gods, usually depicted as wearing winged shoes. The meaning of the name is unclear although it may be related to the same Greek word that gave us 'hermit', and means 'uninhabited'. *Hermione* was the name of the queen in Shakespeare's play *The Winter's Tale*. The name has received a boost in popularity because of the character Hermione Granger in J K Rowling's *Harry Potter* series.

HESTER is a variant of the Hebrew name *Esther*, 'myrtle'. It was widely used by the Puritans in the 17th century. The choice of *Hester* may have been influenced by Greek *hestia*, 'star'. SEE Esther

HETTIE/HETTY is an abbreviation of *Henrietta* but it has been used as a name in its own right. It was the name of a young country girl, Hetty Sorrel, in the novel *Adam Bede* by George Eliot (1819-80).

HILARY/HILLARY is an English form of the Latin name *Hilaria*, 'cheerful female'. Two early saints were called *Hilary*, but they were both men. Today, *Hilary* is almost exclusively reserved for daughters.

HILDA is a Germanic name, often a reduced form of such names as *Brunhilda* but now regularly used on its own. It comes from *hild*, 'battle'. One of the best-known saints of this name was St Hilda of Whitby (614-680). She was of royal birth and a protégée of the Irish saint, *Aidan*. When she was an abbess, she was depicted carrying a crozier, which suggests that she had the powers of a bishop.

HILDEGARD is a Germanic name meaning 'battle guard'. St Hildegard of Bingen (1089-1179) was a scholar, musician and mystic. Some of her music and poetry survive.

HOLLY comes from an Old English noun, *holen*, 'holly, evergreen plant with glossy leaves and red berries'. From the middle of the 20th century, it replaced *Noelle* as a popular name for girls born around the Christmas period. The shrub is used as an emblem of fidelity.

HONEY/HONI These names may be of totally different origins but they are occasionally used as equivalents. *Honey* comes from Old English *hunig*, 'honey'. It has been used as a term of endearment since the 14th century. *Honi* is a Hebrew name related to *Hannah* and meaning 'gracious'.

HONOR/HONOUR *Honor*
is a Latin word meaning 'respect, esteem, reverence'. It was selected by Puritans in the 17th century as a suitable name for daughters. In the 17th century, *honor* without a 'u' was the normal spelling in English and this spelling has been retained in America, where the name continues to be popular. Occasionally, the variants *Honora* and *Honoria* have also been selected.

HOPE is one of the three
divine virtues, the others being *Faith* and *Charity*. All three were chosen by 17th-century Puritans as suitable names for their daughters, and *Hope* has remained in use. The name comes from Old English *hopa* and meant 'desire and expectation'. *Hope* was usually defined as 'a divine virtue by which we desire and firmly expect that God will give us eternal life and the means to attain it.' Some modern *Hopes*

may come from the surname, which is from Old English hop, 'small enclosed valley'.

HYACINTH is the same name
as *Jacintha*. They both come from Greek *Hyakinthos*, the name of the beautiful young man who gave his name to a flower and a precious stone. *Hyakinthos* was, of course, male but since there is a tendency to give flower names to girls, it is easy to understand how the name came to be used for both girls and boys.

NOTABLE NAMESAKES
Halle Berry (b.1966) The only woman of African-American descent to have won the Academy Award for Best Actress; Harriet Beecher Stowe (1811-1896) American abolitionist and novelist whose influential book *Uncle Tom's Cabin* (1852) attacked the cruelty of slavery. When Abraham Lincoln met her it is claimed that he said: 'So you're the

little woman that started this great war!'; **Helen Keller** (1880-1968) the first deafblind person to graduate from college. She was taught to communicate by Anne Sullivan (1886-1936), herself visually impaired. Their story was made into a film, *The Miracle Worker; Hyacinth Bucket* is the snobbish central character of a popular BBC series, *Keeping up Appearances* (1990-96). Hyacinth is played by Patricia Routledge.

I

IDA is a Norman name of Germanic origin. It is derived from *id*, 'work, industry'. Parents who have spent time in Crete may have borrowed the name from Mount Ida. In Greek mythology, this mountain was sacred to Zeus, who was supposed to have been born in a cave on Ida.

ÍDE (pronounced 'ee + da') is an Irish name, often anglicised as *Ita*. It is, however, likely to be a traditional Irish name, possibly derived from Old Irish *ítu*, 'thirst', and implying 'thirsty/hungry for God'. It was the name of an Irish saint who lived from c.480 to c.570. She was the most venerated Irish female saint after St Brigid.

IDUNA (pronounced 'ee + doona') is an English form of the Old Norse name *Iðunnr*, which was probably derived from Old Norse *ið*, 'again' + *unna*, 'to love'. In Scandinavian mythology, *Iðunnr* was the goddess of immortality. She guarded the magic apples of eternal youth. When *Iduna* and her apples were captured by giants, the gods began to grow old. *Iduna*, like *Freya*, has been used by parents who are interested in Scandinavian folklore.

ILEANA is a Romanian form of *Helen*, 'ray of sunlight'. SEE Helen

ILLONA is a form of *Helen*, 'ray of sunlight', that is found in Hungary, Finland and Latvia. *Ilonka* is a pet form in Hungary. SEE Helen

IMELDA is popular in Ireland, Spain and Italy, although it seems to have a Germanic origin. It seems probable that it comes from *irmen*, 'entire, complete' + *hild*, 'battle'. It was the name of a 14th-century saint from Bologna. SEE Emelda

IMMACULATA is from Latin *immaculate*, 'free from sin'. It is a name that is given in honour of Our Lady of the Immaculate Conception. *Immaculada* is the preferred form in Spanish communities.

IMOGEN Shakespeare was the first person to use this name, in his play *Cymbeline*. It seems probable, however, that Shakespeare actually intended the name to be *Innogen*, but it was printed as *Imogen* and not

changed. The intended name is derived from Gaelic *inghean*, meaning 'maiden, daughter'.

NAMES FIRST USED IN SHAKESPEARE'S PLAYS
Aliena in *As You Like It*
Celia in *As You Like It*
Cordelia in *King Lear*
Desdemona in *Othello*
Imogen in *Cymbeline*
Jessica in *The Merchant of Venice*
Mab in *A Midsummer Night's Dream*
Miranda in *The Tempest*

INA is often a short form for any of the names ending in '-ina'. It has been used for *Georgina*, for example. Occasionally, it is used as a pet form of *Agnes*, possibly because of *Ines* and *Inez*, the Italian and Spanish forms of *Agnes*. SEE Agnes

INDIRA is an extremely popular name among Indian parents. It comes from Sanskrit and means 'splendid'. In Hindu mythology, *Indira* was the wife of Vishnu. It was the name of Indira Gandhi (1917-1984), India's first female Prime Minister.

INDU is a Hindi name meaning 'moon'. Like *Indira*, it is a frequent choice of Indian parents worldwide.

INGA is a Swedish form of the name *Inge*, which is popular in Germany and Scandinavia. The name owes its origin to a Scandinavian fertility god called *Ing*, and his name is said to mean 'the foremost one'.

INGRID is a Scandinavian name combining *Ing*, 'fertility god' + *friðr*, 'beautiful'. It became extremely popular throughout the cinema-going world because of the fame of the Swedish actress Ingrid Bergman (1915-82). Occasionally, the form *Ingred* occurs.

IONA (pronounced 'eye' + 'owna') is a small island in the Inner Hebrides. It was chosen by St Colum Cille for a monastic settlement in the middle of the

6th century. Since the early part of the 20th century, *Iona* has been used as a name for girls. The origin of the island's name is unclear and it has been suggested that it includes the Old Norse word *ey*, meaning 'island'. Another possibility is that *Iona* should really be *Ioua*. After Colum Cille established his monastery here, the island was referred to in Gaelic as *I Chaluim Chille*, where 'I' could have meant 'yew'. In the 6th century, the island was covered with yew trees. Alternatively, the 'I' could be a spelling pronunciation of *ey* and so mean 'Colum Cille's island'. When the island was referred to in Latin, it was called *Ioua Insula*, 'yewy island'. It would have been very easy to mistake *Ioua* for *Iona* because, in mediaeval writing, the two would have been identical. There is another twist to the story. The Hebrew word for 'dove' is *Iona* and, of course, Colum Cille was known as 'the dove of the church'.

IRENE In Greek mythology, *Eirene*, 'peace', was the goddess

of peace. *Irene* is the
English equivalent. When
the name was first borrowed,
it was pronounced as three
syllables and sounded like 'I +
reen + ee'. This pronunciation
still occurs but it is most
frequently pronounced as two
syllables, with the stress either on
'I' or 'rene'. In the 8th century, an
Empress called *Irene* ruled the
Byzantine Empire, first as a
regent for her son, then in her
own right.

IRIS was a minor goddess in
Greek mythology. Her name
means 'rainbow'. She was a link
between the gods and humanity,
just as the rainbow is a link
between heaven and earth.
Often, parents choose the name
because it is also the name of a
flower. The flower, however, and
the part of the eye are both
named after the goddess,
because both flowers and eyes
were thought to reflect the
colours of the rainbow.

IRMA is normally regarded as
an abbreviated form of
Ermintrude, which comes from

ermen, 'complete' + *traut*,
'beloved'. It was popular among
the Normans and continues to
have a following, mainly in the
United States. SEE Erma

ISABEL/ISHBEL/ISOBEL
Isabel is a Spanish form of
Elizabeth, a Hebrew name
meaning 'God is my oath'. The
form can be explained in this
way. The initial syllable was
interpreted as 'el', the definite
article, and then dropped, leaving
'Izabeth'. The Spanish language
avoids words ending in 'th', so 'l'
was substituted. *Isabel* has been
regarded as a distinct name for
centuries. Many modern parents
prefer the *Isobel* spelling. *Isabella*
is the Italian form and the ending
in 'bella', meaning 'beautiful',
has added to its attractiveness. A
further suggestion regarding
Isabel is that it is not a form of
Elizabeth but has an older Semitic
origin and means 'daughter of
Baal', that is, 'daughter of the
Lord'.

ISADORA/ISIDORA is a
female form of the Greek name
Isidoros, which comes from

Egyptian *Isis*, the goddess of fertility + *doron*, 'gift'. One of the best-known saints to carry the name was St Isidore the farmer (c. 1080-1130). He worked as a farm labourer near Madrid and was said to finish his ploughing faster than anyone else because his plough was pulled by a team of white oxen, driven by angels. The dancer Isadora Duncan (1878-1927) helped to popularise the name in the 20th century.

ISEULT is one of several spellings of this mythological princess. According to tradition, she was Irish and was pledged to King Mark of Cornwall. Mark sent his nephew *Tristram* to Ireland to collect *Iseult* but they became lovers instead. Iseult's name has also been spelt *Esyllt*, *Isolde* and *Yseult*. It probably means 'beautiful to look at'. She gave her name to the Chapelizod area of Dublin.

ISLA This is the name of a river in Perthshire but it has become a very popular name in Scotland and beyond. The river seems to take its name from Gaelic *aileach*, 'rocky place' and this would have been pronouned like 'eye + lach', which is close to today's pronunciation of both the girl's name and the river.

ISOLDE (pronounced 'ee + zolda') This is a variant of *Iseult*, 'beautiful'. SEE Iseult

ITA is an anglicised form of *Íde*, which comes from an Old Irish noun, *ítu*, 'thirst', implying 'thirsty/hungry for God'. SEE Íde

IVANA/IVANNA was originally found mainly in the Czech Republic and Russia but its use is currently much wider. It is a female form of *Ivan*, which is one of the many variants of the Hebrew name meaning 'God is gracious'. SEE Ivan

IVES Usually, *Ives/Yves* is a boy's name, but it was also the name of an Irish nun who died around AD 450 and gave her name to St Ives in Cornwall. Her Irish name was *Ia*, which may be related to *iamh*, meaning 'enclosure'. St Ia's name is also found in Porthia, 'the port of Ia', in Cornwall.

IVY is one of the many plant names given to girls. It comes from Old English *ifig* and refers to a plant that clings to walls and trees. It often suggests 'committed and unswervingly loyal'.

NOTABLE NAMESAKES
**Imelda Staunton (b.1956)
English actress best known
for her performances in
Vera Drake and *Harry Potter
and the Order of the
Phoenix*; Indira Gandhi
(1917-84) was in her fourth
term as Prime Minister of
India when she was
assassinated; Iris Murdoch
(1919-99) Dublin-born
philosopher and novelist;
Ivana Trump (b. 1949),
Czech athlete and fashion
model, formerly married to
Donald Trump, one of
America's wealthiest
entrepreneurs.**

J

JACINTA/JACINTHA

Jacinta is the Spanish form of *Hyacinth*. The spelling *Jacintha* occurs almost as frequently. And a few parents have used *Jacynth*. SEE Hyacinth

JACKIE used to be a boy's name but it is currently as widely used for a girl. It is usually an abbreviation of *Jacqueline* or the equivalent of *Jacqui*, but it has occasionally been used as a name in its own right. SEE Jacqueline

JACKLYN is a modern form of *Jacqueline*, the female diminutive form of *Jacques*, 'supplanter'. SEE Jacqueline

JACQUELINE is a female diminutive form of *Jacques*, the French equivalent of *James*, 'supplanter'. It is popular both inside and outside France and several anglicised variants occur, including *Jackeline*, *Jackelyn*, *Jacklyn*, *Jacquelyn*, and the pet forms *Jackie* and *Jacky* are now more widely used for girls than boys.

JADE is a precious stone that has been popular in jewellery because of its attractive green colour. It came into English from Spanish *piedra de ijada*, 'stone of the bowel', and it was believed that wearing it could have a beneficial impact on intestinal problems. *Jade* became increasingly popular in the English-speaking world during the second half of the 20th century.

JAIME There are at least two explanations of this name, which is usually pronounced like *Jamie*. It can be from the French expression *j'aime*, 'I love' or a modified spelling of *Jamie*, based on the Spanish name *Jaime*, which may not, in fact, be related to *James*.

JAN is usually an abbreviation of names such as *Janet* or *Janice* but, occasionally, it is the use of a European form of *John* as a girl's name. In this context, *Jana* also occurs. The use of *Jana*, 'God is gracious', has increased in English-speaking communities as Polish speakers emigrate. SEE Janet and Janice

JANAH is a modified spelling of *Jana*, 'God is gracious'.

JANE is a female form of *John*, 'God is gracious'. The Normans introduced it as *Je(h)anne* and *Jane* has remained a favourite since the 11th century. It occurs alone and in such combinations as *Mary-Jane* and *Sarah-Jane*. Lady Jane Grey (1537-54) was a niece of King Henry VIII and was Queen of England for nine days. She was put on the throne in an attempt to prevent the succession of Mary, who was Catholic. She is often referred to as the 'Nine-Day Queen' and her short reign gave rise to the expression 'a nine day wonder'. *Janey* is sometimes used as a pet form.

JANET/JANETTE *Janet* began life as a diminutive form of *Jane*. It was popular until the 15th century but then almost disappeared, although it occurred sporadically in Scotland. It became fashionable in the 19th century and has been frequently used since then. The form *Janette*

is much later than *Janet* and is likely to be a blend of *Janet* and *Jeannette*. SEE Jane and Jeanette

JANICE is derived from *Jane*, 'God is gracious'. It seems to be a 19th-century blend of *Jane* with the ending '-ice' that occurs in names such as *Berenice*. Occasionally, *Janis* occurs. This may be a spelling difference only or the name could be the result of a blend with a name like *Doris*.

JANINA/JANINE Both these names are derived from *Jane*, 'God is gracious'. *Janine* is probably an anglicised spelling of French *Jeannine*, 'little Jane', and *Janina* is a latinised equivalent. SEE Jane

JASMIN/JASMINE/ YASMIN The Persian name of the flower was *yasmin* and this name was modified when the plant was introduced to Western Europe in the early 16th century. *Jasmin* and *Jasmine* are equally popular spellings. More recently, *Yasmin* has joined their ranks. Flowers are frequently chosen as names for daughters.

JAYNE is a variant spelling of *Jane*, 'God is gracious'. SEE Jane

JEAN Like *Jane*, *Jean* is derived from the Norman name *Je(h)anne*, which is a feminine form of *John*, 'God is gracious'. It was one of the most popular names for girls in the first half of the 20th century. Its abbreviated form, *Jeanie*, is also found. In parts of the United States, the French variant, *Jeanne*, is pronounced like *Jeanie*. SEE Jane

JEANETTE/JEANNETTE These are taken from the French female diminutive form of *Jean*, 'God is gracious'. In English, they are pronounced like *Janet* although, occasionally, the 'J' is pronounced in the French way and the second syllable is stressed. SEE Janet

JEANNE is the French female form of *Jean*, 'God is gracious'. It is sometimes pronounced like *Jeanie*.

JEMIMA is a Hebrew name

meaning 'dove'. It is the name of Job's daughter:

And he called the name of the first [daughter] Jemima; and the name of the second Kezia; and the name of the third, Keren-happuch.

Book of Job, Chapter 14: 14)

Jemima was popular in Victorian times and has seen increased usage in the late 20th century.

JENA/JENNA is Arabic for 'little bird'. It is a likely choice for parents looking for a name that is easy to spell, easy to pronounce and not as widespread as *Jane*.

JENNIFER is a Cornish name meaning 'fair, beautiful and smooth'. It is essentially the same name as *Guinevere* and the first part of both names is related to Irish *fionn*, 'fair'. This name became popular in the early 20th century as people looked for Celtic names for their children. The abbreviated forms *Jenni*, *Jennie* and *Jenny* occur widely. They have also been used as pet forms of *Jean*.

JERUSHA (pronounced 'jer +

oosha') is a Hebrew name meaning 'possession'. In the Old Testament, *Jerusha* was the wife of King Uzziah. *Jerusha* was seen as symbolising female virtues and was thus attractive to Puritans and to Americans. It is less widely used now than a century ago but it continues to be selected when parents want an unusual name or when they want to name a child after someone called *Jerry*.

JESSICA is one of the many names that we owe to Shakespeare. He chose it as the name of Shylock's daughter in *The Merchant of Venice*, and he gave her some of the loveliest lines in the play. It is not absolutely clear why Shakespeare chose *Jessica* as the name for a Jewish girl. Perhaps he created it as a female form of *Jesse*, 'gift', or it may be an example of poetic licence. It is sometimes abbreviated to *Jess* and *Jessie*.

JILL has been used as a complete given name for about 500 years but it is almost certainly an abbreviation of

Julian(ne) and its variant *Gillian*, both meaning either 'child of Jupiter' or 'young girl'. By the 16ᵗʰ century, *Jill* was so widely used as a girl's name that it had come to mean 'girl' in the same way as *Sheila* came to represent 'woman' in Australia. A rhyme from 1529 puts it this way:

> *What availeth lordship*
> *Yourself for to kill*
> *With care and with thought*
> *How Jack shall have Jill.*

Occasionally, *Jill* occurs as an abbreviation of *Jillian*, a modern spelling of *Gillian*. SEE Gillian

JO is usually an abbreviated form of *Josephine*, 'God shall add', but it is also used as a pet form for many names that begin with 'Jo-'. SEE Josephine

JOAN used to be one of the most popular names for girls in the Middle Ages. It was a female form of Latin *Jo(h)annes*, 'God is gracious'. It became popular again in the 20ᵗʰ century because of the canonisation of Joan of Arc in 1927. Joan of Arc (c.1412-31) was also known as the 'Maid of

Orléans'. She led the French armies against the English and was responsible for seeing that Charles VII was crowned King of France. She was handed over to the English, tried for heresy and burnt at the stake.

JOANNA When Latin was the language of Christendom and births were recorded in Latin, *Joanna* was used as the Latin equivalent of *Joan*. It became popular as a name in its own right in the Victorian era. SEE Joan

JOANNE Good stories do not necessarily follow a straight line and this statement is true also of names. *Joanne* was originally a French female form of *John*, 'God is gracious'. In English, this was transformed into *Joan*. In the early 20ᵗʰ century, it was re-borrowed and became extremely popular. *Joanne* can also be the result of blending *Jo* and *Anne*.

JOANKA This popular Polish name is a female diminutive form of *John*, 'God is gracious'.

JOCASTA In Greek

mythology, *Jocasta* was a Theban woman who unwittingly married her own son, *Oedipus*. When she discovered the truth, she hanged herself. The meaning of *Jocasta* is uncertain, but it is sometimes linked to Latin *jocari*, 'to be cheerful, to joke', probably because *Jocasta* is a Latin form. The Greek name was *Iokaste*.

JOCELYN is derived from a favourite Norman name, sometimes spelt *Joslanus* or *Joslinus*. There are two possible origins. It may be of Germanic origin and referred to 'a man of the Gaut tribe'. It may also be of Breton origin and refer to someone called after St Judoc, 'lord'. *Jocelyn* was a man's name originally but it is now almost exclusively female. Occasionally it is spelt *Jocelin*, *Joceline* and *Joyceline*.

JODI/JODIE/JODY It is often thought that *Jodie* is a form of *Judith*, 'praised', and it may well be, but the truth is that nobody is absolutely certain. It began to be popular in the 20th century and is used for both boys and girls.

JOLENE may be a female form of *Joel*, 'God is God' (Jehovah is the Lord) , or it may be a created name. In Australia, in particular, in the 20th century, many female names such as *Dorene*, *Jolene*, *Marlene* and *Noellene* became popular. The names were probably the result of blending a name with '-ene', usually regarded as a diminutive. The name may also have been popularised by Dolly Parton's country and western song, 'Jolene', which had the lines:

> *Jolene, Jolene, Jolene, Jolene*
> *I'm begging of you, please don't*
> *take my man.*

JONI is a modern spelling of *Joanie*, 'God is gracious'. SEE Joan

JONQUIL This is one of the many flower names bestowed on daughters, especially during the 20th century. It comes from Latin *jonquilla*, which is a diminutive of *juncus*, 'rush'. The flower resembles the narcissus but has rush-like leaves.

JORDAN This name was

popular for both boys and girls at the time of the Crusades (11ᵗʰ-13ᵗʰ centuries). Crusaders often brought home water from the River Jordan which was used for baptising children. The children were often called *Jordan* to commemorate their christening. The river Jordan flows between Israel and Jordan. It gets its Hebrew name, *Yarden*, from a verb meaning 'flow down' and the river is sacred to Christians, Jews and Muslims. The name began to be popular again in the 20ᵗʰ century, mainly for boys, but it is now used for both, as it was 1000 years ago.

JOSEPHINE is a French female form of the Hebrew name *Joseph*, 'God will add', but it has been popular throughout the world, possibly because it was the name of Napoleon's first wife. Napoleon married the widow Josephine de Beauharnais (1763-1814) in 1796 and divorced her in 1809. By all accounts, *Josephine* was exceptionally beautiful and would almost certainly have remained Empress

if she had given Napoleon an heir. There are several abbreviations of the name, the most widely used being *Jo*, *JoJo*, *Josetta*, *Josie* and *Fifi*. SEE Fifi

JOY refers to the quality of happiness or 'exultation of spirit', and is a name that many parents choose as a wish for their child. It is like *Faith* and *Hope* in being the name of an attractive virtue. *Joy* was regarded as a gift of God and early Christians were encouraged to 'be joyful in the Lord'. The 'Exultet' hymn that is sung during the Easter Vigil Mass was written somewhere between the 5th and the 7th centuries. It encourages the faithful to rejoice:

> *Exult, all creation around God's throne!*
> *Jesus Christ, our King, is risen!*
> *Sound the trumpet of salvation!*

JOYCE is a Norman name, almost certainly related to *Jocelyn*. It is likely that it comes from the name of a 7th-century Breton saint, *Judoc*, whose name means 'lord'. *Joyce* has been a surname since the 14th century. Many parents have probably reinterpreted the name and linked it to 'rejoice'. Like *Joy*, it is then felt to be an appropriate name for a girl.

JUANITA (pronounced 'hu + ann + eeta'/'jew + ann + eeta') is one of the most frequently used names among Spanish speakers. It is a diminutive female form of *Juan*, 'God is gracious'.

JUDITH is a Hebrew name that is widely used in both Christian and Jewish families. It comes from *Yehudit* and means 'woman from Judea'. In the Old Testament, *Judith* was the wife of Jacob's brother *Esau*. A different *Judith* is the heroine of the apocryphal *Book of Judith*. In this, *Judith* manages to save her people by seducing *Holofernes*, the general of the invading Assyrian army, and cutting off his head while he slept.

JUDY is an abbreviation of *Judith* but it is regularly used as a name in its own right. It was popularised in the 20th century because of the fame of the singer and actress Judy Garland (1922-69). Her 1939 film *The Wizard of Oz* has been watched and enjoyed by generations of children. Her real name was Frances Ethel Gumm.

JULIA is a Roman name, based on the family name *Julius*, possibly meaning 'youthful' or 'child of Jupiter'. It is sometimes abbreviated to *Jules*.

JULIAN/JULIANNE

Today, this is usually a boy's name but in the past it was given to both sons and daughters. It comes from Latin *Julianus*, a name that is derived from *Julius*, 'youthful, child of Jupiter'. One of the best-known bearers of the name was St Julian of Norwich (c.1342-c.1413). She lived as a recluse and is renowned for her writings, in which she describes her visions. SEE Julia

JULIANA is the Latin female form of *Julianus*. The precise meaning of the name is uncertain

113

but it is derived from *Julius* and possibly means 'youthful, child of Jupiter'. SEE Julia

JULIE is the French form of *Julia*, 'youthful'. An interesting bearer of this name was Julie Clery (1771-1845). She was born in Marseilles but her ancestry was Irish. She and her sister Desirée were judged to be among the most beautiful women of their day. *Julie* married Napoleon's brother, Joseph. He was made King of Naples and then of Spain by his brother. Desirée's husband became Charles XIV of Sweden. She had earlier been engaged to Napoleon before he met Josephine.

JULIET/JULIETTE *Juliet* is a form of the French diminutive *Juliette*, which is from *Julia*. Shakespeare ensured the appeal of *Juliet* by giving it to the young heroine of *Romeo and Juliet*. SEE Julia

JUNE/JUNO is one of the months of the year that is given to a daughter, often to one born at this time of the year. The month takes its name from *Junius mensis*, 'month of June', which was thought to be sacred to the goddess Juno, the wife of Jupiter.

JUSTINA/JUSTINE These are female forms of *Justin*, 'just person'. Some children are called after the 2nd-century saint Justin the Martyr, but most are given the name because people find it attractive in both sound and meaning.

NOTABLE NAMESAKES Jane Austen (1775-1817) one of the most admired novelists in the English language. Her novels, especially *Emma* and *Pride and Prejudice,* have been filmed many times; **Jenny Lind (1820-87)** Swedish opera singer, internationally renowed as the 'Swedish Nightingale'; **Joan of Arc (1412-31)** France's national heroine. She led the French army to victory over the

English, most notably at Orléans in 1429. She was burnt at the stake by the English when she was nineteen and was canonised in 1920; Joni Mitchell (b. 1943) Canadian folksinger, songwriter and painter.

K

KABIRA (pronounced 'cab + ee + ra') is an Arabic name meaning 'powerful'. It is a female form of *Kabir* and is sometimes given to a daughter to honour a male relative who is no longer living.

KAEDE (pronounced 'ka + ey +dey') is an example of how plants are used for daughters in almost all cultures. This one means 'maple' in Japanese. The maple is valued for its beauty and for the sweetness that some species of maple provide.

KAITLIN/KAITLYN In the United States, in particular, the Irish name *Caitlín* has been anglicised and pronounced like 'kate + lynn'. Early in the 20th century, the Irish spelling was used but, more recently, a variety of spellings has occurred. *Kaitlin* and *Kaitlyn* are the most widely used of the 'K' variants, but we also find *Katelyn* and *Kaytlyn*. SEE Caitlin and Catherine

KAREN/KARIN These variants are Scandinavian pet forms of *Catherine*, 'purity'. *Karen* is found mainly in Denmark and Norway, whereas *Karin* is the preferred spelling in Sweden. Both have been widely used in English speaking communities since the middle of the 20th century. SEE Catherine

KASUMI is a Japanese word for 'mist'. It carries overtones of spirituality rather than weather.

KATHARINE/KATHERINE These are alternative spellings of *Catherine*. They come from the Greek name, *Aikaterine*, which may be linked to *Hecate*, 'the distant one', a Greek goddess of enchantment.

Katharine is the most widely used form in the United States. For almost 2000 years, the name has been linked to the Greek adjective, *katharos*, 'pure' and *Katherine* has been interpreted as meaning 'purity'. Shakespeare uses *Katharina* in *The Taming of the Shrew* and *Katharine* in *Love's Labour's Lost*. Because there have been several saints of this name, many variants are found. The best known of these are: *Katarina, Katharina, Katheryn, Kathleen, Kathlene, Kathryn, Katrin* and *Katrina*. The best-known pet forms are *Kate, Katey, Katie, Kathie, Kathy, Katy, Kay, Kit* and *Kitty*. SEE Catherine

KATHLEEN seems to have originated in Ireland, where it was used as an anglicised form of *Caitlín*. SEE Caitlin

KATIE/KATY Although these are abbreviated pet forms of *Katherine*, they have become popular as independent names. *Katy* was given prominence by the novels of Susan Coolidge (1835-1905), who wrote the perennially attractive children's books *What Katy Did*, *What Katy Did at School* and *What Katy Did Next*. These books follow the adventures of a tomboy growing up in America in the 1860s. All three books are still in print.

KAY is used for two purposes. It can be an abbreviation for any name beginning with the letter 'K' or it can be a pet form of *Katherine*, 'purity'. SEE Catherine

KAYLA can be from a Hebrew name meaning 'crown' or it can be a form of Irish *Keela*. The Irish name has the variants *Keela, Keeley* and *Kyla*. They all seem to come from *cadhla*, 'beautiful enough to occur in poetry'.

KEIKO is a well-known Japanese name meaning 'respectful child'. In Japanese society, respect for one's elders is the norm.

KELLY is an anglicised spelling of the Irish surname Ó Ceallaigh, meaning 'descendant of Kelly'. The exact meaning of *Kelly* is debated. It may come from *ceallach*, 'hermit', or it may mean 'strife'. Whatever its precise origin – and meanings of names of such antiquity are always debatable – the name is widely used for daughters, with and without Irish links. Occasionally, the spellings *Kelli* and *Keli* occur. The name *Ceallach* was used by some of the Vikings who settled in Ireland. When they moved to England, they took the name with them. Kelleythorpe in Yorkshire means 'Kiallakr's settlement'. *Kiallakr* was the Old Norse form of *Ceallach*.

KERRY is popular among Irish emigrants with links to County Kerry. In this case, the name comes from *ciar*, 'dark'. It is also possible that it is a spelling of Welsh *Ceri*, 'beloved'. SEE Ceri

KESIA/KEZIA/KESIAH is a Hebrew name meaning 'cassia, spice similar to cinnamon'. In the Old Testament, *Keziah* was a daughter of Job. The name has been widely used by people of African descent. It seems probable that it is similar to an African name. The pet forms *Kezzie* and *Kizzie* occur.

KEYNE St Keyne was an early Celtic saint who lived either in the 5th or the 6th century. She was probably Welsh and her name may be related to *cun*, 'beautiful'. According to tradition, almost all of her family became saints but *Keyne* had a well with interesting properties. Newlyweds were advised to drink from the well and the one who drank from it first would be the boss in the house.

KHALIDA (pronounced 'cal + ee + da'/'hal + ee + da') is an Arabic name meaning 'eternal'. It is possible that the name is related to *Khaldi*, the name of the supreme god in ancient Armenia.

KIKU is a Japanese name meaning 'chrysanthemum'. It is an example of the widespread tradition of calling a daughter after a beautiful flower. The significance of this name in Japan is linked to the fact that the hereditary monarchy is called 'the Chrysanthemum Throne'.

KIM was at first used as a name for boys but now it is popular for girls as well. It may come from *Kimberley*, a city in South Africa that has been a rich source of diamond mining since the second half of the 19th century. The city was called after Lord Kimberley, whose name means 'Cyneburg's clearing', and *Cyneburg* was a woman's name meaning 'royal manor'. It is also possible that *Kim* is a borrowing from Rudyard Kipling's novel *Kim*. The novel was published in 1901 and was widely read. The hero of the novel was called Kimball O'Hara. In Vietnamese, *Kim* means 'golden'.

KIRSTIN has been adopted from the Danish and Norwegian form of *Christine*, which means 'follower of the Messiah'. SEE Christina

KIRSTIE/KIRSTY This is a Scottish pet form of *Christina*, 'follower of the Messiah', that has become an independent name and widely used in English-speaking communities.

KIT is usually a pet form of *Katherine*, 'purity', but it is occasionally used as a substitute for *Christina*, 'follower of the Messiah'. *Kit* used to be a regular shortened form of *Christopher*, 'bearer of Christ, the Messiah'.

KORA(H) is usually thought to be a latinised Greek name, deriving from *kore*, 'maiden'. In Greek mythology, *Kore* was the daughter of Zeus and she married Hades, the god of the underworld. The form *Korah* almost certainly takes the 'h' ending because of the influence of names such as *Deborah* and *Sarah*.

KRYSTYN/KRYSTYNA These are popular Polish variants of *Christina*, 'follower of Christ, the Messiah'.

KYLA is a form of Irish *cadhla*, 'exceptionally beautiful'.

KYLIE is an aboriginal Australian word for 'boomerang'. It may also be a blend of the surname *Kyle*, 'slender' + *Kelly*. The name has been popularised throughout the world by the Australian singer and actress Kylie Minogue (b.1968).

L

LACEY is a Norman surname. It was introduced by soldiers from Lassy in Calvados and has links with the Knights Templar, the religious and military order established for the protection of pilgrims to the Holy Land in the early 12th century. It has become a girl's name probably because of the suggested link with 'lace'.

LAETITIA/LETITIA

(pronounced 'le + tisha') This name comes from Latin *laetitia*, meaning 'joy'. It was popular among parents who wanted to reflect their joy at their daughter's birth in the child's name. In Victorian times, *Lettice* was a widely-used abbreviation. Its similarity to 'lettuce' and the appearance of Lettice Leaf as a comic character has weakened the appeal of the abbreviation.

LAMIA/LAMYA

(pronounced 'lam + ee + a') This name, of Greek origin, was popularised by a poem of the same name written by John Keats (1785-1821) in 1819. In Greek mythology, the word refers to a mythical spirit that can assume the shape of a beautiful woman. In Keats's poem, *Lamia* is transformed into a beautiful woman by Hermes. She falls in love with Lyceus and they are blissfully happy. *Lamia* does not want Lyceus to publish their joy but he wants everyone to meet her. At the wedding feast he arranges, one of the guests is a philosopher called Apollonius. He realises that *Lamia* is not human and, when he calls her name, she vanishes.

LANA became popular in the 1950s when the film star Lana Turner (1921-95) was at the height of her fame. Her name was created for her and so its origins are uncertain. (Her real name was *Julia* and the family called her *Judy*.) It is possible that it is a form of *Alanna*, which comes from Irish *a leanbh*, meaning 'child' but implying 'darling'. In South America, *lana* is an Amerindian word for a type of tree that produces a dye that is used as body paint.

LANI is one of the many Hawaiian names that began to be used more widely in the 1960s. *Lani* means 'sky, heaven'. A compound form of the name, *Lei*, 'flower' + *lani*, 'heavenly' occurs in a song sung by Bing Crosby in 1937 and by Elvis Presley in 1960. Lani McIntyre was part of the backing group for the Crosby version. SEE Leilani.

LARA is a pet form of *Larissa*, which may come from Latin *larix*, 'larch', or from *Larisa*, the name of the chief city of ancient Thessaly. It is the name of one of the heroines of Boris Pasternak's novel *Dr Zhivago* (1957). The 1965 film, starring Julie Christie as *Lara*, widened the appeal of the name. 'Lara's Theme' written by Maurice Jarre remains one of the most recognizable movie themes ever written. For some parents, *Lara* is regarded as a variant of *Laura*, 'laurel'.

LARISSA was the full name of Boris Pasternak's heroine in *Dr Zhivago*, although she is known by the Russian pet form, *Lara*. It is not certain what the name means. *Larisa* is the name of a city in eastern Greece, close to the Aegean Sea, and *Larissa* is the name of a Byzantine saint, about whom little is known. It is possible that the name is an example of using the name of a plant for a girl. *Larix* is the Latin name for the larch.

LAURA is the feminine form of *Laurus*, a Latin name meaning 'laurel'. The laurel wreath was an emblem of victory. There are several historical *Lauras* but two warrant special attention. St. Laura was a 9th-century Spanish nun who was admired for the courage with which she faced martyrdom. *Laura* was also the name of the woman to whom the Italian poet Petrarch (1304-74) addressed a sequence of sonnets. Because of Petrarch's fame, *Laura* was used as a shorthand expression for an exceptionally beautiful woman.

LAUREL is derived from the English name for a kind of bay tree. The leaves of the laurel

have been used for medicinal purposes for thousands of years and they were also thought to ward off lightning. In ancient Greece and Rome, the foliage was woven into crowns as symbols of victory and honour.

LAUREN is a 20th-century coinage. It may be a feminine form of French *Laurent*, 'man from Laurentum', or a blend of *Laura* and a name such as *Karen*.

LAYLA/LAILA/LEILA (pronounced 'lay + la') is an Arabic name meaning 'night'. It has been used by poets since the 7th century. *Layla* is the name of the central character in poems by the 7th-century Arab poet referred to as *Qays*, and *Leila* is a character in Lord Byron's *Don Juan*. The name became internationally known in 1969 when Leila Khaled (b. 1944) was part of a group that hijacked a TWA plane on its way from Rome to Athens. They flew the plane to Damascus, passing over the city of Haifa, where Leila Khaled was born. Eric Clapton's *Layla* is considered one of rock music's definitive love songs.

LEAH (pronounced 'lee + a'/'lay + a') is a Hebrew name meaning 'weary, languid'. In the Old Testament, *Leah* was the daughter of *Laban* and the elder sister of *Rachel*. *Jacob* wanted to marry *Rachel* but, after working for *Laban* for seven years, was persuaded to marry *Leah* first. He worked another seven years for *Rachel*.

LEANNE is almost certainly a blend of *Lee*, 'wood, clearing' and *Anne*, 'God has favoured me'. SEE Lee

LEDA In Greek mythology, *Leda* was Queen of Sparta and the mother of Helen of Troy. When she was swimming in the river Eurotas, Zeus visited her in the form of a swan and their daughter, *Helen*, hatched from an egg. Some parents use the name because of WB Yeats's poem 'Leda and the Swan'. The meaning of *Leda* is uncertain. It is possible that it is linked to Greek *alethia*, 'truth'.

LEE is sometimes used as an abbreviation of *Leah*, 'weary', but it is frequently the result of using a surname as a given name. It can come from the English surname *leah*, which can mean 'wood' or 'clearing'; it may be from Welsh *lle*, 'place' or the god *Llew*, 'radiant light'; it is possible that it comes from Irish *laoi*, meaning 'poem', or from the River Lee in Cork; it is also the second most widely used family name in China. In this case, it is sometimes spelt *Li* and means 'pear'.

LEIGH is a variant of the surname *Lee*, which comes from *leah*, 'clearing, wood'.

LEILA is an Arabic name meaning 'night'. SEE Layla

LEILANI (pronounced 'lay + lanee') is a Hawaiian name made up of *lei*, 'flower' + *lani*, 'heaven, heavenly'. The song, 'Sweet Leilani' has been sung by many but was popularised by Bing Crosby in 1937 and by Elvis Presley in 1960. Bing Crosby sang it in the film *Waikiki*

Wedding, earning an Academy Award for the 'Song of the Year' and giving Crosby his first gold record. SEE Lani

LENA has been used as a pet form of several names such as *Helena*, 'ray of sunshine', and of *Lenora*, which is usually regarded as related to *Helen*. Now, it is regularly used as an independent name.

LENORA/LENORE

Children's names are often abbreviated, expanded and modified in different generations. *Lenora* started life as an abbreviation of *Eleanora*, which is usually regarded as an expanded form of *Helen*, 'ray of sunshine'. *Lenore* is the French variant but has been a popular girls' name for several hundred years. Edgar Allen Poe (1809-49) immortalised the name in his poem about 'the rare and radiant maiden, whom the angels named Lenore'. SEE Eleanor

LEONORA is an abbreviated form of *Eleanora*. The spelling has been influenced by *Leonie*,

'little lioness'. SEE Eleanor

LESLEY is often assumed to be the female form of Leslie, which is a town in Fife. The meaning of the town is uncertain. It may be from Old Norse *lioss*, 'bright' + *leah*, 'clearing'. It is also possible that the name is Gaelic and involves a compound such as *lios*, 'ring fort' + *laoch*, 'warrior'. The spelling *Lesley* is often reserved for daughters, but in the past both spellings were used for men.

LEXI/LEXIE occurs as an abbreviation of *Alexandra*, 'defender of man', and more recently as an independent name. SEE Alexandra

LEYLA is a variant spelling of an Arabic name meaning 'night'. SEE Layla

LIANA/LIANE *Liane* is from French and means 'tropical climbing plant'. *Liana* is a latinised version of the French name. Coincidentally, the Chinese have *Lian*, 'graceful willow' as a name for a daughter. SEE Leanne

LIDIA is a modification of *Lydia*, a Greek name, meaning 'woman from Lydia'. SEE Lydia

LILIAN/LILLIAN This name is almost certainly a variant of *Elizabeth*, 'God is my oath', and it appears on children's birth certificates 300 years before *Lily* first appears. Some parents may choose *Lilian* as a blend of *Lily* and *Anne*.

LILY is also used as a pet form of *Elizabeth*, 'God is my oath', but it began to be used as an independent name in the 19th century and it is likely that it is another example of parents choosing the name of a flower for a daughter. In Christian tradition, the lily is a symbol of purity. Occasionally, *Lili* is preferred. *Lili* is a German name that was popularised by the song 'Lili Marlene', which was written in 1917 but sung during World War II by soldiers on both sides.

LINDA The origin of *Linda* is uncertain. It may be a form of German *lind*, 'lime tree', or it may be an abbreviation of *Belinda*, which is also of uncertain origin, but may mean 'beautiful shield' or 'beauty and light'. SEE Belinda

LINDSAY/LINDSEY is a surname that has become a popular given name. It is probably derived from *Linissae*, which is a blend of *Lindon*, the original name for Lincoln + *eg*, 'island'. *Lindon* is probably a Celtic name similar to Welsh *llyn*, meaning 'lake'. The name therefore suggests 'island lake'.

LINETTE is an alternative spelling of Lyn(n)ette, 'little image'. SEE Lynette

LISA/LIZA is an abbreviated form of *Elizabeth*, 'God is my oath'. The form with 'z' has been traditionally used in English but the form with 's', which is more recent, is probably a reflection of French *Lise* or German *Liese*.

LOIS The New Testament refers to a *Lois*, who was the grandmother of *Timothy*, to whom St Paul wrote two epistles. For parents not familiar with the New Testament, the name will forever be linked to Lois Lane, the feisty reporter who was loved by Clark Kent, Superman. It is not certain what *Lois* means. It is likely that the name is Greek, since *Timothy* is Greek. This fact would rule out a link with *Louise* and *Eloise*, both of which are Germanic. A possibility is that it is linked to Greek *loion*, 'better, more desirable'. The name is pronounced like 'low + iss'.

LOLA is a Spanish pet form of *Dolores*, which comes from *Maria de los Dolores*, 'Mary of Sorrows'. SEE Dolores

LORELEI According to a German tradition, a beautiful woman with long golden hair sat on the Lorelei rock in the River Rhine, near Coblenz, and lured sailors to their death by singing. In spite of the siren link, *Lorelei* has been given to daughters.

LORETO is the name of a town near the east coast of Italy. According to Christian tradition, the house of Nazareth in which Jesus lived was carried to Loreto by angels in 1295. The house and the area became a place of pilgrimage, linked especially to Our Lady, who was given the title of Our Lady of Loreto. Because of the story, Our Lady of Loreto became the patroness of aviators and people who fly. The house has some interesting features that link it to the Holy Land. It is possible that the 'angels' who carried the house were Crusaders. It is likely that the name *Loreto* is linked to *laurus*, 'laurel'. *Lori* is sometimes used as an abbreviated form.

LORETTA has virtually replaced the older form, *Lauretta*, which links the name with Latin *laurus*, 'bay-tree laurel'. *Loretta* is a latinised frm of *Loreto*. SEE Loreto

LORI is used as an abbreviated form of *Loreto*, *Loretta* and *Lorraine* as well as occurring as a name in its own right. SEE Loreto and Lorraine

LORNA This is another example of a name that was coined by a writer. RD Blackmore (1825-1900) wrote the novel

Lorna Doone in 1869. It is possible that he based the name on *Lorraine*, 'people of Lothar', or it may be related to an Old English word, *lorn*, meaning 'lost, abandoned'. *Lorna* had been stolen from her real parents and was thus, in a sense, 'abandoned'.

LORRAINE is a Norman name for someone from Lorraine, which is a province in northeast France. The area probably owes its name to a Germanic tribe called the *Lotharingi*, 'the people of Lothar', and this is related to *Luther*, 'people's army'. The name began to be used for girls in the 19th century and has sometimes been linked to French *la reine*, 'the queen'. The Lorraine cross (one vertical and two horizontal bars) was the symbol of Joan of Arc and was adopted by the forces of General de Gaulle during World War II.

LOUISA/LOUISE These are female forms of *Louis*, which is Germanic in origin and means 'famed in war'. *Louisa* is the latinate form of French *Louise*.

LUCIA (pronounced 'loo + chee + a'/'loose + eea') is the feminine form of an Old Roman name, *Lucius*, which is derived from Latin *lux*, 'light'. St Lucia (also known as St Lucy) was an early Christian martyr, who died at the beginning of the 4th century. She was one of the most popular saints of the Middle Ages and versions of her name are found throughout Europe.

LUCINDA is a blend of *Lucy*, 'light', and one of the names that end in '-inda', such as *Linda* or *Belinda*. It was first used by the Spanish writer Miguel de Cervantes (1547-1616) in his novel *Don Quixote*. His creation may have been influenced by the Roman Goddess, *Lucina*, who was identified with the moon goddess, *Diana*. *Cindy* is a popular pet form.

LUCY is the most widely-used version of *Lucia* in the English-speaking world. It comes from French *Lucie*.

LUISA is a popular Polish form of *Louisa*, 'famed in war'. SEE Louisa

LULU is a pet name for any of the 'L' names that begin with the sound 'lu'. It is rarely an independent name but is widely used in family circles.

LYDIA is of Greek origin and means 'woman from Lydia'. Lydia was a region in west Asia Minor. It was a powerful kingdom in the 7th century BC, but it was eventually absorbed into the Persian Empire. The last king of Lydia was Croesus (c.560-546BC), who was renowned as the richest man in the world. It was probably under his rule that Lydia became the first country in the world to use coins. *Lydia* began to be widely used in the 18th century. It is, for example, the name of the heroine in *The Rivals*, a play by Richard Brinsley Sheridan (1751-1816).

LYNETTE/LYNNETTE This name seems to have been used for the first time by the poet Alfred Lord Tennyson (1809-92) in *Idylls of the King*, a series of poems dealing with the Arthurian legend. Tennyson used *Lynette* in his poem 'Gareth and Lynette' (1872). It was an anglicisation of the Welsh name *Eluned*, 'beautiful image'. For most modern parents, *Lynette* is a diminutive of *Lynn*.

LYNN is one of the many names that can have several different origins. It may be from Welsh *llyn*, 'lake', or the place name, *Lyn* in Dorset, which comes from Old English *hlynn*, 'torrent'. In some instances, it is a reduced form of *Linda*, 'lime tree', or a modified spelling of the '-line' ending of names such as *Caroline*, 'person'.

NOTABLE NAMESAKES
Laura Ashley (1925-85) Welsh designer of fabrics, clothes and furnishings. Audrey Hepburn wore one of her headscarves in *Roman Holiday* in 1953; Lena Horne (b. 1917) American singer

with a wide repertoire of African-American and jazz music; Louisa May Alcott (1832- 88) American writer, best known for her novel, *Little Women*, published in 1868; Lynn Redgrave (b. 1943) English actress working mainly in England and the United States.

M

MAB Shakespeare is the first to use this name and its origin is debated. It may come from Welsh *maban*, 'my child', or Irish *Mabh*, who may be linked to the Irish goddess *Medb* and her reincarnation, the legendary Queen of Connacht. Percy Bysshe Shelley (1792-1822) wrote a poem, 'Queen Mab', in 1813.

MABEL is a modified form of Old French *amabel*, 'lovely', an appropriate choice for a daughter.

Some parents link the name to modern French, *ma belle*, 'my beautiful one'. *Mabs* is used as an abbreviated form and this abbreviation suggests a link with 'Queen of the Fairies'. SEE Mab

MADELEINE/MADELINE
This is the French form of *Magdalen*. All the variants come from the Greek and Latin forms of the saint's name, *Maria Magdalene*, 'Mary of Magdala', to whom Jesus appears after the Resurrection. In early Christian tradition, Mary Magdalen was believed to be the reformed sinner who washed the feet of Jesus with her tears and wiped them with her hair.
SEE Magdalen

MADGE is a variant of *Mag(gie)*, which is a pet form of *Margaret*, 'pearl'. SEE Margaret

MADHUR is a Hindi name meaning 'sweet'. It is frequently chosen by Indian parents, including those living outside India.

MADONNA This name has been used in Italian as a title for the mother of Jesus. It means 'my lady'. The name is recognised throughout the world because of the entertainer, Madonna (b. 1958). Her full name is Madonna Louise Veronica Ciccone.

MAE is a modified spelling of *May*. It was the spelling used by the film actress and comedienne, Mae West (1893-1980), whose full name was Mary Jane West. She gave her name to an inflatable life jacket. SEE May

MAEVE is the English spelling of an Irish name that was originally represented as *Medb* and is usually spelt *Méabh* in modern Irish. It rhymes with 'save' and is occasionally spelt *Mave*. In Irish mythology, she was a goddess who was reincarnated as Queen Maeve of Connacht, and who is one of the main characters in the epic *Táin Bó Cuailnge*, 'The Cattle Raid of Cooney'. The goddess *Medb* is thought to be the source of *Mab*, the Queen of the Fairies in English literature. SEE Mab

MAGDA is the usual German equivalent of *Magdalen* and it has been adopted as an independent name in the English-speaking world. SEE Magdalen

MAGDALEN St Mary Magdalen's name comes from Latin, *Maria Magdalene*, 'Mary of Magadala'. Magdala was a town on the shore of the Sea of Galilee. Its name means 'tower', so *Magdalen* is sometimes taken to mean 'tower of strength'. It is likely that the traditional picture of Mary Magdalen is a composite of three different women called *Mary*. One appears in St Luke's Gospel (Chapter 8: 2) as the woman 'out of whom went seven devils'. The second also appears in St Luke (Chapter 7:37ff). She is described as 'a sinner' who 'stood at his feet …weeping, and began to wash his feet with tears, and did wipe them with the hair of her head.' The third is the woman to whom Jesus appeared after his resurrection in the Gospel of St John. This saint has always been extremely popular because she was thought to be a sinner, like most people, and her name occurs in many languages and in a wide variety of forms, including *Madalaine, Madaleine, Madaline, Madeleine, Madeline, Madalyn, Magdalane, Magdalen, Magdaliene, Magdalin, Magdaline* and *Magdalyn*.

MAGGIE is a popular abbreviation of *Margaret*, 'pearl'. SEE Margaret

MAHALIA is a Hebrew name meaning 'tenderness'. It was popularised in the 20th century by the gospel singer Mahalia Jackson (1912-72).

MAISIE In Scotland, *Maisie* is often regarded as a pet form of *Margaret*, 'pearl', whereas in Ireland it is usually a variant of *Mary* or its Irish equivalent, *Máire*.

MAMIE is a pet form of both *Margaret* and *Mary*, which were, at one time, the most popular English names for girls.

MANDY is an abbreviated form of *Amanda*, 'beloved', but it is regularly selected as an independent name. It was given a boost with the film *Mandy* (1952), in which a child is helped to deal with her deafness.

MARCELLA is the female form of the Roman family name *Marcellus*, which is a pet form of *Marcus* and may be related to the god *Mars*. *Marcella* was often chosen by parents who had a devotion to the 3rd-century martyr, St Marcel.

MARCIA is derived from the Latin name *Marcus*, and this was probably derived from *Mars*, the name of the god of war. There are several saints of this name but none of them has had a strong impact on the public imagination. Occasionally, especially in the United States, the spelling *Marsha* is also used. Two pet forms, *Marcie* and *Marcy* occur both as variants of *Marcia* and as independent names.

MARGARET probably owes its origins to Greek *margaron*, 'pearl'. The English form comes from Latin *Margarita* and French

Marguerite. *Margaret* has been a popular choice for daughters since the 4th century at the latest. St Margaret of Antioch was the patroness of childbirth and so she was regularly invoked by mothers. The name exists in at least 25 variants; has given rise to independent names such as *Margery* and *Margo*; and is the origin of the surnames *Madge* and *Maggs*, two of the very few English surnames derived from women's names. Some of the popular variants include *Mairéad*, *Margareta*, *Margaretta*, *Margarita* and *Margaretha*. Popular pet forms include *Greta*, *Gretchen*, *Madge*, *Maggie*, *Mags*, *Meg*, *Peg*, *Peggy* and *Rita*.

MARGE is a pet form of *Margery*, which is itself a pet form of *Margaret*, 'pearl'. SEE Margery

MARGERY/MARJORIE

was the most widely-used form of *Margaret* in the Middle Ages and it has been regarded as an independent name for at least three centuries. The spelling with 'j' is much later but is now probably the preferred form. SEE Margaret

MARGO(T) *Margot* was a French pet form of *Marguerite*, 'pearl', but had an independent identity before it was borrowed into English. Because the final 't' was not pronounced, it was often dropped and *Margo* is now the preferred spelling.

MARIA is the Latin form of *Mary*, 'sea of bitterness'. The original Latin name was *Mariam*, which is closer to the Hebrew form, *Maryam*. However, people equated *Mariam* with the Latin accusative case and formed a new nominative case, *Maria*. *Maria* was frequently heard in the Latin prayer, 'Ave Maria', but such prayers were eliminated in most brands of Protestantism. When it was re-introduced to England in the 18th century, *Maria* was pronounced 'mar + eye + a' and, although that pronunciation is still occasionally heard, modern parents seem to prefer 'mar + ee + a'. The spelling *Mariah* occurs but is not widespread. SEE Mary

MARIAN/MARION

These spellings were used almost interchangeably until the 18th century. They both come from a French pet form of *Marie*, 'sea of bitterness', but they have become independent names, sometimes equated with the double-barrelled *Marie-Anne* or *Mary-Anne*. Many will associate the name with Maid Marian of Robin Hood fame. SEE Margaret

MARIANNE is either a variant of *Marian* or a blend of *Marie*, 'sea of bitterness', and *Anne*, 'God has favoured me'. This name came to represent the Republic of France and the goddess of liberty towards the end of the 18th century.

MARIE is the French form of *Maria*, 'sea of bitterness', but it has been used in English since the time of the Normans. It is sometimes pronounced with the stress on the first syllable and sometimes with the stress on the second. SEE Mary

MARIGOLD is one of the many flower names given to daughters. The yellow flower was originally called 'gold' and this is the term Chaucer uses in the *Knight's Tale*, when he describes jealousy as wearing 'a garland of golds'. The flower was renamed in honour of Our Lady.

MARILYN is a 20th-century creation and is probably a blend of *Marie* and the ending 'lyn' from popular names such as *Carolyn*. SEE Mary and Lynn

MARINA looks like a diminutive of *Maria*, but it predates Christianity. It comes from the Roman family name *Marinus*, which was probably derived from *Mars*, the god of war, but was equated with the adjective *marinus*, 'relating to the sea'.

MARION is a variant of *Marian*. SEE Marian

MARISA is, like *Marilyn*, a 20th-century variation on *Mary*, 'sea of bitterness'. The ending may have been borrowed from *Teresa* or *Lisa*.

MARJORIE This is a modern

spelling of *Margery*, which is a form of *Margaret*, 'pearl'. SEE Margery

MARLEEN/MARLENE

This name may have been borrowed from Germany, where Marlene is a pet form of the compound *Maria Magdalene*, or it may be a blend of *Mary* and *Eileen* or *Kathleen*. Usually, they are pronounced like 'mar + lean' but, occasionally, *Marlene* is given a three-syllable pronunciation similar to 'mar + lane + a'. The name was popularised by the film actress Marlene Dietrich (1901- 92).

MARTHA appears in the New Testament as the sister of Mary and Lazarus. In St Luke's Gospel, she is reminded by Jesus that it is more important to concentrate on spiritual matters rather than on household chores. Her name seems to mean 'lady' and it is thus similar in implication to *Madonna*. Occasionally, the spelling *Marta* occurs but it is relatively unusual in English.

MARTINA This name goes back to Roman times, when it was the female equivalent of *Martinus*, a name that came from *Mars*, the god of war. It has been used as a Christian name since the 3rd century at least. In the 20th century, its popularity was largely due to the enthusiasm for the canonisation of Martin de Porres (1579-1639), a lay Dominican brother who was the son of a Spanish dignitary and a freed black slave in Peru. He is the patron saint of the poor and of race relations. *Martine* is the French and German form of the name and it is almost as widely used as *Martina*. *Marti* is a popular pet form.

MARVA is popular among African Americans, in particular. It comes ultimately from Latin *mirabile*, 'wonder, marvel, miracle', but was borrowed from French *merveille*.

MARY *Mary*, in all its variations, has been the most widely-used of all female names for the last 2000 years although it is currently experiencing a drop in popularity. It is the English form of *Maria*, which is a Latin form of Hebrew *Maryam*. Its meaning is uncertain and scholars will continue to argue about whether it means 'sea of bitterness' or 'rebelliousness' or 'longed for child'. Recent discussion suggests that it may actually be Egyptian in origin, possibly coming from *mr*, 'love'. St Jerome linked it to *stilla maris*, 'drop of the sea', and this was easily modified to *stella maris*, 'star of the sea', a title frequently used for Our Lady. This was the name of the mother of Jesus and of hundreds of saints. It has been chosen for queens and peasants, and has, until the late 20th century seemed unassailable as the world's favourite name for girls. It has appeared in a range of variants, including *Máire*, *Máiri*, *Mara*, *Maria*, *Mariah*, *Mariam*, *Marica*, *Marie*, *Marieke*, *Marija*, *Maritsa*, *Marya*, *Maryam*, *Maura*, *Maeryem*, *Mhairi*, *Mhàiri*, *Miri*, *Miriam*, *Mirjam* and *Moira*. It has also been used in compounds such as *Mary-Anne* and *Marie-Antoinette*.

MATILDA is a Latin form of a Germanic name that was popular among the Normans. It is the equivalent of modern German *Mehthild*, and comes from *math*, 'might' + *hild*, 'battle', suggesting 'strong in battle'. The usual pronunciation of the name in Norman times was *Maud* and that fact explains why the same woman was called both Queen Matilda (1102-67) and Empress Maud. She was the legitimate heir to the throne but she was opposed by her cousin Stephen, and their fight triggered a vicious civil war in England between 1135 and 1148. It is not easy to see the link between *Matilda* and *Maud* but it can be explained in this way. *Matilda* was merely the formal, Latin form of a name that was probably pronounced like 'Mat' + 'auld'. The 't' was pronounced as Cockneys pronounce it in 'matter', that is, it almost disappears. This would have given 'Ma'auld'. The 'l' was often dropped as we drop it in 'walk' and 'salmon', resulting in a pronunciation close to

'Ma-aud'. The pet form *Mattie* is regularly employed.

MAUD is a vernacular form of the latinised Norman name *Matilda*. *Maud* was popularised in the 19th century by Alfred Lord Tennyson (1809-92) in his poem, *Maud: a monodrama*, with its well-known stanza:

> *Come into the garden, Maud,*
> *For the black bat, night, has flown,*
> *Come into the garden, Maud,*
> *I am here at the gate alone;*
> *And the woodbine spices are wafted abroad,*
> *And the musk of the rose is blown.*

SEE Matilda

MAUREEN is an Irish diminutive of *Máire*, 'sea of bitterness'. It is composed of *Máire* + *ín* and is usually written *Móirín* in Irish. The variant spellings *Maurene* and *Maurine* are also used. SEE Mary

MAVIS This word has been used for the 'song-thrush' since the 14th century and it came into English from Old French *mauvis*, which has the same meaning. It does not seem to have been used as a girl's name before the 19th century and it is very possible that its selection was helped by the existence of *Maeve*. The second syllable may have been influenced by the ending of such names as *Berenice* and *Janice*. SEE Maeve

MAXINE is a 20th-century creation, coming from *Maximilian*, 'greatest' + the ending '-ine' from such names as *Caroline*, *Emmeline* and *Gwendoline*. The second syllable of *Maxine* rhymes with 'green'.

MAY was originally used as a pet form of both *Margaret* and *Mary*. Since the 20th century, it has often been used for a daughter born during the month of May, possibly linked to the tradition of a 'May Queen', when a pretty girl was garlanded with flowers. SEE Margaret and Mary

MEG is a popular abbreviation of *Margaret*, 'pearl'. SEE Margaret

MEGAN is a Welsh pet form of *Margaret* which is now regularly treated as an independent name. It has now surpassed *Margaret* in

GIRLS

popularity. SEE Margaret

MELANIE is a French form of Latin *Melania*, which comes from a Greek word *melas*, 'dark, black'. There are at least two saints called *Melania* and the likelihood is that they were of African origin.

MELINDA is a 20th-century coinage, probably the result of combining the first syllable of *Melanie* with *Linda*, 'lime tree'. It could also simply be a rhyming variant of *Belinda*. Rhyming pairs such as *Molly* and *Polly* are quite common. SEE Belinda

MELISSA may come from the Greek word *Melissa*, meaning 'bee' and suggesting sweetness and industry. It is also possible that it is an anglicised form of *Maolíosa*, 'devotee of Jesus'. There are sixteen Irish saints who have borne this name, all of them men, but the 'a' ending may have encouraged parents to think of it as a girl's name.

MELODY became popular in the 20th century when many parents broke away from

centuries of using a small group of names and sought something that embodied a wish for their child. The name comes from Greek *melodia*, 'to sing songs'. It suggests harmony and its similarity to names such as *Melanie* has helped it to become a modern favourite.

MERCEDES is, like *Dolores*, *Loreto* and *Pilar*, derived from one of the many titles of Our Lady. Maria de las Mercedes is a Spanish equivalent of 'Our Lady of Mercies'. The Latin word *mercedes* means 'ransom, wages', but Christ's death was seen as the paying of a ransom for the sin of Adam, and his mother was regarded as helping in the ransom.

MERCY is a French word that comes from Latin *Mercedes* and it has taken on the meaning of 'kindness and forbearance'. This is one of the virtue names adopted by 17th-century Puritans for their daughters and it continues to be widely used in Africa.

MEREDITH is from Welsh *Meredydd*, 'great lord'. It has been a surname since the 12th century and is currently popular as a given name for both boys and girls. The girl's name is sometimes abbreviated to *Merry*.

MERIEL is a variant of *Muriel*, 'bright sea', but it is often regarded as equivalent to *Merle*, 'blackbird', and is occasionally used as an abbreviation of *Mary-Louise*. SEE Muriel

MERLE is from French and means 'blackbird' and the name was often used to imply beautiful singing. In this, it resembles *Melody*. Merle Oberon (1911-79) gave the name prominence in the first half of the 20th century, especially in her highly praised performance as *Cathy* in *Wuthering Heights*.

MERLIN/MERLYN In the Arthurian legend, *Merlin* is the name of the magician who helps Arthur in his desire to create an earthly paradise in Camelot. His name is Celtic in origin and probably means 'sea fort'. The word *merlin* meaning 'falcon' does not seem to be related to the legendary magician but it may have helped to preserve the name.

MERYL may be a form of *Meriel* or *Merle* or, as in the case of the film actress Meryl Streep (b. 1949), an abbreviated form of *Mary-Louise*.

MIA was almost unknown as a name choice before the 20th century, when it became extremely popular. It is a pet form of *Maria*, 'sea of bitterness', in several language communities. It is also possibly a borrowing from Italian phrase such as *Mama Mia*, where it means 'my' or it may be a form of *Mimi*, the heroine of *La Bohème*. (*Mimi* is an Italian pet-name for *Maria*!) There is no evidence that parents worried about its meaning. They simply appear to have liked it, maybe because it is easy to say – and spell – and maybe they felt it made a change from *Mary*. Mia Farrow (b. 1945) gave the name prominence by appearing in over forty films. She was actually named Maria de Lourdes Villiers-Farrow. SEE Mary

MICAELA/MICHAELA

These are the Spanish and German female forms of *Michael*, 'Who is like God?' They are currently almost as widely used as the French equivalent, *Michelle*. The abbreviations *Mickie* and *Mikki* are fashionable

MICHI is a Japanese choice meaning 'clear pathway' and embodying a wish that the daughter may find her way easily through life. The related name, *Michiko*, means 'wise and beautiful child'.

MIGNON is a French word meaning 'darling' and, like *Chèrie*, 'dear', it is occasionally used by English speakers. It is pronounced in the French way.

MILDRED is less popular now than it was over a millennium ago. It comes from an Old English combination of *mild*, 'mild, gentle' + *þryð*, 'strength, power'.

MILLICENT looks as if it combines the Latin words for 'one thousand' and 'one hundred'. In fact, it is a Germanic name that was popularised by the Normans in the form of *Melisende*. (In the early 9th century, Charlemagne's daughter was called *Melisenda*.) This name was a combination of *amal*, 'labour' + *swinth*, 'strength' and implied 'hardworking and strong'. Its pet form *Millie* is now more popular than its source name.

MINA is now a well-established independent name but it seems to have originated as an abbreviation of *Wilhelmina*, 'will to protect', or, in spite of the different spelling, *Philomena*, 'daughter of light'. It is usually pronounced to rhyme with *Sheena*. There is another name, *Mina* or *Minah*, pronounced to rhyme with *Dinah*. It comes from Hindi *maina*, 'bird'.

MINERVA In Roman mythology, *Minerva* was the goddess of wisdom and her name means 'full of intelligence'. Her symbol is an owl.

MINNIE is a pet form of both *Mary*, 'sea of bitterness', and also of names that end in *Mina*. SEE Mary

MIRABEL/MIRABELLE

This name comes from Latin *mirabilis*, 'wondrous', and has been used since at least the 14th century. It probably started being used because parents thought of their daughter as a miracle. The form ending in *-belle* has reinterpreted the second syllable as meaning 'beautiful' in French.

MIRANDA comes from Latin *miranda*, 'admirable, lovely'. It was first used as a girl's name by Shakespeare, who gave it to the heroine in his last play, *The Tempest*. *Mandy* is occasionally used as a pet form.

MIREILLE is a French name that began to be used more widely in the middle of the 20th century. It was a French poet Frédéric Mistral (1830-1914) who created the name, possibly from a Provençal word *mirar*, 'to admire', although he suggested

that it was a variant of *Miriam*.

MIRIAM is a variant of the Hebrew name *Maryam*, which may mean 'sea of bitterness' or 'rebelliousness' or 'longed-for child'. In the Old Testament, *Miriam* was the sister of Moses and Aaron. Because Miriam and her brothers lived in Egypt, it is possible that her name is actually Egyptian in origin and may mean 'love'. SEE Mary

MITZI is a German and Swiss pet form of *Maria*, 'sea of bitterness'. SEE Mary

MOIRA/MOYRA These are anglicised versions of Irish and Scottish *Máire*. SEE Mary

MONA There are at least four possible sources for *Mona*. It may be of Irish origin, coming from *Muadhnait*, 'noble lady'. An Old English word for 'moon' was *mona* and this meaning may well have influenced the choice of some parents. The name will almost always be linked to the Mona Lisa painting by Leonardo da Vinci (1452-1519) where *Mona*

is an abbreviation of
Madonna, 'my lady', but
equivalent to 'Madam'.
Finally, the name is used in
Arabic, where it is a form of
Muna, meaning 'wished for,
desired'.

MONICA was the mother of
St Augustine of Hippo. She was
born in North Africa and is a
model of perseverance. She died
around AD 88, having prayed for
40 years for her son's conversion.
Her name seems to come from
the Latin verb *monere*, 'to advise'
and so may mean 'advisor'.
Monika is a less common variant
and, occasionally, *Mona* is used as
an abbreviation.

MORAG is a Scottish name
that has gained international
usage. There are two possible
meanings. It may be a
combination of *mór*, 'great, big' +
óg, 'young', or the first syllable
may be related to *muir*, 'sea'.

MORGAN is based on an old
Welsh name that probably means
'bright sea' or 'sea circle'. It was
the name of King Arthur's

half-sister, Morgan le Fay, who
was Queen of Avalon and who
took Arthur to Avalon to heal his
wounds after he was fatally
injured in battle.

MORNA is from the Irish
endearment, *a mhuirne*, 'beloved,
darling'. The form has probably
been influenced by *Mona*. It is
derived from an Old Celtic name
probably meaning 'bright sea' or
'sea circle'. SEE Mona

MORWENNA is a Cornish
name meaning 'maiden' and is
closely related to Welsh *morwyn*.
The name is similar to the Irish
use of *Colleen*, 'maiden'.

MOYA is an anglicised form of
Irish *Máire*, 'sea of bitterness'.
SEE Mary

MURIEL seems so
quintessentially English and yet
it is a Celtic name, probably
meaning 'bright sea'. Variants of
the name are found in all of the
Celtic languages. It was so
popular with the Bretons who
came with the Normans that it
had established itself as a
surname by the end of the 12th

century. The daughter of a Viking king of Dublin was called *Myrgjol*, which is an Old Norse version of the Irish form, *Muirgheal*. SEE Meriel

MYFANWY is a Welsh name, probably deriving from *my*, 'my' + *banw*, 'woman'. It is sometimes abbreviated to *Myf* and *Fanny*.

MYRNA In the 1940s and 1950s, Myrna Loy (1905-93) was one of the most popular film stars in Hollywood. Her name is a form of an Irish endearment, *a mhuirne*, 'dearest, darling' but the star's roots were in Wales, rather than Ireland. Her father was on a train in 1905, shortly before she was born, and passed through a Nebraskan station called Myrna. He liked the name so much that he gave it to his daughter. SEE Morna

MYRTLE is one of many names taken from a plant. It comes from Latin *myrtilla* which refers to an evergreen shrub with white, scented flowers.

NOTABLE NAMESAKES
Maeve Binchy (b. 1940) bestselling Irish writer and novelist whose books translate worldwide; Marie Clay (1929-2007) New Zealand expert on literacy, best known for her innovation Reading Recovery techniques; Margaret Thatcher (b. 1925) First woman Prime Minister of the UK, a post she held between 1979 and 1990; Marianne Faithfull (b.1960) English singer and musician who has worked with many top performers including David Bowie and the Rolling Stones; Marilyn Monroe (1926-1962) iconic Hollywood actress who starred in such films as *Some Like It Hot*.

N

NAAVA/NAVA is a Hebrew name meaning 'beautiful'. It is most widely used in the Jewish community.

NADIA is a Russian name meaning 'hope'. It is one of several Russian names such as Sonia and Tania that gained widespread popularity in the 20th century. SEE Nadine

NADINE This name, like *Nadia*, comes from Russian *Nadezhda*, 'hope'. *Nadine* became popular in France in the early years of the 20th century and then spread throughout the world.

NADZIA is a Polish form of *Nadia*, 'hope'. SEE Nadia

NALANI There are a number of Hawaiian names that end in *ani*, including *Lani*, 'sky, heavens', and *Leilani*, 'flowers of heaven'. This one means 'heavenly peace'. The meaning is striking and the sounds are easy to pronounce. Each syllable is given equal weight.

NAN Although *Nan* started as a rhyming form of *Anne*, 'graceful, God has favoured me', it has been used as a name in its own right for at least two centuries. It is derived from Hebrew *Hannah*. SEE Anne and Hannah

NANA can be a modified form of *Nan*, 'God has favoured me, graceful'. It can also be a Japanese name meaning 'apple'. SEE Anne

NANCY Several opinions have been expressed about this name. It has been suggested that it is a pet form of *Constance*, 'steadfast and loyal', or a pet form of *Anne*, 'God has favoured me'. It may well be both. The name has also been used with two other references. It has occasionally been selected by parents with a connection to Nancy in north-eastern France and it is sometimes used in the West Indies as a celebration of *Nancy* stories. These are stories that were carried to the Americas by Africans. Many of them have a hero called *Anansi*, 'the spider'. SEE Anne and Constance

NANETTE is a diminutive of *Nan*, 'graceful'. SEE Nan

NANI is a Hawaiian name meaning 'splendour and beauty'. It could be used as a variant of *Anne* or *Nan*. The first syllable is longer than is usual with *Nan*.

NAOKO (pronounced 'na + o + ko') In Japan, *Naoko* is popular partly because of its meaning, 'obedient child'. In a society where respect for one's elders is expected, an obedient child is a blessing.

NAOMI This Old Testament name means 'pleasantness'. It was the name of Ruth's mother-in-law. Ruth refused to leave Naomi when her husband died. Naomi arranged for Ruth to marry her dead husband's relative, Boaz, and their son was the grandfather of King David. *Naomi* has two pronunciations, the first and more widespread rhymes it with 'hay + omee'. Recently, a second pronunciation rhyming with 'hay +ome + ee'

has been used. There is also a Japanese *Naomi*, pronounced like 'na + o + me'. It means 'beautiful above all'.

NATALIE *Natalie* comes from Latin *natalis dies*, 'day of the birth', and it was traditionally given to a child who was born on or around Christmas Day. When Vasco da Gama entered what is now Durban harbour on Christmas Day 1497, he named the land *Terra Natalis*. It is now 'Kwazulu-Natal'. *Natalie* and occasionally *Nathalie* have also been used as the feminine form of *Nathaniel*, 'gift of God'. The Russian form of the name, *Natalya*, is occasionally used.

NATASHA Many Russian names and pet names became popular in Europe in the 20th century. *Natasha* is a pet form of *Natalya*, 'born on Christmas Day', but it is used for daughters born at any time of the year. SEE Natalie

NATSUKO In Japan, a child born in the summer months is

often regarded as being especially lucky. This name means 'summer child' and it carries overtones of good luck and happiness.

NATSUMI is related to *Natsuko*. It means 'beautiful summer' and the summer is beautiful because the family has been blessed by a summer child. SEE Natsuko

NDIDI This popular Igbo name is found not only in Nigeria but wherever Igbo speakers have settled. The name means 'patience' and this fact helps explain why *Patience* is often chosen as a Christian name. It reflects the local customs. The name is pronounced like 'ndeedee'.

NELL Generally, *Nell* is a form of *Helen*, meaning 'sunbeam', but it can also be a female form of *Niall* or *Neal*, both meaning 'champion'. The Irish name was pronounced 'Nell' in the parts of England where Vikings from Ireland settled and it gave rise to the surnames *Nell* and *Nelson*. Many people associate the name with Nell Gwyn (1650-87), the actress and mistress of King Charles II. Her name was actually *Eleanor*, which may be a form of *Helen* or may mean 'foreign'.

NERICE This can be a form of *Nerys*, meaning 'lady', or a reduced form of *Nerissa*, 'sea nymph'. SEE Nerissa and Nerys

NERISSA is a name that comes from Greek. In Greek mythology, *Nereus* was a sea god and the father of the *nereids* or 'sea nymphs'. Nymphs were beautiful, semi-divine maidens that inhabited the sea and the woods and were a personification of aspects of nature.

NERYS The 20th century saw a rise in the use of Welsh names in Wales, but since many of the names were extremely pretty they soon spread to other parts of the world. The spelling with 'y' is the more usual, although *Nerice* has also been used. It is a female form of *ner*, meaning 'lord'. Its meaning of 'lady' is not exactly the same as English 'lady', which can either mean 'woman' or 'woman of high social rank'. *Nerys* means 'lady' in the sense of having the innate virtues that are often associated with a kind, generous, intelligent female.

NESTA is a Welsh name that is found throughout the world, especially where people of Welsh ancestry have settled. It is a latinised form of *Nest*, a pet form of *Agnes*, which means 'holy' but which has for centuries been associated with Latin *agnus*, 'lamb'.

NGOSI is extremely popular among the Igbo communities of Nigeria and elsewhere. It means 'blessing'. In Igbo culture, children are seen as the greatest blessing that a man and a woman could ask for. The children are a blessing while the parents are alive and when they are dead. As long as their children survive, the parents will never be forgotten. The name is pronounced like 'ngo +see'.

NIABI (pronounced 'nee +a + bee') Native American names have been reintroduced into society by Native Americans who are proud of their heritage and by other Americans who empathise with the ecologically-minded people who once roamed the entire continent. *Niabi* means 'fawn' and could be an interesting choice for a gentle girl.

NICOLA is the feminine form of *Nicholas* and means 'people's victory'. This form is used in Italy for a boy, but in the English-speaking world it is almost invariably feminine. The usual abbreviations are *Nickie* and, more recently, *Nikki*.

NICOLE is the French female form of *Nicholas*, 'people's victory', but it is now probably more widely used outside France. Whereas the 'col' in *Nicola* is pronounced like the mountain 'col', the second syllable of *Nicole* is also pronounced like 'coal'.

NINA This is now an independent name but it started in Russia as a pet form of *Anna*, 'grace'. It is also used occasionally as the Spanish equivalent of 'daughter'. At first, it may seem strange to call a child 'daughter', but the custom occurs in many cultures. Irish *Alana* (*a leanbh*) also means 'child', although it has the additional meaning of 'darling'.

NOELLE was originally found only in France, where it was given to a child born on or around *Noël*, 'Christmas Day'. The name is often used with *Marie* in France, giving *Marie-Noelle*, but it is now used worldwide and is not so closely linked to Christmas.

NOMUSA (pronounced 'no + moo + sa') is found widely in southern Africa. It is an Ndebele name meaning 'merciful'.

NONI/NONIE These are pet forms of *Nora*, 'honour'. They rhyme with 'pony', not 'bonny'. SEE Nora

NORA/NORAH is less popular now than it once was and it is usually regarded as an independent name. It was originally an abbreviated form of *Honora*, from Latin *honor*,

'honour', or *Eleanora*, which has been linked to *Helen*, 'sunbeam', for centuries, although it may mean 'foreign'. *Eleanora* has also produced the independent names *Leonora* and *Lenore*. Occasionally, *Norah* is spelt with an 'h'. This makes the name resemble Hebrew names such as *Hannah* and *Sarah*. SEE Eleanora and Honora

NOREEN *Nora* was once one of the most popular names in Ireland and it gave rise to the diminutive *Noreen*, 'little honourable one'. *Noreen* was also widely used in Australia in the 20th century, where it was often spelt *Norene* and *Norine*.

NORMA seems to have come into existence in the 19th century. It may derive from Latin *norma*, 'rule, norm', but it is more likely to be a form of *Norman* and mean 'northerner, Viking'.

NUALA is regularly used now as an independent name, but it was originally an abbreviation of the Irish name *Fionnuala*, from *fionn*, 'fair, beautiful' + *ghuala*, 'shoulders', a phrase suggesting great beauty. In Irish mythology, *Fionnuala* was the daughter of Lir. She and her three brothers were transformed into swans by their stepmother. SEE Fionnuala

NUO Chinese names are beginning to spread beyond China. *Nuo* means 'graceful' and is semantically similar to *Anne* and *Hannah*.

NUYING is a popular Chinese name, meaning 'flower girl'. It suggests the link between the beauty of a flower and a little girl and does not imply 'a girl who sells flowers'.

NOTABLE NAMESAKES
Nadia Comăneci (b.1961) Romanian gymnast and winner of five Olympic gold medals; Naomi Campbell (b. 1970) English supermodel and company director of the Design House of Naomi Campbell; Nicole Kidman (b.1967) Academy Award winning Australian actress.

Star of *The Hours* and *Moulin Rouge*;. Nina Simone (1933-2003) African American singer, songwriter, pianist, and civil rights activist.

O

OCTAVIA comes from Latin *octavius/octavia*, meaning 'eighth child' originally but used without this meaning even in Roman times.

ODETTE is a French name, related to *Odo* and *Otto*, 'prosperity, wealth, good fortune'. This name was popularised by the Second World War heroine Odette Marie Celine Sansom (1912-1995). A film called *Odette* and based on her story was made in 1950. It starred Anna Neagle in the title role.

ODILE is related to *Odette*. It is a French form of the Germanic name *Odila*, meaning 'prosperity,

147

good fortune'. *Odile* is the name of the patron saint of Alsace. She was born blind in the 8th century but gained her sight when she was baptised. She became a nun and was renowned for her piety.

OKSANA/OXANA

This is a popular Ukrainian name. It is a Russian version of Greek *Xenia*, meaning 'hospitality'.

OLAMIDE

(pronounced 'oh + lam + ee + day') is popular in Nigeria and among Nigerians who have settled elsewhere. It is a Yoruba name meaning 'wealth has come into our family'.

OLGA

is regarded as a typical Russian name and so it is, but its history is, like that of many names, a little bit more complex. It is a Russian version of *Helga*, 'holy'. The name was carried to Russia by the Vikings, probably in the 9th century.

OLIVE

This is one of the many examples of plant names that have been given to children, especially girls. It comes from Latin *oliva*, 'olive, olive tree'.

The olive branch has been an emblem of peace at least as far back as the biblical story of Noah. Noah sent a dove out of the ark to find out if the waters had subsided. When it returned with an olive twig in its beak, Noah knew that peace had been restored between God and human beings.

OLIVIA

Shakespeare seems to have been the first person to use this name. He gave it to a character in *Twelfth Night*. She was young, attractive and wealthy but did not fully understand her needs or her strengths. Shakespeare would have known the name *Olive* and the Latin *oliva*, 'olive, olive tree', but the writer who used the word 'punk' as early as 1603: *She may be a punk...* (*Measure for Measure*) probably enjoyed playing with names, possibly to stress the uniqueness of the character.

OLWEN/OLWIN/OLWYN

All these spellings are found for this Welsh name. In Welsh mythology, *Olwen* is a beautiful maiden who loves *Culhwch*. Her name comes from *ol*, 'track, footprint' + *gwen*, 'white, fair, beautiful'. Olwen's father insists that *Culhwch* must complete several spectacularly difficult tasks before being allowed to marry *Olwen*. *Culhwch* succeeds in fulfilling the tasks and winning his beautiful wife.

OLYMPIA This name was originally found only in Greece but it can now be found world wide. It comes from *Olympia*, a plain in Greece that was the site of the original Olympic Games. It was also where Zeus went when he sought peace.

ONEIDA This name is Native American and means 'standing rock'. The Oneida people were part of the Iriquois Nation that lived in the New York State area before the influx of Europeans. *Oneida* is most widely used in the United States partly because of the founding of the Oneida Community, a religious group established in New York State in 1848. Its aim was to return Christians to early beliefs and practices.

ONYEKACHUKWU (pronounced 'on + yay + ka + chook + oo') This significant Igbo name is found throughout Nigeria and wherever Igbos have settled. It is often abbreviated to *Onyeka*. Both mean 'Who is greater than God?'

OONA/OONAGH is an anglicised form of Irish *Una*, which probably comes from *uan*, 'lamb'. The *Oona* spelling represents the pronunciation and the *Oonagh* form is a visual reminder that the name is not English. SEE Una

OPAL Girls have often been given the names of gems and precious stones. An 'opal' is an iridescent gemstone, particularly appropriate for daughters born in October. It comes from the Sanskrit noun *upala*, 'jewel'. There was a tradition that opal stones were unlucky but this has a very simple explanation. An opal can shrink in certain temperatures and can slip out of its setting. The diminutive *Opaline* is occasionally used.

OPHELIA is another of Shakespeare's innovations (SEE Olivia and Regan). The name comes from a Greek name, *Ophelos*, 'help'. According to Ben Jonson, Shakespeare knew 'small Latin and less Greek' so it is uncertain whether he knew the meaning of the name of his tragic heroine. It seems likely that he did. *Ophelia* certainly needed help. She was rejected by Hamlet although he had sworn eternal love; her brother was in France; and her father was murdered by the man she loved. Many of us have an image of *Ophelia* that is based on the John Everett Millais (1829-96) painting, which shows a beautiful young girl, bedecked with flowers, floating on the water.

OPHRAH/OPRAH is a Hebrew name meaning 'fawn, young deer' and it was originally a man's name. Oprah Winfrey, the American television personality, has made her form of the name more widely known and more frequently used, and yet hers comes from a child's inability to pronounce *Orpah*, her given name.

ORFHLAITH/ORLA (rhymes with 'for + ma') is one of the most popular names for girls in Ireland. It comes from *ór*, 'gold' + *flaith*, 'princess'. It has royal and antiquity connections in that it was the name of Brian Boru's sister.

OTTILIE is another French form of *Odila*, a Germanic name, related to *Otto* and meaning 'prosperity'. It was popular in Victorian times but may well be in for a revival. Otylia is the Polish equivalent of the name.

OWENA is a female form of *Owen*, a name that is found in different variants in all the Celtic languages. This form is linked most closely with Wales. It seems to mean 'well born' or 'yew born'. The Celts were particularly interested in trees and this interest is reflected in the names they chose for children and for places. *Terenure*, for example, means 'land of the yew tree'.

OXANA SEE Oksana

P

PADDY/PAT/PATSY These are very popular pet forms for *Patricia*, 'nobly born'. SEE Patricia

PAGE/PAIGE In the Middle Ages, a *page* was a young boy, often of noble blood, who was attached to a member of the nobility as an assistant, or to be trained in the behaviour suitable to a person of rank. The title was extended to any boy in livery or to a boy at a wedding who helps to carry the bride's train. In our gender-aware society, the term has been extended to girls and, in this way, and also because of the use of *Page* as a surname, it has become a given name exclusively for girls.

PALLAS (pronounced 'palace') is the name of the Greek goddess of wisdom. It was used as an alternative name for *Athene*, the goddess to whom Athens was dedicated. *Pallas* is the equivalent of Roman *Minerva*. Since *Minerva* means 'full of sense', it is probable that *Pallas* had a similar implication.

PALOMA is the Spanish word for 'dove' and it is thus an appropriate choice for a girl. It is the equivalent of *Columba*. *Paloma*

is extremely popular in Hispanic circles in America and its attractive sound and meaning has encouraged its spread into English-speaking communities.

PAMELA is so widespread now that it is hard to believe that it only came into existence in the late 16th century. *Pamela* seems to have been created by the courtier poet, Sir Philip Sidney (1554-86), and it is uncertain where he got his inspiration. It is possible that he combined *pame*, an old spelling of 'palm', the tree associated with Christ's triumphal entry into Jerusalem on Palm Sunday, with *Ella*, a name popularised by the Normans and meaning 'other'. Samuel Richardson's novel of 1740 was called *Pamela or Virtue Rewarded* and its popularity encouraged the spread of the name.

PANDORA In Greek mythology, *Pandora* was the first human woman and she got her name, which means 'all gifted', because each of the gods gave her a gift. She is, in two ways, the

equivalent of *Eve*. First, she is the mother of all humanity and second, she is blamed for bringing evil into the world. Zeus sent *Pandora* to earth with a jar or box. If she had kept it closed, the world would have received every conceivable blessing. *Pandora* opened it, of course, and all the evils of the world were released. In spite of *Pandora's* bad press, the meaning of this name is actually very positive.

PANSY used to be a popular girl's name, similar in its inspiration to *Daisy* and *Violet*. The name comes from French *pensée*, meaning 'thought' and suggesting that the child would always be in the parents' thoughts. The name has been associated with two negative forces. One is that it took on the meaning of 'effeminate' and the second was the comic strip appearance of *Pansy Potter*, the Strong Man's daughter in *The Beano* in 1938 and again in *Sparky* in 1965.

PAOLA is an Italian form of *Paula*, 'little one'. SEE Paula

PATIENCE is one of the Seven Virtues. It comes from the Latin *patientia*, 'the ability to endure suffering or trials with calm resignation'. In the 17th century Puritans began to call their daughters after the four so-called Cardinal Virtues, namely justice, prudence, temperance and patience (or fortitude), and the so-called Theological Virtues, namely faith, hope and charity. *Patience* was popularised by the reputation of the poet Patience Strong (1907-90). Her morally uplifting verses continue to be printed in cards and calendars and many people have taken comfort from her words on death and bereavement.

PATRICIA is the female equivalent of *Patrick*. It has always been a favourite in Ireland and, to a lesser extent, in France. *Patricia* is from the same root as the adjective 'patrician', which came from Latin *patricius*, 'nobly born', and referred to a member of a noble family in ancient Rome. Constantine I, who was the first Christian emperor, used the adjective for an officer appointed by him to represent his Byzantine empire.

NAMES FROM VIRTUES

Amity
Charity
Chastity
Clemency
Comfort
Constance
Faith
Felicity
Fidelity
Gloria
Grace
Harmony
Honor/Honour
Hope
Joy
Mercy
Patience
Prudence
Serena
Verity

PAULA is one of the many female names related to Latin *paulus/paula*, 'small'. When one considers the impact made by St Paul, the apostle, it is not surprising that many early Christians and martyrs bore the name of *Paula*. It is less popular now than it was in the past but it is a name that could again become fashionable.

PAULETTE is French for 'little Paula'. It was rarely used by English-speaking parents until the mid 20th century, when Paulette Goddard (1905-90) was at the height of her fame. Like many exceptionally beautiful Hollywood stars, she married several times, her best-known husband being Charlie Chaplin. Goddard was actually born Pauline Levy, but Hollywood moguls decided that *Paulette* had more 'class'.

PAULINA is the feminine form of Latin *Paulinus*, which meant 'little Paul' or 'little, little one'. It was used more frequently in English than *Pauline*. Shakespeare used the name for an outstandingly strong character in *The Winter's Tale. Paulina* stands up against the king's injustice and, by means of her unfailing loyalty, is the instrument for uniting the king and queen with each other and with their daughter, *Perdita*. Occasionally, the spelling *Paulena* occurs.

PAULINE is the French form of *Paulina* but it has now become more popular worldwide. SEE Paulina

PEARL is one of several jewels that began to be used for little girls in the 19th century. *Opal* and *Ruby* are others. Occasionally, a child called *Margaret*, 'pearl', is given the pet name *Pearl*, especially if there are several other *Margarets* in the family.

PEGGIE/PEGGY is a pet form of *Margaret*, which has *Maggie* and *Meggie* as shortened variants. It is useful to give a child a name that has several variants. As a name, *Peggie* has much to recommend it but, as a child grows up, she may prefer *Mags* or *Margaret*. It may seem strange that *Peggie* and *Maggie* are alternative pet forms of the same name but, in children's language, rhyming pairs are common. We find them in *bow-wow*, *Humpty Dumpty* and *pell-mell*. SEE Margaret

PENELOPE is from Greek *penelops*, 'duck'. At first sight, it may seem strange to call a child after a bird but 'my duck' is used as an endearment in parts of England, and many beautiful names, such as *Rachel* and *Rebecca*, are taken from words for animals. In Greek mythology, *Penelope* was the wife of *Odysseus* (referred to as *Ulysses* in Latin). When Odysseus did not return immediately from the Trojan War, *Penelope* was approached by many suitors, but she remained faithful to her husband. She told each of her suitors that she would marry him when she had finished the weaving she was doing, but each night she unpicked all the weaving she had done during the day. Her name came to represent chastity, faithfulness and intelligence. *Penny* is the usual abbreviation.

PEONY is one of many girls' names derived from flowers or shrubs. The name comes from Greek *Paion*, 'physician of the gods'. The peony has attractive globular flowers in varying shades and was cultivated widely because of its value as a medicinal plant.

PERDITA is chosen by parents who are interested in Shakespeare. He chose it as the name of the daughter of Hermione and Leontes in *The Winter's Tale*. *Perdita* means 'one who was lost'. *Perdita* was 'lost' but, like the Prodigal Son, she was found and restored to her parents. One actress to play the part of *Perdita* was Mary Robinson (1758-1800). The Prince of Wales, later George IV, saw her in the role and was so struck by her beauty and wit that she became his mistress.

PERSEPHONE (pronounced 'per + sef + on + ee') Few parents will choose this name but it could be a way of distinguishing a child who has a common surname, such as *Jones*. In Greek mythology, she was a goddess who was carried off and made Queen of the Underworld. Her mother would not give up the search for her daughter and was rewarded in that *Persephone* was allowed to spend part of every year on earth. The *Persephone* story is a myth symbolising the annual return of spring.

PETA is a female form of *Peter*. It comes from Greek *petros*, rock, stone'. It is not as frequently used as *Petra*.

PETRA is a female form of *Peter*, from Greek *petros*, 'rock, stone'. The tendency is to pronounce the first syllable to rhyme with 'met' rather than 'meet'. Coincidentally, *Petra* is the name of an ancient walled city in Jordan. It was originally carved out of the red sandstone of the local cliffs and can only be reached through narrow pathways. When the poet John William Burgon first saw it in 1845, he described it as:

A rose-red city – half as old as Time!

PETRINA is a form of *Peter*, 'rock'. It is a combination of *Petra* and the diminutive ending found in *Paulina*. This name is stressed on the second syllable, a fact that explains its pet form, *Trina*. SEE Petra

PETRONEL/PETRONELA /PETRONELLA This female version of *Peter*, 'rock', has been used for almost 2000 years and was the name of an early martyr. The variant without the final vowel occurred quite widely in the Middle Ages.

PETULA This is a 20th-century name and no one is absolutely certain of its meaning. It may come from Latin *petulare*, 'to ask, request', and may suggest that the child was longed for. It is possible, too, that it is a blend of the flowers, *petunia* and *primula*. The name was popularised by Petula Clark (b. 1932), who has been a star of radio, film and television for almost 60 years. Her father joked that he gave his daughter the name by putting together the names of two girl friends, *Pet* and *Ulla*.

PHILIPA/PHILIPPA/ PHILLIPA/PHILLIPPA

The most frequently employed spelling of this name is with *Philippa* but all the variants of this female form of *Philip*, 'lover of horses' are regularly employed. In the past, both women and men used *Philip* but there was a growing tendency to separate the forms for the two genders. *Pippa* is a popular pet form.

PHILIPPINA

This female variant of *Philip* means 'little horse lover'. It has also been interpreted as 'lover of pain' in the Christian sense of learning to endure pain for the purpose of associating oneself with the sufferings of Christ.

PHILLIDA/PHYLLIDA

Originally, this was a variant of *Phyllis*, 'green foliage', but it is used as a name in its own right. SEE Phyllis

PHILLIS

This spelling is occasionally used for *Phyllis*, 'green foliage'. Some parents prefer this spelling and they are in good company. John Milton (1608-74)

uses *Phillis* as a generic name for a beautiful country girl in his poem *L'Allegro*:

Herbs and other country messes,
Which the neat-handed Phillis
dresses. SEE Phyllis

PHILOMENA

comes from the combination of the Greek words *philein*, 'to love' + *menos*, 'strength'. *Filomena* was the name of at least one early saint. There has been some debate over the name of another saint, whose relics were found in the catacombs in 1802. The inscription seemed to read: *Filumina pax tecum*, which was first interpreted as 'Peace be with you, Philomena'. Other scholars suggested that the inscription may have meant 'Peace be with you, beloved', because Greek *philoumena* meant 'beloved, well loved'. Still others suggested that the inscription may have meant 'Peace be with you, daughter of light', where *filumina* was a reduced form of *filia*, 'daughter' + *luminae*, 'of light'. Because of the debate, many parents stopped using this name, but since all three interpretations have their attractions, the scholarly arguments should not deter parents. The usual abbreviations are *Phil* and *Mena*.

PHOEBE In Greek mythology, *Phoebe* was a Titan and the daughter of *Uranus*, god of heaven, and *Gaia*, goddess of the earth. Her name comes from Greek *phoibos*, 'bright', and she was later sometimes equated with *Artemis*, the moon goddess. The name is pronounced like 'fee + bee'.

PHYLLIS In Greek mythology, *Phyllis*, whose name means 'green foliage', was the daughter of King Sithon of Thrace. She fell irretrievably in love with Demophon, a young Greek warrior, on his return from Troy. Demophon explained that he had to go to Athens first but promised to return on a particular day so that they could get married. Demophon was delayed in Athens and was unable to return to Thrace to keep his word. *Phyllis*, who reminds one a little of Madame Butterfly, believed that she had been betrayed. In despair, she hanged herself, but the gods felt pity for the great love she had shown, so they transformed her into a living almond tree. Demophon returned too late to save *Phyllis*. He hugged the almond tree but she was unable to return to the land of the living.

PIA (pronounced 'pee + a') is the female form of Latin *pius*, 'holy, reverent'. The name is popular in many parts of Europe, especially Italy. It began to be widely used after Ingrid Bergman (1915-82) used the name for her daughter. The name occurs in Sweden but it was suggested that Ingrid Bergman's daughter was named after the initials in the phrase 'Peter (her first husband) Ingrid Always'.

PILAR (pronounced 'pee + lar') is a Spanish name that has gained a degree of popularity worldwide. The name comes from the Spanish word *pilar*, meaning 'pillar, column'. According to tradition, St James the Apostle travelled to Spain to preach the

Gospel. He stopped at Saragossa and became depressed by his lack of success in converting the people. While he was praying, Our Lady appeared to him and gave him a statue of herself and a 'pillar' of jasper wood and told him to build her a temple, using the image and the 'pillar'. James built a chapel and dedicated it to Our Lady of the Pillar. The statue and the jasper column are still preserved. The words 'pillar' and 'column' probably suggest something large to most modern people but, even as recently as the 16th century, Cardinal Wolsey (1475-1530) used a 'pillar' as a symbol of the dignity of his office. We do not know the exact size of his 'pillar' but it was certainly capable of being carried by a young man.

PIPER means 'one who plays a pipe, musician'. It is not used widely but was popularised during the 20th century by the film actress Piper Laurie. Laurie's real name was Rosetta Jacobs but the studio managers did not think that was sufficiently memorable.

PIPPA started off as a reduced form of *Philippa*, 'lover of horses', but it has taken on an independent existence. It was used by the Victorian poet Robert Browning (1812-89) for his poem, *Pippa Passes* (1841) which contains the chorus that many parents learnt at school:

> *The year's at the spring*
> *And day's at the morn;*
> *Morning's at seven;*
> *The hillside's dew-pearled;*
> *The lark's on the wing;*
> *The snail's on the thorn:*
> *God's in his heaven –*
> *All's right with the world!*

SEE Philippa

PLACIDA comes from the Latin adjective *placida*, 'calm, serene, gentle'. It was the name of countless nuns and of the children who were called after them.

POLLY is a pet form of *Mary*, which may mean 'bitter'. One of the many forms of *Mary* is *Molly*, and *Polly* is a rhyming equivalent. Rhyming pet forms are far from uncommon. We find them in

GIRLS

such pairs as *Meggie* and *Peggie* and *Rick* and *Dick*. *Polly* was joined to *Anna* by Eleanor Hodgman Porter (1868-1920) for her ever-cheerful character, *Pollyanna*.

POPPY There are two equally possible etymologies for this girl's name. The first is that it comes from the flower which occurs in several vivid colours. The second is that it may owe its origin to French *poupée*, 'doll'.

PORTIA Anyone who has seen or read *The Merchant of Venice* will remember *Portia*, the wife of Bassanio, who dresses as a male advocate to defend *Antonio*, the merchant. The name comes from an old Roman name, *Porcius*, which was probably a nickname from *porcus*, 'hog, pig'. The form *Portia* or *Porcia* was used in Rome. It was, for example, the name of the wife of Marcus Junius Brutus (85-42 BC), who conspired against Julius Caesar.

PREETA is a Hindi name meaning 'love'. It is similar in implication to *Preeti*.

PRIMROSE is from Latin *prima rosa* meaning 'earliest rose'. It is not a rose but it is an attractive spring flower. It is one of many flower names given to daughters.

PRISCILLA is the name of the woman with whom St Paul stayed when he was in Corinth. Her name seems to be from the Roman name *Priscius*, based on a nickname and meaning 'ancient'. The name was popular with reforming Christians in the 17th century. A male form, *Priscillian*, was the name of a 4th-century bishop of Avila. The pet form, *Cilla*, is now used as an independent name.

PRUDENCE is from Latin *prudentia*, 'foresight, sagacity, skill'. It is one of many virtues adopted by Puritans for their daughters in the 17th century. It continues to be used today especially among African Christians. *Pru* and *Prue* are both used as abbreviations.

PRUNELLA has two possible origins. It may be from Latin

pruna, 'plum'. This would link the name to others derived from flowers or shrubs. It may also come from French *prunelle*, 'sloe, the fruit of the blackthorn'. *Prunella* is used in English for a strong silk material. It got its name from French because it was usually the colour of the sloe.

PURITY The meaning of this name is self-evident. It comes from Latin *puritas*, 'purity', and has been used sporadically since the 17th century as a means of giving a daughter a virtue to live up to.

NOTABLE NAMESAKES
Paloma Picasso (b.1949) fashion designer and the daughter of Pablo Picasso; Patty Duke (1956) American actress who promotes awareness of mental health issues; Paula Radcliffe (b. 1973) English long-distance runner who holds many records, including the Marathon; Penelope Cruz (b.1974)

Spanish actress and dancer; Prunella Scales (b.1932) English actress who played Sybil in the television series *Fawlty Towers.*

Q

There are very few girls' names that begin with 'Q' and those that occur in English-speaking communities are taken from other cultures and from surnames. There is a tendency to use the 'q' spelling for exotic names such as *Quetzalcoatl*, the 'Plumed Serpent' of the Toltec and Aztec civilizations. He was the god of the morning and evening star, and regarded as the symbol of death followed by resurrection. Occasionally, too, Arabic names are written with 'q' to indicate a particular glottal sound that does not occur in Celtic or Germanic languages. Since the Arabic script is totally different from the scripts used in

Western Europe, the use of 'q' or 'k' is only a rough approximation.

QADIRA is the female form of Arabic *Qadir*, meaning 'powerful'. It is sometimes written with a 'Q' rather than a 'K' to indicate that the first syllable is not to be pronounced exactly like English 'cad'.

QUASHEE (pronounced 'quash + ee') This name has been found in the Caribbean since the 17th century. It is an anglicised spelling of the Ashanti name *Kwasi*, 'born on Sunday'. It has been used for both boys and girls. SEE Kwasi

QUEENIE is much less popular now than it once was, although it continues to be used in African societies where there is a local name such as *Shufai*, which means 'female chief, queen'. It is likely that the English name came from Old English *cwene*, meaning 'woman, female', rather than from *cwen*, meaning 'queen' but the first word was lost and people

equated *Queenie* with a female monarch and thus as a suitable name for the little queen of the household.

QUINTINA (pronounced 'quin + ten + a') is occasionally used as a female form of *Quentin*. It is a diminutive and means 'little fifth child'.

R

RACHEL is a Hebrew name meaning 'ewe'. It has been, and continues to be, a popular choice worldwide. It occurs in a number of variants, including *Rachael*, *Rachelle*, *Rahel*, *Raquel* and *Rochelle*. *Rachel* appears in the Old Testament as the daughter of Laban. *Jacob* loves her and works for Laban for seven years for the right to marry her. After this time, he is tricked into marrying Rachel's older sister *Leah* and has to work for another seven years for his beloved *Rachel*.

RADHA is a significant figure in Hindu mysticism. She is the favourite lover of Krishna and the reincarnation of *Lakshmi*, the goddess of prosperity. *Radha*, which is pronounced like 'rad + ha', is symbolic of the human spirit's desire for unity with God.

RAE occurs as an independent name, found most frequently in Australia. It may have developed from a shortened form of *Rachel* and mean 'ewe' or it may be a female equivalent of *Ray*, from *Raymond*, 'strength and protection'. A third possibility is that it is the surname *Rae*, which has been used in Scotland since the 13th century and means 'roe'.

RAHEL is the Polish equivalent of *Rachel*, 'ewe'. SEE Rachel

RAMANI (pronounced 'ra + man + ee') is a Hindi name meaning 'beautiful girl', a very

fitting title for a new baby.

RAMONA is Spanish and is the female form of *Ramon*, which is a variant of *Raymond*, 'strength and protection'. It was popularised by the song 'Ramona', which was written for a film of the same name, which was released in 1928. It has been revived many times and has been sung by many top performers, including Louis Armstrong, Jim Reeves and the Bachelors.

RANA/RANEE/RANI is a Hindi name meaning 'queen'. The term was also used as a title for members of the royal family that ruled Nepal between 1846 and 1951.

REBECCA is a Hebrew name. Its meaning is uncertain. It may mean 'young cow' or 'noose' but these unflattering meanings are overcome by *Rebecca's* important role in the Old Testament. She is the wife of *Isaac* and the mother of *Jacob*. Indeed, it was *Rebecca* who decided that Jacob, rather than his elder twin brother *Esau*, should gain his father's blessing and become the link between Abraham and the future chosen people. When *Rebecca* left her home, she was blessed by her family and told:

Thou art our sister; be thou the mother of thousands of millions…
Book of Genesis, Chap. 24, verse 60.
Rebecca occurs in a variety of forms, the most popular being *Rebeca(h)* and *Rebeka(h)*. It has also given rise to such pet forms as *Becka*, *Beckie*, *Becky*, *Bekki* and *Bekky*.

REGAN The first recorded use of *Regan* as a given name was in Shakespeare's play, *King Lear*. *Regan* was one of Lear's three daughters. It is uncertain where Shakespeare got the name, but since the story of Lear is based on Celtic mythology, it is reasonable to assume that he thought it was Celtic. He may have linked it to *Regina*, the Latin word for 'queen', or to the Irish surname *Reagan/Regan*, meaning 'little king'. The first syllable is sometimes rhymed with 'me' and sometimes with 'may'.

REGINA is the Latin word for 'queen'. It has been used for monarchs, especially in court cases, such as *Regina v. Brown*, and as a title of Our Lady, *Regina Coeli*, 'Queen of Heaven'. The second syllable is sometimes pronounced like 'Jean' and sometimes to rhyme with 'mine'.

RENATA is from Latin *renatus*, meaning 'reborn'. It was used by early Christians to indicate that, by baptism, they were reborn in Christ. The French equivalent is *Renée* and, although that is a name in its own right, it is sometimes treated as an abbreviated form of *Irene*, 'peace'.

RENÉE is the French female form of *René*, meaning 'born again'. SEE Renata

RHEA In Greek mythology, *Rhea* was a Titan and the mother of Zeus. Her husband Cronus was obsessed by the thought that his children would betray him so he ate all *Rhea's* children except Zeus, whom *Rhea* managed to save. In Roman mythology, *Rhea Silva* was the mother of *Romulus*

and *Remus*. The name is
pronounced in two different
ways. Some parents rhyme it
with 'see a', while others rhyme
it with 'say a'.

RHIANON/RHIANNON

This popular Welsh name means
'goddess, eternal spirit'. It is also
used by people who are not of
Welsh ancestry and they tend to
pronounce the name to rhyme
with 'see + cannon'.

RHODA comes from the
Greek word *rhodon*, 'rose'. (It is
probable that the island of
Rhodes has the same origin.)
This is one of the many flower
names taken over as names for
daughters.

RHONA looks like a Welsh or
Greek name but it seems to have
originated in Scotland. It may be a
female form of *Ronan*, 'seal child',
or of *Ronald*, 'mighty rule'. *Rhona*
may also have been influenced by
names such as *Mona* and *Shona*.
The 'h' in *Rhona* is not
pronounced. It seems to have
been introduced to parallel names
such as *Rhiannon* and *Rhoda*.

RIHANA is an Arabic
name meaning 'sweet
basil'. It is thus one of the
many names from a variety of
cultures that reflect an interest
in flowers, plants and herbs. The
use of 'sweet' in the English
translation means that this
particular variety is more
aromatic than usual. This
particular plant was famed for its
medicinal powers.

RITA started life as a pet form
of *Margarita* or *Margherita*, the
Spanish and Italian forms of
Margaret, 'pearl'. It is regularly
used, however, as a full name.
SEE Margaret

RIVKA is a Hebrew form of
Rebecca, 'young cow' or 'noose'.
SEE Rebecca

ROBERTA is a female form of
Robert, 'bright fame'. It does not
occur as frequently as its
abbreviations, *Bobbie* and *Bobby*.

ROBIN/ROBYN is a pet
form of *Robert* and was originally
always a male name. The shift
from male to female occurred
during the 20th century. While

Robin is still used for both girls and boys, the 'y' spelling is almost exclusively female.

ROMA is the name of Italy's capital and it has been used for centuries as a girl's given name. The city of Rome takes its name from *Romulus*, one of twin boys fed by a she-wolf and brought up by shepherds. *Roma* tends to be mainly Catholic but this is a tendency and not an absolute rule. *Roma* has two other possible sources. It can be one of the names of the goddess *Lakshmi* in Hindi mythology and it can be from Romani, where *rom* is '(hu)man' and *roma* is the plural.

ROMOLA (The first syllable rhymes with 'dom' or 'dome') Like *Roma*, this name is taken from the city of Rome and suggests 'Roman'. *Romola* is the title of a novel by George Eliot (1819-80).

ROSA This is the Spanish and Italian form of 'rose', one of the most perennially popular flower names. SEE Rose

ROSALEE/ROSALIA/ ROSALIE These are all derivatives of Latin *rosa*, 'rose'. St Rosalia was a 12th-century Italian saint. SEE Rose

ROSALEEN is an Irish form of Rosalind, which is usually interpreted as a 'rose' name but is, in fact, from German *hrod*, 'fame' + *lind*, 'wood'. SEE Rosalind

ROSALIND is one of the many names of Germanic origin introduced by the Normans. It is a combination of *hrod*, 'fame' + *lind*, 'wood', and owed some of its popularity to being interpreted as the wood of the cross of Christ. Shakespeare uses the name *Rosalind* for the heroine of his play *As You Like It*.

ROSAMOND/ ROSAMUND Like *Rosalind*, this is a Germanic name, combining the words *hrod*, 'fame' + *mund*, 'protection'. It was given a new interpretation as *rosa*, 'rose'+ *mundi*, 'of the world', a title given to Mary in the Litany of the Blessed Virgin Mary.

ROSANNA is a blend of *Rose* + *Anna*, 'grace', suggesting 'rose of grace' or 'graceful rose'. It is one of the many blends in which *Rose* occurs. We have, for example, *Rose-Anne*, *Rose-Mary* as well as *Mary-Rose*. SEE Rose

ROSE The rose bush produces flowers that are colourful and fragrant and the rose has been regarded as a symbol of beauty for thousands of years and in a variety of cultures. In the *Song of Solomon*, for example, the speaker claims:

> *I am the rose of Sharon, and the lily of the valleys*

One of the titles of Our Lady is *Rosa sine spina*, 'a rose without thorns', and Ophelia described Hamlet as:

> *The expectancy and rose of the fair state...Hamlet*, Act 3, Scene 1.

There are numerous modifications of this name, including *Rosa*, *Rosie*, *Rosalee*, *Rosalie*, *Rosena*, *Rosetta*, *Rosita*, *Rosy* and *Roz*.

ROSEMARIE/ROSEMARY

This name may be regarded as a blend of *Rose* + *Marie*, the French form of *Mary*, or as a modified form of *Rosemary*. This name has two possible origins. It may be a blend of two widely-used names or the name of an aromatic shrub. The herb takes its name from Latin *ros marinus*, 'dew of the sea'. Parents may choose to interpret their daughter's name as a blend or as a herb that is associated with remembrance.

ROSENA This is a diminutive of *Rose*. SEE Rose

ROWENA When Sir Walter Scott (1771-1832) wrote *Ivanhoe*, he used the name of *Rowena* for the Saxon heroine. *Rowena* is also said to be the daughter of *Hengist*, one of the leaders of the Saxon invasion of England in the 5th century. It is likely that the name is a blend of *hrod*, 'fame' + *wynn*, 'joy', suggesting 'the joy of fame'. However, since the name is first used by Geoffrey of Monmouth in the 12th century, it is just possible that it is a combination of Welsh *rhodd*, 'gift' + *gwen*, 'fair, beautiful'.

ROXANA/ ROXANNA/ ROXANNE

These are variants of Greek *Roxanç*, the name of Alexander the Great's Persian wife. Her name is said to mean 'dawn'. The forms *Roxie* and *Roxy* are favoured pet forms.

ROZ

is usually an abbreviation of one of the *Rose* compounds. This form is a favourite in Poland. SEE Rose

ROZALIA

is a popular name in Poland. SEE Rosalee

RUBY

A 'ruby' is a precious stone that can vary in colour from pale rose pink to deep crimson. It has traditionally been associated with great value, as in the *Book of Proverbs*:

*Who can find a virtuous woman?...
her price is far above rubies.*

The word is related to Latin *rubeus*, 'red'.

RUTH

is a Hebrew name. Its meaning is debated but it suggests 'devoted friendship'. The Bible tells the story of *Ruth* in considerable detail. She was a Moabite woman in a strange land, and John Keats has immortalised her in his 'Ode to a Nightingale' when he describes how the nightingale's song may have been heard and felt:

*Through the sad heart of Ruth,
when, sick for home,
She stood in tears amid the alien
corn.*

Later, when her husband dies, she refuses to leave her mother-in-law Naomi, telling her:

*...whither thou goes, I will go; and
where thou lodgest, I will lodge; thy
people shall be my people; and thy
God my God.*

NOTABLE NAMESAKES
Rachel Green was the name of the character played by Jennifer Aniston in the long-running American TV series, *Friends*.; Rebecca de Mornay (b. 1959) American actress and producer; Renee Fleming (b. 1959) American soprano who sings classical opera and also jazz; Roberta Flack (b. 1937) African American singer of jazz, folk

and gospel music; **Ruth
Rendell (b.1930)** British
popular crime writer who
introduces psychological
realism into her novels. One
of her memorable
characters is Inspector
Wexford.

S

SABHA/SADHBH is a
traditional Irish name meaning
'peacefulness, tranquillity'. The
first version is pronounced like
'saw + va' and the second tends
to rhyme with 'hive'. It is not as
popular now as it once was but,
with the renewed interest in
Celtic traditions, it could come
into its own again.

SABINE is found mainly in
French and German-speaking
communities. It is pronounced
like 'sab +een' in French and
'zab +eena' in German. It comes
from Latin *Sabina*, 'a Sabine
woman'. The Sabines inhabited a

central region of the
Apennines in Italy. They
were renowned for their
industry and their beliefs,
which differed considerably from
those of their Roman neighbours.
According to legend, the Romans
attacked a Sabine district and
carried off many of their women.
The Sabine men raised an army
to attack the Romans and bring
their women home, but the
Sabine women acted as
peacemakers between the two
groups and stayed with their
Roman husbands.

SABIRA is an attractive Arabic
name meaning 'patient, serene,
uncomplaining'. It resembles a
Hebrew name *Sabra*, which is a
name for a Jewish person born in
Israel. It is possible that it is
related to *sabrah*, 'prickly pear'.

SABRINA is an ancient name
for the River Severn. It was
recorded by Tacitus in the 2nd
century and by St Bede in the 8th
century. It is not possible to be
certain what *Sabrina* means but it
is undoubtedly Celtic in that
Sabrann is an old Irish form for

the river Lee. Geoffrey of Monmouth, in his *Historia Regum Britanniae* (c. 1139), suggests that the name comes from the daughter of King Locrine who was drowned in the river. In his masque *Comus* (1637), John Milton (1608-74) uses the name *Sabrina* for the spirit of the River Severn and addresses her as:

> Sabrina fair,
> Listen where thou are sitting
> Under the glassy, cool, translucent wave,
> In twisted braids of lilies…
>
> (lines 859-62)

SACHA (pronounced 'sash + a') is the French form of Russian *Sasha*, which is a form of *Alexander*, meaning 'defender of men'. Although both forms were originally male, the 'a' ending has encouraged their acceptance as girls' names in English.

SACHIKO (pronounced 'satch + ee + ko') is a popular Japanese name meaning 'child of bliss, child that is a source of great happiness'.

SADIE is generally regarded as a pet form of *Sarah*, 'princess', but it has gained status as an independent name, possibly due to Sadie Hawkins, a character in the *Li'l Abner* cartoon strip, created by Al Capp, the pen name of Alfred Caplin (1909-79). SEE Sara(h)

SAIRA (pronounced 'sigh + ra'/'Sarah') is often regarded as a variant of *Sara(h)*, 'princess', but it can also be an Arabic name meaning 'traveller'. SEE Sara(h)

SAKURA is a Japanese name meaning 'cherry blossom' and cherry blossom is a symbol of good fortune.

SALLY is a pet form of *Sarah*, 'princess', but many parents treat it as a full given name. The interchange of 'l' for 'r' is also seen in *Hal* from *Harry*. The attractiveness of *Sally* has been enhanced by the fact that 'a sally' is an excursion. The 'Sally Lunn' is a sponge tea-cake that has been popular since the 18th century. *Sal* is sometimes used as an abbreviation. SEE Sarah

SALOME is a Greek form of
Hebrew *Shalom* meaning 'peace'.
The meaning is attractive but
the name was not widely used
until the 20th century. According
to Christian tradition, *Salome* was
the daughter of Herodias and the
step-daughter of King Herod.
She danced for her step-father
and he was so pleased by her
performance that he offered her
anything she chose to ask for.
She chose the head of John the
Baptist, who had criticised her
mother and who was in one of
the king's prisons.

SAMANTHA does not seem
to have existed before the 18th
century, although it has grown
dramatically in popularity since
its first appearance in the United
States. It is almost certainly a
feminine form of *Samuel*,
meaning 'God listened', but the
ending is unexpected in that it
does not occur in other feminised
names. Double names are widely
used in the southern states –
names such as *Nancy-May* or
Billie-Jean – so it is possible that
Sam was doubled with *Anthea*,
'flower-like', producing first

Sam-Anthea and then
Samantha. The name is
regularly shortened to *Sam*.

SANDRA is an abbreviation of
two names, *Alexandra*, 'defender',
and *Cassandra*, 'prophet', but the
abbreviation is now more
widespread than the two sources
put together. SEE Alexandra and
Cassandra

SANDIE/SANDY is an
abbreviation of *Alexandra*,
Cassandra and, more recently,
Sandra. *Sandie* and *Sandy* were
popularised in the second half of
the 20th century by the singer
Sandy Shaw (b.1947) who was, at
one time, the best-selling female
singer in the British Isles. SEE
Sandra

SAOIRSE is an Irish name
meaning 'freedom'. It is thus
similar in meaning to *Uhuru* in
Swahili and, like *Uhuru*, it
became popular just before and
after independence. It is usually
pronounced like 'seer + sha'.

SARA(H) is the Hebrew name
of Abraham's wife. She conceived
a son, *Isaac*, in her old age. Like a

large number of significant characters in both the Old and New Testaments, she had her name changed. Originally, she was called *Sarai*, probably meaning 'argumentative', but, in Chapter 17 of the *Book of Genesis*, God told Abraham: *As for Sarai thy wife, thou shalt not call her name Sarai, but Sarah shall her name be. Sarah* means 'princess'. The spelling *Sara* without the 'h' is as popular as *Sarah*. There is a Christian legend about Mary, Martha, Lazarus and their maidservant, *Sara*. According to this apocryphal story, the four of them moved to Provence in France and Sara became the patron saint of Gypsies.

SASHA is a Russian pet name from *Alexander*. SEE Sacha

SCARLETT *Gone with the Wind* was written by Margaret Mitchell in 1936. Scarlett O'Hara was the name of the feisty heroine, who struggled to retain the family estate after the American Civil War. Scarlet(t) has been a surname since 1185. It comes

from French *escarlate*, the name of a rich fabric, often red but also blue, green and brown. The retailers of this material were known as, for example, Ralph le Escarlet, and in this way the surname was established. Many people will know that Will Scarlet was the name of one of Robin Hood's inner circle. In Mitchell's novel, *Scarlett* was the surname of the heroine's grandmother.

SCYLLA is pronounced like *Cilla*. The name occurs in Greek mythology as the name of a female sea creature who lured sailors to their death. The name was later applied to a dangerous rock in the Strait of Messina.

SELENA/SELINA In Greek mythology, *Selena* was the moon goddess, also known as *Artemis*. She fell in love with a mortal, Endymion, and Zeus was persuaded to grant him eternal life and youth. There was, however, a catch. He retained his youthful immortality only if he remained asleep forever.

SELMA is, for many parents, a

pet form of *Anselma*, the female form of *Anselm*, 'God is my protection'. It may also be interpreted as a form of Arabic *Selim*, 'peace'. Both interpretations are positive and help explain the growing popularity of the name.

SERAPHIA is the perfect choice for a little girl who is an angel. The Hebrew form *seraphim*, 'angels', only occurs in the plural, but 'seraph' is regarded as a singular. It may be related to *seraph*, 'to burn'. *Seraphia* is used mainly in Catholic countries, as is *Seraphina*, 'little angel'.

SERENA comes from Latin *serenus*, 'calm'. It is similar to names such as *Joy* or *Prudence*, in that it indicates the parents' hope for the child. In this case, it is the hope that the child's life will be peaceful and serene. It is said that there is a Chinese curse that is equivalent to: 'May you live in exciting times.' At first sight, this does not seem much of a curse, but perhaps there is much to be said for quiet, peaceful times.

SHANNON is the name of an Irish river and has become a very popular name, especially in Australia, where it has been used for both girls and boys. Like many river names, this one is ancient, although it seems to be related to *sean*, 'old' and would suggest 'wisdom'.

SHARON is a place name in Israel. It probably means 'level plain'. Chapter 2 of the *Song of Solomon* begins:

I am the rose of Sharon, and the lily of the valleys.

Some Catholic commentators have taken this as a reference to the mother of Jesus.
Occasionally, the name is spelt *Sharron*.

SHEBA is the Hebrew name for an inhabitant of Saba, a kingdom in the south west of Arabia. The name of the kingdom has been transferred to an Old Testament woman. According to the first *Book of Kings*, *Sheba* heard of the wisdom of Solomon and travelled to Jerusalem to find out if the reports were true. When she tested Solomon's wisdom, she decided that he was even wiser than people had said. The meaning of her name is unknown but she is associated with beauty, power, intelligence and good judgement.

SHEENA is a phonetic spelling of the Scots Gaelic name *Sìne*, which is a form of *Jean*. It is derived from the Hebrew name *Johanan*, meaning 'God is gracious'. SEE Jean

SHEILA comes from the Irish Gaelic name *Síle*, pronounced like 'she + la'. Other spellings of the name are *Shelagh* and *Sheelagh*, but they are all pronounced the same way. It is possible that *Síle* is a form of *Celia*, which may mean 'heavenly'. At one time, *Sheila* was used so frequently in Australia that it became a generic name for 'woman'. SEE Cecilia

SHELLEY is the name of towns in Derbyshire, Sussex, Suffolk and Yorkshire. The name comes from Old English *scylf*, 'slope,

ledge' + *leah*, 'clearing'. It has also been a surname since the 13th century, best known perhaps because of the Romantic poet Percy Bysshe Shelley (1792-1822). *Shelley* has grown in popularity since the middle of the 20th century and has almost replaced *Shirley*, a name that seems similar but is, in fact, unrelated.

SHERYL is a variant of *Cheryl* and may be a blend of *Sherry*, 'rich wine' + *Beryl*, 'precious stone'. SEE Cheryl

SHIRLEY has been a surname since 1219. *Shirley* occurs as a place name in five English shires and means 'shire clearing'. Like most surnames, it was originally given to sons, but that tendency changed in the mid 19th century when Charlotte Brontë gave the name to the heroine of her novel, *Shirley*.

SHOSHANA is a Hebrew name meaning 'lily'. It is normally anglicised to *Susan* in English-speaking communities. SEE Susan

SIAN is the Welsh equivalent of English *Jean* or *Jane*, meaning 'God is gracious'. It used to be confined to Wales but, although it is still linked to Welsh people, it is found widely throughout the British Isles. SEE Jane

SIDNEE/SIDONIE/ SIDONY This name has two possible origins. It can be a female form of Latin *Sidonius*, person from Sidon, a city in Lebanon. According to tradition, this was the Latin name of an Irish monk whose name is commemorated in *Saint-Saens*. The second origin is that it is a female form of *Sidney*, which may come from Old English *sid* + *ieg*, 'wide + island', or from the French place name *St Denis*. SEE Sidney

SÍLE (pronounced 'Sheila')is an Irish name that is usually regarded as equivalent to *Celia*, 'heavenly'. It is found mainly in Ireland but the anglicised form, *Sheila*, is an international name. SEE Celia and Sheila

SILVANA/SYLVANA is a female form of Latin *sylvana*, meaning 'goddess of the woods'. A related root is found in the state of *Pennsylvania*, 'Penn's wooded area', which was founded by William Penn in 1682. In Roman mythology, *Silvanus* was a woodland deity, similar to the Greek *Pan*.

SILVIA/SYLVIA is probably derived from the Latin noun *silva*, 'woods'. In Roman mythology, Rhea *Silvia* was a princess of Alba Longa and the mother of *Romulus* and *Remus*, the legendary founders of Rome. Their father was the god, Mars. As babies, they were placed in a basket on the river Tiber because their mother was a Vestal Virgin. They were rescued by a she-wolf who fed them until they were taken in by a shepherd and his wife. SEE Rhea

SIMONE (pronounced 'sim +own'/'seem + own') is a French female form of *Simon*, 'rock', but its popularity has seen it spread far beyond the boundaries of France. *Simon* was a common Hebrew name. It was the original name of St Peter and also of Simon of Cyrene, who helped Christ carry his cross to Calvary. The French actress, Simone Signoret (1920-85) helped to popularise *Simone* in English-speaking areas. Her appearance in the very successful film *Room at the Top* (1959) earned her numerous awards, including an Oscar.

SINDY was originally an abbreviation of *Cynthia*, 'moon goddess', but it has attained the status of a full name. It is also regularly spelt *Cindy*.

SÌNE (pronounced 'she + na') is a Scots Gaelic form of *Jean/Jane*, 'God is gracious'. This form is rare outside Scotland but the anglicised form *Sheena* is well-known.

SINEAD is an Irish equivalent of *Jeannette*, a female form of *Jean*, 'God is gracious'. A number of French names arrived in Ireland with the Normans and, although traditional Irish names such as *Oisín* were retained, others, such as *D'arcy*, were absorbed into the

name bank. It is pronounced like 'shin + aid'.

SIOBHAN is an Irish equivalent of *Joan*, 'God is gracious'. It has become popular throughout the English-speaking world where it is normally pronounced like 'shiv + awn'. SEE Joan

SIOFRA is an Irish name meaning 'little pixie, water sprite, changeling'. It is sometimes used as an Irish equivalent of *Josephine*. The usual pronunciation is like 'sho + fra', although it is sometimes pronounced like 'she +offra'.

SITA is a popular Hindi name largely because it is the name of a goddess who is seen as a symbol of female virtue. According to Hindu tradition, *Sita*, which rhymes with 'Rita', is the eternal wife of Vishnu, but she chose to allow herself to live an arduous life on earth in order to provide a role model for human beings.

SKYE During the second half of the 20th century, natural phenomena, such as rivers, trees and flowers became increasingly popular as given names. *Skye* may be from the island of Skye or it may be a fancy spelling of *sky*, which comes from an Old Norse noun *sky*, meaning 'cloud' but also, by extension, 'shadow' and 'soul'.

SONIA/SONYA

is a Russian borrowing that has become steadily more popular since the early days of the 20th century. In spite of its appearance, it is a pet form of *Sophia*, 'wisdom'. Like *Tania*, another Russian borrowing, the ending varies between 'ia' and 'ya' but the variants are pronounced the same.

SOPHIA

comes from a Greek noun meaning 'wisdom'. According to Christian tradition, St Sophia was the mother of three virgin martyrs, Faith, Hope and Charity. She died three days after they were martyred, while praying at their grave. St Sophia is highly regarded in the Orthodox Church, where her feast day is celebrated on 30 September. In the past, the name was regularly pronounced like 'Soph + eye + a' but it is currently more usual to pronounce it like 'soph +ee + a'. A popular pet form is *Sophie*, also spelt *Sophy*.

SORCHA

(pronounced 'sor + ha'/'sor + ka') is an Irish given name of considerable antiquity and means 'brightness, light'. This is an indigenous Irish name, not a modification of one from Hebrew, Greek, Latin, French or English.

STACEY/STACY

started life as an abbreviation of *Anastasia*, 'resurrection', but has become a popular given name for both girls and boys. It is likely that it is becoming an exclusively female name. Whereas *Anastasia* can be pronounced with the '-tas-' rhyming with both 'has' and 'haze', *Stacey* rhymes with *Gracie*.

STELLA

is the Latin word for 'star'. Parents have often chosen natural objects or phenomena for their children. In Sanskrit, for example, *Chandra* means 'moon' and essentially the same implication is conveyed by *Selena*.

STEPHANIE is the French form of Greek *stephanos*, 'garland' or 'crown'. The male name *Stephen* has always been popular in Christian circles because St Stephen is reputed to have been the first Christian martyr. According to tradition, the men who stoned Stephen to death left their cloaks with St Paul for safe keeping.

SUKEY/SUKI/SUKIE

These are pet forms of *Susan*, 'lily', and they were popular in the past. They could easily become popular again. Many will remember the nursery rhyme:

Polly put the kettle on,
Polly put the kettle on,
Polly put the kettle on,
We'll all have tea.
Sukey take it off again,
Sukey take it off again,
Sukey take it off again,
They've all gone away.

SUSAN/SUSANNA(H)

come from the Hebrew given name *Shoshana*, 'lily'. This name has been popular throughout Europe since early Christian times. It occurs in a wide range of forms and abbreviations, including *Sue*, *Suki*, *Susanne*, *Susette*, *Susi*, *Susie*, *Suzanna*, *Suzanne*, *Suzette*, *Suzi* and *Zsa-Zsa*.

SYBIL with a 'y', is the usual spelling of this name, although *Sibil* also occurs. The name is originally from Greek but was taken into English from Old French *Sibille*. A 'sybil' was a prophetess, a woman who was consulted because of her ability to divine the future. The variation in use between 'y' and 'i' was extremely common in English. If we are to judge from printed versions of his plays, Shakespeare often spelt 'it' as 'yt'.

SYDNEY This is the spelling of the capital city of New South Wales. The surname and the place names were written as both 'Sidney' and 'Sydney'. This spelling is now used more frequently for girls than for boys. SEE Sidnee

SYLVIA is now the more popular spelling of the Latin name, meaning 'wood, forest, woodland'. SEE Silvia

SYLWIA This is a Polish form of Sylvia. SEE Silvia

NOTABLE NAMESAKES
Sarah Bernhardt (1844-1923) French actress who played many famous roles, including the title role in *Hamlet* on the European and American stage; Shirley Bassey (b. 1937) Welsh singer, best-known, perhaps, for singing the theme song for three James Bond films; Simone de Beauvoir (1908-96) French writer and philosopher who wrote a treatise on the exploitation of women in *The Second Sex* (1949); Stella McCartney (b. 1971) fashion designer and the daughter of Paul and Linda McCartney.

T

TABITHA has the same meaning as *Dorcas*. They both mean 'gazelle', with *Tabitha* coming from Hebrew and *Dorcas* from Greek. We find a reference to *Tabitha* in the *Acts of the Apostles* (Chapter 9). She was raised from the dead by Peter. *Tabbie* or *Tabby* are sometimes used as abbreviations and they are sometimes equated – incorrectly – with 'tabby', the name for a striped cat. It seems likely that the cat takes its name from an Arabic name for a section of Baghdad where 'tabby' or 'striped taffeta' was manufactured.

TAKAKO is a Japanese name meaning 'eminent child'. It is pronounced like 'tack + a + ko'.

TAKARA is Japanese and means 'treasure'. It rhymes with 'Tara' and the first syllable is pronounced like 'tack'.

TALITHA is a Hebrew word meaning 'little girl'. It became a given name because of the story

GIRLS

in *St Mark's Gospel*, Chapter 5, where Christ is approached by Jairus and asked to heal his daughter. By the time Christ reaches Jairus's house, he is told that the little girl is dead. He goes into the room where the child is and says, *Talitha, cumi*, 'Little girl, get up.' The usual pronunciation is like 'tal' (like 'Sal') + 'eetha'.

TALLULA(H) is a Native American name that is said to mean 'laughing water'. It is found in the name of Tallulah Falls in Georgia. Spellings of the name vary. Sometimes it has an 'h'. In this it resembles *Sara* and *Sarah*. The name became familiar because of the actress Tallulah Bankhead (1902-68). She was the daughter of the Speaker of the House of Representatives in the United States and became a popular actress. She is reported to have said: 'If I had my life to live over again, I'd make the same mistakes, but I'd make them earlier.'

TAMAR may be derived from the Hebrew name for 'palm tree'.

It was the name of King David's daughter and also of his grand-daughter because Absalom called his daughter *Tamar*. It may also be from the River Tamar that flows through Devon and Cornwall or from the river of the same name in Tasmania that was named after it. River names are often old and this one is no exception. It is a Celtic name meaning 'dark' and is related to Old Irish *temen*, 'dark', and to Sanskrit *tamas*, 'darkness'. Children, daughters in particular, have been called after rivers. We can think, for example, of *Afton* and *Shannon*. SEE Tamara

TAMARA is a Russian name, taken from Hebrew *tamar*, meaning 'palm tree'. It is likely that it was first given as a name to daughters in the hope that they would be as beautiful and as fruitful as the tree. Occasionally, the name is abbreviated to *Tammie*, although that has become a name in its own right.

TAMMIE/TAMMY This name may be an abbreviation of any name beginning with 'Tam-'

but it has been widely used as a given name since the Debbie Reynolds film, *Tammy and the Bachelor* (1957). The title song of the film with the chorus of '*Tammy, Tammy, Tammy's in love*' was a worldwide hit.

TAMORA is the name of the Queen of the Goths in Shakespeare's play *Titus Andronicus*. It is not clear where Shakespeare got this name but it may be related to *Tamar*.

TAMSIN is a variant of *Thomasina*, 'twin'. It used to be found only in Cornwall but it is growing in popularity throughout the world. SEE Thomasina

TANIA/TANYA Both these forms gained popularity in the 1970s. They could be abbreviations of Russian *Tatiana* or of *Titania*, the Fairy Queen in Shakespeare's *A Midsummer Night's Dream*. Her name is derived from *Titan*. The Titans were a race of Greek gods who were expelled from heaven by Zeus. They were supposed to be gigantic in terms of size,

intellect and beauty. SEE Tatiana

TANSEY/TANSY is one of the many plant names that have been bestowed on daughters. The name comes to us from Latin *athanasia* but it is derived from a Greek word meaning 'immortal'. The plant is usually spelt 'tansy' but the form with 'e' is equally widespread as a girl's name.

TARA is the name of a hill in County Meath. It has been linked to mythical characters for millennia and has also been the seat of the High King of Ireland. The name is probably related to modern *tor*, 'hill', and it was used in Margaret Mitchell's novel *Gone with the Wind* as the name of the O'Hara estate. *Tara* has two other interesting connections. It is the name of an edible fern in Tasmania and New Zealand and it is a Sanskrit word for 'star'.

TATIANA has always been a popular Russian name because of the Orthodox saints who bore this name in the early Christian period. It is a feminine form of Latin *Tatianus* and this seems to be derived from the name of an old Roman family, *Tatius*, possibly meaning 'truth'. A 2nd-century Christian philosopher was called *Tatian* and this, too, could have encouraged the spread of the name.

TEGAN is Welsh and is almost certainly related to *tegwch*, 'beauty'.

TEODORY is a Polish form of *Theodora*, 'gift of God'. SEE Theodora

TEODOZJI is a Polish form of *Theodosia*, 'gift of God'. SEE Theodora

TERESA is a popular Christian name that occurs in a variety of forms, including *Teressa*, *Theresa*, *Theresia*, *Therese* and *Treasa*. This particular spelling was originally Spanish but has spread worldwide because of St Teresa of Avila's writings, especially *The Way of Perfection*. The meaning of the name is debated but it seems to be linked to Latin *terra* and so might mean 'cultivator'. It has a number

of pet forms, including *Teri*, *Terri*, *Terry*, *Tess*, *Tessa* and *Tessie*.

TERESITA means 'little Teresa'. It has given rise to *Zita*.

TESS is a form of *Teresa* but it has taken on a life of its own thanks mainly to the success of Thomas Hardy's novel *Tess of the d'Urbervilles*: *A Pure Woman*, first published in 1891 and never out of print since that date. SEE Teresa

TESSA is derived from *Teresa* but has been used independently since the 19th century. It is just possible that it is an abbreviated form of *contessa*, 'a countess'. SEE Teresa

THALIA is the name of the Greek muse of comedy and she is also one of the Graces and was believed to preside over festivities. Her name means 'luxuriant'. The name has also been given to an exotic aquatic herbaceous plant.

THEA is often used as an abbreviated form of *Dorothea*, 'gift of God'. SEE Dorothea

THECLA is the name of a class of butterflies but it has been a girl's name for at least two millennia. It is made up of two Greek words *theos*, 'God', and *kleia*, 'glory', and suggests 'the glory of God'. According to Christian tradition, Thecla of Icolium was converted by St Paul and was the first female martyr.

THELMA Credit for the creation of this name has gone to Marie Correlli whose 1887 novel was entitled *Thelma*. In the novel, *Thelma* is Norwegian but the origin is uncertain. It may be a blend of *Thor*, 'god of thunder' + *Selma*, which may be related to both *Salaam* and *Shalom*, greetings meaning 'Peace'. There is a further possibility that it may be a contraction of Greek *thelema*, meaning 'will, determination'.

THEODORA is the feminine form of *Theodore*, derived from Greek and meaning 'gift of God'. It combines the same two Greek words as *Dorothea* and the names are anagrams of each other. A 6th-century Byzantine empress was called *Theodora* (c. 500-548).

She was the wife of Justinian and was said to be an actress from a poor background. In this she resembles Nell Gwynn who was a mistress of Charles II. *Theodora* was also both intelligent and wise and is reputed to have advised her husband on political and theological matters.

THEODOSIA is related to *Theodora* in the sense that the name combines Greek *theos* 'God' + *dosis*, 'giving, bestowing'. Most children called *Theodosia* take their name from the Emperor Theodosius I (c. 346-395). He was a devout Christian and banned any form of pagan worship in the empire. In the 5th century, Saint Theodosius founded a monastery near Bethlehem.

THEOPHILA is the feminine form of Theophilus, which comes from Greek *theos*, 'God' + *philos*, 'friend'. St Luke addressed his Gospel and the *Acts of the Apostles* to *Theophilus* and both male and female forms were the names of early Christian saints.

THOMASINA is a female diminutive form of *Thomas*, a Hebrew name meaning 'twin'.

THORA is a female form of the Scandinavian god of thunder, Thor. According to the mythology, she was married to the Danish king Elf.

TIA is the Spanish and Portuguese equivalent of 'aunt'. It is also used as an abbreviation of names such as *Laurentia*, laurel'.

TIFFANY is from Greek *Theophaneia*, the word for the Feast of the Epiphany on 6th January, a feast dedicated to the manifestation of Christ to the Gentiles in the form of the Magi. The Greek word means 'God + revelation'. In the Middle Ages, the Feast was regularly called *Tiffany* and the name was often given to a daughter born on 6 January. The name received an unexpected boost from Charles Louis Tiffany, who founded the New York jewellers, Tiffany and Company. The 1961 Audrey Hepburn film *Breakfast at Tiffany's* helped to establish *Tiffany* as a favourite name of the second half of the 20th century. *Tiffany* is also the name of a very fine muslin material.

TILDA is a pet form of *Matilda*, 'might in battle'. SEE Matilda

TILLY is a pet form of *Matilda*, 'might in battle'. It is a little less formal than *Tilda*. SEE Matilda

TINA is an abbreviation of such names as *Augustina*, 'great, magnificent', and *Christina*, 'Christian'. It is also an acronym of a phrase used by Mrs Thatcher in a 1980 speech: *There is no alternative*.

TITANIA is the name of the queen of the fairies in Shakespeare's play *A Midsummer Night's Dream*. *Titania* comes from Greek *Titan*, the name of an ancient Greek god who was expelled from heaven by Zeus. Titan's descendants retained many of their supernatural powers, making *Titania* an excellent choice for a fairy queen.

TONY is occasionally used as an abbreviation of *Antoinette*, 'little flower'. SEE Antoinette

TORI is a very popular abbreviation of *Victoria*, 'female conqueror'. SEE Victoria

TRACEY/TRACIE/TRACY has been used as a surname since the 12th century. It was based on one of the French towns such as Tracy-sur-Mer, which meant 'domain belonging to Thracius, on the sea'. There is no single 'correct' spelling as each of these variants has been used for centuries as surnames. *Tracey* and *Tracy* especially are also used as variants of Teresa. SEE Teresa

TRICIA is a popular abbreviation of *Patricia*, 'one of noble birth', but it is also regularly used as a name in its own right. SEE Patricia

TRILBY In 1894, George du Maurier wrote a novel called *Trilby*, whose heroine of the same name was a beautiful artist's model who became a wonderful singer under the control of Svengali. The trilby hat was called after her because it was worn in a stage version of the novel. It is uncertain where du Maurier got the name from, but it is likely to be a blend of *trill*, 'the singing of a bird' + 'by', 'settlement, as in Derby'.

TRINA was originally an abbreviation of *Catriona*, *Katrina*, 'pure', *Petrina*, little rock' or *Trinity*, 'belief in three persons in one God', but it now occurs as a given name. SEE Catriona and Petrina

TRINITY is occasionally used as a girl's name, often as a translation of the more popular Spanish *Trinidad*. The name comes ultimately from Latin *trinus*, meaning 'threefold', but it is selected because of the Christian belief that there are three persons in the one God. *Trina* is occasionally used as an abbreviation.

TRISHA is an abbreviation of *Patricia*, 'one of noble birth', but it is now used as a name in its own right. SEE Patricia

TRIXIE is a pet form of *Beatrice* or *Beatrix*, 'blessed traveller'. SEE Beatrice

TRUDA is a popular Polish abbreviation of *Ermintrude*, 'completely loved', and *Gertrude*, 'well loved spear'. SEE Ermintrude and Gertrude

TRUDIE/TRUDY Both these forms are regularly used as versions of *Ermintrude*, 'completely loved', and *Gertrude*, 'well loved spear'. SEE Ermintrude and Gertrude

TUESDAY Although several months of the year, for example, *May*, have been used as girls' names, *Tuesday* is the only day of the week to have occurred in English. The practice of calling children after the day of the week on which they were born is, however, widely practised in Africa. Tuesday Weld (b. 1943) was an actress who starred opposite Elvis Presley in *Wild in the Country* (1961), and this undoubtedly caused *Tuesday* to be selected by other parents. *Tuesday* means 'day of the war god'. The Germanic war god, sometimes spelt *Tiw*, has been equated with Mars, the Roman war god. That is why French has *mardi* for the same day of the week.

NOTABLE NAMESAKES
Tammy Wynette (1942-98) American singer and composer. Her single, 'Stand by Your Man' was one of the biggest selling country music songs of all time; Teresa is the name of several saints including St Teresa of Avila (1515-82), St Teresa of Portugal (13th century) and Mother Teresa of Calcutta (1910-97); Teri Hatcher (b.1964) American actress best-known for playing Lois in *Lois and Clark: The New Adventures of Superman* (1993-97) and Susan Mayer in *Desperate Housewives*; Tori Amos (b. 1961) American pianist and singer.

U

ULRICA (pronounced 'ool + reek + a') is used as an English spelling of either German *Ulrike*, meaning 'prosperity and power', or of the Swedish equivalent *Ulrika*. All three forms are fashionable and all three are pronounced essentially the same way.

UME/UMEKA (pronounced 'oo + may') is a Japanese name that means 'plum blossom' and this blossom is symbolic of trust and devotion. The longer form *Umeka* means 'plum blossom child' and is often chosen for a child born at the auspicious time of the appearance of the blossom on the plum tree.

UNA is sometimes spelt *Oonagh* and it is a Gaelic name, originally limited to Ireland and Scotland. Because the pronunciation and form are the same as Latin *una*, 'one, alone', the two are usually equated. It seems, however, that *Una* may be an extremely old Celtic name, possibly linked to the tradition of the banshee, the fairy woman who appears to foretell a death in the family.

UNITY has often been used as a translation of *Una*, because of the supposed similarity of meaning. It comes directly from French *unite* and indirectly from Latin *unitas*, 'oneness, agreement'. SEE Una

URSULA This name is a diminutive of Latin *ursa*, 'female bear'. The name has been popular in Christian circles for an extremely long time. According to legend, St Ursula, a 4th-century martyr, was the daughter of the king of Cologne. She asked her future husband for permission to travel for three years before her marriage and the request was granted. She and her companions went to Rome but they were massacred as they returned to Cologne. St Ursula is the patron saint of schoolgirls.

NOTABLE NAMESAKES
Ulrika (1688-1741) became
Queen of Sweden when her

brother, Charles XII died in 1728; Ursula Le Guin (b. 1929) American writer, famed for her science fiction novels, which often deal with social issues; Unity Mitford (1914-48) was one of the noted Mitford sisters.

V

VALDA This name does not seem to occur before the 20th century. It may be an invented form, like *Wanda* or *Wendy*, or a blend of *Val*(erie) + (Lin)*da*. In this case, it would mean 'healthy + shield'. SEE Valerie

VALENCIA is the name of a city and province in east Spain. It may come from Latin *valens*, 'healthy'. The idea of calling a child after a town is widespread. *Roma* is a popular name and *Paris* is beginning to appear.

VALENTINA is a female form of *Valentine*, which comes from *valens*, 'healthy'. *Tina* is used as an abbreviation.

VALERIE is Latin in origin. It comes from *Valeria*, which was the feminine form of an old Roman family name, *Valerius*, which is derived from *valere*, 'to be strong and healthy'.

VALMA/VELMA Sometimes, these names are kept apart but they have both been used as abbreviations of *Wilhelmina*, in which case, they would mean 'desire for protection'. SEE Wilhelmina

VANESSA Writers often invent names and this one was created by Dean Jonathan Swift as a pseudonym for his friend, Esther Vanhomrigh. It is likely that he took the first syllable 'Van' from her surname. It is Dutch and means 'of, from'. It is not certain where he got the 'essa' from. It could be from Latin *esse*, 'to be', or it may be baby talk for *Esther*, 'myrtle'. SEE Esther

VELMA This may be an

abbreviation of Wilhelmina, meaning 'desiring protector'. SEE Wilhelmina

VENTURA is a Spanish choice and means 'good luck' and comes from Latin *advenire*, 'to come about, to happen'.

VERA has two possible origins and meanings. It may be from Latin *vera*, 'truth', or it may have come into the language from Russia, where *Vera* is a popular name, meaning 'faith'. To have a combination of 'truth' and 'faith' is quite a gift for a little girl. The usual English pronunciation rhymes the name with 'hear + a' but the Russian name sounds more like 'vay + ra'.

VERENA may be a diminutive of *Vera*, 'truth', or may come from Old French *ver*, 'springtime'. SEE Vera

VERITY comes from Latin *veritas*, 'truth', via French *verité*. The word 'verity' has been used as an abstract noun in English since 1375 but it does not seem to have been used for children until the 17th century, when

Puritans introduced names of virtues like *Faith* and *Hope* as names for their daughters.

VERNA comes from Latin *vernus*, 'relating to spring'. Spring has always been a time of hope, a time of new beginnings. Poets have written about the season and Wordsworth even suggests that spring can inspire goodness:

One impulse from a vernal wood
May teach you more of man,
Of moral evil and of good
Than all the sages can.

('An Evening Scene')

VERONA may be derived from the Italian town of Verona, or it may be an abbreviation of *Veronica* 'true image, or it may be a female form of *Vernon* and so mean 'alder trees'. SEE Veronica

VERONICA This name has been part of Christian tradition for almost 2000 years. The tradition is that a woman wiped Christ's face with a towel when he was carrying his cross to Calvary. As a reward for her kindness, the image of Christ's face was imprinted on the towel. The woman's name was unknown. It was certainly not *Veronica*, but she was given this name because the Latin phrase for 'true image' is *vera icon* and *Veronica* is an anagram. It is a lovely story that has resulted in a widely-used name. *Veronica* is also the name of a shrub that has blue flowers.

VESPERA comes from Latin *vesper*, 'the evening star'. The Greeks called it *Hesperus*. The 'evening star' was, in fact, the planet Venus. The name is also linked to evening prayers or devotions.

VESTA was the Roman goddess of the home and the hearth and she was the daughter of Saturn. It is also the name of one of the larger asteroids that lies between Mars and Jupiter. The young women who tended the flame in the Temple of *Vesta* in Rome were known as 'vestal virgins'. Her temple was circular and contained no images of the goddess.

VICTORIA can be regarded as the female form of *Victor* or as a direct borrowing from Latin *Victoria*, 'victory, success in battle'. The name was popularised by Queen Victoria (1819-1901), whose reign of 64 years is the longest in British history. Her name has been used in 'Victorian values', a phrase that implies self-reliance and morality. The spectacular waterfall on the Zambia-Zimbabwe border was named the Victoria Falls by David Livingstone in 1855. Its local name translates as 'the smoke that thunders'. The abbreviations *Vicki*, *Vicky*, *Vikki* and *Tori* have all proved popular.

VINCENTIA is the female equivalent of *Vincent*, 'conquering'. The name has often been used as a tribute to St Vincent de Paul (1576-1660), who dedicated most of his life to helping the poor and the underprivileged.

VIOLA is the Latin form of 'violet' and both words have been used for girls' names. Shakespeare chose *Viola* as the name of Sebastian's twin sister in *Twelfth Night*. She falls in love with Duke Orsino and eventually wins his heart. Apart from Shakespeare's usage, the name was not popular before the 20th century.

VIOLET is the English word for Latin *viola* but it has been used as the name of a sweet-smelling flower since the 14th century. *Violet* comes directly from French *violette*, 'a small viola'. It is one of the many flower names to be used for daughters. Occasionally, the form *Violette* is also used.

VIRGINIA can claim a Latin and an English origin. It can be the female form of an old Roman family name, *Verginius* (often written *Virginius* in English). The family name may be related to Latin *virga*, 'rod'. The American state of *Virginia* was the first permanent European settlement in North America. It was called after Queen Elizabeth I, the 'Virgin Queen'. The first child born there in 1587 was called *Virginia* in honour of the queen.

VITA is Latin for 'life' It is a name that is easy to pronounce and meaningful worldwide. It may have been given an impetus by the Italian poet, Dante (1265-1321), whose love for *Beatrice* is described in his *Vita Nuova* (new life). The novelist Vita Sackville-West (1892-1962) used *Vita* as part of her nom-de-plume although her given name was Victoria.

VIVIEN This name can be spelt in a variety of ways, including *Vivian, Vivianne, Vivienne, Vyvien* and *Vyvyan*. They all have the same source in that they come from *Vivianus* which is linked to Latin *vivus*, alive. When the Normans introduced this name to the British Isles, it was used for males, but today it is often considered to be a girl's name. Some people suggest that the ending 'ian' should be preferred for boys and 'ien' for girls. This would be useful, but parents will choose the spelling that they prefer and they have every right to do so.

VONNIE is an abbreviation of both *Veronica* and *Yvonne*. SEE Veronica and Yvonne

---

NOTABLE NAMESAKES
Vanessa-Mae (b. 1978) classical musician who was born in Singapore. She is a virtuoso of both the violin and the piano; Vera Lynn (b. 1917) British singer who became extremely popular during World War II, when she was called 'the Forces' Sweetheart'; Violetta Szabo (1921-45) worked as a British agent during World War II and was immortalised in the 1958 film, *Carve Her Name with Pride* in 1958; Virginia Wolfe (1882-1941) is regarded as one of the finest novelists of the 20th century.

WALLIS is a form of one of the most widely-occurring surnames in the British Isles. It comes from an Old English word for 'foreigner, stranger', but took on the meaning of 'Welsh' and is found in a variety of spellings, including *Wallace*, *Walsh* and *Welch*. *Wallis* was brought into the public domain largely because of the relationship between the Duke of Windsor and his future wife, Wallis Simpson (1896-1986). Her divorce from her husband is widely seen as the reason for Edward VIII's abdication in 1936. She was reputed to have said: 'A woman cannot be too thin or too rich.'

WANDA This name has an uncertain history. It may be Polish or it may be Germanic and have the same meaning as *wand*, 'light, supple rod'. *Wanda* occurs as the title of an 1883 novel by Maria Louise Ramé, under her pseudonym Ouida, which was an approximation to a child's pronunciation of *Louise*.

WENDY came into existence in the 20th century. It was used by JM Barrie for a female character in his play *Peter Pan*. According to his account, he was inspired by a child acquaintance who said 'fwendie' for 'friend'. *Wendy* would therefore imply 'good friend'. It has also been used as an abbreviation of *Gwendolen*, meaning 'beautiful ring'. SEE Gwendolen

WERONIKA is a Polish form of *Veronica*, meaning 'true image'. SEE Veronica

WHITNEY is a surname taken from the Derbyshire town, meaning 'white island'. It is also the name of a woollen material. The reason for its use as a given name is most likely due to the fame of Whitney Houston (b. 1963), the American singer and actress, who has sold well over 50 million singles worldwide.

WILFREDA is a female form of *Wilfrid*, a Germanic name meaning 'will for peace'. It is now less commonly used than its abbreviated form *Freda*. SEE Freda

WILHELMINA is a female form of the German name *Wilhelm*, from the combination of two words, 'will + protection', and suggesting 'protector'. The German name was popular in Europe because of the German emperors, Wilhelm I and II. *Wilhelmina* (1880-1962) was Queen of the Netherlands. During World War II, she established a government in exile in London and frequently used the radio to broadcast to her people.

WILLA is found most widely in the United States but is gradually making its way in Europe too. It can be regarded as a female form of *William* or *Wilfrid* or *Wilbur*. It can also be seen as a 20th-century creation based on 'will'. In this case, 'will' can have a range of meanings including 'desire' and 'longing'.

WILLOW Strange as it might initially seem, the names of trees have often been used for children. Indeed, the Greeks had a type of female spirit or nymph called a *dryad* that lived in trees. We also find names such as *Derry* (oak), *Yvette* (yew) that reinforce the link. A willow is a tree that is often found near water. It has long, slender branches and has been used for millennia in building and folk medicine.

WILMA is a 20th-century coinage. It may be a reduced form of *Wilhelmina* or a feminised form of *Will*. Either way, it suggests 'will power' and 'desire'. SEE Wilhelmina

WINIFRED There are two possible explanations for this name. It may be Welsh in origin and be a combination of 'fair, white, pure' and 'reconciliation' or it may be a combination of two Old English words and mean 'friend of peace'. Either way, the meaning is positive. *Win* and *Winnie* are abbreviated forms.

WINONA is a Native American name meaning 'first daughter'. It has been popularised by the film actress Winona Ryder (b. 1971). She was born in Winona, Minnesota, and was named after the town.

WYNN is an anglicised form of Welsh *gwen*, meaning 'fair, beautiful'. It is sometimes used as a name in its own right or as a modified spelling of *Win*. SEE Gwen

NOTABLE NAMESAKES
Wanda Jackson (b. 1937) American Gospel and rock 'n' roll singer who dated Elvis Presley; Wendy Darling is a character in JM Barrie's play, *Peter Pan* (1904); Wilhelmina (1889-1962) Queen of the Netherlands from 1890-1948, when she abdicated in favour of her daughter, Juliana; Winifred Atwell (1914-83) Trinidad-born pianist who enjoyed great popularity in the 1950s and early 1960s.

X

XANTHE is a Greek name that is occasionally used by English speakers. It means 'yellow, golden' and is pronounced like 'Zanth + ay' (as in 'hay').

XANTHIPPE (pronounced 'zanth + ippay') was the name of the wife of Socrates and it has, unfortunately, taken on her attributes and is thus a name for an ill-tempered woman. Like *Xanthe*, the root of this name is 'yellow, golden'.

XAVIERA is the female form of *Xavier* and is thus Basque in origin and means 'new house'. The name is pronounced in various ways but is usually either equivalent to 'Zav + ee + aira' or 'Zav + eera'.

XENA is Greek and pronounced like 'Zena'. It is related in meaning to 'the hospitality due to a guest'.

XENIA is also Greek and is more widely used than its variant *Xena*. It means 'hospitality' and is pronounced like 'zeen + ya'.

NOTABLE NAMESAKES
Xena, Warrior Princess was an American television series filmed in New Zealand and running between 1995 and 2001. The show was set in ancient Greece but was totally fictional; Xenia Tchoumitcheva (b. 1987) is a Russian model and beauty queen.

YASMEEN/ YASMIN
These are variant spellings for a name that comes from Persian and means 'flower'. The spelling *Jasmine* also occurs. The flower is a climbing plant with beautifully-scented white flowers. SEE Jasmine

YASU is a Japanese name meaning 'tranquil, calm, serene'.

YEKATERINA is a Russian form of *Catherine* and possibly means 'pure' or 'consecrated'. SEE Catherine

YELENA is a Russian form of *Helen*, possibly meaning 'sunbeam', a very appropriate name for any little girl. SEE Helen

YNEZ (pronounced 'ee + nyez') is a French pet form of *Agnes* and means 'holy, pure'. SEE Agnes

YOKO Is a Japanese name that can mean both 'sunlight' and 'ocean child'.

YOLANDA and its French equivalent, *Yolande*, are well known names that can be traced to the 13th century. Its meaning is uncertain but it may be a variant of *Iolanthe*. The meaning of this name is not known for certain, but it is possibly connected to the French name *Violante* which means 'violet'.

YOSHIKO (pronounced 'yo + she + ko') is Japanese and means 'good child'.

YSEULT (pronounced 'ee + solt') is a French form of *Isolde* and it is also spelt *Iseult*. One of the most beautiful legends of the Middle Ages concerned the love story between *Yseult* and *Tristan*. *Tristan* fell in love with *Yseult* even though she was due to marry his uncle. The exact meaning of her name is uncertain. It is possibly derived from a Welsh word meaning 'beautiful'. She certainly represents youth and beauty.

YUKIKO (pronounced 'you + key + ko') is Japanese and is an ideal name for a winter daughter since it means 'snow child'.

YUKO is not an abbreviated form of *Yukiko*, although they both contain the word for 'child'. *Yuko* means 'gracious child'.

YVETTE (pronounced 'ee + vet') is a French female form of *Yves* and means 'yew tree'. The 'Yve' part is Germanic and the 'ette' is French and suggests 'little'.

YVONNE like *Yvette*, is a French name that is now very widely used throughout the world. It comes from *Yves* and means 'yew tree'.

NOTABLE NAMESAKES
Yasmin Le Bon (b. 1964) English supermodel, married to Simon Le Bon, the lead singer in Duran Duran; Yelena Isinbayeva (b. 1982) Russian pole vaulter who won a gold medal in the 2004 Olympics. In 2005, she became the first woman vaulter to clear five metres; Yoko Ono (b. 1933) is a Japanese artist and musician. She married John Lennon in 1969.

Z

ZADA Many Arabic names occur in two forms, one beginning with 's' and the other with 'z'. This name means 'lucky' and is an attractive equivalent of Latin-inspired *Fortunata*. *Sadie* is occasionally used as a pet form.

ZAFIRA/ZAFIRAH is from Arabic and means 'victory'. It could be chosen as an alternative to the ever-popular *Victoria*. Normally the middle syllable is pronounced to rhyme with 'me' but some parents rhyme it with 'my'. As with many names that have Arabic or Hebrew antecedents, the final 'h' is optional in English, as with *Sara(h)* and *Susanna(h)*, for example.

ZAHAR is an alternative form of *Zara* and means *'dawn'*. SEE Zara

ZAKIRA is an Arabic name meaning 'remembrance, commemoration'. It is often chosen to honour a relative who has died, without giving the child the same name. The name is sometimes interpreted as the female equivalent of *Zachary* and there is certainly a link. *Zachary* means 'God has remembered.'

ZANNA is a Spanish form of Susanna and means 'lily'. SEE Susanna

ZARA occurs in both Arabic and Hebrew, partly because the languages are closely related and partly because Islam and Judaism share the Old Testament. In both languages, *Zara* is associated with the 'brightness of the dawn'. Some parents regard *Zara* as an alternative form of *Sarah*, 'princess' but they are quite distinct. SEE Sarah

ZARINA looks like a diminutive of *Zara* and, of course, it could be used in this way, but it is also an Indian name and comes from a Hindi word meaning 'golden'.

ZELDA is now a name in its own right although it was originally an abbreviation of

Griselda, which may mean 'grey battle', although this is not certain. The wife of the novelist F. Scott Fitzgerald was called Zelda and she helped to popularise it. SEE Griselda

ZELIA may have two interpretations. It may come from the same root as 'zeal' and so mean 'fervent, devoted', or it may be an anglicised form of Hebrew *Zilla(h)*, meaning 'shadow'. The form *Zelia* may have been adopted in English because it resembles *Celia* and *Delia*.

ZENA occurs now as a name in its own right with its origins traced to a Greek adjective meaning 'kind, hospitable'. It is also used as an abbreviation of *Zinaida* which is the name of two Russian orthodox saints. The name means 'child of Zeus' but this implies 'child of God'.

ZENIA is used as a pet form of *Zenobia*, 'given life by Zeus', and also as an anglicised form of *Zinnia*, a plant with beautiful flowers. SEE Zenobia and Zinnia

ZENOBIA is from Greek and implies 'given life by Zeus'. It is not widely used outside Greek circles, although three of its variants, *Zenia*, *Zena* and *Zizi*, are interesting possibilities. The earliest *Zenobia* lived in the 3rd century and was a Middle Eastern queen. She conquered Egypt and large tracts of Asia Minor but she was eventually defeated by the Roman Emperor, Aurelian. Romans tended to admire courage so *Zenobia* was not executed but allowed to live out her life in Italy.

ZEP(H)IRA This name may be pronounced with a middle 'p' or 'f' and this choice accounts for the two spellings. It can be a variant of *Zafira*, meaning 'victory', or it may come from Hebrew and mean 'daybreak, dawn', or it may be related to *zephyr* and mean 'warm west wind'. SEE Zafira

ZETA is also occasionally spelt *Zetta*. The form with one 't' rhymes with *Rita*, and the form with 'tt' rhymes with 'Greta'. It may come from an Arabic word meaning 'olive' or it may be the sixth letter of the Greek alphabet.

ZINNIA is the name of a plant that produces beautiful flowers. It is derived from the name of the German botanist, J.G. Zinn, who first classified it.

ZITA is the name of an Italian saint who is the patron of domestic workers. Its meaning is uncertain but it may mean 'child'. The name is also used as a form of *Teresita*, 'little Teresa'. SEE Teresa

ZOE is from a Greek noun meaning 'life'. It has been popular in English-speaking communities since the 19th century, but it has been used as a Christian name for almost two thousand years.

ZOFIA is used widely in Polish communities. It is a form of *Sophia*, meaning 'wisdom'. SEE Sophia

ZSA ZSA is a Hungarian pet form of *Susanna*, 'lily'. The Hungarian-born actress Zsa Zsa

GIRLS

Gabor made the name famous. SEE Susanna

ZULEIKA has two pronunciations. It can be pronounced like 'zoo + like + a' or 'zoo +lake +a'. This name occurs in the *Book of Genesis* (Chapter 39) where *Zuleika* was the wife of an Egyptian called Potiphar. She tried to seduce *Joseph*, the son of Jacob, but in spite of her attractiveness *Joseph* did not weaken.

ZYTA is a Polish form of Teresa. SEE Teresa and Zara

NOTABLE NAMESAKES
Zara Phillips (b. 1981) daughter of Princess Anne and Captain Mark Phillips. She is a renowned equestrian and has won gold medals in European equestrian championships; Zelda Mishkovsky (1914-84) born in Russia and moved with her family to Israel, where she became a poet, renowned for her deep faith and the beauty of her language; Zoe Ball (b. 1970) English radio and television presenter who came third in the *Strictly Come Dancing* television show in 2005.

BOYS' NAMES

BOYS

A

AAPELI (pronounced 'ah + pelli') is a Finnish form of Abel. SEE Abel

AAPO (pronounced 'ah + po') is the Finnish form of Abraham. SEE Abraham

AATAMI (pronounced 'ah + tam + ee') is the Finnish form of Adam. SEE Adam

AARON is currently one of the most popular names for boys in the British Isles. It is from Hebrew and its precise meaning is uncertain, although many believe it means 'mountain of strength'. Aaron was the brother of Moses and he became the first High Priest. Traditionally, *Aaron* was pronounced like 'A' as in 'air' + 'on' but the 21st-century pronunciation is more likely to be 'A' as in 'had' + 'ron'. An alternative spelling is *Aron*. There is also a Welsh name *Aeron* that may have contributed to the popularity of *Aaron*. SEE Aeron

ABDI is a Hebrew name meaning 'my servant, my follower'.

ABDUL is an extremely popular Arabic name. It is composed of two parts *Abd + al*, meaning 'servant of/devotee of' but suggesting 'servant of the most high'. It is similar to the use of 'Mal' as in *Malcolm*, in Irish and Scottish Gaelic.

ABDULLA(H) is related to *Abdul*. It is a form of *abd* 'devotee of' + *Allah*, 'God'. It can be written with or without the final 'h'. It is an extremely popular name for Muslims.

ABEL is from a Hebrew name that is sometimes transcribed as Hevel or Havel. (In the traditional Hebrew script, vowels are omitted and so there is considerable variation in the English equivalents.) The name means 'breath' and the Hebrew form links this son of Adam and Eve with his mother, whose name may also be related to 'breath'. In the Old Testament, *Abel* was the second son of Adam and Eve. His sacrifices found favour with God and his envious brother *Cain* murdered him. *Abele* is the Italian form of this name. SEE Eve, Kane

ABRAHAM is not currently as popular as *Aaron*, but it has been used for millennia as a mark of respect for the first of the Jewish Patriarchs, whose story is told in the *Book of Genesis*, Chapters 11-25. The original form of the name was *Abram* and many scholars believe that it means 'great father, father of a multitude'. Certainly, the first syllable *Ab* is related to Hebrew *Abba*, 'father'. There have been many famous *Abrahams*, including Abraham Lincoln (1809-65), who wanted to abolish slavery in the United States of America and who was assassinated while watching a play.

ABSALOM is an English equivalent of a Hebrew name, *Avshalom*, which combines *ab/av*, 'father' with *shalom*, 'peace', meaning perhaps 'My father is peace' or 'Peace to my father'. If it has the latter meaning, then it is ironic because *Absalom* led a rebellion against his father, King David. The revolt was put down but when he was fleeing from the battle, *Absalom's* hair was caught in a tree and he was killed by Joab, a supporter of *David*. When *David* heard of the death of his beloved son, he uttered a cry that is beautiful even in translation: *O Absalom, my son, my son! O Absalom, my son!*

ADAIR is a Celtic name that has become popular over the recent past. Like many old names, its precise meaning is uncertain but it seems to be related to *doire*, 'oak grove'. It would be attractive to have twins called *Adair* and *Derry* in that the twins would be linked by meaning. *Adair* may have two additional sources. It may be a form of Hebrew *Adaro*, meaning 'noble', or it may be related to *Edgar*, which comes from Old English *ead*, 'prosperity, rich blessing' + *gar*, 'spear'.

ADAM According to the *Book of Genesis*, *Adam* was the first man.

He was created from the earth:

And the Lord God formed man of the dust of the ground, and breathed into his nostrils the breath of life; and man became a living soul.

(Chapter 2: 7)

Adam's name has been interpreted to mean 'man' but it may also come from similar Hebrew words meaning 'red' or 'earth' or from an Assyrian verb *adamu*, 'to make'. *Adam* was extremely popular as a given name in the past as the proliferation of surnames such as Adams, Adamson and Mac Adam suggests and it has become a favourite choice in the last three decades.

ADAMO is the Italian form of *Adam*.

ADI is one of those very simple names that could be popular in any culture. It is almost certainly from Hebrew and means 'jewel' but it may also be a modified form of Arabic *Adil*, which has the meaning of 'justice'.

ADIN may be a form of the popular Irish name *Aidan* or it may be from a Hebrew source meaning 'physical'. SEE Aidan

ADLAI (pronounced 'ad + lie') is, like many widely-used names, capable of more than one interpretation. King David had a herdsman called *Adlai*, which seems to be a reduced form of *Adalia(h)*, meaning 'God is good; God is just'. It is possible that some uses can be traced to a Germanic adjective *adal*, 'noble'.

ADLEY can be a variant of *Adlai* or a name in its own right, with Hebrew and Old English sources. SEE Adlai

ADOK is a Polish name that may be a variant of *Adrian*. SEE Adrian

ADON (pronounced 'ah + don' or to rhyme with 'say don') is from Hebrew and means 'lord God'. It is perhaps linked to *Adonis*, the Greek proper name that owes its origin to Phoenician *adon*, 'god'. When the poet John Keats died, Shelley wrote an elegy called *Adonais*, in which he compared Keats to other poets who had died young but linked him to *Adonis*, whose beauty caused him to become a god. Shelley's choice may be a blend of Greek *Adonis* and Hebrew *Adonai*.

ADRIAN is a widely used form of the Latin *Hadrianus*, 'man from Hadria in northern Italy'. There are many versions of this name, with and without the initial 'h'. It has been the chosen name of a second-century Roman Emperor and several popes. Adrian IV was an Englishman, Nicholas Breakspear (1100-59), the only Englishman ever to become pope. Adrian IV gave Henry II of England support in his desire to take control of Ireland. *Adriano* is a popular variant.

AENGUS (pronounced 'eng + uss' or 'ayn + guss') is the name of an Irish god of love and poetry. It is also, appropriately enough, the name of an 8th-century saint who was said to be so holy that he only conversed with angels. St Aengus was renowned for his love of prayer and solitude and was known as *Céile Dé*, 'Servant of God', a title that became anglicised to *Culdee*. W B Yeats immortalised *Aengus* in his poetry. *Angus* is a well-loved Scottish equivalent. The name seems to come from *aon*, 'one' + *gus*, 'choice' or *gas*, 'warrior' and implies 'outstanding'.

AERON (pronounced 'air + on', or less frequently 'ah + ron') In Welsh mythology, *Aeron* was a supernatural being, godlike, if not quite a god. The name can mean 'berry'. It has occasionally been equated with *Aaron*. SEE Aaron

AESOP (pronounced 'ee + sop') Although large numbers of people in the world are familiar with *Aesop's Fables*, the originator's name has never ranked high on the popularity stakes, possibly because it did not seem to have an etymology. Aesop lived in the 6th century BC and revolutionised story telling in Greece. Aesop, unlike his contemporaries, used animals to dramatise human characteristics, especially weaknesses. This technique was new to Europe but seems to have been a feature of African culture and that may give us a clue to his name. It may be a form of *Ethiop*, meaning not just 'Ethiopian' but 'African'.

AHMED (pronounced 'ach + mid' or 'ah + med') is an extremely popular Arabic name. It means 'most highly praised, most worthy of commendation'. There are many spellings of this name including *Ahmad* and the preferred Turkish variant, *Ahmet*.

AIDAN is a Celtic name that has joined the ranks of *Brian*, *Connor* and *Kevin* in becoming an international favourite. It is a variant form of *Aodh*, a Celtic god of fire, and might be an attractive choice for a redhead! There were several Irish saints called *Aidan*, the best known of which lived in the 7th century. He was made a bishop in Ireland but chose to become a monk on the island of Iona around AD 630. He was not allowed to keep to his chosen life of isolation, prayer and penance but was asked to go as a type of apostle to Lindisfarne in Northumbria. St Bede was a follower of Aidan and lavishly praises him for his dedication to his faith. He died in AD 651 and was described in this way by Bede:

He was a pontiff inspired with a passionate love of virtue, but at the same time full of a surpassing mildness and gentleness.

AINSLEY is one of the many examples of a place name that became a surname and then a popular given name. This one may come from Annesley in Nottinghamshire or Ansley in Warwickshire. The first probably means 'single field or meadow' or even 'Anna's field'. The latter is recorded as early as the 12th century and is from *ansetleah*, meaning 'field or meadow of a hermitage'.

(*The most frequently adopted place names have two syllables but names that have a pattern of consonant + vowel + consonant + vowel + consonant + vowel, such as Dakota, Jericho, Sahara are more attractive to parents than monosyllabic, consonant laden place names such as Gdansk or Minsk.)

AKBAR (pronounced 'ack + bar') is an Arabic name meaning 'greatest'. Like many Arabic names, the main implication is that 'God is great'.

AKIM (pronounced 'ack + eem') is a popular name in Eastern Europe. It started as a pet form of *Joachim* but has become a name in its own right. The Hebrew original means 'established by God' and, according to early Christian tradition, the parents of the Blessed Virgin Mary were Joachim and Anna. The variant *Hakim* is widely used among Muslims. SEE Joachim

AKIO (pronounced 'a + key + o') is a Japanese name, meaning 'bright boy'.

ALAIN is a French form of *Alan*. SEE Alan

ALAN was introduced into the British Isles by the Normans, who were accompanied by many Breton adventurers, including Alan of Brittany, and many will remember Alan a Dale, the minstrel in the Robin Hood stories. The name is Celtic in origin and, since it means 'rock', is a meaning equivalent of *Peter*. *Alan* was popularised in the 1950s by the film star Alan Ladd and it has remained a favourite. Two other forms of the name are also popular, namely, *Allan* and *Allen*. Usually, these are surnames that have become given names again. *Alano* is used in Italy.

ALASDAIR, ALASTAIR

There are many variants of this Scottish form of *Alexander*, including *Alasteir*, *Alaster*, *Alistair*, *Alister*, and the surname *MacAlister* has also become almost as popular as a given name as *MacCauley*. The name means 'defender of men/warriors'. Several early Scottish monarchs were called *Alasdair* and the fame of Alexander the Great (356-323 BC) has ensured the continued appeal of all variants. SEE Alexander

ALBAN

(pronounced 'all + ban' or, less often, to rhyme with 'sal can') There were many parts of the Roman world called *Alba*

from some geographical feature that was white or whitish, from Latin *albus*, 'white', but *Alba* was also an Irish name for Scotland. This name is almost certainly from the Celtic word *alp*, 'rock, mountain'. One of the earliest British martyrs was called *Alban* and although he lived in the 3rd century, his fame continued and St Albans in Hertfordshire was named in his honour.

ALBERT

is of Germanic origin and comes from the combination of *adal*, 'noble' + *berht*, 'bright'. There was an English equivalent, *Athelbeorht*, but that died out after the Norman Conquest of 1066. *Albert* is popular throughout Europe, although the pronunciation may differ and it tends to be *Alberto* in many countries. The name was popularised in England in the 19th century because of Queen Victoria's husband. His name was extended to a watch chain, a bravery medal and a size of notepaper, approximately 9.5 cm x 15 cm.

ALBIN

is a popular variant of

Alban. SEE Alban

ALDEN is an Old English name composed of two elements, *ald*, 'old' + *wine*, 'friend'. It occurs equally frequently in two alternative forms, *Aldin* and *Aldon*. SEE Alvin

ALDO is a popular Italian name derived from a Germanic adjective *ald*, 'old', but implying 'trusted, reliable, wise'.

ALDOUS (pronounced to rhyme with 'all + bus') is an English name that was popular in the Middle Ages and reintroduced to society by the parents of the writer Aldous Huxley (1894-1963). His popularity resulted in the rebirth of the name. Its origins are shrouded in mystery but the first part is from Germanic adjective *ald*, 'old', and the second part may be *hus*, 'house'.

ALED is a popular Welsh name that has begun to be used in many parts of the world. Its meaning is uncertain but it may mean 'noble brow'.

ALEKSANDR SEE Alexander

ALEKSY SEE Alexis

ALESSANDRO SEE Alexander

ALEXANDER is the Latin form of the Greek name, *Alexandros*, which is a combination of *alexein*, 'to defend' + *andros*, a form of 'man'. *Alexander* has been the name of emperors, kings and eight popes. The first of these was the fifth pope in line from St Peter. *Alexander* is the English version of this name but it occurs in some form in every European language and has given rise to such reductions as *Aleck*, *Alex*, *Alick*, *Sandy* and *Sasha*. SEE Sasha

ALEXIS is sometimes used as an abbreviation of *Alexander* but it is a name in its own right. It comes from *alexein*, 'to defend', and means 'helper, defender'. The Greek form is *Alexios* and the Latin version *Alexius* occurs in Europe.

ALFONSO is a variant of *Alphonse*. SEE Alphonse

ALFRED was a king of the southern part of England, known then as Wessex, from 'West Saxon'. He was born in AD 849 and died in AD 899 and is probably best remembered as the king who burned an old lady's cakes rather than as the man who struggled to reintroduce Christian values and education into his kingdom. Alfred's name is from *ælf*, 'elf, fairy, supernatural being' + *ræd*, 'counsel, advice'. He made a treaty with the Vikings and brought peace to Wessex. The name has given rise to *Alf*, *Alfie*, *Alfy* and *Fred*. SEE Frederick

ALI is a well-known Arabic name meaning 'lofty, noble'. The Prophet Muhammad's son-in-law was *Ali* and, for a time, he ruled the Muslim world as Caliph. This *Ali*'s followers were Shi'ites. Many people will know the name from the heavyweight boxing champion, Muhammad Ali, the chosen name of Cassius Clay when he converted to Islam.

ALLAN This version of the name illustrates the close transfer between given names and surnames. It is most likely to be taken from a surname, but, of course, the surname was originally a given name! SEE Alan

ALONSO This is a variant of *Alphonse*. SEE Alphonse

ALONZO SEE Alphonse

ALOYS (pronounced to rhyme with 'al + boys') is a popular German form of *Aloysius*. SEE Aloysius

ALOYSIUS is a Latin version of a dialectal form of *Louis*, 'famous in war'. It became widespread in Europe after the 16th-century Italian saint Aloysius Gonzaga, and appears in a wide range of forms such as *Alabhaois* (Irish), *Alois* (French), *Aloisio* (Portuguese) and *Alojzy* (Polish). In Europe, the name is usually pronounced 'al + oy (rhyming with 'toy) + zee + oos'. In Ireland, it is more likely to be pronounced as 'alo + wish + uss'. With names, it is hard to say 'This pronunciation is right' because the pronunciation differs from one country to another. How many people know – or care – that *Aloysius*, *Ludwig* and *Louis* are all versions of the same name?

ALPHONSE is a widespread form of a name that occurs widely in Europe under such variants as *Alfonse*, *Alfonso*, *Alphonsus*, *Alonso* and *Alonzo*. The name is Germanic in origin and means 'noble and well-prepared'. The abbreviation *Alfie* is regularly used for these variants. Several kings of Portugal and Spain had this name.

ALUN is a Welsh mythological name that appears in the *Mabinogion*, a collection of Welsh legends and myths from the Middle Ages. It seems likely that *Alun* is the Welsh equivalent of the Breton name *Alan* and means 'rock'. SEE Alan

ALVIN is most popular in America. It is a combination of two Old English elements, *ælf*, 'elf, supernatural being' + *wine* 'friend'. The name also occurs as

Alwin and *Elwin*. SEE Elwin

ALVIS can be related to *Elvis*, which has been popular since Elvis Presley became one of the biggest record sellers of all time. *Alvis* is from Old Norse and means 'all wise'. SEE Elvis

AMADEO is a Spanish form of *Amadeus*. SEE Amadeus

AMADEUS comes from two Latin words, *amare*, 'to love', and *deus*, 'God', and it can be interpreted to mean God's love of the child or the child's love of God, or both. Wolfgang Amadeus Mozart (1756-1791) is probably the best known bearer of this name, although, as with all names, there are stories attached to it. It seems that the young Mozart was actually christened *Wolfgang Theophilus* but he latinised his Greek name.

AMADI is an Igbo name that has been carried from Nigeria by Igbo speakers. It means 'rejoicing', a fitting name for a longed-for son.

AMAR is from Sanskrit, where

it means 'immortal'. It has the same meaning as *Ambrose*. It is understandable that parents of all countries want their children to have all that good wishes can bring them.

AMBROSE is from Latin *Ambrosius*, which is based on the Greek name *Ambrosios*, meaning 'immortal'. Appropriately, it was the name of a 4th-century saint, who was a theologian and bishop of Milan. The name occurs in such forms as *Ambros*, *Ambrosi*, *Ambrosio* and *Ambrosius*.

AMERIGO Most of us know that America takes its name from the Italian explorer, Amerigo Vespucci (1451-1512), whose Latin name was *Americus*. What many of us probably don't know is that *Amerigo* is a medieval form of *Henry*, which is a combination of the Germanic elements *haim*, 'home', and *ric*, 'power'. SEE Henry

AMERY (pronounced 'aim + erry') is an Old English name that became a surname and then,

more recently, re-emerged as a given name. Its meaning is uncertain but it may imply 'illustrious ruler'. The variant *Amory* also occurs.

AMIN (pronounced 'ah + mean') is an Arabic name that means 'truthful'. The word is found also in Hebrew with the meaning of 'truth'. It was used at the end of prayers, promises and vows to strengthen or confirm what had been said. Gradually, in the form of *Amen*, it came to be the accepted formulaic conclusion to a prayer.

AMIR (pronounced 'ah + mere') is an Arabic name meaning 'commander' or 'prince'. It comes from the same word as the title *Emir* and is an honourific that is often bestowed on descendants of the Prophet Muhammad.

AMIT (pronounced 'ah + meat') Arabic and Hebrew are related languages so it is not surprising that the same name with similar meanings is found in both. *Amit* is more widely used in

Arabic-influenced communities and has the meaning of 'infinite', with the implication that God's attributes – love, generosity – are immeasurable. In Hebrew, it has taken on the sense of 'friend'. The name also occurs in Sanskrit where it means 'immortal'.

AMOS (pronounced 'aim + oss') is a Hebrew name meaning 'carry' and possibly implying 'carrying a burden'. It was the name of an Old Testament prophet. He wrote the *Book of Amos*, which is considered by many scholars to be the oldest of the prophetic books.

AMRIT (pronounced 'am + reet') is a Sanskrit name, related to *Amit* and meaning 'immortal'. SEE Amit

ANAKONI (pronounced 'anna + coney') is a Hawaiian form of Anthony. SEE Anthony

ANAND is becoming increasingly popular among expatriate Indian families. It means 'happiness' in Sanskrit and embodies the parents' wish

that their son may be blessed by peace and joy.

ANDREJ is a Polish form of one of the most widely used names in the world. SEE Andrew

ANDRÉ is the usual French form of *Andrew*. SEE Andrew

ANDREAS is a Greek form of *Andrew*. SEE Andrew

ANDREW is from a Greek word for 'man, warrior' and *Andreas* tends to be the form used in Greek-speaking communities. The origin is Greek *aner*, 'man', *andros*, 'of a man'. This same root also gave rise to the end of *Alexander*. According to the New Testament, *Andrew* was the brother of *Peter* and Christian tradition claims that he was crucified on an X-shaped cross. He is the patron saint of Scotland and the flag bears his emblem. *Andrew* is also the patron saint of Greece and Russia. The pet forms of this name include *Andie* and *Andy*.

ANEURIN (pronounced 'an +

eye + rin') is an extremely old Welsh name and can be traced back to around AD 600. Its meaning is unclear but it may be a Welsh equivalent of Latin *Honorius*, 'honorable man'.

ANGELO is a popular Italian name meaning 'angel, messenger of God'. According to Jewish, Christian and Islamic traditions, angels are attendants of God and messengers between Him and humans.

ANGUS is the Scottish equivalent of *Aengus* and thus means 'first choice' or 'first among warriors'. It is popular in Scotland and throughout the world where Scots have settled. SEE Aengus

ANIL (pronounced 'an + eel') is an Indian name that comes from Sanskrit and means 'air, wind'. It is an alternative name for the god Vayu, who was the god of the wind. The name is attractive to English speakers partly because it is pronounced like the verb *anneal*, which means 'set on fire', usually metaphorically!

ANNAN is sometimes spelt *Anan* and it can come from the Hebrew word for 'cloud' or from a Ghanaian name for 'fourth child'. *Annan* also occurs in Scotland as a surname and this name may come from an old Celtic word for 'river'. It would thus imply, 'one who lives near a river'.

ANSELM came into English from Italy, where *Anselmo* is found. It was the name of an 11th-century, Italian-born Archbishop of Canterbury. He was famed throughout the Christian world for his wisdom and learning. In spite of its Italian connection, however, the name is almost certainly of Germanic origin, coming from *ans*, 'god' + *helm*, 'helmet'. It could be interpreted as 'God is my protection.'

ANTHONY has been popular throughout Europe in such forms as *Antoine*, *Anton* and *Antonio*. Its origins are unclear because it almost certainly predates Roman times. *Antonius* was adopted by a noble Roman family that included the Roman general, Mark Antony (83-30 BC). The Roman name did not have an 'h' in it. The 'h' was introduced when it was thought to be related to the Greek word, *anthos*, 'flower'. Interestingly, Shakespeare did not use the 'h' for Mark Antony, the friend of Julius Caesar and lover of Cleopatra. There are at least two well-known saints called *Anthony*, the 3rd-century hermit, St Anthony of Egypt, and St Anthony of Padua (1195-1231), who was devoted to the needs of the poor. Many people call on St Anthony for help when they have lost something.

ANTOINE is the usual French form of *Anthony*. SEE Anthony

ANTON is the usual German form of *Anthony*. SEE Anthony

ANTONIO is used in Italy, Spain and Portugal. SEE Anthony

ANWAR is an Arabic name meaning 'brighter'. It was the given name of President Sadat of Egypt, who jointly won the Nobel Peace Prize in 1978 but was assassinated in 1981.

AODH/AEDH was the name of a Celtic god of fire. It was revived in the 20th century due in part to the poetry of W B Yeats and, in particular, to his poem, 'Aedh Wishes for the Cloths of Heaven'.

ARCHIBALD is a Germanic name that was introduced into England by the Normans. It is composed of the elements *ercan*, 'genuine' + *bald*, 'bold, brave, courageous'. It is most popular in Scotland where it also occurs as a surname. The abbreviation *Archie* is regularly used. The 'bald' segment has nothing to do with 'baldness'. No one is really sure where modern 'bald' comes from but the likeliest explanation is that it is a form of 'balled', meaning 'smooth like a ball'.

ARDAL/ARDGHAL (pronounced to rhyme with 'far + call' or 'far + Hal') is an Irish name composed of *árd*, 'high' + *geal*, 'courage'. It is one of several Irish names given to children in the wake of increased Irish pride in their heritage.

ARI is another example of a name that may arise in different cultures. In Hebrew, it means 'lion'; in Old Norse, it meant 'eagle'. Since both these meanings express strength and power and freedom, the name is popular. In Greek communities, *Ari* is used as an abbreviation of *Aristotle*, the name of a Greek philosopher who studied under Plato and taught Alexander the Great.

ARIEL (pronounced to rhyme with 'air + ee + el' or 'ar + ee + el) is a Hebrew name that means 'lion of God'. The form *Arel* is a less frequently used alternative. In the Old Testament, *Ariel* was used metaphorically to refer to Jerusalem. Shakespeare selected *Ariel* as the name for the airy spirit in *The Tempest*, possibly because the name suggested music combined with an ethereal quality. In 1851, one of Saturn's larger moons was discovered and named *Ariel*.

ARMAND is most widely used in France. It is a form of *Herman*, meaning 'soldier, war + man'. SEE Herman

ARMANDEK is a Polish variant of *Armand*. SEE Herman

ARMANDO is an Italian form of *Armand*. SEE Herman

ARNOLD is one of the names of Germanic origin that the Norman conquerors introduced into Britain. It combines two nouns, *arn*, 'eagle' + *wald*, 'power, rule'.
One of the early references to the name belongs to Saint Arnold, a talented musician who lived at the court of Charlemagne, the first Holy Roman Emperor.

ARON is an alternative spelling of *Aaron*, especially popular in Poland. SEE Aaron

ART is a Celtic form of the name that is best known as *Arthur*.

ARTHUR like *Anthony*, rarely had an 'h' until the 16th century. Although his story is surrounded by myth and legend, it is likely that he ruled part of Britain in the 6th century. It is uncertain what his name means. It may be a Celtic word for 'bear' and the bear represented courage, strength and fortitude, or it may have been a Latin form of Greek *arktouros*, 'keeper of bears'. *Arthur's* name will always be linked to the story of the Round Table when chivalry, courtesy and honour were more precious than power and wealth. The name has remained popular because of the enduring appeal of the Arthurian legends.

ARTUR is a Polish variant of *Arthur*. SEE Arthur

ARUN (pronounced to rhyme with 'ah + run') is from Sanskrit, where it means 'reddish brown'. Its meaning may, therefore, overlap that of *Adam*. In Hindu mythology, *Arun* was the charioteer who drove the sun god across the sky, thus creating heat and light.

ASA (pronounced 'ace + a') is a Hebrew name meaning 'doctor, one who heals'. It was the name of an early king of Israel and was the original name of the jazz singer Al Jolson.

ASHER In the Old Testament, *Asher* was the son of Jacob and the ancestor of one of the twelve tribes of Israel. The twelve sons of Jacob were *Asher, Benjamin, Dan, Gad, Issachar, Judah, Manasseh, Naphtali, Reuben, Simeon* and *Zebulun*. Only the tribes of Benjamin and Judah remained in Israel. The others, known as the 'Lost Tribes', were deported to captivity around 720 BC. *Asher* means 'happy, blessed'.

ASHOK(A) is, like many Indian names, from Sanskrit, where it means 'free from sorrow'. It was the name of an emperor of India in the 3rd century BC.

ASHUR can be an alternative spelling of *Asher*. SEE Asher

ASIF is a well-loved Arabic name meaning 'forgiveness'.

217

AUBERON came to the British Isles with the Norman conquerors. Its origins are debated but it may be a Germanic name combining *adal*, 'noble', with *ber*, 'bear', or it may be a form of another Germanic name, *Aubrey*, which combines *alb*, 'elf' + *ric*, 'power'. Shakespeare uses the spelling *Oberon* for the king of the fairies and husband of Titania in *A Midsummer Night's Dream*.

AUBREY is a Norman name derived from the German *Alberic*, a combination of *alb*, 'elf', and *ric*, 'power, rule'. Alberic was thought to be the leader of the elves and this may have encouraged Shakespeare to use a variant for the king of the fairies in *A Midsummer Night's Dream*.

AUGUSTIN/AUGUSTINE is found in one or more variants in most European languages. It comes from the Roman name *Augustus*, meaning 'exalted, illustrious', and it has been the name of emperors and saints. Saint Augustine (AD 354-430) was a theologian from North Africa who wrote movingly about his own life and conversion. Most of us can respond to a prayer that he describes in *Confessions*: 'Give me chastity and continency, but not yet.' The use of a concluding 'e' is optional.

AUGUSTYN This is a Polish form of *Augustin(e)*. SEE Augustin

AUSTEN This is an abbreviated form of *Augustin(e)*. SEE Augustin

AUSTIN This is an abbreviated form of *Augustin(e)*. The Augustinian Friars are also called 'Austin Friars'. Austin in Texas is also a form of this popular name. SEE Augustin

AXEL is a popular Scandinavian name that means 'peace'. It is sometimes equated with *Absalom*. SEE Absalom

AZIZ is used widely throughout the Muslim world. It has two meanings, 'powerful' and 'cherished'.

NOTABLE NAMESAKES

Adam Smith (1723-97)
Scottish philosopher
credited with establishing
modern economics; **Andy
Warhol** (1928-87) American
artist, entrepreneur and
major figure in the Pop Art
scene; **Anton Dvorak**
(1841-1904) Czech
composer, best known for
his *New World Symphony* of
1893; **Arthur Ashe**
(1943-93) African-American
tennis player who won the
Wimbledon Singles title in
1975.

B

BABAR means 'lion'. It is thus
the equivalent of *Leo*. It was the
name of the 16th century Mogul
ruler of India. It probably came
originally from Turkish.
Occasionally *Babru* or *Bablu* is
used as an alternative.

BAHAR (pronounced
'bah + harr') is an Arabic
name meaning 'sailor'. The
Arabs were superb sailors and it
has been suggested that they
were the first to circumnavigate
the world. The name has a strong
aura of respect attached to it.

BAHIR (pronounced 'bah +
here') is an Arabic name almost
certainly meaning 'welcome'. It
is found throughout the Muslim
world and is sometimes spelt
Bachir. The variation in the
central consonant is due to the
fact that English does not have
an exact equivalent of the Arabic
sound.

BALDWIN was an Old
English given name derived
from the elements *bald*, 'bold,
courageous' + *wine*, 'friend'. It
became a surname but has
regained some of its use as a
given name. *Baldwin*
(1058-1118) was the name of a
Flemish leader of the First
Crusade. When the Crusaders
conquered Jerusalem, he
became its first king.

BALFOUR is most widely found in Scotland. The name is believed to come from a Gaelic greeting meaning 'The blessings of God on the harvest'. It is a surname that has become a given name.

BARACK/BARAK/BARAQ

(pronounced 'bah + rack' or 'bah + rakh' where the 'kh' is similar to 'ch' in 'loch') can be either a Hebrew name meaning 'lightning' or a Muslim name meaning 'blessed'. It was the name of an Old Testament military commander. He lived at the time of the prophet *Deborah* who encouraged him to release the Israelites from their bondage. His victory over the Canaanites ensured that the Israelites knew peace and prosperity for 40 years. In parts of Africa, the name is sometimes spelt *Baraka*.

BARDO is a Dutch abbreviation of *Bartholemew*. SEE Bartholemew

BARNABAS is usually listed as an Apostle although he was not one of the original Twelve.

In so far as we know, he was born in Cyprus and was related to St Mark the evangelist. His original name was Joseph but he was given the name *Barnabas*, which means 'son of exhortation' or 'son of consolation' because of his success as a preacher. When St Paul was converted, many of the early Christians had misgivings about him but *Barnabas* acted as his sponsor. The name has become popular over the last decade especially in its anglicised form of *Barnaby*. *Barney* is frequently used as an abbreviation, although it is also used as an abbreviation of *Bernard*.

BARNABY is an English equivalent of *Barnabas* and so means 'son of consolation' or 'son of exhortation'.

BARNARD In the past, *Barnard* was often given as an alternative spelling of *Bernard* and this form is still widely used as a surname and also as an American form, where the stress is placed on the second and not the first syllable. SEE Bernard

BARNET can be a variation of *Bernard*, an abbreviation of *Barnabas*, or a name in its own right, probably coming from Old English *Beornheard*, 'brave man' or 'brave child'. It is possible that *beorn* is related to *bairn*. SEE Barnabas and Bernard

BARNEY is regularly used as a given name in its own right but it originated as an abbreviated form of *Barnabas* or *Barnard*. SEE Barnabas and Bernard

BARRY is an Irish name, almost certainly coming from *bearach*, 'spear'. It is also a frequent surname, as in Kevin Barry.

BART is a shortened form of *Bartholomew* and means son of Talmai or Tholmai. It has further been suggested that *Talmai* comes from 'furrows' and so *Bart* may mean 'son of a farmer or sailor'. SEE Bartholomew

BARTHOLOMEW The name *Bartholomaios* is from Hebrew and means 'son of Talmai' or 'son of Tholmai'. It may also mean 'son of furrows'. King David's father-in-law was

called *Bartholomew*. The Irish name *Parthalán* and the surname *Mac Partlan* have this ancient Hebrew name as their source.

BARTOLOMEO is a form of *Bartholomew* found in countries where Italian, Spanish and Portuguese are spoken. SEE Bartholomew

BARUCH (pronounced 'bah + rookh') has been a favourite name in certain families and it is often the full name for children who are called *Barry*. It means 'blessed'. In the Old Testament, Baruch was a disciple of the prophet Jeremiah and his writings foretold the destruction of the Temple of Jerusalem in 588 BC. SEE Barry

BASIL is from a Greek adjective meaning 'like a king'. The popular herb, basil, got its name because it was used in royal medications and balms. In the 4th century, St Basil the Elder and his wife, Macrina, suffered for their faith. They had ten children, three of whom, including Basil the Great, became saints. He was a defender of the Oriental Church and is cherished in Orthodox Christianity because of his struggles against heresies.

BASILIO is an Italian form of *Basil*. SEE Basil

BAUDOUIN (pronounced to rhyme with 'go + dwin'. The final vowel is nasalised in the French pronunciation. *Baudouin* is a Belgian form of *Baldwin* and a name favoured by the Belgian royal family. SEE Baldwin

BAZYLI Bazyli (pronounced 'bah + zee + lee') is a Polish form of *Basil*. SEE Basil

BEAU (pronounced like 'bow' in 'bow and arrow') was popular in French-speaking communities and is the name of the film star Beau Bridges. It comes from the French adjective *beau*, 'handsome', and is also used as a noun to indicate a handsome well-dressed young man. The female equivalent *Belle* or *Bella* is also used. The name *Beauregard*, meaning 'beautiful to look at', is still found in some families in the southern states of America.

BEDE Few people outside religious orders are called *Bede* and yet it is a name with a link to an intellectually gifted saint. *Bede* comes from the Old English verb *biddan*, 'to pray', and gradually the noun came to mean 'prayer' and then 'an object to help in saying the rosary'. In fact, modern 'beads' come from the same word although few people wearing a necklace of beads would think of using them as an aid to prayer! St Bede was a disciple and admirer of St Aidan, who helped to spread Christianity in Northumberland. He is thought to have died while translating the Lord's Prayer into English.

BEN can be an abbreviation of both *Benedict* and *Benjamin*. It can mean 'son' in Hebrew. It is currently used as a name in its own right. SEE Benedict and Benjamin

BENDYK (pronounced 'ben + deek) is a Polish form of *Benedict*. SEE Benedict

BENEDETTO is an Italian form of *Benedict*. SEE Benedict

BENEDICT comes from Church Latin *benedictus*, which meant 'blessed'. It is composed of two elements *bene*, 'well' + *dicere* 'to speak'. Saint Benedict was an Italian monk (AD 480-550) who founded the Benedictine Monastic Order in the 6th century. Virtually all Christian monks continue to adhere to his rules. *Benedict* has also been chosen by 16 popes, the most recent of whom became pope in 2005. *Ben* is also used as an abbreviation of *Benedict*. An English St Benedict who died about AD 628 introduced stone walls and stained glass windows into English churches.

BENIAMINO (pronounced 'ben + yam + eeno') is an Italian form of *Bejamin*. SEE Benjamin

BENITO 'little Ben' is an Italian abbreviation of *Benedict*. SEE Benedict

BENJAMIN in its reduced form *Ben*, is currently one of the most popular names in Ireland and England. It comes from Hebrew and means 'son of my right hand'. In the Old Testament, *Benjamin* was the twelfth son of Jacob. His mother, Rachel, died shortly after giving birth to him and he was especially loved because of this. *Benjamin* was the founder of one of the twelve tribes of Israel. This was the given name of Benjamin Franklin, one of the founding fathers of the United States.

BENNET In the Middle Ages, this was the usual English form of *Benedict*. It ceased to be used as a given name but was widely used as a surname. Often today's use of *Bennet* or its variant *Bennett* come from use of a surname as a given name.

BENOIT is a French form of *Benedict*. SEE Benedict

BERNARD is a Germanic name that is made up of the elements for 'bear' and 'strong, brave'. It continues to be a favourite name worldwide and is found in such forms as *Barnard*,

Barnet, Bernardo, Bernhardt as well as in the abbreviations *Barney* and *Bernie*.

BERT is a popular abbreviated form of many names including *Albert, Bertram, Bertrand, Gilbert* and *Robert*. *Bert* may come from a Germanic adjective meaning 'bright and famous'.

BERTRAM The Normans introduced this Germanic name into the British Isles after the Norman Conquest of 1066. It seems to be a blend of *berth*, 'bright, famous' + *hramn*, 'raven'. In Germanic culture, the raven symbolised intelligence and acumen. The name would have been attractive to Celts, among whom the raven was also a symbolic bird.

BERTRAND is a medieval variant of *Bertram*. Since the second syllable, meaning 'raven' ended in 'mn', a difficult combination, some speakers ended the name with 'm' and others with 'n'. The addition of a 'd' is not unusual. After all 'yon'

and 'yonder' are related. SEE Bertram

BEVAN is a Welsh name from *ap*, 'son of' + *Evan*, 'John', and meaning 'son of God's graciousness'. SEE John

BHAGAT is from Arabic and suggests 'joy, rejoicing, celebration'. Arabic-speaking parents, like parents of all languages, are delighted at the birth of a son and so this name is popular. The name is pronounced like 'ba + gat' but the initial 'B' is pronounced with an accompanying puff of air.

BHASKAR is a widely-used Indian name which comes from two Sanskrit words meaning 'light + creating'. It is one of the names given to the Hindu god *Shiva* and to the sun. In English-speaking communities, the name is pronounced like 'bass +car'. In Indian circles the 'Bh' is pronounced like 'b' but accompanied by a puff of breath. SEE Shiva

BIBIANO is a Spanish form of Vivian and is a male name. Vivian was a popular Norman name, meaning 'lively'. SEE Vivian

BJORN (pronounced 'b + yorn') is a traditional Scandinavian name, meaning 'bear' and suggesting 'strength and tenacity'. It has spread beyond its original homeland and is popular in Germany.

BLAIN/BLAINE was a bishop in Scotland during the 6th century but it is likely that he was born in Ireland. He was certainly educated there but went to Scotland to preach to the Picts. His monastery became the Cathedral of Dunblane. It is not certain what his name means but it may be related to *bladhm*, 'flame', and it rhymes with 'gain'.

BLAIR is most frequently found as a surname in Scotland and the north of England but, like a lot of surnames, it has recently been used as a given name. The meaning of *Blair* is uncertain but it probably means 'man from the plains or the meadow lands'.

BLAISE Many people with sore throats have sought the help of St Blaise, who was probably a 4th century Armenian saint. His name possibly means 'torch, firebrand'. According to legend, Blaise was able to cure both humans and animals. The animals used to come on their own to his cave and wait until he had finished praying. (Many human visitors were less considerate!) It is hard to overestimate the strength of Blaise's appeal but an indication is that in England in 1222, the Church insisted that all labouring men and women should have a holiday on the feast of St Blaise, 3 February.

BOB is an abbreviation of *Robert*, one of the many Germanic names introduced into the British Isles by the Normans. It means 'bright fame' and it had a large number of reduced forms, including *Bobby*, *Dob*, *Hob*, *Nob*, Rab and *Robin*. SEE Robert

BOGDAN is a widely used Polish name meaning 'God's gift'. It is thus the Polish equivalent of *Theodore*.

BONIFACE is still popular in Africa but it was once much more widespread in Europe. It looks as if it means 'bonny + face' meaning handsome but, in fact, it comes from Liturgical Latin *bonum*, 'good' + *fatum*, 'destiny, fate', and suggests that the recipient of the name will lead a happy, fulfilled life. There have been nine popes called *Boniface*, the last one holding the papacy between 1389 and 1414. Of the many saints and holy people with this name, one of the most illustrious was St Boniface, the Apostle of Germany, who was martyred in the middle of the 8th century. Tradition has it that St Boniface was from England but he has also been claimed by Ireland and Scotland.

BONIFACY is the Polish form of *Boniface*. SEE Boniface

BORIS Like a lot of Russian names such as *Tania*, this became popular in English-speaking communities in the second half of the 20th century. *Boris* seemed especially attractive after Boris Becker, at seventeen, became the youngest player ever to win the Men's Singles Title at Wimbledon in 1985. The name occurs most widely in Russia, as both *Boris* and *Borislav*, but it is not of Russian origin. Its meaning is uncertain but it has been suggested that it means either 'wolf' or 'small'. It has been the name of at least one saint and of several rulers in both Bulgaria and Russia.

BORYS is the Polish form of *Boris* and *Boryslaw* is equally widely used. SEE Boris

BOYD is a frequently occurring surname that derives from a Gaelic nickname, *buidhe*, 'yellow gold'. In the Celtic languages, the adjective followed the noun and a fair-headed individual was likely to be called, for example, *Sean Buidhe*. It is easy to see how the nickname became a surname and eventually a given name.

BRAD is often used as a name in its own right, particularly in Australia and the USA. Originally, it was an abbreviated form of *Bradford*, *Bradley* or, less frequently, *Bradshaw*. In each of these cases, the 'brad' syllable was from Old English and meant 'broad'. SEE Bradley

BRADFORD There are at least nine towns in England called *Bradford*, a name that comes from the Old English words *brad*, 'broad, wide' and *ford*, 'ford, river crossing'. People often adopted the name of their birthplace as a surname and this led to the adoption of *Bradford* as a given name.

BRADLEY is an Old English place name composed of *brad*, 'broad, wide' + *leah*, 'clearing, wood'. *Bradley* is found as a surname in all English-speaking settlements and *Brad* is often a reduction of the surname.

BRADY may be either an Irish or an English surname. The Irish variant may come from *bradán*, 'salmon', possibly referring to the salmon of wisdom. Even one mouthful of this mythical salmon would make one as wise as Solomon. The English variant is a

combination of *brad*, 'broad, wide' + *ey*, 'island'. This name is pronounced to rhyme with 'lady', not 'laddie', and it is rarely abbreviated.

BRAM is a name that was popularised by Bram Stoker (1847-1912), who gave the world one of its most enduring horror stories in *Dracula* (1897). For him, it was an abbreviation of *Abraham*, meaning 'father of a multitude', but it is used as a given name in its own right. SEE Abraham

BRAN can be a Celtic name meaning 'raven' and symbolising spirituality. It can be a reduced form of the given name *Brandon* or an abbreviation of the surnames *Brandon* and *Branwell*. *Brandon* is a town in Durham and comes from the Old English compound *brom*, 'broom, whin, furze' + *dun*, 'hill'. *Branwell* was the name that the Brontës used for Patrick Branwell Brontë, the brother of Charlotte, Emily and Anne. *Branwell* is a Cornish town and probably means 'Brant's well'. SEE Brandon

227

BRANDON occurs occasionally as a variant of *Brendan* but it can also come from one of the many towns of this name in England. Most of the towns get their name from Old English *brom*, 'broom, whin, furze' + *dun*, 'hill' but the first syllable may also mean 'brand' as in 'firebrand'.

BRENDAN is one of the most popular Celtic names in the world. There were two Irish St Brendans in the 6th century and probably many more since that time. The most illustrious Brendan was the Kerry saint, who was born near Tralee in or around AD 484 and died in AD 577, and who is reputed to have sailed to America, which he called the 'Land of Delight'. The meaning of his name is as strongly debated as the likelihood of his voyage. It may be from *bran*, 'raven', symbolising Celtic spirituality, or from a Welsh noun meaning 'king'.

BRETT is a name given to the Bretons that accompanied William the Conqueror in 1066.

It occurs most frequently as a surname and parallels *Welsh* in having an ethnic reference. It is popular as a given name in Australia and the United States of America.

BRIAN is one of a set of Irish names like *Brendan* and *Sean* that have spread worldwide. Its exact meaning is unclear but it seems to mean 'eminence, hill' and in this it can be linked to Welsh *Bryn*. Brian Boru was the Munster king who became High King of Ireland and defeated the Vikings in their attempts to conquer Ireland in the 11th century. He was victorious in the Battle of Clontarf (1014), but he himself was killed in the battle.

BRODERICK is a Welsh name that has spread beyond Wales. It comes from *ap* , 'son of' + *Roderick*, 'fame and power'.

BRUCE became a popular given name in memory of the Scottish patriot, Robert the Bruce (1274-1329). The meaning of the name is debated. It certainly arrived in the British Isles in the

11th century with the Norman Conquerors and may be a form of the Belgian town of Bruges.

BRUNO is related to 'brown' and was almost certainly a nickname meaning 'brown-haired'. It has until recently been most popular in Germany. There are at least two St Brunos. One, born in Germany, founded the monastic order of Carthusians in 1084. The other, who was an Italian, was renowned for his wisdom and was an adviser to four popes.

BRYAN is a variant spelling of *Brian*. SEE Brian

BRYN is a Welsh name possibly related to *Brian* and meaning 'hill, height'. The famous American College *Bryn Mawr*, 'big hill', was founded near Philadelphia in 1880 by the Quakers.

BYRAM and Byron are now well established given names and both come from the Old English phrase *æt þæm byrum*, 'at the cowsheds'. SEE Byron

BYRON Lord Byron (1788-1824), the romantic poet, became an overnight sensation with the publication of *Childe Harold's Pilgrimage* (1812) and although his readers were shocked by the rumours of his wild lifestyle, his poetry made him a wealthy man. He died of malaria trying to help in the Greek fight for independence.

NOTABLE NAMESAKES
Baruch (Benedict) de Spinoza (1632-77) Dutch philosopher of Portuguese Jewish origin; Beniamino Gigli (1890-1957) Italian singer, often regarded as being one of the best operatic tenors of all time; Bertrand Russell (1872-1970) British philosopher and pacifist; Bob Hope (1903-2003) born in England but achieved fame in America as a comedian and film actor; Brad Pitt (1963) American

film actor and producer who has often been voted one of the world's handsomest men.

C

CADMAN/CAEDMON

These names may be variants or they may come from totally different sources. They may mean 'Cada's man', in the same way that Cadbury means 'Cada's settlement'. *Cada* was an Old English name that meant 'spirit'. The second variant is the name of the first Anglo-Saxon to write religious poetry in Old English. He was a herdsman at a monastic settlement near Whitby. This settlement had very close links with Ireland and so *Caed* may mean 'free' or 'battle' and *mon*, 'man'. Readers who enjoy Ellis Peters (1913-95) will remember the monk called Brother *Cadfael*. His name is almost certainly Welsh, where the *Cad* means 'battle'.

CAIN is of Hebrew origin and may mean 'possessed'. He was the son of *Adam* and *Eve*, and the brother of *Abel*. According to the *Book of Genesis*, *Cain* killed *Abel* because *Abel's* offerings seemed to be more acceptable to God. Because of its biblical associations, *Cain* is unlikely to be used but the alternative spelling *Kane* is extremely popular. It is possible that *Cain* will be rescued from its negative associations. It can come from Irish *cian*, 'dark one', or *Cathán*, 'war champion'. SEE Kane

CALE is a frequently used abbreviation of *Caleb* or it could be related to Irish *caol*, 'slender'. SEE Caleb

CALEB is a Hebrew name. Its etymology has been debated but it may mean 'hound', a meaning that would link it to *Cuchulain*, 'the hound of Cullen'. In the Old Testament, *Caleb* left Egypt with Moses and was blessed in that he was permitted to see and to enter the Promised Land.

CALUM/CALLUM is a Scots Gaelic form of *columba*, 'the dove'. The Irish equivalent is *Colm*. The spelling with 'll' is the more usual one. Boys to whom this name is given are being linked to the dove of peace and purity. They are also being associated with the Holy Spirit, who appeared in the form of a dove and whose blessings include wisdom, understanding and fortitude. SEE Colm

CALVIN tends to be reserved for Puritans or Non-Conformists. It comes from the surname of John Calvin (1509-64), the French theologian and reformer. His name is a dialectal diminutive of *chauve*, 'bald', and so means 'little bald one'. *Cal* is sometimes used as an abbreviation.

CALVINO is an Italian variant of *Calvin*. SEE Calvin

CAMERON is one of the many Gaelic surnames adopted as a given name. It is the name of a major Scottish clan and comes from *cam*, 'crooked' + *srón*,

'nose'. (Noses were apparently of more significance in the days before plastic surgery!) It has been argued that *Courtney* means 'short nose' and the French scholar Pascal (1623-62) is reputed to have claimed: 'If Cleopatra's nose had been shorter, the whole face of the world would have changed.'

CAMILO/CAMILLO is a male equivalent of *Camilla*. It comes from an old Roman family name, *Camillus*. Its meaning is uncertain. It may suggest 'noble'. It is rarely found outside Spanish circles.

CAMPBELL The *Campbells* were and are one of the great Scottish clans. Their name has been debated and may have several etymologies. It may come from *cam*, 'crooked' + *beul*, 'mouth', or from *de campo bello*, 'concerning the field of battle', or *cath*, battle' + *maol*, 'chieftain'. *Campbell* is one of many Gaelic surnames adopted as a given name.

CANUTE (pronounced 'can + oot' or 'k + noot') is only found occasionally but the form *Knut* is growing in popularity. *Canute* was king of England (1017-35) and also king of Denmark and Norway. While he was king, England experienced peace and some prosperity. The name is old and its meaning debatable but Old Norse had two possible origins. 'Knot' was *knutr* and 'knuckle' was *knuta*. *Canute* is best remembered for a story which may have little validity. Some of his ministers told him that he was all-powerful and could do anything. Canute showed them that he was only human by ordering the sea to turn back. The sea ignored him, as *Canute* knew it would. SEE Knut

CARADOC/CARADOG (pronounced 'car + a + dock') is a Welsh name that goes back at least two millennia. The first part of the name, *cara*, means 'beloved' and the second part is uncertain. *Caradoc* was a Welsh hero who stood up against the might of the Roman army in the first century. He was defeated but impressed the Romans with his courage.

CAREY/CARY (rhymes with 'Mary' or, less frequently, 'marry'). This name occurs almost equally in both spellings. It comes from a Somerset river called *Cary*, which is of Celtic origin and may be related to *caer*, 'fortress' or to Irish *ciar*, 'dark'. The name was popularised by the film star Cary Grant, who usually played the role of a suave, attractive gentleman.

CARL is an alternative spelling of *Karl*, the German form of *Charles*. Old English had *ceorl* and Old Norse had *karl*, meaning 'man, male, ordinary person rather than a noble'. This form of *Charles* has become very popular throughout Europe although *Karl* is perhaps catching up. SEE Charles and Karl

CARLO is an Italian form of *Charles*. SEE Charles

CARLOS is a Spanish form of *Charles*. It is based on *Carolus*, the

Latin form of the Germanic name. SEE Charles

CARMICHAEL is a Celtic surname that is becoming more widely used as a given name. The name means 'Michael's fort' and the 'Michael' referred to is the Archangel whose Hebrew name means 'Who is like God?' The name is found throughout the British Isles but especially in Scotland. There is a lovely Scottish ballad that has Mary, Queen of Scots, describe her feelings on the morning that she was executed by her cousin, Queen Elizabeth in 1587. The refrain is:

Last night there were four Maries,
Tonight, there'll be but three.
There was Mary Seaton and Mary Beaton
And Mary Carmichael and me.
SEE Michael

CAROL used to be a boy's name. It was an anglicised form of Latin *Carolus*. As so often happens, as soon as *Carol* was adopted as a girl's name, it ceased to be widely used for boys. SEE Carl and Charles

CAROLUS is the Latin form of the Germanic name that means 'male, ordinary person'. SEE Charles

CARROLL may have two sources. It may be a modified spelling of *Carl* or it may be an anglicised spelling of an Irish surname that means 'warrior'. SEE Charles

CARSON is a surname that is becoming fashionable. It means 'son of Carr' and the 'Carr' may be from Old English *carr*, 'rock', or from an abbreviation of a given name such as Scandinavian, *Kare*, pronounced to rhyme with 'car + ray' or English *Carlton*.

CARY is an alternative spelling of *Carey*. SEE Carey

CARYL is now most frequently used as a girl's name although it was originally a variant of both *Carl* and *Carroll*. SEE Carroll and Charles

CASEY is an Irish surname that is now regularly used as a given name. It means 'watchful, vigilant'.

BOYS

CASIMIR (pronounced 'caz + ee + mere') is a popular Polish name that means 'bringer of peace'. It is also regularly spelt *Kasimir*.

CASPAR is used in Germany and Eastern Europe as the equivalent of English *Jasper*. The name seems to be of Persian origin and means 'keeper of treasure'. Although there is no biblical support for the claim, Christians have believed that *Caspar* was the name of one of the Magi who brought presents of gold, frankincense and myrrh to honour the baby Jesus. The names of the other Magi were *Balthasar* and *Melchior*, neither of which has achieved the same degree of acceptance as *Caspar*, possibly because of the cartoon 'Caspar the friendly Ghost'.

CAVAN/CAVIN may be interpreted in a variety of ways. It may be the adoption of a county name as a given name. In this, it would resemble *Derry* and *Kerry*, or it may be a modified form of *Caoimhín*, 'handsome'. It is also possible that it is derived from *caoimhneas*, 'gentleness', and is a name in its own right. SEE Kevin

CECIL is not as widespread now as it once was but it is a name with a long history of use. There are two competing views regarding its origin. It may come from a Welsh form of a name for 'Sixth', coming from Latin *Sextus*, or it may be derived from the old Latin surname *Caecilius* that also gave us *Cecilia*. The Roman name may have come from a nickname, *Caecus*, 'blind'. The Cecils were an exceptionally powerful family from the 16th century. William Cecil (1520-98) was Queen Elizabeth's closest advisor and Secretary of State. He became Lord Burghley and acquired great power and wealth for his family. The surname became a given name and spread throughout the English-speaking world.

CEDRIC Just as Shakespeare gave the world *Cordelia*, Sir Walter Scott created *Cedric* as the name of a character in his novel *Ivanhoe* (1819). It is possible that Scott based *Cedric* on the Old

English name *Cerdic*. It is also possible that it comes from a Gaelic word meaning 'first choice' or that it is a blend where the second syllable parallels such names as *Baldric*, 'brave ruler', where the 'ric' is a Germanic word that comes from the same root as German *reich*. The name is pronounced in two ways: the first syllable may rhyme with 'red' or 'reed'.

CEPHAS (pronounced 'sea + fas') is extremely well known but not widely used. It is from Aramaic, *kefa*, 'stone, rock', and was the name given to St Peter.

CHAD is the modern equivalent of *Ceadda*, the name of a 7th-century saint and bishop of Mercia. There was a cult in his honour from the time of his death in 672. St Bede was a devotee of St Chad and is supposed to have advised people that dust from Chad's grave could be used to cure illnesses in both people and animals if mixed with water and drunk. The meaning of *Chad* is uncertain but it may be connected with Old English *cedelc*, a herb sometimes called 'field mustard'. Modern use of *Chad* possibly owes more to Chad Valley toys than to the English saint. The toys were called after the valley through which the river Chad runs. The African country, Chad, is a source of some recent uses.

BOY'S NAME TO GIRL

Some names that were once exclusively given to boys have now become more popular for girls:

Beverley

Charlie

Evelyn

Hilary

Jocelyn

Jody

Jordan

Kelly

Kerry

Robin

Shirley

Sidney

CHAIM is a popular Jewish name. It comes from Hebrew *chayyim* and means 'life'. It is sometimes written as *Hyam*. The initial 'Ch' is often pronounced like 'h' in English but the original sound is closer to the 'ch' in Scottish 'loch'.

CHANDLER For over a decade, the television series *Friends* was extremely popular and, as one of the friends was *Chandler*, it is understandable that he gave a boost to the popularity of this name. It is a trade name coming from Old French, *chandelier*, 'candle maker, seller of candles'. Like many trade names, such as 'Barber' and 'Butler', *Chandler* became a surname and then a given name.

CHARLES is a perennially favoured name worldwide and it appears in such forms as *Carl*, *Carlo*, *Carlos*, *Carolus*, *Carroll*, *Carey*, *Cary*, *Charley*, *Charlie*, *Chas*, *Chuck*, *Karel*, *Karl*, *Karel*, *Searluis* and *Tearlach* and it has given rise to several female variants. The name is from a Germanic noun that meant 'man, ordinary person' and is from the same root as English *churl*, which originally simply meant 'a male human being, a husband'. The name has been held by many rulers including Charlemagne (742-814), who became the Holy Roman Emperor in AD 800 , and the ill-fated Charles I of England, who was executed in 1649. It became popular in Scotland and Ireland in the 18th century because of Bonnie Prince Charlie, the 'Young Pretender', whose attempt to reclaim the British throne was finally defeated in 1745.

CHARLTON There are over eight towns in England with this name, which derives from Old English *ceorlatun*, 'settlement of ordinary people'. The place name became a surname and then a given name. One reason why surnames become given names is that there is a tradition of giving the eldest son his mother's surname as a middle name. Often the middle name is preferred. The actor Charlton Heston got his name in this way.

CHAS is a popular abbreviated form of *Charles*. SEE Charles

CHESTER A *chester* is a walled city or town that was originally occupied by the Romans. It comes from Latin *castra*, a 'camp', and the different regions of England pronounced the name differently, resulting in such place names as *Cirencester*, *Manchester* and *Tadcaster*. People often used the place they came from as a surname and the surname *Chester* became a popular given name. It has produced two popular abbreviated forms: *Ches* and *Chet*.

CHET SEE Chester

CHRÉTIEN is the French form of *Christian*, 'follower of Christ'. SEE Christian

CHRISTIAN is the normal adjective from *Christ*, which comes from Greek *Khristos*, 'the anointed one, the Messiah'. *Christian*, 'follower of Christ', became popular as a given name in England in the Middle Ages and its popularity was increased by Christian, the central character in John Bunyan's allegorical novel, *The Pilgrim's Progress* (1678-84), and by Fletcher Christian (1764-93), the first mate on Captain Bligh's ship, HMS *Bounty*. In April 1789, Christian led a mutiny and took over the ship. The mutineers settled on the island of Pitcairn in 1790.

CHRISTOPHE is a French form of *Christopher*, 'bearer of Christ'. SEE Christopher

CHRISTOPHER is one of the most frequently used names in the 21st century. It comes from Greek *Khristos*, 'Christ' + *pherein*, 'to bear or carry'. The name appears to go back to a legendary 3rd-century saint, who has become the patron of travellers. According to tradition, *Christopher* was a very big man who used to carry people across a river when it was too rough to travel by boat. One stormy night, a little boy asked him to take him across the river. As he went across, Christopher noticed that the child was getting heavier and heavier. Eventually, it was revealed that the little boy was the Christ child and that Christopher was carrying both him and the weight of the world's sins on his shoulders. The usual abbreviations are *Chris*, *Christie*, *Christy*, *Kit*, *Kris* and *Kriss*. Variants of the name include *Christophero* and *Christophorus*.

CHUCK is an American abbreviation of *Charles*.

CIAN (pronounced 'key + in') is one of the many Irish names to become popular outside Ireland. It comes from Gaelic *cian*, 'ancient'. It is occasionally used as an equivalent of *Kane*, although the Irish surname *O'Kane* comes from a different source and means 'warrior'. SEE Kane

CIARÁN is an Irish name meaning 'little dark one'. It has been the name of at least 26 Irish saints. One of them, St Ciarán of Saighir, died around AD 530. He is often said to be the 'first' apostle of Ireland in that he was St Patrick's precursor.

CLARENCE is derived from an English royal title, the Duke of Clarence. This, or its Latin equivalent, *Dux Clarentiae*, was the 14th-century title of Edward III's son. He took the title because his wife was a rich heiress from Clare, Suffolk. The Suffolk town takes its name from the local river and may come from either Old English *clayar*, 'gentle', or from an even older Celtic name, similar to Welsh *claear*, 'lukewarm'. In spite of appearances, the name is unrelated to the girl's name *Clare*.

CLARK Anyone who has ever read or watched a film or television programme about Superman will know that *Clark Kent* was his name when he was functioning as a reporter! *Clark* comes from a surname which owes its origin to Latin *clericus*, 'a man in holy orders'. It is, in origin, the same name as 'clerk'. In medieval England, 'er' was usually pronounced 'ar' and *Derby*, for example, was written 'er' but pronounced like 'ar'.

CLAUD/CLAUDE came into English from French, where the final 'e' is used. It has its origin in an ancient Roman family name which comes from the nickname *claudus*, 'lame'. The Latin form was *Claudius* and it was the name of a Roman Emperor (10 BC – AD 54) who succeeded Caligula. *Claudius* is credited with restoring law and order to the empire.

CLAUDIO is an Italian form of *Claud*. SEE Claud

CLAUS (rhymes with 'house') is an abbreviation of German *Niklaus*, one of the many forms of *Nicholas*, 'victory of the people'. SEE Klaus and Nicholas

CLEMENT is an English form of Latin *clemens*, 'merciful, mild, gentle, kind'. One of the earliest popes was called *Clement*. He held the papacy from about AD 88 -97 and was probably the third pope after St Peter. Several other popes and saints have had this name, which is currently experiencing a revival.

CLIFF comes from Old English *clif*, 'steep rock-face'. It was originally adopted as a given name from the surname *Clifford*, the name of several English towns meaning 'ford at the cliff or slope'. *Cliff* is now a given name in its own right.

CLIFFORD means 'ford at the cliff'. SEE Cliff

CLINT It is possible that some 'Clints' derive their name from the Yorkshire town of Clint, which comes from Danish *klint*, 'hill' although most are likely to be from an abbreviated form of *Clinton*, a surname combining Danish *klint*, 'hill', and *tun*, 'settlement'. *Cliff*, *Clint* and *Craig* are all strong names that became popular in the 20th century. They are all linked to 'rock' and might even be thought of as a modern form of *Peter*.

CLINTON SEE Clint

CLIVE is derived from Old English *clif*, 'steep rock-face', and is a variant of *Cliff*. It became very popular in England because of Lord Robert Clive of India (1725-74). He was a British general and colonial administrator who did much to reform the administration of India.

CLYDE It is perhaps more usual for girls to be called after rivers, if we think of *Afton*, for example, or *Shannon*, but *Clyde* seems to be taken from the river in Glasgow. The origin of the river's name is debated but it may come from Old English *clud*, 'rock', or from Celtic adjectives meaning 'warm' or 'noisy'.

CODY is a surname that has been widely used for both girls and boys since the middle of the 20th century. In this it resembles *Jody*. It is possible that the surname comes from Old Norse *koddi*, 'pillow, bag', but its exact meaning is uncertain.

COLIN has been popular in Europe since the Middle Ages. It is likely that it is a diminutive of *Col*, a pet form of *Nicholas*, 'victory to the people'. The name may have arisen independently in Ireland and Scotland, where it may come from the Gaelic word

for 'pup'. To modern ears, 'pup' does not have the same connotation as in Gaelic society, where *cú/conn* meant 'dog, hound' but could be used to imply 'warrior'.

COLM is the Irish equivalent of *Callum*. It comes from Latin *columba*, 'dove'. The name was held by one of the most famous of Irish saints, St Columba (521-97) or *Colmcille*, 'the dove of the church'. He was a missionary who established the monastery of Iona, from where Celtic Christianity spread throughout Scotland, England and many parts of Europe. SEE Callum

COLMAN (pronounced 'coal + man') is, like *Colm*, derived from Latin *columba*, 'dove', and it is the name of many early Irish saints. The surname *Colman/Coleman* may come from the given name, or English *Colman* may mean 'Col's man' and either imply 'a devotee of St Nicholas' or a man who worked for *Nicholas*. SEE Nicholas

CON is an abbreviation of

several names beginning with *Con*, including *Connor* and *Constantine*. The form *Conn* with double 'n' is an Irish name, meaning 'noble'.

CONAL/CONALL/ CONNELL is an Irish given

name that may derive from *Conn*, 'noble', or *con(n)*, 'hound, warrior'. It can also come from the surname *O'Connell*, although this originally meant 'descendant of Conal'.

CONAN (rhymes with 'go

man') is related to Irish *Conn*, 'noble'. He appears in the mythological stories surrounding Finn Mac Cool. *Conan* became a surname and the surname was passed on as a middle name to Arthur Conan Doyle (1859-1930), the creator of Sherlock Holmes. *Conan the Barbarian* was a fantasy hero created by the American writer, Robert E Howard (1906-36) and brought to the screen by Arnold Swarzenegger in 1982.

CONNOR This ancient Irish

name has become universally popular and is now as likely to be found in Australia as in Ireland. This was the name of a great Irish king who lived at the time of Christ and who appears in the mythological cycles preserved by the early Christian monks. The meaning is debated. It may mean 'lover of hounds' or 'noble warrior'. Either way, it is a name that is likely to become as popular as *Seán*. It is just possible that *Connor* has been influenced by Middle English *connen*, 'to know, to have great understanding', in that a *conner* would be 'a knowledgeable person'.

CONRAD This German name

is also spelt *Konrad* and means 'brave advice'. It is the name of at least one 10th-century saint and it was popularised by the novelist Joseph Conrad (1857-1024), who was born in Poland but wrote his novels in English.

CONSTANTINE This is the

English and French form of Latin *Constantinus*, meaning 'absolutely steadfast'. It was adopted by

Christians because the Roman Emperor Constantine the Great (AD 288-337) adopted Christianity as the official religion of the Empire. It is sometimes abbreviated to *Con* and also appears as *Constantino* in Italy.

COREY/CORY The form with 'e' is a relatively common Irish surname that has been adopted as a given name. It may come from Irish and mean 'visitor' or it may be a modified form of the Germanic name, *Godfrey* from *god*, 'God, good' + *frid*, 'peace', and suggest 'the peace of God'. If we think of the latter meaning, this name is almost a salutation. Every time it is spoken, it is a wish for 'peace'.

CORMAC is an old Gaelic name. Its age is indicated by the position of *mac*, 'son'. The first syllable comes from an old word for 'raven', *corb*. In Celtic tradition, the raven symbolised the spirit world. An ancient bearer of this name, Cormac Mac Airt, was reputed to be the wisest man in the world.

CORNELIUS is the name of an old Roman family and may come from Latin *cornu*, 'horn' but the exact implication of the name has been lost. The abbreviation *Con* is occasionally used for *Cornelius*.

COSMO is the Italian form of Cosmas and is now more popular than the anglicised Greek form, which was *Kosmas*, a name that is related to 'cosmos' and implies 'natural order and beauty'. The names *Cosmas* and *Damian* regularly co-occur because they are early 4th-century brothers and saints. A variant of the name in the de Medici family was *Cosimo*. *Cosimo de Medici* (1389-1464) was an Italian statesman and banker. He became the ruler of Florence in 1434 and used his great wealth to promote painting and the arts. He is often regarded as a founding father of the Renaissance.

COURTNEY is a surname that has been used as a given name for both girls and boys. It was a noble Norman name and may derive from one of the towns in northern France called *Courtenay*, 'realm of Curtius', or it may be the result of a nickname *court nez*, 'short nose'.

CRAIG is a Gaelic name derived from *carraig*, 'rock'. There are similar forms in Irish, Scots Gaelic and Welsh and it is probable that they are the source of English 'crag'. The name implies 'rock' and it is extremely popular worldwide, partly because it has also been adopted from the Scottish surname, Craig.

CRISPIAN/CRISPIN The variant with 'a' was widespread in the Middle Ages but *Crispin* seems to be the preferred form now. Both come from an old Roman family name, *Crispus*, 'with curly hair'. St Crispin was a 3rd-century martyr. He and his brother Crispinian, reputedly lived in what is now France, and supported their preaching by working as shoemakers. The name is referred to in Shakespeare's *Henry V* because

the Battle of Agincourt took place on 25 October, the feast day of St Crispin:

> *Then will he strip his sleeve and show his scars*
> *And say: 'These wounds I had on Crispin's day.'*

CURT was originally used in England and Germany as an abbreviated form of *Konrad*, the Germans preferring *Kurt*, which is also popular now in English-speaking communities. It is not related to the English adjective 'curt', which comes from French *court*, meaning 'short, brusque'. SEE Conrad

CURTIS has also given rise to the abbreviation *Curt* so parents may select their preferred meaning. *Curtis* comes from an old French adjective, *curteis*, 'courteous'. It was regularly used as a nickname and became a surname. In the Middle Ages, the adjective 'courteous' implied much more than it does now and suggested 'having the manners of a prince, being gracious, mannerly and respectful'.

CUTHBERT is one of the many Germanic '-bert' names to be adopted worldwide. We also have *Albert* and *Robert*, for example. The first syllable comes from a verb meaning 'to know' and so suggests 'knowledge' and the second syllable is the same word that has given us 'bright'. St Cuthbert was a 7th-century bishop of Lindisfarne. He died in 687 and many miracles were attributed to him. St Cuthbert was trained in Celtic Christianity and was directly in line from St Aidan. SEE Aidan

CYPRIAN comes from Greek and means 'one from Cyprus'. The Latin form was *Cyprius*. The name became popular throughout Christendom because of St Cyprian, who died around AD 258. He was a martyr and was one of the earliest scholars to write about the necessity for church unity.

CYREK continues to be popular in Poland. The name comes from the 4th-century martyr St Cyricus, who is reputed to have been killed as a child with his mother. He is the patron saint of children.

CYRIL comes from the Greek word *kyrios*, 'lord', and it was the name of several saints, the best known of whom is the Greek missionary priest who has given his name to the Cyrillic alphabet that is used to write Russian and many of the Slavic languages. St Cyril is highly regarded in the Orthodox church because he taught through the medium of the Slavic languages. He lived from 826-69.

CYRUS like *Cyril*, comes from Greek *kirios*, 'lord', although it may be Persian in origin. It was certainly the name of several Persian rulers. Cyrus the Great, for example, died around 530 BC and founded an empire that included Syria, Palestine and most of Asia Minor. He is reputed to have ruled with wisdom and kindness. Certainly, he was benign in setting free the Jews from their Babylonian captivity.

CYRYL is the Polish form of *Cyril*. SEE Cyril

D

NOTABLE NAMESAKES
Calvin Klein (b. 1942)
American fashion designer
whose name is also used on
perfumes and jewellery;
Cecil B deMille (1881-1954)
one of the most successful
film-makers of the first half
of the 20th century. Noted
for lavish spectaculars such
as *The Ten Commandments*,
he also produced hundreds
of silent films; Cliff Richard
(b. 1940) Indian-born
English singer whose career
has spanned six decades;
Colin Firth (b. 1960) English
actor whose performance as
Mr Darcy in the BBC
television series, *Pride and
Prejudice* (1995) brought
him international acclaim.

DACEY (pronounced 'dace + ee') is an Irish name meaning 'southerner'. It is related to *Desmond*. SEE Desmond

DAHAB (pronounced 'dah + hab') is an Arabic name meaning 'gold'. Gold has been valued in virtually all cultures and, since time immemorial, parents have regarded their children as precious. That is why they often choose to name their children after precious metals or jewels.

DAI (pronounced 'die') is a Welsh form of *David*, 'beloved'. SEE David

DAIKI (pronounced 'die + key') is a popular Japanese name for a son. It means 'of great value'. Without children, many parents feel that life is meaningless and a child that comes after a long wait is exceptionally valuable.

DALE has been a surname since the 13th century. It means 'one

BOYS

who lives in a dale or valley'. The surname became a given name originally in the United States but now it is found in most English-speaking communities. It is now also given to girls.

DALEY/DALY Irish surnames make particularly good given names because the majority of them were originally given names! *Daley* comes from *Ó Dálaigh*, 'descendant of Dálach' and *Dalach* comes from *dáil*, 'assembly'. *Daley* would thus be the equivalent of 'councillor'. *Daley* and *Daly* have both been used as surnames since the 13th century but some of the uses may be a modified form of *Dale*.

DALTON is a surname based on place names that are found throughout northern England and means 'one who lives in a valley settlement'. The name became popular because of the fame of John Dalton (1766-1844) who is regarded as the father of atomic theory. He also gave the first comprehensive description of 'daltonism' or colour blindness.

DALZIEL For most Scots, this surname is pronounced like 'dee + yell' and it has developed from the name of a barony in Lanarkshire into a surname and now a given name. The spelling with 'z' is actually a mistake. The older spelling was *Dalyhel* or *Dalʒel* with 'ʒ' representing the 'y' sound. It was replaced by 'z' for ease of printing. The meaning is debated but members of the family claim that it means 'the beautiful meadow'.

DAMIAN/DAMIEN This is the name of a 4th century saint who was martyred with his brother, *Cosmas*. The name comes from Greek *Damianos* and it seems to be derived from a verb meaning 'to tame' or 'to subdue'. The form with 'ien' was originally French but it was popularised by Father Damien (1840-89), a Flemish missionary priest who dedicated his life to the service of the lepers of Hawaii. He eventually caught the disease himself and is honoured on 15 April in Hawaii. *Damiano* is the variant used in Italy, Spain and Portugal.

DAMON is a Greek name meaning 'to tame, to subdue'. In Greek mythology, *Damon* and Pythias were close friends who lived in Syracuse in the 4th century BC. Pythias was sentenced to death by Dionysius I. He wanted to put his affairs in order before dying, so *Damon* agreed to take his place in prison. When Pythias returned on the day of execution, Dionysius was so impressed by the courage and love shown by the two young men that he pardoned Pythias.

DAN Today, *Dan* is generally an abbreviated form of *Daniel* but it is an independent Hebrew name meaning 'judge'. In the Old Testament, *Dan* is a Hebrew prophet, the son of Jacob. It is also the name of a town in the north of Israel where the tribe of *Dan* settled.

DANA (pronounced 'dan + a' or 'dane + a') was popularised by the American film actor Dana Andrews (1909-92). His given name was the surname of a friend of his father's. The surname means 'Dane' and meant 'person who lived under the Danes in England'.

DANIEL This is one of the top ten choices for parents in Ireland, England, France and Germany since the 1990s, and it has been a top American choice since the 1950s. The fact that it has also been used as a surname since the 12th century indicates that it has been a popular choice for a long time. The Old Testament *Daniel* lived in the 6th century BC. He was a prophet who spent his life in captivity in Babylon. He was thrown into the Lion's Den but emerged unscathed. *Dan* and *Danny* are popular abbreviations.

DANTE (pronounced 'dan + tay') probably comes from Latin *durant*, meaning 'lasting, enduring'. Dante Alighieri (1265-1321) was an Italian poet who composed an epic, *The Divine Comedy*, that describes the progression of a soul from Hell, through Purgatory and finally into Paradise. Dante's epic was admired and imitated by poets throughout Europe. The name *dante* also occurs as the name of an African animal but this is probably unrelated.

DARBY/DERBY This word can be a city, a surname and a given name and it can have at least two etymologies. The English city derives from an Old Scandinavian form, *diurby*, meaning 'settlement where there are deer'. It has been used as a surname since the 12th century and has been pronounced like 'dar + by' since the late Middle Ages. In Ireland, the form *Darby* is the usual spelling. It is often regarded as an anglicised form of *Diarmaid*, 'without envy'.

DARCY is a Norman surname originally given to people who had come from Arcy in northern France. The Irish surname may come from John D'Arcy, who settled in Ireland during the 14th century. The surname was also used by Irish families called *Ó Dorchaidhe*, 'descendant of the dark-haired one'. The surname became a given name partly because of the custom, in certain circles, of addressing or referring to a man by his surname.

DARIEN is possibly a variant of *Darren* but it is also possible that it was inspired by a line in a sonnet by John Keats (1795-1821) as he described the Spaniard explorer Cortez:

Silent, upon a peak in Darien

The place name once referred to the entire Isthmus of Panama. A group of Scottish settlers established a colony in Darien in the late 17th century but conditions were hard and the colony failed.

DARRELL Like *Darcy*, this name started life as a Norman surname reflecting the fact that certain families had come from *Airelle* in France. *Darrell* is the most frequently used spelling although *Darell*, *Darrel*, *Daryl* and *Darryl* also occur. It began to be used as a given name in the 19th century and has been popular ever since. The town's name may be linked to the Latin adjective *aereus*, 'airy'.

DARREN is currently widely used throughout the English-speaking world. It is possible that it comes from the Norman name adopted by settlers from Airaines. The Irish name is likely to have its origin in *dara*, 'oak tree'. Like *Darrell*, this name has a range of spellings including *Darin*, *Daron* and *Darrin*.

DAVID has been one of the most widely used given names in the British Isles. It is the name of the patron saint of Wales and was the given name of two Scottish kings. *David* is a Hebrew name, probably meaning 'beloved'. In the Old Testament, David lived about 1000 years before Christ and was one of the most famous of the kings of Israel. He was the son of Jesse and when he was a boy he killed the Philistine giant, Goliath, with his slingshot. King David has usually been given credit for writing the Psalms, although many scholars doubt that they are the work of one man. David's son was *Solomon* and, according to Hebraic tradition, the Messiah was to be descended from *David*. *Dave*, *Davey*, *Davie* and *Davy* are widely used abbreviations.

DAVIES/DAVIS Both these forms mean 'son of Davy' and they have been surnames for over 700 years. They are currently in use as given names, largely due to the growing tradition of giving a son his mother's maiden name as one of his names. SEE David

DEAN/DEANE *Dean* is widely used as a place name in England. It comes from an Old English word *denu*, 'valley'. Over time, people adopted *Dean* as a surname and passed it on to their sons. There is a second explanation for some *Deans*. They take their surname from Old French *dien*, 'dean', in the same way as butlers' sons adopted 'Butler' or bakers' children began to be known as *Baker*. *Dean* experienced a burst of popularity during and after the 1950s due to the fame of the film actor, James Dean (1931-55). For many, he symbolised youth culture.

DECLAN is a version of the long-established Gaelic name, *Deaglán*, possibly meaning 'full of goodness'. This is the name of a 5th-century Irish saint who was born in Waterford and trained to be a priest in Rome. He knew St Patrick but did not owe his conversion to him. St Declan was honoured for centuries and many miracles were attributed to him, including the sinking of a fleet of pirates who were about to attack Ireland. Recently, the abbreviation *Deckie* has begun to be used.

DEKKEL is a widespread Arabic name meaning 'date palm'. In some cultures, the date is symbolic in the same way as bread and wine are in others.

DEL is regularly used as an abbreviation of *Derek*, 'gift of God', but it is also used in African American and Caribbean communities as a prefix to created names such as *Delmar*, 'noble and famous' and also 'from the sea', and *Delroy*, 'of the king'. A similar use is made of *La* for

girls' names, producing such coinages as *Lalene*, *Latonia* and *Latoyah*. SEE Dell

DELANEY/DELANY is a popular Irish surname, meaning 'trained warrior'. It can also be a version of a Norman name deriving from *aunaie*, 'alder grove'. A 12th century version of the name was *Del Aunei* or *De Launay*. Like many Irish surnames, it makes a very attractive given name.

DELL The Middle English word *delle*, 'hole, valley', has given rise to a surname and to place names such as *Arundel*, 'hoar-hound valley'. Although *Dell* was originally a boy's name, there is evidence that it is being given increasingly to girls.

DEMING is a Chinese name, sometimes spelt as two words, *De Ming*, and pronounced like 'day + ming'. This name means 'virtue bright' and is given by parents in China with essentially the same intention as Puritan parents calling a child *Patience*.

DEMOS (pronounced 'day +

mos' or 'dee + mos') is used mainly in the Greek community. It is often an abbreviation of *Demosthenes*, 'power of the people'. *Demosthenes* was an Athenian statesman who overcame a stammer by training himself to speak with pebbles in his mouth. (There are kinder methods of achieving the same end.) He was an orator who spoke fearlessly against aggressive rulers.

DEMPSEY is an anglicised form of the Irish surname, *Ó Díomasaigh*, 'descendant of the proud one'. It started to be used as a given name in the United States but is no longer limited to this region. Jack Dempsey (1895-1983) was heavyweight boxing champion of the world between 1919 and 1926. His fame popularised the name in America.

DENIS/DENNIS The spelling with one 'n' is the norm in France and is used for its patron saint. The spelling with '-nn-' is usual elsewhere. This name comes from Greek *Dionysius*

and its meaning is uncertain. The first two syllables are related to *Zeus* and *deus*, meaning 'god' so the name probably implies 'godlike'. This meaning would fit with the facts in that *Dionysius* was probably a Persian rather than a Greek god and so not fully integrated into the classical pantheon. The French patron saint died around AD 250. He was born in Italy and his Latin name was *Dionysius*. He was sent from Rome to help in the conversion of Gaul and became bishop of Paris. Later, he was martyred by order of the Emperor Valerian. The French devotion to St Denis was strong for over 1000 years and many of the Norman soldiers and officers were called after him.

DENZEL/DENZIL is a Cornish name, usually said to be composed of *Denis + el* and meaning 'little Denis'. It is also possible that it has been influenced by the Cornish noun *danas*, 'fallow deer'. The Cornish diminutive ending *el* would thus make the name mean 'little deer', an exact equivalent of Irish *Oisín*. It has been a surname since the 12th century and a given name since the 16th. The Academy Award-winning actor, Denzel Washington (b.1954), has popularised the name in America. SEE Denis and Oisín

DERBY This given name is often derived from the name of the English city, meaning 'deer settlement'. It began to be used as a surname in the 12th century. SEE Darby

DEREK/DERRICK Forms of *Derek* have been used as surnames since the early 16th century, when Dutch settlers introduced this form of the Germanic name *Theodoric*, 'power of the tribe'. SEE Dirk

DERMOT is an anglicised form of the Gaelic name *Diarmaid*, 'without envy'. It has a variety of spellings including *Dermid*, *Diarmid* and *Diarmuid*. In Scotland the surname *Mac Diarmaid* is regularly pronounced like *Mac Dermott*, which also

occurs. There have been several Irish saints of this name. A 6th-century saint, for example, was the spiritual director of St Ciarán of Clonmacnois, which became the greatest monastic settlement in Ireland.

DERRY is often an abbreviation of other names such as *Alexander* or *Andrew*, but it can be used to reflect a connection with the city of *Derry* or one of the many towns beginning with *Derry* and meaning 'oak grove'.

DESMOND looks like *Edmond* or *Esmond* and its spelling has certainly been influenced by these Germanic names. *Desmond* is, however, an Irish name originally applied to someone from *Deas Mumhán*, 'south Munster'. The Old Irish *Des-Muma* was a territory in southwest Ireland taking in Kerry and Limerick. The Fitzgeralds became 'Earls of Desmond' in the 14th century. *Desmond* is no longer limited to the south of Ireland and has been spread throughout the world by Irish emigrants. The usual abbreviations are *Des*, *Desi* and *Dessie*. In each of these, the 's' is pronounced like 'z'.

DEVEN/DEVIN/DEVON

This name can have a number of possible origins. It may be from Old French *devin*, which is the same word as modern 'divine' but implying 'excellence' rather than supernatural powers. It can also be a place name and imply 'from Devon'. The county of Devon is from Celtic *Dubona*, 'black water'. It may also derive from the Irish surname *Devine*, which can be an Anglicisation of *Ó Daimhín*, 'descendant of the little stag', or of *Ó Duibhín*, 'descendant of the little dark one'.

DEVENISH is most likely to

come from Old English *defenisc*, 'man from Devon'. It has been used as a surname since the beginning of the 13th century and is found as both a surname and a given name in the Caribbean.

DEWAIN This is the least

widely used variant of *Duane*. SEE Duane

DEWI (pronounced 'dew +

ee') is a Welsh form of *David*, 'beloved', and it is experiencing a revival in use. The 5th-century St David, who is the patron saint of Wales, was known as St Dewi. SEE David

DEXTER has two origins. It

may come from Latin *dexter*, 'right, handy, dexterous', and has many positive connotations, including the meaning of 'lucky, auspicious'. *Dexter* can also come from a surname that is based on a trade and has been in use since the 13th century. It comes from Old English *deag*, 'dye' + *ester*, 'female ending'. In Old English, male and female versions of the same trade were differentiated and this is seen in surnames. *Baker*, for example, meant 'male cook', whereas *Baxter* meant 'female cook'. A similar gender distinction was made between *Dyer* and *Dexter* and *Webber*, 'weaver', and *Webster*.

DIARMAID/DIARMID/ DIARMUID (pronounced 'jeer

+ mid', 'deer + mid' or 'der + mot') These spellings are used for the same name which seems to be based on Gaelic *di*, 'without' + *(h)airmit*, 'envy', and which is sometimes translated as 'free man'. Several Irish saints have borne this name. The 8th-century Diarmaid founded a hermitage called *Díseart Diarmada* in Kildare in AD 818. This was one of the earliest 'Deserts' to appear in Ireland. Many Irish monks sought solitude so as to be totally at one with God and these hermitages gave rise to such place names as *Desertmartin* and *Desertmore*. SEE Dermot

DICK *Dick* and *Dickie* are popular abbreviations of *Richard*, 'powerful and strong'. The popularity of *Richard* can be seen in the proliferation of pet names and in the fact that it has given rise to such surnames as *Dickens*, *Dickenson*, *Dickie*, *Dicks* and *Dix* as well as several beginning with 'R'. In the Middle Ages, *Dickon* was one of the most popular abbreviations of *Richard* but that pet name has disappeared. SEE Richard

DIEGO (pronounced 'dee +

egg + o') is a Spanish form of *Jacob* or *James*, 'one who supplants'. It was popularised by Diego Maradona (b. 1960), the Argentine player whom many regard as the most talented footballer of all time. At first glance, it is hard to see how *James*, *Jacob* and *Diego* are related, but the links can be explained. It is also possible that *Diego* has been influenced by the Latin name *Didacus*, meaning 'instructed'. SEE Jacob

DIETER (rhymes with 'Peter') is a German name that has spread beyond Germany and Austria. It comes from an Old German name meaning 'army of the people' and it became extremely popular among German speakers in the early 20th century.

DILLON is an Irish surname that has recently become a given name, possibly under the influence of Welsh *Dylan*. The Irish name may mean 'ray of light' or 'faithful'. *Dillon* can also be a Welsh and English surname. In this latter case, the name probably comes from *Dilwyn* in Herefordshire. *Dilwyn* may have a Welsh source but it has also been influenced by the Old English word *dilge* meaning 'secret place, place of concealment'. SEE Dylan

DINO (pronounced 'dean + o') is an Italian name, possibly derived from Latin *decanus*, 'deacon, dean'. SEE Dean

DION (pronounced 'dee + on') comes from Greek *Dionysius*, 'godlike'. It is essentially the same name as *Dennis* but seems to be more attractive to many parents at the moment. SEE Denis

DIONIZY (pronounced 'dee + on + ee + zee') is a popular Polish form of *Denis*. SEE Denis

DIRK This is a form of *Derek*, 'power of the people', that is found in the Netherlands and parts of Belgium and Germany. It was given prominence in the 20th century by the popularity of the actor Dirk Bogarde (1921-99). The noun *dirk* meaning 'dagger' may also have contributed to the use of this name. In English, *Dirk* rhymes with 'work' but, on the

continent, the 'dir' is pronounced like 'deer'.

DIXON can be a direct use of the surname which is another form of Dickson, 'son of Richard'. It has also been used by some parents as an abbreviated form of *Benedict*, 'blessed'. SEE Benedict and Dick

DOBRÉE/DOBRY

(pronounced 'doe + bree') This name has limited circulation but, like many names, carries a history with it. The Huguenot Dobrées fled to London to avoid persecution. The name has been preserved as both a surname and a given name. It comes from *d'Aubry*, meaning 'from the white poplar grove'.

DOMHNAL/DOMHNALL /DÓNAL (pronounced 'doe + nal') These are variants of a widely-used name deriving from *domhan*, 'world', and suggesting 'ruler of the world'. The name is equally popular in Ireland and Scotland and has gained a foothold in communities with no or few Gaelic connections. SEE Donald

DOMINIC is a form of Latin *Domenicus*, which comes from *dominus*, 'lord'. Many children in the past were given this name in honour of St Dominic (c.1170-1221). He was born in Spain and named Domingo de Guzman. In 1216, he founded the Order of Preachers, or Dominicans, in Toulouse. This name is popular throughout the world and occurs in such forms as *Domenico* and *Domingo* as well as in the abbreviated forms of *Dom* and *Nic*.

DONALD is the usual international form of *Dónal*, 'ruler of the world'. The 'd' ending was added in the Middle Ages and is also found in *Dugald* for *Dougal* or *Dugal*, 'dark-haired foreigner or Dane'. *Donald* has given rise to the surname *Mac Donald*, the name of one of the biggest clans in Scotland. *Don* and *Donnie* are pet forms. SEE Domhnal

DONAT is a Polish name meaning 'gift'. It comes from Latin *donation*, 'gift, present'. For most Poles, the name is in honour of St Donatus. SEE Donatus

DONATO This form is used in Italy, Portugal and Spain. It means 'gift'. SEE Donatus

DONATUS *Donatus* is a Latin name meaning 'gift' and usually implying 'gift of God'. It is widely used in Africa as a Christian name, as for example, Donatus Nwoga, the Nigerian poet and academic. St Donatus, who died in AD 874, was the bishop of Fiesole, not far from Florence in Italy, but he was an Irishman who happened to stop off in Fiesole when returning to Ireland from Rome. The people of Fiesole needed a bishop and Donatus was seen as a gift from God. Even though he was an exile, *Donatus* never forgot Ireland. He wrote a life of St Brigid and established hospices throughout his diocese where travellers to and from Rome could find safe accommodation.

DONCHADH/ DONNCHADH/ DUNCHADH (pronounced
'done + uhuh') These are earlier forms of *Duncan*, a name that is used throughout the world. It

means 'dark-haired warrior' and it occurred in both Ireland and Scotland. Duncan (c.1001-1039) was king of Scotland and the historical figure Shakespeare introduces into *Macbeth*. For dramatic purposes, Shakespeare causes Duncan to be murdered by Macbeth, but he actually died in battle. SEE Duncan

DONG is widely used in China. It means both 'east' and 'winter' and is sometimes written with a 'u'. The related, and equally popular, *Donghai*, means 'east sea'.

DONOVAN This Irish surname is one of many that has been adopted as a given name. It comes from *Ó Donndubháin*, 'descendant of Donndubhán', and the name means either 'the little dark one' or 'the little dark prince'. The name has been well liked, partly because of its link with O'Donovan Rossa (1831-1915), the Cork patriot.

DORIAN *Dorian* may be a modified form of the Irish surname *Ó Deoradháin*, which means 'descendant of the little exile'. This link might explain why it was first used by Oscar Wilde (1854-1900) in his novel, *The Portrait of Dorian Gray*. In the story, Dorian Gray was an exceptionally handsome young man who managed to stay young and attractive while his portrait in the attic aged and showed all the signs of Dorian's misspent life. Whatever one might think of Dorian Gray, the name *Dorian* is worth considering.

DOUGAL The Irish and the Scots distinguished between the fair-haired Vikings from Norway, who were called *finn*, 'fair' + *gall*, 'foreigner', and the dark-haired Danes who were called *dubh*, 'dark, black' + *gall*, 'foreigner'. Both descriptions became given names. *Dougal* was the more popular form in Scotland, whereas the same name became *Doyle* in Ireland. In Scotland, too, it gave rise to the Mac Dougals.

DOUGLAS Versions of this old Celtic name are found throughout the British Isles. It

crops up as *Dulais* and *Dulas*
in Wales, as *Dawlish* in
England, and as Douglas in
the Isle of Man and Scotland.
It comes from a combination of
dubh, 'dark, black' + *glas*, 'water'.
The name gave rise to one of the
most important clans in Scotland.
It is not a version of *Dougal*,
although they share a common
element. *Douglas* is the older
name and is now popular among
people with no Celtic
connections.

DREW For most people, *Drew*
is an abbreviated form of *Andrew*,
'warrior', but it may also be
related to Gaelic *draoi*, 'magic',
and thus related to *Druid*. *Drew* is
regularly used as an independent
name and is particularly popular
in Australia. SEE Andrew

DROSTAN/DRUSTAN

This Irish name is likely to be
the ancestor of *Tristan*. It was the
name of a monk who died in Iona
around AD 610. It is not certain
what his name meant but it may
be linked to *druas*, meaning 'light
dew'.

DUANE/DWAIN/DWANE/DWAYNE
This name has
been popular for about 50 years.
It comes from the Irish surname
Ó Dubháin, 'descendant of the
little dark one', and it is
frequently used by African
Americans and by families from
the Caribbean.

DUB This name sounds like an
abbreviation of *Dublin*. It is,
however a Zulu name meaning
'zebra'. It tends to be pronounced
to rhyme with 'tube', not 'tub'.

DUGAL/DUGALD
These
are variant spellings of *Dougal*,
'dark foreigner, Dane'. SEE
Dougal

DUNCAN *Duncan* used to be
limited to Ireland and Scotland
but now it is found worldwide.
It comes from *Donnchadh*, 'brown
warrior', and it has been used as
a surname in the north of
England since the 12th century
and in Somerset since the 13th.
The '-can' ending is probably
due to a link with *ceann*, 'head'.
St *Dunchadh*, who died around
AD 717, was the abbot of Iona for

the last seven years of his life.

DUNE Dune is a Zulu name meaning 'headman' or 'chief'. It is pronounced as two syllables and rhymes with *Una*.

DUNSTAN is an Old English name, composed of *don(n)*, 'dark, brown' + *stan*, 'stone'. It seems likely that the first syllable was borrowed from the Celtic languages. In the 10th century, St Dunstan was the Archbishop of Canterbury.

DUSTAN/DUSTIN This given name has only been popular since the second half of the 20th century, although it has been the name of a town for much longer and a surname since the 12th century. The Northamptonshire town may simply mean 'dusty settlement' but the given name may have its roots in Scandinavian mythology. It seems to come from *Thorsteinn*, 'the stone of the thunder god Thor'. *Dustan* is occasionally abbreviated to *Dusty*.

DWAIN/DWAYNE These are variant spellings of *Duane*, 'descendant of the little dark one'. SEE Duane

DWIGHT has been an English surname since the 14th century and a given name for just over 100 years. The name was popularised by Dwight D. Eisenhower (1890-1969), who was the allied commander during World War II and later President of the United States. It comes from the name *Diot*, which died out in the Middle Ages but which is a form of *Dionisia*, 'goddess'. SEE Denis

DYLAN is a Welsh name that was given a worldwide exposure by the poet Dylan Thomas (1914-53). The name may be related to Irish *Dillon*, 'ray of light' or 'faithful', but it is more likely that it comes from Welsh *dy*, 'great' + *llanw*, 'sea', suggesting 'son of the great sea'. SEE Dillon

NOTABLE NAMESAKES
Dale Carnegie (1888-1955) American writer, best known for his book *How to Win Friends and Influence*

BOYS

People which has not been out of print since first published in 1936; David Beckham (b.1975) once the world's highest-paid professional footballer, captained the English national team on fifty-eight occasions (2000-06). Has become an advertising brand and fashion icon; Derek Edward (Del Boy) Trotter is the fictional hero of the BBC comedy series *Only Fools and Horses*. The part is played by David Jason (b. 1940); Douglas MacArthur (1880-1964) American General who was, in part, responsible for the conduct of World War II in the Pacific.

E

EAMON/EAMONN

(pronounced 'aim + on') is the Irish equivalent of the Germanic name, *Edmund*, 'prosperity and protection'. It has a variety of spellings, including *Éamon* and *Éamonn*. It is extremely popular at the moment, especially in Ireland and among Irish people living in England. SEE Edmond

EBEN/EBENEZER Most

people regard *Eben* as a reduced form of the Hebrew name *Ebenezer*, 'stone of help', but it has had a separate existence for centuries and means 'stone'. It is thus semantically similar to *Cephas* and *Peter*. In the *First Book of Samuel*, *Ebenezer* is the name of the memorial stone set up by Samuel after his victory at Mizpeh, when the Israelites recovered the ark from the Philistines. The full name was popular in Victorian times and was the name of the 'hero' of Charles Dickens's novel, *A Christmas Carol*. Today, the shortened form is much more widespread.

EDAN (pronounced 'ee + den' and 'aid + den')is occasionally used as a spelling of the Irish name, *Aidan*, 'flame', although it may also be linked to *éadan*, 'brow of a hill', a feature that occurs in such place names as Edenderry or Edenmore. It is also possible that the African American community, in which it often appears, uses *Edan* as a modified spelling of *Eden*. This comes from Hebrew *eden*, meaning 'pleasure, delight', although it may also have been influenced by Sumerian *eden*, meaning 'plain'. SEE Aidan

EDGAR All of the 'Ed-' names are Germanic in origin. Many existed in England before the Norman Conquest of 1066 but many more were carried to the British Isles by the Normans. *Edgar* is composed of *ead*, 'prosperity' + *gar*, 'spear', and may be interpreted as 'prosperous warrior' in that the spear was often used as a metaphor for a warrior. One of

the 10th-century kings of England who became a saint was called 'Edgar the Peaceful'. The abbreviations *Ed* and *Eddie* are occasionally used.

EDISON is a surname meaning 'son of prosperity'. It began to be used as a given name in the United States as a tribute to Thomas Edison (1847-1931). He was a prolific inventor who gave the world the aphorism: 'Genius is one per cent inspiration and ninety-nine per cent perspiration'. SEE Edgar

EDMOND/EDMUND This Germanic name is made up of the two elements, *ead*, 'prosperity' + *mund*, 'protection'. The spelling with 'o' comes later than the spelling with 'u' but they are currently equally popular. There are several saints of this name including the 9th-century king of East Anglia, often called Edmund the Martyr (c. 847-870). He was defeated by the Danes but refused to give up his Christian faith and was executed by being shot with arrows. Like *Edgar* and *Edward*, this name can be abbreviated to *Ed* and *Eddie*.

EDOUARD is a French form of *Edward*, 'prosperity's guardian'. SEE Edward

EDWARD has always been the most widely used of the 'Ed-' names. It has been used by eight English kings since the 13th century and by many saints, including Edward the Confessor, both saint and king, who died in 1066 and whose death triggered the Norman Invasion of England. It occurs in several variants throughout Europe including *Edouard* and *Edouardo*. Its widely used pet forms are *Ed*, *Eddie*, *Ned*, *Ted* and *Teddy*.

EDWIN was once extremely popular but is now less so. It is composed of *ead*, 'prosperity' + *wine*, 'friend'. Like the other 'Ed-' names, it was popular in Anglo-Saxon royal families and it is abbreviated to *Ed* and *Eddie*.

EGAN is an Irish name that is currently very popular. It comes from *Aodhgan*, 'flame', and it has given rise to the surnames *Egan*, *Hagan* and *O'Hagan*. In the past, the first syllable of the name rhymed with 'may' but it is now more usual to rhyme it with 'me'. *Egan* has been caught up in the transformation of 'ay' sounds to 'ee' because 'tay' for 'tea' was considered uneducated.

EGBERT It is probably true to say that this is the only '-bert' name that no longer appears on any list of popular names and yet it has a long history and means 'bright sword', from *ecg*, 'edge, sword' + *beorht*, 'bright, famous'. It has been revived on at least two occasions, the last one being in the 19th century.

ELDRIDGE This surname comes from the Old English name *Æðelric*, 'noble ruler'. It is used as a given name in Sierra Leone and among African Americans in the United States. A variant, *Eldric*, is the given name of golfer Tiger Woods.

ELI (pronounced 'eel+ eye') The meaning of this Hebrew name is debated. It may mean 'highest' or it may incorporate the unit *el*, which can mean 'God'. Combining the two gives the parent the possibility of 'God in the highest'. In the Old Testament, *Eli* was the priest chosen by God to train *Samuel*.

ELIAS Early in the first century, many of the biblical texts were translated into Greek, and Hebrew names were also modified. *Elias* is the Greek equivalent of *Elijah*, 'God is the Lord'. *Elias* was popular in the Middle Ages and gave rise to the surnames *Ellis*, *Ellison*, *Eliot* and *Elliot*. The name experienced a second wave of popularity among the early Puritans but it is rare now outside Jewish circles.

ELIOT/ELLIOT/ELLIOTT The proverb 'What goes around comes around' could apply to names. *Élie* occurred as the Old French form of *Elias*, 'God is the Lord', and it was used as a given name. *Éliot* developed as a diminutive and became a surname in the 12th century. *Eliot* and its variants began to be used again as

a first name in the 19th century. The name was readily adopted in England because it was similar in form to the Old English name, *Æþel gyð*, 'noble combat'.

ELISHA (pronounced 'ell + eye + sha' but 'ell + ee + sha' also occurs) is the name of an Old Testament prophet who probably lived in the 9th century BC. He was the successor of *Elias/Elijah* and he is best known for curing Naaman, the Syrian soldier who had leprosy. *Elisha* means 'God is my help'

ELLERY is a form of *Hilary*, which comes from Latin *hilaris*, 'cheerful', and is closely related to the modern adjective, 'hilarious'. It was the name of several saints, the earliest, St Hilarius of Poitiers, dying in the 4th century. SEE Hilary

ELLIS is a form of *Elias*, 'God is the Lord'. SEE Elias

ELMER is not as popular now as it once was or as popular as its meaning might suggest. It comes from an Old English name,

Æðelmær, 'noble and famous'.

ELMO is an alternative name for St Erasmus, who died around AD 300. It means 'pleasant, friendly, affable', and it occurs most frequently in the phrase 'St Elmo's fire'. This phenomenon involves the appearance of a light around a ship's mast or aircraft usually during an electric storm.

ELROY is essentially the same name as *Leroy*, 'the king'. It is either an anagram of *Leroy* or a blend of the French and Spanish forms *le roi* and *el rey*. SEE Leroy

ELTON is a place name in at least six English counties. It may be a form of 'Ella's settlement' or, in certain cases, it can mean 'settlement where eels are found'. The name has been used as a surname since the 13th century and has been popularised in the second half of the 20th century by the singer-songwriter, Elton John (b.1947).

ELVIS This name will forever be associated with Elvis Presley (1935-77). It is universally known and widely used especially among Africans and African Americans and yet its meaning is uncertain. It has been suggested that it may mean 'all wise', but it is most likely to be a modified form of a surname such as *Elvy*, 'elf war'. It was the second name of the singer's father. Whatever the name means, it is now closely linked to the singing style of one of the icons of 20th-century music.

EMIL/ÉMILE/EMILIO

These are variants of an old Roman name, *Aemilius*, probably from a nickname, meaning 'rival'. They are popular in Europe and, with the movement of people, especially young people, they are now found in all countries in the European Union.

EMLYN is found in Wales and seems to be a form of Latin *Aemilius* and is thus related to *Emil*. *Emlyn* also occurs as a surname in England and this form seems to have been introduced by the Normans. It may be from the same Latin source or from one of the many Germanic names the Normans modified. In this case, it is probably from *Adalhelm*, 'noble protector'. SEE Emil

EMMANUEL and, less frequently, *Immanuel* are from Hebrew and mean 'God with us'. The Old and the New Testament references to the name both deal with the coming of the Messiah. In Isaiah, there is the prophecy:

> *Behold, a virgin shall conceive and bear a son, and shall call his name Immanuel (7:17)… the stretching out of his wings shall fill the breadth of thy land, O Immanuel (8.8).*

Matthew's Gospel refers to Isaiah's prophecy:

> *Behold, a virgin shall be with child, and shall bring forth a son, and they shall call his name Emmanuel, which being interpreted is 'God with us'. (1:23)*

The Spanish form, *Manuel*, is extremely popular and *Emmanuel* is widely used by African communities. *Manny* is a regular abbreviation.

EMMET has been a surname in England since the 12th century. It can have three possible origins. It may be from the Lancashire place name, Emmot, which is from Old English *eagemot*, 'meeting place of streams'. It may also be one of the relatively few surnames in English that is based on a woman's name. *Emmot* was a popular pet form of *Emma*, 'entirely loved'. The third possibility is that it comes from the English dialect word *emmet*, meaning 'ant' and sometimes used as a nickname for someone who was extremely industrious. In Ireland, the use of *Emmet* as a given name is due to the respect and affection that people still have for the patriot, Robert Emmet (1778-1803). In the past, most Irish children knew by heart the speech he made from the dock: *Let no man write my epitaph …*

EMRYS (pronounced 'em + rees') is a Welsh name usually considered to be a form of *Ambrose*, 'immortal'. Like many Celtic borrowings, there is a good chance that it paralleled an indigenous name, possibly involving *rhys*, 'ardour'.

ENDA Many Irish men who bear this name spend a great deal of time explaining that it is a man's name and not a variant of *Edna*. St Enda, who died around AD 530, has often been called the father of Irish monasticism. He established a monastery on Inishmore, the largest of the Aran Islands. The monastery was renowned for its austerity and sanctity. It was also a centre of study where other saints found the peace they needed to renew their spiritual lives. The meaning of his name is uncertain but the suggestion that it may derive from *éan*, 'bird', is appropriate for a man with so few ties to the earth.

ENGELBERT is transparently a German name meaning 'bright angel'. It was selected by the singer, Engelbert Humperdinck, as a means of gaining attention. His real name was Arnold George Dorsey (b. 1936) and his choice raises the interesting question:

'How important is a name if one wants to be famous?' Dorsey took the name of the German composer, Engelbert Humperdinck (1854-1921) who is perhaps best remembered for his 1893 opera, *Hänsel und Gretel*.

ENOCH This Hebrew name means 'experienced' and, considering the claim that *Enoch* lived for 365 years, he probably gained a great deal of experience! The Old Testament has two *Enochs*, the first being the son of *Cain* and the second the father of *Methuselah*, who is said to have lived for 969 years, making his father's long life seem brief. *Enoch* became popular in England with the rise of Puritanism and it continues to be used, especially in Wales.

ENRICO is an Italian form of *Henry*, 'home power'. It is still popular among Italians and among music lovers in honour of the tenor Enrico Caruso (1873-1921).

EOGHAN/EOIN (pronounced 'Owen') is a Gaelic name that may well predate

Christianity. It may be composed of early Celtic forms and mean 'yew tree born'. For centuries it has been linked to the Greek name *Eugenios*, 'nobly born', but it is almost certainly not simply an Irish equivalent of a Greek name. It is found in the name of the county Tyrone, which is an anglicised form of *Tír Eoghain*, 'Eoghan's land'. The link between *Eoghan* and *Eugene* goes back at least to the 6th century, when the Tyrone man, St Eoghan, was also referred to as *Eugene*. He was captured as a boy by pirates, probably from Scotland. Eventually, he returned home and established several monasteries, including one at Ardstraw in his home county. *Eoghan* is pronounced like *Owen* and often spelt as both *Eoin* and *Owen*.

EPHRAIM The second of Jacob's twelve sons was called *Ephraim*, a name that the *Book of Genesis* suggests means 'fruitful'. This name is not widely used outside Jewish circles. It is often abbreviated to *Ephie*, pronounced like 'ee + fee'.

ERC was a contemporary of St Patrick. He was one of the people who did not want Patrick to light his fire on the Hill of Slane to celebrate the first Easter Sunday in Ireland. Later, he was baptised by Patrick and made a bishop. According to tradition, St Erc, whose name may be related to *earc*, 'reptile', was the teacher of St Brendan the Navigator. Although *Eric* has a Germanic etymology, it is just possible that *Erc* was adopted by Irish Vikings in the same way that *Niall* was.

ERIC is traditionally regarded as a Scandinavian name, coming from *e*, 'always, forever' + *rik*, 'power', and meaning 'eternal power'. It was not used in England before the time of the Vikings but was reinforced by the Normans. It was the name of Leif Ericsson's father, Eric the Red. Leif Ericsson, like St Brendan, is often credited with 'discovering America', perhaps another reason for linking Irish *Erc* and Scandinavian *Eric*.

ERNEST This name will almost always suggest the name of Oscar Wilde's play, *The Importance of Being Earnest*. *Ernest* comes from a Germanic noun, *earnest*, meaning 'seriousness' or 'battle'. It is from the same root as the English adjective 'earnest'. It has been the name of dukes and lords and was extremely popular, especially in the first half of the 20th century. *Ernie* is often used as an abbreviation. *Ernst* is the German equivalent and *Ernesto* is found in Italy, Spain and Portugal.

ERROL can be from a Scottish place name or an English surname. The origin of the Perthshire town is uncertain but it may be related to the Old Celtic word meaning 'strong river'. (The same word is used for the river Aire.) It is also possible that it comes from *earnleah*, 'eagle wood'. The English *Errol* comes from the Old English name *Eoforwulf*, 'boar wolf'. The name was popularised by the Australian film actor, Errol Flynn (1909-59).

ESAU It is not likely that many children will be called *Esau* and yet it is very well known within Jewish and non-Jewish circles. *Esau* was the older of the twin sons of Isaac and Rebecca. He sold his birthright to his brother *Jacob* for 'a mess of potage' (Genesis: 25). *Rachel* helped *Jacob* to win the blessing of *Isaac*, who was blind, and *Jacob*, rather than *Esau* became the patriarch, whose children initiated the twelve tribes of Israel.

ETAN is often used as the Jewish form of *Ethan*, 'firmness, steadfastness'. SEE Ethan

ETHAN Since the 1990s, *Ethan* has become one of the most popular names in the English-speaking world. It is a Hebrew name, meaning 'firmness' and the only thing we know about the Old Testament character, who appears in the first *Book of Kings*, is that he was a wise man, although not as wise as Solomon.

ETIENNE is the French form of *Stephen*, 'garland, crown'. SEE Stephen

EUGENE has been a popular name for at least two thousand years. It comes from the Greek name *Eugenios*, which is related to the Greek word *eugenes*, meaning 'well born'. It is, thus, similar in meaning to *Patrick*. *Eugene* was the name of several saints and four popes. Other famous bearers include the Irish-American playwright, Eugene O'Neill. *Gene* is frequently used as an abbreviation.

EUSTACE started life as the French form of two Greek names, *Eustakhios*, 'good grapes', and *Eustathios*, 'good standing'. St Eustace was a popular Norman saint, whose authenticity cannot be vouched for. According to tradition, he was a first-century Roman general who became a Christian and was martyred with his entire family. He is the patron saint of hunters, a fact that endeared him to the Normans.

EVAN is a Welsh form of the Hebrew name, *John*, meaning 'God is gracious'. The older form of the name was *Ieuan* and this name is often equated with *Ewan*, although they have different origins. SEE Ewan

EVELYN is used today mainly as a girl's name but for centuries it has been a surname and a boy's given name. The interesting fact is that it seems to come from a female Norman name, *Aveline*, which seems to have been a diminutive form of *Eve*, 'life'. SEE Eve

EWAN is an anglicised form of Gaelic *Eoghan*, 'well born' or 'yew born'. SEE Owen

EWART is the name of a town in Northumberland. It comes from Old English *ea*, 'river' + *worþ*, 'enclosure, homestead'. *Ewart* has also been used as a surname since the early 13th century. The surname has two possible meanings. It can be a Norman form of *Edward*, 'guardian of prosperity', or it can come from an Old English phrase *eowu*, 'ewe' + *hierde*, 'keeper, herder'. *Ewart* started to become popular as a given name in the 1990s.

EYTAN is a modified spelling of *Ethan*, 'firmness'. SEE Ethan

EZEKIEL Although Ezekiel is no longer popular outside Jewish circles, the abbreviated form *Zeke* is extremely fashionable. *Ezekiel*, whose name means 'strength of God', was a Hebrew prophet who lived in the 6th century BC. He prophesied the destruction of Jerusalem but offered hope for the coming of a Messiah.

EZRA is a Hebrew name, meaning 'help'. *Ezra* was a reforming priest who worked hard to ensure that the Jewish people would be true to their rules and obligations. The name was popular with Puritans, who saw themselves as performing for Christianity what *Ezra* attempted for Judaism in the 5th and 4th centuries BC.

NOTABLE NAMESAKES
Eamon deValera (1882-1975) President of Ireland from 1959 to 1973. A dominant figure in Irish politics, he was instrumental in Ireland's fight for independence and also served as prime minister; Edgar Allen Poe (1809-49) American poet and writer, famed for his short stories of mystery and the macabre; Ethan Hawke (b. 1970) American film actor and director; Ezra Pound (1885-1972) American poet and critic often honoured as a leading light in the Modernist Movement.

F

FABIAN/FABIEN has been popular in parts of Europe since it was borne by a 3rd-century pope who was martyred. The name was originally a Latin family name that probably came from *faba*, 'bean'. The Roman General, Fabius Cunctator, who died in 203 BC, gave the Latin form of the name a great deal of prestige. After Hannibal had defeated the Roman army in 216 BC, Fabius pursued a policy of cautious delaying tactics in order to defeat Hannibal. His tactics gained him the name of *Cunctator*, 'delayer'. The Normans introduced the two spellings of the name. *Fabien* is the preferred form in France and *Fabiano* is widely used in Hispanic communities throughout the world.

FAISAL is a popular Arabic name meaning 'decisive judge'. It was the name of the king who ruled Saudi Arabia from 1964-75. The first syllable is often pronounced like 'face'.

FARID is used in India and in the Arabic-speaking world. It comes from an Arabic word, *farada*, meaning 'to be unique'. It was the name of a 13th-century Persian poet.

FARLEIGH/FARLEY are places in several English counties, including Derbyshire and Hampshire. They come from Old English *fearn*, 'fern, fern-covered' + *leah*, clearing'. The place name was adopted as a surname in the 13th century and passed on to sons if it was a mother's maiden name. *Farley* was popularised in the 20th century by the actor Farley Granger (b. 1925).

FEARGAL/FEARGHAL (pronounced 'fir +gull') is a traditional Gaelic name that comes from *fear*, 'man' + *gal*, 'valour'. In the 8th century, it was the name of a monk who left his monastery to make a pilgrimage to the Holy Land but remained in Europe and spent a great deal of his time converting the people of Carinthia, Austria. *Feargal*, who was known in Latin as *Virgil*, was a holy man but he was also a free thinker and was reported to Rome for his views on the nature and structure of our planet.

FEARGHAS/FEARGHUS/ FERGUS (pronounced 'fir + guss') This old Gaelic name has two possible meanings. It may come from *fear*, 'man' + *gus*, 'vigour, choice', or the first syllable may be a form of *fearr*, 'best'. *Fearghas* is the traditional Irish form; *Fearghus* is the Scottish form; but *Fergus* is the preferred spelling throughout the world. According to Irish legend, Fergus gave up his Ulster throne for a year to allow his wife's son *Conchobhar* (Conor) to test his leadership qualities. Conor liked the job, however, and refused to relinquish the throne to his stepfather. *Fergus* joined forces with Queen Maeve to fight against Ulster. *Fergus* was eventually killed by Ailill, Maeve's consort, when he found him swimming naked with Maeve.

FEIDHLIM/FELIM/PHELIM

(pronounced 'fail + im') These three spellings are used for an Irish name with strong Munster links. It was the name of several Munster kings and it probably comes from *feidhil*, meaning 'constant, enduring'.

FELIX

is the Latin word for 'lucky, happy, fortunate'. It was the name of several early saints who counted themselves 'lucky' to die for their faith. The phrase *felix culpa*, 'fortunate fault' was used for the sin of Adam and Eve because, although the sin was a fault, it brought about the blessing of Christ's birth and our redemption. Variant forms, including *Felicio* and *Feliks*, are found throughout Europe. The older pronunciation rhymed the first syllable with 'mail' but many parents now rhyme it with 'meal'.

FEMI

(pronounced 'fame + ee') The Yoruba name *Olufemi*, meaning 'God loves me', is regularly abbreviated to *Femi*.

FERDINAND

This is one of many Germanic names that have found their way into virtually all European languages. It probably means 'prepared for a journey' or 'peaceful but prepared'. The usual Spanish forms are *Hernando* and *Fernando*. *Ferdinando* is used in Italy and *Ferdie* is often used as a pet form. Ferdinand of Aragon (1452-1516) was the Spanish monarch who sponsored Christopher Columbus on his voyages of discovery. His daughter was Catherine of Aragon, the first wife of Henry VIII.

FERGAL is the usual spelling of this ancient Irish name that means 'man of valour'. SEE Feargal

FERGUS has become the most widely-used spelling of this Gaelic name, which means 'man of vigour'. SEE Fearghas

FERNANDO/FERNÃO

These are, respectively, the Spanish and Portuguese versions of *Ferdinand*, 'prepared'. Fernão do Po was a Portuguese explorer who mapped the West African coast in the late 15th century. In 1472, he named an island off the coast of Cameroon after himself and it retained the name for over 500 years. It is currently called Bioko. SEE Ferdinand

FIDEL (pronounced 'fee + dell') is a Spanish name from Latin *fidelis*, 'faithful'. It is more common than *Fidelio*, especially among people who admire Fidel Castro (b. 1926). In 1959, he led a revolution in Cuba that overthrew President Batista. Castro became Prime Minister and retained the title until 1976, when he became President. He held that post without interruption until 31 July, 2006, when he transferred power to his brother while he received medical attention. On 24 February, 2008 he announced his retirement.

FINBAR/FIONNBARR/FIONNBHARR

has been a popular name in Ireland for centuries but it is currently found worldwide, especially in families with Irish links. The name comes from *fionn*, 'fair' + *barr*, 'head'. An early *Finbar* was born in County Cork and died around AD 633. There are many wonder tales associated with him, one being that he was led by an angel to an area where he founded a monastery that developed into the city of Cork. Barry Island, off the coast of Wales, is called after him.

FINDLAY/FINDLEY/FINLAY/FINLEY

has been a surname since the 13th century.

It comes from Gaelic *fionn*, 'fair' + *laoch*, 'hero, warrior'. It was found mainly in Scotland but is now used more widely as a given name.

FINN/FIONN is a Gaelic word meaning 'fair-haired'. The adjective was applied to the Norwegian Vikings who were *finn*, 'fair' + *gall*, 'foreigner, stranger'. Fionn Mac Cumhail or Finn Mac Cool is one of the best-known mythological heroes of Ireland. He is the traditional builder of the Giant's Causeway and is also linked to Fingal's Cave on the Hebridean Island of Staffa. *Finn* and his Fianna (band of warriors) have much in common with the Arthurian Cycle of Arthur and his Knights of the Round Table. In particular, they are both betrayed by a beautiful young wife and a close friend.

FINTAN/FIONNTÁN In Irish mythology, *Fintan* lived at the time of Noah and the Flood. He managed to survive because he transformed himself into a salmon. He is reputed to have

eaten the nuts of knowledge which had no punishment attached to them, unlike the fruit of the tree of knowledge in the Garden of Eden. Fintan, the Salmon of Knowledge, lived in the River Boyne and was greatly sought after because anyone who ate the salmon would have infinite knowledge. The meaning of his name is uncertain but it may be composed of *fionn*, 'fair' + *táin*, 'wealth in cattle'. *Fintan* was the name of several Irish saints, including St Fintan of Clonenagh who died in AD 603 after establishing a monastery where the monks lived on vegetables, barley bread and water.

FLOYD is based on an English pronunciation of Welsh *Llwyd*, 'grey-haired', sometimes anglicised as *Lloyd*. The Welsh sound represented by 'll' and found in such place names as Llanvair, 'Mary's church', is not found in English.

FORD In Old English, *ford* meant 'shallow place in a river where one could wade across'. It has been used as a surname since the 14th century and as a given name since the 19th century. Ford Madox Ford (1873-1939) was a writer. His name illustrates *Ford* in both functions.

FRANCIS In Latin, *Franciscus* meant 'French man'. The popularity of the name, *Francis* is due to St Francis of Assisi (1182-1226), who was christened *Giovanni*, 'John', but nicknamed *Francesco* because his father, who was a rich merchant, had business links with France. St Francis was renowned for his love of animals and for his devoted service of the poor. He founded the Franciscan Order in 1209. *Francis* occurs in a wide variety of forms, including *Francesco*, *Francisco*, *Proinsias* and in the pet forms *Frank* and *Frankie* as well as *Frans* and *Franz*. *Franchot* is a diminutive that occurs occasionally in France.

FRANK Although *Frank* is used as a pet form of *Francis*, it is also a Germanic name in its own right. The name was applied to the Germanic tribe that

eventually settled in what is now France in the 6th century. They probably got the name from *franca*, 'javelin, knife', and they gave their name to France. The Franks were free and so the word gradually took on the meaning of 'free' and then 'open'.

FRANKLIN illustrates the intricate patterns of development of many given names. The term *franklin* meant 'free man, freeholder' in 13th-century England. It comes from Latin *francalis*, '(land) held without dues'. It began to be used as a surname in the 15th century. It was the surname of Benjamin Franklin (1706-90) who was an American inventor and statesman. He was one of the signatories of the Peace Treaty between America and England after the American War of Independence. Franklin D Roosevelt (1882-1945) was the 32nd President of the USA (1933-45), the only US president to be elected to a third term in office.

FRASER/FRAZER is a Scottish surname that seems to be of Norman origin. It seems likely that the name started as a nickname for 'curly-haired' rather like the technique in Irish where *Máire Catach* is 'Curly-haired Mary'. An early form is *Freselière*. It has occasionally been claimed that the name comes from French *fraise*, 'strawberry' but this is likely to be a folk etymology. The use of 'z' is most likely to occur in the USA.

FREDERIC/FREDERICK

This name is of Germanic origin and is one of the many names introduced into the British Isles by the Normans. It comes from *fred*, 'peace' + *ric*, 'power', and it is popular throughout Europe. The form without 'k' is French but many parents like it. Other variants are *Frederik*, *Fredric*, *Fredrick* and *Fryderyk*. The abbreviated form *Fred* has been widely used as a full name and had a surge of popularity in the 1990s.

FRITZ is a form of *Frederick*, 'peaceful power', that is extremely popular in the USA.

> **NOTABLE NAMESAKES**
> **Floyd Patterson (1935-2006) American boxer and, at 21, the youngest ever to hold the world heavyweight championship; Frank Sinatra (1915-98) hugely popular singer for over forty years and an academy-award winning actor; Franz Lizst (1811-86) Hungarian composer and virtuoso pianist; Freddie Laker (1922-2006) British airline entrepreneur who set up Laker Airlines and was the first to offer 'no frills flights' in 1966.**

G

GABRIEL is a well-known Hebrew name meaning 'man of God' or possibly 'messenger of

God'. Gabriel is the archangel that is associated in Judaism, Christianity and Islam with messages from God. In The Old Testament, he appeared twice to Daniel, once to explain Daniel's vision to him and later (Chapter 9: 22):

And he [i.e. Gabriel] informed me, and said, 'O Daniel, I am now come forth to give thee skill and understanding.

In The New Testament, he announces the births of John the Baptist and Jesus to Zacharias and Mary respectively. In Islam, *Gabriel* is regarded as the angel who revealed the Koran to the Prophet Muhammad. *Gabriello* occurs in Italian, Spanish and Portuguese and the abbreviations *Gabe and Gabie* are used. *Gay* was also widely used in the past but is found less frequently.

GAGAN (pronounced 'gag + an') is an Indian name that takes its meaning from the Sanskrit word for 'sky'.

GALE Occasionally, two languages have a similar word for the same phenomenon and that can encourage its adoption. Old English, *gal*, 'light, pleasant, merry', was similar to a Norman adjective, *gail*, 'joyous, gay'. The adjective was used as a nickname from the early 12th century before becoming a surname in the 13th. Today it is used as a given name and the spelling differentiates it from the girl's name, *Gail*.

GALVAN/GALVIN This boy's name is taken from an Irish surname that may mean 'exceptionally fair', or it may come from *gealbhán*, 'sparrow'.

GANDHI There are interesting preferences in languages with regard to naming. In Irish, for example, 'F' is a productive letter when it comes to both male and female names. In India, 'G' is very widely used. *Gandhi* means 'sun'.

GANNON was an Irish leader after whom the town of Dungannon in County Tyrone was named. The meaning of *Gannon* is uncertain but it is probably derived from *gean*, 'love, affection'.

GARETH continues to be a popular name in Wales and in many parts of the world with Welsh links. It seems likely that *Gareth* is related to Welsh *gwared*, 'gentle', but we cannot rule out the possibility that it is a Welsh form of *Gerard*, 'spear brave', a name that was popular among the Normans. *Gareth* is a knight in the Arthurian tales. SEE Gerald and Gerard

GARFIELD is a surname probably based on Old English *gara*, 'a triangular strip of land' + *feld*, 'land free from wood, plain'. It has been used as a given name since the early 20th century. The Caribbean cricketer, Gary Sobers, (b. 1936) was named *Garfield*. *Garfield* is a comic strip cat that is featured in over 2,500 newspapers worldwide. Whether this wide coverage will increase the usage of the name remains to be seen.

GARRET/GARRETT This popular name resembles Welsh *Gareth* but they may have different origins. It seems probable that *Garret(t)* is a form of either *Gerald*, 'spear rule' or *Gerard*, 'spear brave'. *Garret(t)* has been used as a surname since the 12th century. SEE Gerald and Gerard

GARTH may be a form of *Gareth* or *Garret* but it is most likely to come from a surname that is derived from an Old Norse noun, *garðr*, meaning 'enclosure'. The name probably shifted from the enclosure to one who looked after the enclosure. In this way, it could easily become a surname, as it did in the north of England in the 14th century.

GARY was virtually unknown as a boy's name until the film actor Gary Cooper (1901-61) made it one of the most popular names in America. Like many stars' names, *Gary* was a stage name, thought to be more striking than *Frank*. Cooper was named after *Gary*, an Indiana town, but the town was named after Elbert Henry Gary (1846-1927). It seems likely that *Gary* comes from *gar*, 'spear', but it is possible that it is also from the Irish surname, *Garry*, which comes from *Mac Fhearadhaigh*, 'son of the manly one'.

GASTON can be an English surname coming from *gærstun*, 'grass enclosure', or it can be a French name deriving ultimately from Norman *gascon*, 'a man from Gascony'. Gascony is in the foothills of the Pyrenees but it was ruled by England between 1154 and 1453.

GAVIN is almost certainly Welsh in origin and may come from *gwalch*, 'hawk' + *gwyn*, 'white, fair'. This is the same name as *Gawain*, who was a knight of the Round Table and the nephew of King Arthur. The name seems to have died out everywhere except in Scotland, but it is now popular in Ireland, Wales and England.

GAWAIN is a form of *Gavin*. The form with 'w' was found mainly in Wales and Cornwall. In the earliest Arthurian legends, *Gawain* is the perfect knight, pure, courageous and courteous. The 14th-century alliterative

poem, *Sir Gawain and the Green Knight*, describes some of his adventures. SEE Gavin

GENE is an abbreviated form of *Eugene*, 'well-born, noble'. It is now regularly used as a given name in its own right, particularly in the USA. SEE Eugene

GEOFFREY is a Norman name of Germanic origin. It is not certain what it comes from, but it was already in widespread use when it was given to the historian Geoffrey of Monmouth in 1100, and to the poet Geoffrey Chaucer, when he was born around 1340. It is possible that *Geoffrey* is a form of *Godfrey*, 'God's peace', or a combination *gawia*, 'territory' + *fred*, 'peace'. It has an equally popular variant *Jeffrey* and the abbreviations *Geoff* and *Jeff* are widely used.

GEORGE is one of the most popular names throughout Europe and, indeed, throughout the world. It owes its origin to the Greek name, *Georgios*, which comes from the Greek word *georgos* meaning 'farmer' or 'earthwork'. St George was a legendary dragon slayer who is said to have been martyred near Lydda in Palestine, possibly in the early 4th century. He is the patron saint of England, Portugal and Catalonia. If he existed at all, he was probably born in Palestine. *George* has been the name of six kings of England, two kings of Greece, and the first president of the United States, George Washington. Other famous bearers include authors George Eliot and George Sand, both female novelists. Other popular versions of the name include *Georges*, *Georgy*, *Giorgio*, *Jorge* and *Jurgen*.

GERAINT

(The 'g' is pronounced as in 'garden' and the second syllable rhymes with 'pint') This medieval name has become increasingly popular in Wales over the last half century. The story of *Geraint* and *Enid* is found in the Arthurian legends and features prominently in Alfred Lord Tennyson's *Idylls of the King*. *Geraint* learns about Guinevere's adultery with Lancelot and doubts Enid's faithfulness but her devotion to him gradually convinces him of her innocence. It is not certain what the name means, although most commentators suggest that it is from Greek *Gerontios*, 'old man'.

GERALD

is a Germanic name popularised by the Normans. It is probably a blend of *gar*, 'spear' + *wald*, 'rule'. This name gave rise to the Irish surname, *FitzGerald*, 'son of Gerald'. The FitzGeralds became the Earls of Kildare and, although nominally under England's jurisdiction, had almost virtual autonomy, especially in the 15th century. Other forms of the name include, *Gearalt*, *Giraldo* and *Giraud*. *Gerry* is a widely used abbreviation.

GERARD/GERRARD

Like *Gerald*, *Gerard* is a Germanic name that was popularised by the Normans. It is composed of two elements, *gar*, 'spear' + *hard*, 'brave, strong'. Even in the Middle Ages, *Gerald* and *Gerard* were confused, with the same individual apparently using the forms as alternatives. Indeed, both names were often written *Gerad* or *Jerad*, giving rise to several surnames, including *Garrad*, *Garrat*, *Garrett* and *Jarrett*. Variants include *Gearóid*, *Gérard*, *Gerardo*, *Gerhard* and *Gerhardt*. *Gerry* is the most popular abbreviation.

GERMANUS is the name of a 5th-century saint who was the Bishop of Auxerre. Although his name is from Latin *germanus*, a noun and adjective used to describe people living in central and northern Europe, its origin is unclear. It is possible that this was the name given by the Gauls to their neighbours and that the word comes from a Celtic language. The Celtic derivations suggested are Old Irish *gair*, 'neighbour' or Irish *gairm* 'battle-cry'. According to several scholars, *Germani* was originally the name of a group of Celtic people in north-eastern Gaul. It was then transferred from these to their Teutonic conquerors, and afterwards extended to all the Teutonic peoples. A link with 'battle-cry' is suggested by the story of St Germanus (c. 378-448), who was probably a Breton. He led an army of Bretons against pagan Picts and Scots, using the battle-cry 'Halleluiah'.

GERVAISE/GERVASE This name was popular among the Normans but, although the first element looks like Germanic *gar*, 'spear', the second element has never been identified. Since St Gervasius was an early Christian martyr, it is possible that his name is not Germanic at all. *Gerwazy* is a popular Polish variant.

GIANNI is an abbreviated Italian form of *Giovanni*, meaning 'God is gracious'. SEE John

GIDEON is a Hebrew name. It occurs in the Old Testament where *Gideon* is a warrior and a judge. Under his leadership, the Israelites defeat the Midianites. His name is singularly appropriate since it means 'the one who cuts down'. *Gideon* is particularly popular in the USA. The Midianites were the descendants of *Midian*, 'strife, judgement', and he was the son of Abraham and his concubine *Keturah*.

GILBERT is a Norman name of Germanic origin. It is a combination of *gisil*, 'pledge' + *berth*, 'bright'. St Gilbert of Sempringham (c. 1083-1189) was the founder of the only religious order founded in England. The Gilbertines were disbanded when Henry VIII dissolved the monasteries by the parliamentary acts of 1536 and 1539. William Schwenck Gilbert (1836-1911) was the librettist who collaborated with Arthur Sullivan in the writing of the Gilbert and Sullivan light operas.

GILES It is not clear when St Giles lived. It may have been in the 6th or 8th century but his fame throughout Europe caused *Giles* to be one of the most popular names in the Middle Ages, and it has continued to have a following since then. The saint was known as *Aegidius*, which is a latinised form of Greek *Aigidios*, which in turn comes from *aigidion*, 'kid, young goat', but this was modified in France. One of the stories told about the saint relates to his love of animals. He left Athens to live in a cave as a hermit in France. A royal hunting party was following a deer which sought refuge in the cave. Giles stood in front of the animal and was wounded with an arrow. An idea of his popularity may be gained from the fact that, at one time, over 150 churches in England were dedicated to him. Other spellings of the name include *Gilles* and *Gyles*. The initial 'g' is usually pronounced like 'j' in 'jam' but there is a modern tendency to use the French pronunciation of 'g' as in 'gendarme' and to rhyme the name with 'heal'.

GIOVANNI is an Italian form of *John*, 'God is gracious'. SEE John

GIUSEPPE (pronounced 'jee + oo + seppy' is an Italian form of *Joseph*, 'God shall add'. SEE Joseph

GLEN/GLENN This name comes directly from Gaelic *gleann*, 'glen, valley'. It became a surname in Scotland in the early 13th century and has been a given name for over a century. Its popularity was boosted by the film star Glenn Ford (1916-2006). Ford was born in Canada and was christened Gwyllyn Samuel Newton Ford by his Welsh parents. The studios thought that Glenn Ford was more memorable.

GLYN/GLYNN is the Welsh equivalent of *Glen* and also means 'valley'. It evolved in essentially the same way: a person was denoted by his locality, in this case a valley; the name became a surname and then a given name. It is currently very popular among Welsh people. *Glyn* was used as a surname in the 14th century but forms such as *John de Glin* are found from the 12th century.

GODFREY is a Norman name of Germanic origin. It combines two words, *god*, 'God, good' + *frid*, 'peace', implying 'God's peace'.

The name was often confused with *Geoffrey*, a fact that accounts for the '-frey' ending. *Godfrey* was extremely popular among the Normans. It was the name of a saint who was the bishop of Amiens. Godfrey de Bouillon (d. 1100) was the name of the leader of the First Crusade in which Jerusalem was taken. The name continues to be widely used, especially in Africa.

GORDON As a surname, *Gordon* seems to have arisen in Scotland. It is the name of an important clan with its roots in an area known as Gordon in Berwickshire. Since some of the Normans came from Gourdon in Saône-et-Loire, it is possible that the French place name helped to reinforce the attractiveness of *Gordon*, which was a surname as early as 1220. The meaning of *Gordon* is uncertain. It may come from Old English *gara*, 'triangular strip of land, corner piece of land' + *dun*, 'hill, fortress'. It is not certain when *Gordon* became a given name, but it was widely used in Victorian times as a mark of respect for the British general, Charles George Gordon (1833-85) who died leading his army at Khartoum. The spelling *Gorden* is also found.

GRAEME/GRAHAM/ GRAHAME

Like *Gordon*, *Graham* was a place name that became a surname, especially in Scotland, and has more recently been used as a given name. *Graham* is an old form of Grantham in Lincolnshire. Grantham probably comes from Old English *grand*, 'gravel, sand bank' + *ham*, 'village, estate'. The variants are almost equally widely used with *Graham* being slightly more popular than the other two.

GRANT

started life as a Norman nickname for someone who was big, tall, or occasionally the oldest son. It comes from *grand*, 'big, large'. *Grant* became a surname as early as the 12th century and has been a given name for almost 200 years. In the United States, it was sometimes given to a son as a mark of respect for Ulysses S. Grant

(1822-85). He was an important general in the American Civil War and was the one who accepted the surrender of Robert E. Lee and his confederate army. He behaved honourably towards the defeated army, refusing to allow his troops to cheer their victory by saying: 'The war is over. The rebels are our countrymen again.'

GRANVILLE

was an aristocratic Norman name taken from one of the many French towns called 'Grande Ville', 'great town'. Guillaume de Gran(de)ville gradually developed into William Granville and, as with many surnames, a son was often named *Granville* when it was his mother's surname. Nowadays, it is a given name used most frequently in the north of England.

GREGORY

has been a popular name for 2000 years. It comes from Greek, *Gregorios*, meaning 'watchful', and was widely used among the early Christians, who were instructed to be ever vigilant and watchful for the

Second Coming of Christ. *Gregory* was the name of several saints, including St Gregory the Great (c.540-604), who sent St Augustine to England in 596 to convert the Angles. He was also a pope, the first of many to bear the name of *Gregory*. The adjective 'Gregorian' is used for church music sung as plainsong, and we use the 'Gregorian Calendar', which was introduced in 1582 by Pope Gregory XIII to bring the calendar back into line with the solar year. He did this by cutting out ten days. He also changed the time of New Year's Day from March 25 to January 1. There are many variants of *Gregory*, including *Greagoir*, *Grégoire*, Gregor and *Gregorio*.

GUIDO (The 'g' as in 'garden' and the rest as both 'ee + doe' and 'wee + doe') is a Norman name with a Germanic background. It probably comes from *witu*, meaning 'wood'. The link between *witu* and *Guido* is similar to the link between 'guardian' and 'warden' or 'Guillaume' and 'William'. In Norman French, there was a tendency to pronounce 'w' as if it were 'g' as in 'good'. At the time, *Guido* was regularly written as *Wido*. *Guy* was often used as an abbreviation. Guy Fawkes (1570-1606) often used *Guido* as his name.

GUILLAUME (The 'g' as in 'garden'; and has two main pronunciations, namely, 'gee + ohm' and, less widely 'gwee + ohm') is a French form of *William*, 'the will to protect, willing protector'. SEE William

GUSTAVE has become more widely popular in the last 30 years. This is a French form of Swedish *Gustaf* or *Gustav* and this is made up of Old Norse *goð*, 'god' or *gaut*, 'Goth' + *stafr*, 'staff', suggesting 'the staff of God' or 'the staff of the Goths'. In its Latin form, *Gustavus*, it was borne by members of the Swedish monarchy. Its popularity in England in the past is suggested by the first lines of a William Brighty Rands (1823-82) poem:

> *Godfrey Gordon Gustavus Gore –*
> *(No doubt you have heard the name*

before) –
Was a boy who never would
shut a door.

GUY is an abbreviated form of
Guido, 'wood', but it has been
used for centuries as a name in
its own right. There is also an
Old French word 'gui' meaning
'guide' and this could have
contributed to the use of *Guy* in
France.

(1813-1901) one of the most
influential composers of
Italian opera in the 19th
century. Works include
***Rigoletto* and *La Traviata*;**
Gustave Holst (1874-34)
English musician and
composer, best known for
his *The Planets Suite*.

H

HABIB (pronounced 'ha +
beeb') is an Arabic name
meaning 'beloved'. It is used by
both Christians and Muslims and
is particularly popular among
people of Lebanese and Syrian
origins.

HADLEIGH is an English
surname based on towns that are
found in at least five different
shires. The towns take their
names from Old English *hæþ*,
'heather-covered' + *leah*,
'clearing'. Less frequently, a
child is named *Hadley*.

HAKEEM/HAKIM is an Arabic name meaning 'wise'. Possibly because of its attractive meaning, it is popular throughout the Islamic world.

HADRIAN means 'man from Hadria, Italy'. It is the same name as *Adrian* and the vacillation between using the initial 'H' and dropping it is clear when we realise that the Adriatic Sea takes its name from Hadria, as does the Emperor Hadrian (AD 76-138). Hadrian became emperor at the age of 17. He was determined to secure the borders of the Roman Empire and toured all the provinces with this in mind. He inaugurated the building of a 120-kilometer wall stretching from the west coast of northern England to the east. The wall was begun in AD 122 and was between 2.5 and 3 metres thick. SEE Adrian

HAL is an abbreviation of *Harry*, 'home power'. SEE: Henry

HAMISH is a Scottish form of *James*, 'supplanter'. In Gaelic, the first consonant of the address

form of the name *Seumas* is pronounced like 'h' and *Hamish* is an anglicised form of this pronunciation. SEE: James

HANK is found mainly in the USA, where it is usually an abbreviated form of *Henry*, 'home power'. In the Middle Ages, it was popular in England as a pet form of *Hankin*, from *Johannes*, 'God is gracious', plus the diminutive ending '-kin'.

HANS is a popular pet form of *Johannes*, 'God is gracious', in many parts of Europe. It was the name of the Danish writer Hans Christian Andersen (1805-75). The diminutive of *Hans* is also known to every child who has heard the story of *Hansel and Gretel*, 'little John and little Margaret'.

HAROLD is an Old English name that is made up of *here*, 'army' + *weald*, 'rule'. It is very similar to the Viking form of the same meaning, *Haraldr*. Harold II (c. 1019-66), was the last Anglo-Saxon king of England. He

BOYS

was defeated by William the Conqueror at the Battle of Hastings in 1066 and, probably because of that, the name dropped out of favour until it was reintroduced in the 19th century. It is often abbreviated to *Harry*.

HARRY has been a popular name in England for well over 1000 years and its popularity shows little sign of diminishing. It has been used as an abbreviated form of both *Harold*, 'army rule', and *Henry*, 'home power'. In fact, it seems likely that *Harry* was the usual pronunciation of *Henry* in the Middle Ages. The Normans did not pronounce the 'n' and 'er' was regularly pronounced like 'ar', as it is in 'clerk' and 'Derby'. SEE Harold and Henry

HARVEY is quite widely used as a given name, especially in the USA. It comes from the surname *Harvey*, which the Normans introduced as the given name *Hervé*, 'battle worthy'. The Normans almost certainly adopted the name from the

Bretons who accompanied them to England in 1066. The original Breton form was *Aeruiu*.

HASHEEM/HASHIM This Arabic name means 'destroyer of evil' and it is widely used throughout the world. The spelling with '-im' is often preferred by Muslims but both spellings occur.

HECTOR is a Greek name that seems to be related to the Greek verb *ekhein*, meaning 'to restrain'. In Greek mythology, *Hector* was the eldest son of King Priam of Troy and the older brother of *Paris*. He was killed by the Greek hero, *Achilles*. He tied Hector's body to his chariot and drove round the walls of Troy three times to show the Trojans that their champion was dead. *Hector* has been more popular in Gaelic-influenced communities because it resembles a Gaelic name, *Eachdonn*, meaning 'brown horse'.

HENRY This Germanic name was carried to the British Isles by the Normans. It is made up of

288

haim, 'home' + *ric*, 'power'. *Henry* was the name of eight English kings, the last one being Henry VIII (1491-1547). It was also the name of one of the greatest explorers, Henry the Navigator (1394-1460). Henry the Navigator was the third son of the king of Portugal. He explored the west coast of Africa and laid the foundations for Portuguese expansion worldwide. Several other forms of this popular name are found, including *Eanraí*, *Eanruig*, *Hendrick*, *Henri*, *Heinrich* and the Polish form, *Henryk*. *Hal*, *Hank* and *Harry* are the most frequent abbreviations.

HERBERT This is one of the many Germanic names introduced by the Vikings. It is a combination of *heri*, 'army' + *berth*, 'famous, bright'. *Herbert* became a surname in the 12th century. As the surname became more widespread, the use of *Herbert* as a given name diminished until the 19th century when, possibly because of the British crown's link with Germany, names of German origin began again to feature as

the choice of parents for their sons. The usual abbreviations are *Bert*, *Bertie*, *Herb* and *Herbie*.

HERMAN/HERMANN is a Germanic name that has been popularised by German settlers around the world. The form with one 'n' is English. It was introduced by the Normans and is made up of *here*, 'army' + *man*, 'man'.

HILAIRE (pronounced 'hill + air') is the French form of Latin *Hilarius*, 'the cheerful man'. This form of the name was popularised by Hilaire Belloc (1870-1953). Belloc was a prolific writer of essays, poetry and light verse. He is often remembered for such quatrains as:

> *When I am dead*
> *I hope it may be said:*
> *'His sins were scarlet*
> *But his books were read.'*

HILARY is now usually regarded as a girl's name but it was used for centuries for boys. It comes from Latin *hilaris*, 'cheerful', and is an anglicised form of *Hilarius*, 'the cheerful man'.

HORACE is an English form of *Horatius*. The meaning of this ancient Latin name is unclear but it may be linked to *hora*, 'hour', and may have reminded Romans of the motto often found on sundials: *Horas non numero nisi serenas*, 'I do not count the hours unless they are happy'. The Roman poet, Horace (65-8 BC), was greatly admired by Shakespeare's contemporaries. His odes celebrate love, friendship and good wine.

HORATIO Largely due to the fame of Horatio Nelson (1758-1805), who was killed at the Battle of Trafalgar, *Horatio* became one of the most popular names in 19th-century England. Like *Horace*, it comes from Latin *Horatius* but the exact meaning of the name is uncertain, although it may derive from *hora*, 'hour'. *Horatio* is the Italian form of the name. Shakespeare chose this name for the only character in *Hamlet* that the Prince trusts and respects.

HOWARD This is an English surname that may come from several sources. It may be a form of Old German *Hugihard*, 'heart, spirit, mind + brave'; it may be from Scandinavian *ha*, 'high' + *weard*, 'guard'; or it may, in some cases, have a humbler origin and come from Old English *eowu*, 'ewe' + *hierde*, 'herd' and thus be equivalent to 'shepherd'. It has often been linked to Wales, possibly because of the perceived link to *Howell*, an English form of *Hywel*, 'eminent'.

HOWELL/HYWEL The ancient Welsh name *Hywel* means 'eminent' and it has, in the 20th century, become popular among Welsh people and people with links to Wales. In the English form *Howell*, it has been used as a surname since the 12th century and has given rise to the surname Powell, from *ap*, 'son of' + *Howell*.

HUBERT is a Germanic name introduced by the Normans. It is made up of the two elements, *hug*, 'heart, mind, spirit' + *berth*, 'brave, famous, bright'. St Hubert was a bishop of Maastricht who died in AD 727. He is said to have been converted on Good Friday. He was out hunting and found a stag with a crucifix in his antlers.

HUGH/HUW This name is found widely and has given rise to the Irish surname *McHugh* as well as to *Hughes*, 'son of Hugh', and *Pugh*, 'son of Hugh' in Wales. It is a Germanic name, widely used by the Normans. It comes from *hug*, 'heart, mind, spirit' and the 'g' is likely to have been pronounced more like 'h' than 'g'. In Ireland, it is often thought to be the equivalent of *Aodh*, 'fire'.

HUGO is the Latin form of *Hugh*, 'heart, mind, spirit'. The Normans used *Hugh* and *Hugo* interchangeably. SEE Hugh

HUMPHREY/HUMPHRY This is a Germanic name favoured by the Normans, who often seem to have spelt it *Hunfrid*. The older spelling indicates its meaning, which is a combination of *hun*, 'bear cub, warrior' + *frid*, 'peace'. The 'ph' spelling was introduced because of the influence of Greek spelling such as *phi*, the 21st letter of the Greek alphabet. *Humfrey*, *Umfrey* and variants such as *Humfray* have been used as surnames since the 13th century.

HUSSAIN/HUSSEIN This Arabic name is extremely popular as both a given name and a surname in the Arab world. It is a pet form of *Hasan* and means 'handsome, beautiful'. It comes from an Arabic verb *hasuna*, 'to be good'. Al-Hasan was the son of *Ali* and the grandson of the Prophet Muhammad. Al-Hussein was another son of *Ali*. The massacre of his family caused the rift between Shi'ite and Sunni Muslims.

HYACINTH In Greek mythology, *Hyacinth* was the name of a handsome boy who was loved and accidentally killed by Apollo. A dark lily grew on the spot where his blood fell. The meaning of the name is uncertain but it now refers to a precious stone and a flower related to the lily. St Hyacinth was a 3rd-century martyr and the name continues to flourish in Africa, and in Poland in the form of *Jacek*. SEE: Jacek

HYAM/CHAIM/CHAYAM

This is a Jewish name taken from a Hebrew noun meaning 'life'. It was – and remains – popular among Yiddish-speaking Jews. The writer, Chaim Potok (1929-2002), wrote in both Yiddish and English. His best-known novel, *The Chosen*, was published in 1967. SEE Chaim

NOTABLE NAMESAKES
Hank Marvin (b. 1941) lead guitarist with 'The Shadows', formerly Cliff Richard's backing band; Harry Potter – hero of seven fantasy novels published by JK Rowling between 1997 and 2007. Now a major film series; Harold Pinter (b. 1930) Nobel prize-winning playwright, poet and actor.

His early plays which used language sparingly gave rise to the adjective 'pinteresque'; Herbert Von Karajan (1908-89) an Austrian and one of the most admired orchestra conductors of the 20th century; Humphrey Bogart (1899-1957) award-winning American actor. One of his most famous performances was with Ingrid Bergman in the 1942 film *Casablanca*.

IAIN/IAN This is a Scottish form of *John*, 'God is gracious'. The form *Iain* used to be found only among Gaelic speakers but it is now as widely used as *Ian*. SEE John

IBRAHIM tends to be an Islamic form of *Abraham*, 'father of many'. SEE Abraham

IDRIS (pronounced 'eed + dris' or 'id + ris') is a Welsh name made up of the constituents *iud*, 'lord' + *ris*, 'ardent'. In Welsh mythology, *Idris* was a giant who lived in Snowdonia. As sometimes happens, *Idris* is also an Arabic name. In Islamic tradition, *Idris* was a prophet who was taken body and soul into heaven. He was said to have been the first person to use a needle to sew garments and is thus seen as a patron of tailors.

IEUAN (pronounced 'you + an') is a Welsh form of *John*, 'God is gracious'. SEE John

IGNATIUS is a modified form of *Egnatius*, the name of a Roman family. Its meaning is unclear. *Ignatius* became a popular Christian name because it was interpreted as being derived from *ignis*, 'fire'. One of the best-known saints to bear this name was St Ignatius of Loyola (1491-1556). He was a Spanish theologian and the founder of the Society of Jesus, more widely known as the Jesuits. There are several variants of his name in regular use. These include *Ignace*, *Ignacio* and *Ignazio*. The abbreviation *Iggie* occurs.

IGOR (pronounced 'ee + gor') This Russian name comes from the Scandinavian compound, *Ingvar*, where *Ing*, means 'fertility god' + *var*, 'warrior'. The 9th-century Vikings took the name to Russia and it has been used outside Russia for at least 100 years.

IMMANUEL is the variant of *Emmanuel* that is used in the *King James Bible*. It means 'God is with us'. SEE Emmanuel

INIGO/IÑIGO is a medieval Spanish form of *Ignatius* and is best known now because of Inigo Jones (1573-1652), who is regarded by many as the first architect in England to be named for his work. He also contributed to stage design. Jones seems to have been born in Smithfield in London, the son of a Welsh cloth-worker who was also called *Inigo*.

IORWYN (pronounced 'yor + win') is a Welsh name that began to be used in the 19th century as Welsh people took a keen interest in their history and traditions. It seems to come from *ior*, 'lord' + *gwyn* 'fair, holy'.

IRA (pronounced 'eye + ra') is a Hebrew name meaning 'watchful'. It was one of the Old Testament names favoured by the Puritans in the 17th century and carried by them to America.

IRVIN/IRVINE/IRVING It is probable that these variants are derived from places in Scotland, such as Irvine in Ayrshire and Irving in Dumfries. Although the two places are quite distinct, the surnames have been used almost interchangeably, even within the one family, since the 15th century. It is not clear what the place names mean. The first element may be from Old English *gyr*, 'mud, marsh', or they may be forms of *eofor*, 'boar' + *wine*, 'friend'. It is possible, however, that the towns are of Celtic origin. Some children have been named after Washington Irving (1783-1859) who wrote 'Rip Van Winkle'.

ISAAC *Isaac* is a Hebrew name that means 'he laughs'. He was the son of *Abraham* and *Sarah*, and the father of *Jacob* and *Esau*. *Abraham* showed his total devotion to God by being willing to sacrifice *Isaac*, but the sacrifice was stopped by an angel. *Isaac* has been used as a surname since the early 12th century and it was adopted by Puritans in the 17th century. Sometimes *Zack* is used as an abbreviation although this is more usual with *Zachary*.

ISHMAEL (pronounced 'ish + my + el' or 'eesh + my + el') Like *Isaac*, *Ishmael* was a son of *Abraham*. His mother, *Hagar*, was the hand-maiden of *Sarah*, Abraham's wife. When Sarah had a son, *Isaac*, in her old age, *Ishmael* and his mother were driven away. The meaning of *Ishmael* is uncertain but it seems to mean 'God will hear'. He is believed to be the ancestor of Muhammad and the Arab nations.

IVAN is a Russian form of *John*, 'God is gracious'. SEE John

IVES (pronounced 'eve' or

'ives') This name was very popular with the Bretons who accompanied William the Conqueror to England. It seems to be of Germanic origin and may come from *iwa*, 'yew', although it may have been reinforced by Old English *ifig*, 'ivy'. It is also possible that it is a modified Celtic name, related to Irish *iamh*, 'enclosure'. SEE Yves

IVOR (pronounced 'eye + vor') is often associated with Wales but it is a Scandinavian name made up of *yr*, 'yew' + *herr*, 'army', implying 'archers'.

J

JACEK (pronounced 'yat + seck')is one of the most popular names in Poland. Its English equivalent is *Hyacinth*. SEE Hyacinth

JACK Many people think that *Jack* is a form of *Jacob*. It started life, however, as a pet form of *John*, 'God is gracious'. Its form comes from a Middle English variety, *Jankin*, 'little John', where '-kin' is a diminutive.

Jankin was reinterpreted as *Jank + in*. Then the '-in' was dropped, the 'n' was lost and *Jack* remained. In the 1980s, many parents, especially in England, went through what might be called a 'monosyllabic phase'. Hundreds of sons were named *Fred*, *Jack*, *Joe*, *Sam* and *Zach*.

JACOB The Hebrew name *Ya'akov* has, over time, given rise to an extremely long list of variants, including *Diego*, *Jacob*, *Jacobus*, *Jacques*, *James*, *Hamish* and *Seamus* – and this does not include the dozens of pet forms! The Old Testament Patriarch was the son of *Isaac* and *Rebecca*, the twin brother of *Esau*, whom he supplanted, and the father of the twelve tribes of Israel. There is debate about the meaning of his name. The most usual interpretation is that his name means 'supplanter' because he tricked his elder twin brother into giving up his birthright for 'a mess of pottage'. The biblical support for this meaning comes from the *Book of Genesis*, Chapter 27, verse 36:

And he [Esau] said: 'Is not he rightly named Jacob? For he hath supplanted me these two times: he took away my birthright; and behold, now he hath taken away my blessing.

An alternative derivation is that Ya'akov means 'heel' because when he was born, his hand held on to Esau's heel.

How did Ya'akov become James? The basic facts are these:

➢ Iakobos is the Greek equivalent of Ya'akov. (The 'Ia' was pronounced like 'Ya')

➢ Iakobos first became Iacobus in Latin and then Iacomus

➢ Iacobus gave Iaco, Iago and Jacques

➢ Sant Iago gave Santiago and, when the 'San' was dropped, the Spanish had Tiago and Diego

➢ In parts of France, Iacomus became Gemmes and this gave English James.

JAKE was a medieval variant of *Jack* but it has become popular in its own right. It is also sometimes used as an abbreviation of *Jacob*.
SEE Jack

JAMAL (pronounced 'jam + al') is a widely-used Arabic name meaning 'beauty'. Many Muslim children are given this name in honour of Jamal al-Din al-Afghani (1839-97). He promoted unity among all Muslims and was opposed to foreign rule in Muslim lands.

JAMES was originally a variant of *Jacob*, 'supplanter', but for centuries it has been thought of as a separate name. It is one of the most perennially popular of all biblical names and has been abbreviated to *Jamie*, *Jas*, *Jay*, *Jem*, *Jemmy*, *Jim*, *Jimmie* and *Jimmy*. SEE Jacob

JAN can be a form of *John*, 'God is gracious'. Medieval records show that *Jan* was widely used in England and may have been a spelling pronunciation. It may also have been imported from the continent, in which case it would have been pronounced like 'Yan'. This form is current in the Czech Republic, Germany, Poland, Scandinavia, Slovenia and the Netherlands. SEE John

JARED/JARID/ JARRAD/JARRETT

When a name has been popular over a long period of time, we often find many variants. These names – and several less common versions – have been used as given names and surnames since Norman times. The most likely explanation is that they are forms of *Gerald*, 'spear rule', or *Gerard*, 'brave spear'. It is not easy to be certain because the names were regularly confused, even in the 11th century. An alternative etymology is that some of these names come from a Hebrew name, *Yarad* or *Yered*, meaning 'descent'. SEE Gerald and Gerard

JARLATH/JARLETH is a popular Irish name. The Irish equivalent is *Íarlaith* and this is a combination of *íar*, 'west, western' + *flaith*, 'lord'. There are at least two Irish saints of this name. The earlier was the third bishop of Armagh between 467 and 481; the second was a 6th-century Galway monk.

JASON was one of the most popular boys' names in the 1980s and 1990s. It is less widespread now. It comes from the Greek name *Iason*, which takes its meaning from the verb 'to heal'. In Greek mythology, *Jason* was the son of a king in Thessaly. He set sail in a ship called the *Argo* with a group of heroes (known as Argonauts) in search of the Golden Fleece that would enable him to win back his kingdom from an uncle. The Golden Fleece was guarded by a dragon that never slept but, with the help of his lover, Medea, who was a sorceress, Jason managed to win the fleece. *Jason* was used in the *Acts of the Apostles* as a variant of *Joshua*, 'God is salvation'. SEE Joshua

JASPER Apart from the song, 'O, Sir Jasper', few people use the name today, but it was extremely popular in the past and may be due for a revival. It is also used in parts of Europe in the form of *Caspar*. *Jasper/Caspar* is, according to Christian tradition, the name of one of the three Magi to bring gifts to the

infant Jesus. His name seems to be of Persian origin and means 'treasurer'. SEE Caspar

JAY is often used as a pronunciation of the letter 'J' and it has been used for the many names beginning with this letter. *Jay* is also used by Indian families. In this case, it comes from Sanskrit, *jaya*, meaning 'triumph, victory'.

JEAN is the French form of *John*, 'God is gracious'. It comes from *Jehan*, a medieval form of Latin *Johannes*. It has been and remains an extremely popular name in France and is widely used in such compounds as *Jean-Jacques* and *Jean-Paul*. SEE John

JED is popular in the USA and is occasionally used as an abbreviation of *Gerald* or *Gerard*. Often, it is a pet form of the Hebrew name, *Jedidiah*, 'beloved of God'. This was the name given to Solomon to mark him out as specially chosen by God.

JEFFERSON This has been a surname since the 14th century and means 'son of Geoffrey' and *Geoffrey* probably means 'land of peace'. Sons have been given their mother's surname for centuries and, since *Jefferson* was a common surname, the usage spread. *Jefferson* was also given to American children in honour of Thomas Jefferson (1743-1826), a leader in the war of Independence and the third President of the USA. SEE Geoffrey

JEFFREY is an alternative spelling of *Geoffrey*, 'land of peace', and the two spellings have been equally popular since the 12th century. *Jeff* and *Geoff* are often used as pet forms. SEE Geoffrey

JEREMIAH is an anglicised form of the Hebrew name *Yirmiyahu*, 'God has lifted (me) up' or 'God has appointed (me)'. *Jeremiah* (c.650-c.585 BC) was one of the major prophets of Judaism and is credited with the authorship of the *Book of Jeremiah* and *Lamentations*. *Jeremiah* witnessed the destruction of Jerusalem by the Babylonians in

the 6th century BC. The name was very popular in the Victorian period but it is less popular today than the modified form, *Jeremy*.

JEREMY is a simplified form of *Jeremiah*. SEE Jeremiah

JEROME looks as if it is related to *Jeremy* but it has a different background. It comes from Greek *Hieronymos*, 'holy name'. St Jerome (c.331-c.419) became a secretary to Pope Damasus in 382 and began to translate the New Testament and the Psalms into Latin. When Damasus died in 385, St Jerome left Rome and travelled to Bethlehem, where he completed the translation of the entire Bible.

JESSE Like *Aaron* and *Ethan*, *Jesse* has become popular in the 21st century. It comes from the Hebrew name *Yishai*, 'gift'. According to the *Book of Samuel*, *Jesse* was the name of King David's father and is considered to be a direct ancestor of Jesus. Some African Americans are called *Jesse* in honour of the athlete Jesse Owens (1913-80). He was the grandson of a slave and brought great pride to all African Americans by winning four gold medals at the 1936 Olympic Games in Berlin.

JOACHIM comes from a Hebrew name *Yehoiachin*, 'established by God, God's judgement'. According to Christian tradition, *St Joachim* was the father of Our Lady and thus the grandfather of Jesus. *Joachim* was popular among early Puritans and remains well liked in Europe.

JOCK is a variant of *Jack* and tends to be found more widely in Scotland than elsewhere. SEE John

JODY seems to have been created in the early 20th century and its origin is debated. It is possible that it is a form of *Jude*, 'praised', or a pet form of *Joseph*, 'God will add'. Adding the diminutive ending 'ie/y' to *Jude* would produce *Judy*, which is a

girl's name, so parents may have preferred *Jody*. Alternatively, *Joey* could have been modified by introducing a 'd'. Whatever the explanation, *Jody* and *Jodie* are popular choices for both boys and girls. SEE Joseph and Jude

JOEL was a minor Hebrew prophet whose dates are uncertain. He may have lived in the fifth or the ninth century BC. His name, *Yo'el* means 'God is God' or, more accurately, 'Yahweh is God'.

JOHN has been one of the most popular names among Christians for almost 2000 years. It comes from the Latin form *Johannes*, which is a modification of Hebrew *Yochanan*, meaning 'God is gracious'. The name was valued by Christians because of John the Baptist, the cousin and forerunner of Jesus, and because of the apostle John, who is believed to have written the fourth gospel. It would be almost impossible to list all the significant bearers of *John* but it was chosen by 23 popes and by kings from England, France,

Hungary, Poland and Portugal. As one would expect with a name that has been popular over such a wide area for so long, there are many variants of *John*, including *Eoin, Gian, Hans, Iaian, Ian, Jan, Janos, Jean, Jon, Sean, Shane, Shawn* and *Zane*.

JONAH was popular among 17th-century Puritans and it began to be fashionable in the 20th century. It comes from Hebrew *Yonah*, 'dove, symbol of peace'. In the Old Testament, *Jonah* was a minor prophet. He was called by God to preach in Nineveh (an ancient city on the east bank of the River Tigris) but disobeyed and tried to escape by sea. He was thrown overboard and swallowed by a large fish, usually assumed to be a whale. After three days, he was thrown up on the shore of Nineveh.

JONATHAN comes from the Hebrew name *Yehonatan*, meaning 'God's gift'. In the Old Testament, *Jonathan* was the son of King Saul and a devoted friend of *David*. He and his father were killed by the Philistines at the battle of Mount Gilboa. Occasionally, the name is spelt *Jonathon*, and is often abbreviated to *Jon*.

JORDAN At the time of the Crusades, there was a tradition of baptising children with water from the River Jordan, in which Jesus was baptised. These children were often called *Jordan* to commemorate their christening. The river flows for about 320 kilometres between Israel and Jordan and gets its Hebrew name, *Yarden*, from a verb meaning 'flow down'. It is sacred to Christians, Jews and Muslims.

JOSEPH like *James* and *John*, continues to be a popular choice. It comes from *Josephus*, which is the Latin form of the Hebrew name *Yosef*, 'God will add'. In the Old Testament, it was the name of Jacob's eleventh son. Because he was his father's favourite, his brothers sent him to Egypt but told *Jacob* that he had died. In Egypt, he became the advisor to the Pharaoh and was eventually responsible for saving the lives of his brothers when there was a famine. In the New Testament, *Joseph* was the name of Mary's husband. As one might expect, there are many forms of *Joseph*, as the panel suggests.

Forms of Joseph

Variant	Language
Josef	Czech
Josef	German
Joseph	English
Joseph	French
Yoseif, 'He shall add'	Hebrew
Jozsef	Hungarian
Seosamh, Iosaf	Irish
Giuseppe	Italian
Josephus	Latin
Juozas	Lithuanian
Jose	Portuguese
Jozef	Polish
Iosif, Osip	Russian
Jose	Spanish

JOSHUA is one of several Hebrew names that experienced a resurgence in popularity during the 20th century. It comes from *Yehoshu'a*, meaning 'God is salvation'. *Joshua* was the name of a major prophet who lived around the 13th century BC. He succeeded Moses as leader of the Israelites and was with them when they entered the 'Promised Land'. The name *Jesus* comes from *Iesos*, which is a Greek modification of *Joshua*.

JUDE is an abbreviated form of both *Judah* and its Greek equivalent *Judas*. It comes from Hebrew *Yehudah*, 'God be praised'. In the form of *Judah*, it was the name of Jacob's fourth son. It was also the name of Judas Iscariot, who betrayed Jesus for thirty pieces of silver, and of one of the apostles, usually known as St Jude and widely appealed to as the 'patron of hopeless cases'.

JULIAN In the past, *Julian* could be used for both girls and boys. It comes from Latin *Julianus*, which is a variant of *Julius*. It is not certain what either of these names means but it has been suggested that they may derive from the Greek adjective *ioulos*, 'with a downy beard'. It was the name of a Roman Emperor who lived from c. AD 331-363. He was Constantine's nephew and is often called Julian the Apostate because he reversed Constantine's decision to make Christianity the state religion. He was killed on a campaign against the Persians and his last words were said to be *Vicisti Galilaee*, 'You have won, Galilean'.

JULIUS is an ancient Roman family name that may possibly come from Greek *ioulos*, 'with a downy beard', possibly an expression for 'young'. It may also be a form of *Jupiter*, the main Roman god. In this case, it would suggest, 'follower of Jupiter' or 'favoured by Jupiter'. The Roman family claimed descent from *Julius* who was the son of Aeneas, the Trojan leader. *Julius* is often associated with Gaius Julius Caesar (100-44 BC), who was one of Rome's most successful generals and statesmen. He was murdered in the Senate by men who thought he wanted to be king. *Jules* is a popular French variant.

JUSTIN comes from Latin *Justinus*, 'the fair/just man'. St Justin (c.100-165) was an early Christian philosopher and martyr. The details of his life are scanty but it seems likely that he was born in Samaria and beheaded in Rome.

NOTABLE NAMESAKES
Jack Lemmon (1925-2001) two-time Academy Award-winning actor and comedian. Starred in classics such as *Some Like It Hot* and *The Odd Couple*; James Dean (1931-55) actor who gained iconic status by playing troubled loners; Jesse James (1847-82) American train and bank robber. He was shot in the back by a bounty hunter; John Lennon (1940-80) English singer, songwriter and co-founder of The Beatles. As a solo artist he wrote and recorded such songs as 'Imagine'. Shot dead in New York on 8 December 1980; Jonah Lomu (b. 1975) New

Zealand rugby player who holds the record for try scoring in the Rugby World Cup series.

K

KAI/KAY/KYE This name began to be a popular choice for parents who wanted an unusual name for their son. It is pronounced to rhyme with 'high' and seems to be taken from the name of one of King Arthur's knights. Sir Kay's name is thought to be a form of Latin *Gaius*. The meaning of the Latin name is uncertain but many parents link it to 'joyful, happy'.

KAMAL (pronounced 'Kam + al') is an Arabic name meaning 'perfect'. In many societies, parents seem to aspire to have perfect sons and daughters.

KANE has been used as a surname for over 900 years. It may have several possible origins. It possibly comes from the Welsh adjective *cain*, 'beautiful'. Since Welsh adjectives followed the noun, this adjective might easily have been mistaken for a surname. It may derive from *Caen* in France, where many Normans came from and where William the Conqueror endowed a monastery. It may come from the Cornish saint, *Keyne*, or from the Gaelic surname *Mac Cathain*, 'son of the warrior'. *Kane* is occasionally used because of the Irish surname *O'Kane*, which comes from *Ó Cathán*, descendant of the 'warrior' or 'war champion'.

KAREEM/KARIM These are variant spellings of one of the most frequently-used names for a Muslim child. It means 'noble'.

KARL is the German and Scandinavian form of *Charles*, 'man'. It was particularly popular in the Austrian royal house and was often combined with other names such as *Karl-Gustav*. It was also the name of the German philosopher, Karl Marx (1818-83). He is credited with being one of the founding fathers of communism.

KAZUKI is a Japanese name with two possible meanings. One is 'shining one' and the second is 'new generation'.

KEANU is a Hawaiian name meaning 'cool, refreshing breeze'. It has been given prominence by the actor Keanu Reeves (b.1964) who is partly Hawaiian.

KEIR is most popular in Scotland. It has been a surname since the 13th century. The surname, which is also written *Kerr*, comes from Old Norse *kjarr*, 'brushwood, marshy ground'. It is also possible that the place name from which the surname comes is from Gaelic *ciar*, 'dark'.

KEITH can also be a Scottish surname that probably comes from a Gaelic word such as *ceiteach*, 'woods'. The name may have started in Scotland but it is now found throughout the world.

KEN is a frequently-used abbreviation of *Kenneth*, 'fire-born'. It is also used as a pet form of the Hebrew name *Kenan* or *Cainan*, 'possession'. In the Old Testament, *Kenan/Cainan* was a great grandson of Adam and Eve.

KENDRICK/KENRICK

This name may have either a Germanic or a Celtic origin. It may be a modified spelling of the Old English name *Ceneric*, 'keen/bold + power', or it may be from Welsh *Cynrig* or Gaelic *Mac Eanraig*, both meaning 'son of Henry'.

KENNEDY is an Irish and Scottish surname. It comes from Ó Cinnéide, 'descendant of Ceannéide'. The name is said to mean either 'ugly head' or 'helmeted head'. *Kennedy* was popular in the second half of the 20th century, mainly because of John Fitzgerald Kennedy (1917-63), the 35th president of the United States.

KENNETH is an anglicised spelling of the Gaelic name *Coinneach*, which is so old that its meaning is uncertain. It may mean 'born of fire'. Kenneth I was king of Scotland in the 9th century. He defeated the Picts

305

and reigned from about AD 844 until 858. *Kenneth* is popular throughout the world, especially in Africa, where it was carried by Scottish missionaries. It is often abbreviated to *Ken*, *Kennie* and *Kenny*.

KERR is a surname that has become a given name in the 20th century. It is less common than *Keir*, 'brushwood, marshy ground', to which it is related. SEE Keir

KERRY comes from County Kerry, which may owe its origin to *ciar*, 'dark'. The name was male in Australia but is now almost exclusively female.

KEVIN In the second half of the 20th century, *Kevin* became one of the most popular names for sons, even among families with no Irish connection. It comes from Irish *Caoimhín*, 'of gentle birth'. St Kevin, who died around AD 618, was an Irish monk who established a monastery in Glendalough. He loved solitude and refused to be

disturbed for the entire 40 days of Lent, during which time he prayed almost incessantly. A story is told to illustrate his love of nature and also his stillness at prayer. When he had his arms outstretched, a blackbird laid an egg in his hand. He kept his arms outstretched until the egg hatched.

KHALID (pronounced 'hal + eed') is a popular Arabic name meaning 'eternal, everlasting'. It is usually, but not exclusively, a Muslim name. It was the given name of a 7th-century military leader, Khahid ibn-al-Walid (c.584-642). He was a friend of the Prophet Muhammad and has the military distinction of never having been defeated.

KHALIL (pronounced 'hal + eel') is an Arabic name popular among Middle East Christians and Muslims. It means 'friend'.

KIERAN is an Irish name that has proved popular outside the Irish diaspora. It comes from *Ciarán*, 'little dark one'. It is also spelt *Kieron* and *Keiron*. Although unrelated, a similar name, *Kiran*, 'sunbeam' is used by Indian parents. SEE Ciarán

KILLIAN is an Irish name, marginally more popular in its Irish form *Cillian*. The name probably comes from *cill*, 'church', or, since it may predate Christianity, from *ciall*, 'good sense, intelligence'. St Killian (c.640-c.689) was born in Ulster but travelled to Europe to help spread Christianity. He was murdered in Bavaria because he condemned the marriage of Duke Gozbert to his dead brother's wife. There are *Killians* throughout Africa where Irish missionaries have been.

KIM There are four possible origins for *Kim*, a name that was popularised by Rudyard Kipling (1865-1936). His novel *Kim* was published in 1901. In it, *Kim* is the orphaned son of an Irish soldier serving in India. Kim manages to reconcile the two aspects of his life: the European and the Indian, revealing the best of both. *Kim* has also been used as an abbreviation of

Kimberley, a town in South Africa that has been a rich source of diamond mining since the second half of the 19th century. The town was called after Lord Kimberley, whose name means 'Cyneburg's clearing' and, unusually, *Cyneburg* was a woman's name, meaning 'royal manor'. Occasionally, *Kim* can be used as an abbreviation of Hebrew *Joachim*, 'established by God'. Finally, it is one of the most frequently occurring names in Vietnam, where it means 'golden'.

KIRK comes from *kirkya*, the Scandinavian equivalent of English 'church', and it was adopted as a surname by people who lived near a church as early as the 13th century. It was popularised by the film actor, Kirk Douglas (b. 1916) and by Captain Kirk of the Starship Enterprise. The *Star Trek* television programmes began in 1966 but continue to be regularly shown. They have spawned six television series, ten films, hundreds of computer games and a dictionary and grammar of

Klingon! The 40th anniversary of the first broadcast was celebrated on 8 September, 2006.

KIT In Elizabethan times, *Kit* was a popular abbreviation of *Christopher*, 'bearer of Christ'. It was so popular that the Caribbean island of St Kitts was originally St Christopher. (Christopher Columbus named it after himself.) It was also the name of a US frontiersman and scout, Kit Carson (1809-68).

KNUT (pronounced 'k + noot') is one of the Scandinavian names that began to be popular in the 19th century as Scandinavian mythology began to be more widely known. It is the same name as *Canute*, who was king of Denmark, England and Norway and who died in 1035. The name means 'knot'.

KOFI is a Ghanaian name meaning 'born on Friday'. In the New World, Akan-speaking slaves preserved the name, although it was often spelt *Coffey*, *Cuffee* or *Cuffy*. In Guyana, South America, a slave leader called *Cuffy* led the first successful slave rebellion since Spartacus, who rebelled against Rome in 73BC. In 1763 Cuffy encouraged the slaves to rebel against their appalling conditions. Plantation after plantation was taken by the rebels and half of the Europeans fled the colony. Cuffy and his rebels held out until 1764, when they were defeated by troops from neighbouring colonies and from Europe.

KONRAD is the German equivalent of *Conrad* and the spelling with 'K' is increasing. It comes from *kuon*, 'bold, brave' + *rad*, 'counsel, advice'. It has been popular in the German-speaking world since the 10th century at the latest but has only made an impact on the English-speaking world in the 19th. SEE Conrad

KUNTO is an Akan name meaning 'third child'. The Akan people are mainly found in Ghana but thousands, perhaps hundreds of thousands, were taken to the New World as part of the Slave Trade. Many African-Americans and Caribbean people trace their ancestry to Ghana.

KURT was originally an abbreviated form of *Konrad*, 'brave counsel', but it is now usually regarded as an independent came. SEE Conrad and Curt

KWAME (pronounced 'kwa + may') is an Akan name, meaning 'born on Saturday'. It is best known perhaps as the name of Ghana's first Prime Minister and President, Kwame Nkrumah (1909-72). His given name was Francis but he changed it to *Kwame* in 1945.

KWASI (pronounced 'kwa + s/zee') like *Kofi*, *Kunto* and *Kwame*, is a Ghanaian name that is still used in the Caribbean. *Kwasi* means 'born on Sunday' and it was often written *Quashie* in Jamaica.

KYE is a spelling of *Kai*, 'happy'. SEE Kai

KYLE is an ancient name. It comes from a surname which derives from a river name in Yorkshire. The river's name is from Welsh *cul*, 'narrow'.

NOTABLE NAMESAKES
Keith Richards (b. 1943) guitarist and founding member of *The Rolling Stones*; Kenneth Branagh (b. 1960) award-winning actor and film director, born in Northern Ireland; Kevin Bacon (b. 1958) American actor and director, who is best known for his performance in *Apollo 13* (1995); Khalil Gibran (1883-1931) born in Lebanon but moved to America where he became an artist and poet; Kofi Annan (b. 1938) Ghanaian politician who served as Secretary-General of the United Nations from 1997-2007; Kurt Vonnegut (1922-2007) American novelist and science fiction writer.

L

LACHLAN/LACHLANN

the 'ch' is pronounced like the
'gh' in 'lough') is a Gaelic name
for a Viking. It means 'land of the
lakes' and it has given rise to the
surname McLaughlin. The form
Lochlan(n) is more likely to occur
in Ireland and *Lachlan(n)* in
Scotland, but that is only a
tendency and not a fixed rule.

LAMAR The meaning of *Lamar*
is uncertain. It may be from
lamar, an old English word
meaning 'amber'; it may be a
modified form of French *la mer*,
'the sea'; or it may be from
Germanic *Landmar*, 'land +
famous'. If the Germanic
explanation is correct, then
Lamar is similar in meaning to
Lambert, which comes from *land
+ berth*, 'bright, famous'.
Lambert Simnel (c.1475-1525)
was a pretender to the English
throne. He wanted to dethrone
Henry VII and was actually
crowned king in Dublin in 1487.
The uprising failed and Simnel

was punished by being given a
lowly job in the kitchen of the
royal household.

LANCE The history of this
name reminds us that we cannot
take meaning for granted. *Lance*
looks like the word for a weapon
and seems to come from Latin
lancea, 'weapon with a long
wooden shaft and a metal head'.
Indeed, some parents may
choose the name because of such
a meaning. It is more likely,
however, that *Lance* comes from a
Germanic name *Lanzo*, 'land
man'. The Normans used it as an
abbreviation for many names
beginning with *Land-* and it had
become a surname by the 12th
century. Many parents select the
name as an abbreviation of
Lancelot, who was a Knight of the
Round Table and the lover of
Queen Guinevere. We do not
know what Lancelot's name
means but *Lancelot* was a Celtic
name that underwent a great
deal of change. In view of the
fact that the Arthurian knight
was originally devout, it is
probable that the first part of his
name was from *llan*, 'church'.

LANCELOT/LAUNCELOT

In the Arthurian legends,
Lancelot was one of the bravest
and best Knights of the Round
Table. He eventually betrayed
King Arthur by having an affair
with Queen Guinevere. This
triggered the war that put an end
to Camelot and Arthur's reign of
peace. It is not easy to say what
Lancelot means. It is often
interpreted as 'lance bearer' but
this is improbable. The spelling
Launcelot is a reflection of the
French pronunciation of the
name. SEE Lance

LAURENT is a French form of
Laurence. SEE Laurence

LAURENCE/LAWRENCE

These spellings are anglicised
forms of *Laurent*, which comes
from Latin *Laurentius*, 'man from
Laurentum'. The town of
Larentum almost certainly took
its name from *laurus*, 'laurel', the
leaves of which have been used
for their medicinal qualities and
also to honour persons of
achievement. There were
several saints called *Laurence*.
One was a martyr who died in
Rome in AD 258. Another
was St Laurence O'Toole
(1128-1180), who is also
known as Lorcan Ó Tuathail.
He was Bishop of Dublin when
the Normans attacked the city in
1170. He realised that the Irish
were unable to resist the might
of the Normans and submitted to
the rule of Henry II. The
spelling with 'w' is almost equally
common. They are both
abbreviated to *Larry*.

LECH In Polish mythology, *Lech*
was the founder of Poland. The
name is popular even though its
meaning is unknown. It may be
related to *Ludwig*, 'war fame'. It
became a symbol of the Polish
desire for freedom when Lech
Walesa (b.1943) founded the
Solidarity Trade Union, which
contributed greatly to the
overthrow of communism in
Poland.

LEE is one of those names that
can have a variety of sources and
meanings. It can be an English
surname from *leah*, which can
mean 'wood' or 'clearing'; it can
come from Welsh *lle*, 'place', or

the god *Llew*, 'radiant light'; it can be from Irish *laoi*, meaning 'poem', or from the River Lee in Cork; it is also the second most widely used family name in China. In this case, it is sometimes spelt *Li* and means 'pear'. Occasionally, the name is spelt *Leigh* but this a variant spelling of *leah*.

LEIF (pronounced 'leaf') is one of the many Scandinavian names that began to be used in the late 19th century when there was renewed interest in northern mythologies. The name means 'beloved'. Leif Ericsson was a Norse explorer who, around the year 1000, sailed westward from Greenland and discovered a country he called *Vinland*. It is thought that he was one of the first Europeans to reach the shores of America.

LEIGH (pronounced 'lee') is a variant form of *Lee*, 'wood, clearing'. see Lee

LEMUEL Most people first come across this name in *Gulliver's Travels* (1726). Lemuel Gulliver was a surgeon on a merchant ship and the book relates his adventures. *Lemuel* is a Hebrew name meaning either 'consecrated to God' or 'devoted to God'.

LEN/LENNY These are popular pet forms of *Leonard*, 'brave as a lion'. see Leonard

LENNOX is a Scottish surname that is now used as a given name. The surname comes from a place name in Dunbartonshire and it is probably of Gaelic origin. It may come from a compound involving *leamhán*, 'elm tree'. The name is popular in the Caribbean.

LEO is the Latin word for 'lion' and it was used as a given name in the Roman Empire. *Leo* was also widely used among early Christians, who saw themselves as 'lions of the true God'. *Leo* occurs as a surname in England as early as the 12th century. The French form, *Leon*, is also popular, especially in the United States.

LEONARD is a Germanic name that was popular among

the Normans, among whom it had become a surname by the 13th century. The Norman name is composed of *leon*, 'lion' + *hard*, 'brave, strong'. St Leonard was a 6th-century miracle worker, who became a hermit and lived in the woods near Limoges. It is said that his prayers helped the king's wife through a difficult birth and so he became the patron saint of women in labour.

LEONARDO is the Italian form of *Leonard*. Most parents who give their sons this name have Leonardo da Vinci (1452-1519) in mind. He was a polymath, as much at home in the fields of anatomy and hydraulics as in art.

LEOPOLD looks as if it includes the word *leo* but, in fact, it does not. It is a Germanic name made up of the words *liut*, 'people' + *bold*, 'brave'. The spelling was altered because of the popularity of *Leo* and *Leonard*. Queen Victoria had a son called *Leopold*. He was given the name in honour of a great-uncle, King Leopold of the Belgians.

LEROY is almost certainly from French, *le roi*, 'the king'. It is popular in the Caribbean and the southern states of America, where it tends to be pronounced like 'lee + roy'.

LESLIE is usually regarded as the male form of a Scottish place name, which is a town in Fife. The meaning of the town is uncertain. It is probable that it comes from Old Norse *lioss*, 'bright' + *leah*, 'clearing'. It is also possible that the name is Gaelic and involves a compound such as *lios*, 'ring fort' + *laoch*, 'warrior'. The spelling *Lesley* is often reserved for daughters, but traditionally, the two spellings were used for men. *Les* is a widely-used abbreviation.

LESTER is derived from a surname that is based on the city of Leicester, which was originally written *Ligeracæster*, 'Roman fort on the Ligera River'. The name of the river is Celtic and is probably from the same root as the River Loire, which used to be *Ligeris*. The meaning of the root is uncertain. It may simply mean 'river'.

LEVI (usually pronounced 'leave + eye') is a Hebrew name meaning 'attached, pledged, united'. It was the name of Jacob's third son and it gave rise to the Levites, the tribe of *Levi*, regarded as the priestly caste. Today, many people will associate *Levi* with jeans. This trademark owes its origin to Levi Strauss (1829- 1902), who was the original manufacturer of this type of denim garment.

LEWIS In Norman times, *Lewis* was a regular alternative spelling of *Louis*, which was a form of the Germanic name *Hlod*, 'fame' + *wig*, 'battle'. SEE Louis

LIAM is an Irish form of *William*, which was a popular Norman form of the Germanic name *Wilhelm*, 'will + helmet/ protection'. It looks as if the Irish simply selected the second half of *William*, but it is more likely that *Liam* is an Irish pronunciation of *Guillaume*, a French form of *William*. *Liam* has

become extremely popular in the English-speaking world, possibly as a result of the international fame of the actor Liam Neeson (b. 1952). SEE William

LINUS is a Greek name that has become popular in the 20th century. It is the name of St Peter's successor, who was the second pope. It is not certain what *Linus* means but it is probable that it is related to Latin, *linum*, meaning 'flax, flax-coloured'. In Greek mythology, *Linus* is the name of two characters. The first was a son of *Apollo* and he was linked to a dirge that was sung to lament the dying vegetation in Autumn. The second was a musician who was famed for the wonder of his music, and for the fact that he taught Hercules.

LLEWELLYN/LLYWELYN is a Welsh name that probably comes from *llew*, 'lion', although it may also be related to *Lugh*, an ancient Celtic sun god. The widespread nature of the god's influence is indicated by the fact that Leiden, Lyons and London were all dedicated to him. *Llewellyn* was the name of two medieval Welsh heroes, *Llewellyn the Great* (1173-1240) and his grandson, who died in 1242 fighting to free Wales.

LLOYD comes from Welsh *llwyd*, meaning 'grey'. It is an exceptionally common Welsh surname and has been used as a surname since the early 14th century. The English have difficulty pronouncing the Welsh sound represented by 'll' and so have been recording it as *Floyd* since the 15th century.

LOCHLANN is another form of *Lachlann*, 'land of the lakes'. SEE Lachlan

LOUIS is the modern French form of the Germanic name *Ludwig*, which comes from *hlod*, 'fame' + *wig*, 'war'. *Louis* has been the name of 18 French kings, including St Louis (1214-70). According to one story told about him, he had great devotion to the presence of Jesus in the hosts preserved in the tabernacle of the altar. Once, a

servant ran to tell him that Jesus was appearing in another part of the palace. Louis IX refused to go, saying that he could 'see' Jesus every morning at Mass. The State of Louisiana was called after Louis XIV (1638-1715).

LUCAS is a Latin form of the Greek name *Loukas*, meaning 'man from Lucania'. Because of the Latin word, *lux*, 'light', the name is often said to mean 'light'. In the Middle Ages, it was common to write *Lucas* in formal documents but *Luke* on less formal occasions, and it has been a surname since the 12th century. Some modern usage may derive from the surname. SEE Luke

LUDO is an abbreviation of *Ludovic*, another form of the Germanic name *Ludwig*, 'famed in war'. It may also owe its popularity to the fact the *ludo* is a Latin word meaning 'I play'.

LUKE is the English form of Latin *Lucas*. The name has remained popular for 2000 years, largely because of St Luke, the evangelist. Traditionally, he has been described as a doctor, possibly because his gospel shows more interest in ailments than the other three. The name got extra prominence in the 20th century because of Luke Skywalker in the *Star Wars* trilogy.

LUTHER comes from a German surname that is a compound of *liut*, 'people + *heri*, 'army'. It is widely used as a given name by evangelical Christians in honour of Martin Luther (1483-1546), who is generally credited with bringing about the Protestant Reformation. The name became even more widely used among African Americans after the assassination of Martin Luther King (1929-68).

LYLE is a spelling of a French surname based on *l'isle*, 'the island'. It has been used as a surname since the early 14th century and began to be used as a given name in the 20th century.

NOTABLE NAMESAKES
Lance Armstrong (b. 1981) American cyclist who has won the Tour de France seven consecutive times; Leonardo DiCaprio (b. 1974) American actor who rose to fame in the award-winning film, *Titanic* (1997); Lester Piggott (b. 1935) one of the greatest flat jockeys of all time; won the Derby nine times; Linus Pauling (1901-94) American scientist who won two Nobel Prizes in different fields; Louis Armstrong (1901-71) perhaps the best-known American jazz musician of all time; Ludovic Kennedy (b. 1919) Scottish journalist, broadcaster and writer.

M

MAC/MACK is used mainly as a nickname for someone whose name begins with the Gaelic prefix *mac*, 'son'.

MACARTAN means 'son of Art' and *Art* probably means 'bear'. This surname, like *Macauley*, 'son of Olaf', and *Mackenzie*, 'son of the handsome one', has begun to be used as a given name.

MAGNUS (pronounced 'man + oos'/'mag + noos') is from Latin *magnus*, 'great'. Charlemagne (742-814) was the Holy Roman Emperor and was also known by his Latin name, *Carolus Magnus*, 'Charles the Great'. The *Magnus* was first used as an independent name by the Scandinavians and they carried it to Ireland and Scotland, where it is now usually written as *Manus*. This, in turn, gave rise to the surname, MacManus. St Magnus of Orkney (c.1075-1116) was a convert to Christianity. He was martyred by his brother *Haakon*, who then became sole ruler of Orkney.

MALACHI/MALACHIAS

(pronounced 'mal + ackee'/ 'mal + ach +eye') This is the name of a minor Hebrew prophet and it means 'messenger of God'. It is usually equated with Irish *Malachy*, 'devotee of St Cellach', and the spelling used for the Irish name is a borrowing from Hebrew.

MALACHY/ MAOILEACHLAINN

(pronounced 'mal + ackee'/ 'mwail + loch + lin') is the name of an Irish saint and Archbishop of Armagh. He lived from 1095-1148 and this was a turbulent time in Ireland when many of the dioceses were in need of reform. His name means 'devotee of St Seachlann' and he is also known as *Maelmaedoc*, 'devotee of St Madoc'. *Malachy* was also the name of a High King of Ireland who fought the Vikings and Brian Boru and died around 1022. He was immortalised in Thomas Moore's melody, 'Let

Erin Remember':

*When Malachy wore the collar
of gold
Which he won from the proud
invader.*

MALCOLM originated in Scotland and means 'devotee of St Columba, the dove'. There have been four Scottish kings called *Malcolm*. Malcolm III (c.1031-93) was the son of King Duncan and he came to the throne after killing Macbeth in battle in 1057. Shakespeare's play *Macbeth* deals with this period, but changes many of the details, partly out of respect for James I, who regarded himself as a direct descendant of *Duncan*.

MALIK/MELLICK (pronounced 'mal + eke') is an Arabic name meaning 'ruler, king'. It is widely used as both a given and a surname in the Arab world, and has some currency among African Americans. SEE Melchior

MANASSEH (pronounced 'man + assay') In the Old Testament, *Manasseh*, 'causing to forget', was the eldest son of *Joseph*, the head of one of the twelve tribes of Israel and a Hebrew patriarch. His name is popular in Africa and among African Americans.

MANFRED was a popular Norman name and was widely used in Germany in the first half of the 20th century. It probably comes from *man*, 'man' + *frid*, 'peace', although it is possible that the first syllable was originally *magin*, 'strength'.

MANNY is a widely-used abbreviation of *Emmanuel*. SEE Emmanuel

MANSOOR/MANSUR is a popular Arabic name meaning 'victorious'. It was the name of the founder of the city of Baghdad.

MARC is the French form of *Marcus*, 'born under Mars'. SEE Marcus

MARCEL is a French name taken from Latin *Marcellus* and probably meaning 'little follower of Mars'. SEE Marcus

MARCO is the Italian form of *Marcus*, 'born under Mars'. SEE Marcus

MARCUS is the original Latin form of *Mark*. Its meaning is uncertain but it is likely that it is linked to *Mars*, the name of the Roman god of war, and *Mars* is almost certainly from *mas-maris*, 'virile'. *Marcus* was not widely used in the English-speaking world until the early 20th century.

MARIO is an Italian form of *Marius*, 'virile', but it is usually given to a child in honour of *Mary*, the mother of Jesus. Mario Lanza (1921-59), the singer and film actor, helped to popularise the name in the 1950s. SEE Marius

MARIUS is an old Roman family name already well established when Gaius Marius (c.157-86 BC) was a general and politician. The name is probably linked to *Mars*, the Roman god of war, and to the adjective *mas-maris*, 'virile'. It has also been suggested that it may be related to *mare*, 'the sea'. Although the name predated Christianity, *Marius* is occasionally used as the male form of *Maria*, the Latin form of *Mary*.

MARK In the English-speaking world, *Mark* is the usual name of the second evangelist and companion of both St Peter and St Paul. *Mark* is said to have been buried in Venice in the 9th century and he is the patron saint of the city. In Arthurian legend, *Mark* was the name of the king of Cornwall, the uncle of *Tristan* (or sometimes *Tristram*) and the promised husband of *Iseult*.

MARLON occurs as an English surname. It is a variant of *Merlin*, 'sea fortress', and it was used as a given name as early as the 17th century. In spite of this history, however, most parents who now choose the name do so in memory of the actor Marlon Brando (1924-2004).

MARMADUKE is traditionally regarded as an English name. It is, however, a modification of the name of the

Irish saint, *Mael-Maedoc* (1095-1148), also known as *Malachy*. SEE Malachy

MARSHAL/MARSHALL

This name, which refers to a high-ranking military officer, goes back through English to French *mareschal*, 'commander', through Latin *mariscalcus*, 'officer', to the Old German elements *marah*, 'horse' + *scalc*, 'servant'. It is sometimes linked to the Roman god *Mars* but that association is a coincidence. Marshall McLuhan (1911-80), the Canadian writer, is probably the best-known bearer of the name.

MARTIN is from the Latin

name *Martinus*, and was originally derived from *Mars*, the Roman god of war and probably means 'virile'. Variants of the name are found throughout European languages, partly because of the fame of St Martin de Tours, a French bishop who died around AD 397. More recently, it has been associated with St Martin de Porres (1579-1639), a lay Dominican brother who was the

son of a Spanish dignitary and a freed black slave. Several other Martins have been prominent in helping to promote the name. These include Martin Luther (1483-1546) and Martin Luther King (1929-68).

MARVIN/MERVIN This has

been a popular surname since the 12th century. The different pronunciations can be accounted for by the fact that medieval 'er' was regularly pronounced 'ar' as it is in *clerk* and *Derby*. It may come from Old English *Merewine*, 'lake friend', from Welsh *Merfyn*, 'famous', or from Welsh *Myrddyn*, 'sea fortress'. The name is popular with African Americans. Marvin Gay II (1939-84), better known as Marvin Gaye, was a musician and rhythm and blues singer.

MATHIAS/MATTHIAS

This is the Greek form of the Hebrew name *Mattathia*, 'gift of God' and it is often used as a means of distinguishing the apostle and evangelist *Matthew* from the disciple chosen to replace Judas Iscariot. It is widely used in Germany and in West Africa.

MATTHEW is the English version of the Hebrew name *Mattathia*, 'gift of God'. It is usually preserved for St Matthew, the apostle, tax-collector and author of the first gospel. Occasionally, the form *Mathew* occurs. It has several abbreviated forms, including *Mat*, *Matt*, *Mattie* and *Matty*.

MAURICE comes from the Latin name *Mauritius*, meaning 'Moor' and applied in the Middle Ages to someone from North Africa or to someone with a dark complexion. The name was introduced by the Normans and took the form of *Muirgheas* in Ireland, although *Muirgheas* is meaningful and suggests 'sea choice'. St Maurice was a 3rd- century soldier who became a Christian and was martyred for refusing to make sacrifices to idols. He was regularly depicted as an African. This Norman name gave rise to the surname *Morris*, which has been borrowed as a given name. SEE Morris

MAX is now often selected as an independent name although it was formerly an abbreviation of *Maximilian*, 'greatest', or *Maxwell*, 'great well' or 'Magnus's well'. SEE Maximilian and Maxwell

MAXIMILIAN is from the Latin name *Maximilianus*, which is a derivative of *Maximus*, 'greatest'. It was the name of a 3rd-century martyr and also the name of the Emperor of Mexico from 1864 to 1867. *Maximilian* (1832-67) was the brother of Emperor Franz Josef of Austria (1830-1916). *Maximilian* was executed by firing squad after a popular uprising in Mexico against an imposed emperor.

MAXWELL is now a given name but it is derived from the Scottish surname which, in turn, is from the place name. *Maxwell* was originally Maccaswell. *Maccas* was an Irish form of *Magnus*, 'great', and 'well' could be either a well or running water.

MEL is an Irish name that has been given exposure by the actor Mel Gibson (b. 1956). St Mel was a contemporary of St Patrick, who made him a bishop. St Mel (d. c. 490), whose name may mean 'devotee' or 'honey', was involved in St Brigid's becoming a nun and, according to tradition, accidentally made her a bishop! Perhaps it was not an error after all, as it has been suggested that St Hilda (614-80) of Whitby was also a bishop.

MELCHIOR (pronounced 'mel + key + or') is the traditional name of one of the three wise men, or 'Magi', who visited the infant Jesus with gifts. *Melchior* is related to modern Arabic *Malik*, 'king', and seems to mean 'king's city'.

MEREDITH is from Welsh *Meredydd*, 'great lord'. It has been a surname since the 12th century and is currently popular as a given name for both boys and girls.

MERLIN Anyone who has been exposed to the Arthurian legend will know of Merlin, the magician who guides Arthur in his quest for the creation of a heaven on earth at Camelot. In Geoffrey of Monmouth's 12th-century *Historia Regum Britanniae*, *Merlin* is called *Myrddyn*, 'sea fortress', and he uses his magic to bring the stones of Stonehenge from Naas in Ireland. When the legends were translated into French, *Myrddyn* became *Myrddlin* and then, by association with *merlin*, 'falcon', his name became *Merlin*. The name is currently also used for daughters.

MERRICK is a surname that is based on *Meuric*, a Welsh form of Maurice. It illustrates an interesting circle where a given name becomes a surname and then a given name again. SEE Maurice

MERVIN/MERVYN This name is almost certainly from *Myrrdyn*, 'sea fortress', the same name that gave *Merlin*. It is also possible that it is linked to *Merfyn*, 'sea famous'. SEE Merlin

MICHA (pronounced 'meeh + hah') is the name of a minor prophet in the Old Testament. It means 'Who is like God?' and is related to one of the most widely used names in the world, *Michael*.

MICHAEL is from the Hebrew name *Mika'el*, 'Who is like God?' In the Old Testament, *Michael* is an archangel who is God's messenger and leader of the hosts of angels. He defeated Lucifer and sent him and his followers hurtling out of heaven. In the *Book of Revelation*, he is described as the leader of heaven's armies. There are many saints called after him, as well as Byzantine emperors and a Russian Czar.

More recently, St Michael the archangel has been chosen as a brand name for Marks and Spencer plc. *Michael* has been – and continues to be – a popular choice for parents worldwide. It is often abbreviated to *Mick*, *Mickie*, *Micky* and *Mike*.

Forms of Michael

Variant	Language
Michal	Czech, Slovak
Michaë	Dutch
Micheál	Irish
Micheil	Scots Gaelic
Michel	French, German
Michelef	Italian
Miguel	Spanish, Portugese
Mihael	Slovene
Mihail	Romanian
Mihailo	Serbian
Mihály	Hungarian
Mihhaelo	Esperanto
Mihkel	Estonian
Mihovil	Croatian
Mikael	Scandinavian
Mikaere	Maori
Mikel	Basque
Mikelis	Latvian
Mikhail	Russian, Bulgarian
Mikhailo	Ukrainian

MILES was a Norman name and, although it has never been as widely used as the name of a saint, it has been used steadily since the 12th century. It has the same form as Latin *miles*, 'soldier', and some parents may choose it for that reason. It is also possible that it is linked to the Slavic element *mil* or *mir* meaning 'mercy' as in *Miroslav*, or to *Michael*. SEE Michael

MILO was used by the Normans as a latinised form of *Miles* as early as 1086. The meaning of *Milo* is therefore as uncertain as *Miles* and may be interpreted as 'soldier', 'peace' or 'Who is like God?' In favour of a Latin origin for the name is the fact that Milo of Croton lived in the 6th century BC and was renowned as a wrestler and strong man. He is supposed to have died trying to split a tree with his fist.

MILTON There are many villages and towns in England of this name and they can mean either 'mill town' or 'middle town'. *Milton* became a surname in the early 14th century and has, more recently, been used as a given name.

MITCHELL is a surname that comes from an English pronunciation of the French name *Michel*, 'Who is like God?' It has become an independent name and its abbreviation, *Mitch*,

is also gaining independence.

MOHENDRA is a frequently-used Indian name meaning 'great Indra'. *Indra* is a goddess and the name probably means 'splendid'.

MONTAGUE was a Norman surname that came from *mont*, 'hill' + *aigu*, 'pointed'. Drogo de Montaigu was one of the nobles who accompanied William the Conqueror to England in 1066. The name began to be used as a given name in the 19th century. The abbreviation, *Monty*, is often used.

MORGAN is derived from an Old Celtic name probably meaning 'bright sea' or 'sea circle'. It was the name of King Arthur's stepsister, Morgan le Fay, who was Queen of Avalon and who spirited *Arthur* away to heal his wounds after he was fatally injured in battle.

MORRIS is a surname based on *Meurisse*, an early Norman variant of *Maurice*, 'dark'. *Morris* was often used as a given name until about the 17th century but it has regained favour and is slightly more widely used than *Maurice*. SEE Maurice

MUBARAK is an Arabic name, meaning 'blessed'. It is interesting how many cultures have favoured a son with such a name. Although cross-language equivalences are never easy, the meaning of 'blessed' is carried by Old English *Eadig*, Latin *Benedictus*, Greek *Macaire* and Indonesian *Rachmad*.

MUHAMMAD/ MUHAMMED is almost certainly the most popular name for boys in the world. It is the name of the Prophet of Islam who lived from c. 570-632. He was born in Mecca and wrote the Koran around 610. He faced opposition and fled to Medina with his followers in 622. The Islamic calendar dates from AD 622. The name *Muhammed* means 'worthy of praise'. It occurs in many variants, including *Mahomet*, *Mohamad* and *Mehmet*.

MUNGO is first recorded in Scotland in the 6th century as an alternative name for St Kentigern. It was the name of the Scottish explorer, Mungo Park (1771-1806), who sought the source of the River Niger. The name is glossed in Latin as *carissimus amicus*, 'dearest friend', but that meaning would seem to rule out a Gaelic origin for the name.

MUNRO is a well-known surname, also spelt *Monroe*. The surname and given name come from a place in Scotland near the Roe river and meaning 'mouth of the red river'. Hugh Thomas Munro (1856-1919) published a list of all 277 mountains in Scotland that are at least 914 metres high in 1891 and these mountains are often called 'munros'.

MURRAY is often from the Gaelic name *Muireach*, 'sea traveller'. The surname *Murray* is sometimes from this source and sometimes from the province of Moray in Scotland.

MUSTAFA/MUSTAPHA is Arabic and means 'the chosen

one'. It was a term of respect given to the Prophet Muhammad.

Mustafa Kamal (1881-1938) was given the name *Ataturk*, 'father of the Turks', in 1934 for his efforts to turn Turkey into a modern secular state when he was President.

MYLES is an alternative spelling of *Miles*, 'soldier'. SEE Miles

NOTABLE NAMESAKES
Marc Bolan (1947-77) guitarist who helped found the rock group *Tyrannosaurus Rex*; Marcel Marceau (1923-2007) French mime artist who joined the French resistance during World War II and saved the lives of many Jewish children; Marvin Hamlish (b. 1944) American composer, pianist and conductor; Maurice Chevalier (1888-1972) French singer of such hits as 'Louise (1929) and 'Thank Heaven for Little Girls'. Michael Schumacher (b. 1969) German Formula One driver and seven times world champion; Muhammad Ali (b. 1942) (formerly Cassius Clay) African American three-time World Heavyweight Champion boxer. In 1999 Ali was named 'Sportsman of the Century' by the BBC.

N

NAAMAN (pronounced 'nay + man') is the name of the Syrian whose leprosy is healed by Elisha. Elisha instructs Naaman to wash in the Jordan and, although he believes the Syrian rivers are superior, he does as he is instructed and is healed.

NABIL (pronounced 'nab + eel') is a popular Arabic name meaning 'noble, gracious'.

NADIR (pronounced 'nad + ear') is an Arabic name meaning 'precious'. It is widely used in the Arab world and is occasionally spelt *Nadeer*.

NATHAN comes from a Hebrew word meaning 'gift'. In the Bible, *Nathan* was a minor prophet who lived at the time of King David. In spite of David's power, *Nathan* reproached him for the sin of taking another man's wife. *Nathan* is one of a handful of Hebrew names that have become popular since the 1990s. (*Aaron* and *Ethan* are two others.) It is sometimes abbreviated to *Nat*.

NATHANIEL is a Hebrew name meaning 'gift of god'. It is equivalent to the Greek name *Theodore*. In chapter one of St John's Gospel, *Nathaniel* is praised by Jesus: *Behold an Israelite indeed, in whom there is no guile.* Occasionally, the name is spelt *Nathanael* but this is rare outside Jewish circles.

NEAL There are many spellings for this name, which comes originally from *Niall* and is related to *niadh*, 'champion'. It is the basis of the surnames *Mac Neill*, *Neal* and *O'Neill* and versions of the surname have been used in England since the 11th century. This name illustrates the way that certain names travel. The Vikings in Ireland adopted *Niall* and took it to Iceland and Norway as *Njall*. When they moved to Normandy, the name went with them and was introduced into England after 1066. It was latinised as *Nigellus*, giving the world a new name, *Nigel*. *Nelson* was one of the surnames based on it and then that became a given name, as with Nelson Mandela. SEE Niall and Nigel

NELSON has been used as a surname since the early 14th century. It comes from *Niall*, 'champion' and means 'son of the champion'. Horatio Nelson (1758-1805) became a national hero in England because of his victories at sea during the Napoleonic Wars, and his popularity led to the extended use of both *Horatio* and *Nelson* as given names. Many columns and pillars were erected in Nelson's honour. The Dublin monument, Nelson's Pillar, was erected between 1808 and 1809 and blown up by Republicans in 1966.

NEVILLE is a Norman surname, derived from one of the many places in France called either *Néville* or *Neuville* and meaning 'new settlement'. It has become increasingly popular as a given name since the 17th century.

NEVIN/NIVEN These given names are both based on surnames. The likelihood is that they come from Gaelic *naoimhín*, 'little saint', and this is a very positive meaning.

NIALL is the Irish form of the name that also occurs as *Neal*, *Neil* and *Nils*. It means 'champion' and it is pronounced in two ways. It can rhyme with 'be + still' or 'by + still', with both pronunciations being equally popular. One of the earliest *Nialls* on record is *Niall of the Nine Hostages*, who was king of Tara in the 4th century. We cannot

be certain how he got his name but he either held or was given a hostage by every group he defeated.

NICHOLAS In the 21st century, *Nicholas* is popular worldwide and it has been chosen regularly by parents for at least 1600 years. *Nicholas* is from two Greek words, *nike* meaning 'victory + *laos*, 'people'. One saint to hold this name was St Nicholas of Myra in Turkey, who died around AD 326 and who is better known as Santa Claus. The name has several pet forms, including *Col*, *Colin*, *Nick*, *Nickie* and *Klaus*. The term 'Old Nick', which refers to the devil, is almost certainly an abbreviation of (*I*)*niq(uity)* although some people argue that it owes its origin to Niccolo Machiavelli (1469-1527). In the past, *Nicolas*, without the 'h' was widely used and this gave rise to such surnames as *Coll* and *Cowl*.

NICO can be a Greek name meaning 'victory', but it is usually an abbreviation of *Nicholas*.

NICOLAI/NIKOLAI These variants of *Nicholas* are popular in Russian and Poland. SEE Nicholas

NICODEMUS This Greek name means 'victory of the people'. *Nicodemus* occurs in the New Testament, where he is a Pharisee and a member of the Sanhedrin, the highest court of justice in Jerusalem at the time of Jesus. The Gospel of St John tells us that Joseph of Arimathaea asked Pilate for Christ's body and adds:

> *And there came also Nicodemus, which at the first came to Jesus by night, and brought a mixture of myrrh and aloes, about an hundred pound weight.*
>
> (Chapter 19, verse 39)

Nick is frequently used as an abbreviation.

NIGEL is one of the many variants of *Niall*, 'champion'. *Niall* was sometimes represented as *Nihel* and this was turned into Latin as *Nigellus*. It should be remembered that, until the 16th century, it was normal for a child's baptism to be recorded in

Latin. *Nigellus* was then thought to be a form of Latin *niger*, 'black', and *Nigel* was said to mean 'black-haired'. Parents may interpret the name as they choose. SEE Neal

NIKODEM is the Polish form of *Nicodemus*, 'victory of the people'.

NILS is, and has been, a popular name choice in the Scandinavian countries since the Vikings settled in Ireland. They borrowed *Niall*, 'champion', and carried versions of it to Iceland, Sweden, Norway, Denmark, England and France. SEE Neal

NOAH is a Hebrew name meaning 'comfort, peace'. The biblical *Noah* was a patriarch, represented as being about ten generations removed from *Adam*. According to the *Book of Genesis*, Noah built the ark and saved his family and two representatives of every species of animal from the Flood that destroyed the world.

NOAM is a Hebrew name meaning 'friendship'. Prior to the

1960s, it was adopted by Jewish people who wished to give their children quintessentially Hebrew names. The name has been given prominence by Noam Chomsky (b. 1928) who revolutionised the teaching of linguistics from the late 1950s onwards. Many parents who have enjoyed Chomskyan linguistics have called their sons *Noam*.

NOBU is a popular choice for a son in Japan. It means 'truth', a virtue that every parent would aspire to for their child.

NOEL The Latin phrase, *natalis dies domini*, 'birth day of the Lord' was shortened in Old French to *nael* and this developed into *Noël*, an extremely popular name for a boy born close to Christmas Day. The surname *Newell* is a 12th-century surname based on *Noel*.

NORBERT There are many Germanic names that end in *bert*, 'bright'. *Norbert* is less popular than *Albert* or *Robert* but it is still found throughout the world, mainly due to the interest in St Norbert (c. 1080-1134). St Norbert, whose name means 'north + bright', founded an order of monks called Norbertines. The Normans introduced this name into England.

NORMAN This given name means 'north man' or 'Norse man', a term regularly given to the Vikings and used in English before the Norman Conquest of 1066. Starting in the 8th century, the Vikings spread from Scandinavia to many parts of Europe, including England, France, Germany, Ireland, Russia and Scotland. The section of France called Normandy takes its name from the *Normans*.

NORRIS is from the Anglo-Norman surname *Noreis*, 'northerner', a name that is found throughout the British Isles. Occasionally, the surname comes from Norman French *norrice*, 'nurse'. Use of the given name is recorded from the 12th century.

NORTHROP This unusual name means 'northern farm/hamlet'.

It was given prominence by the
Canadian literary critic Northrop
Frye (1912-91), one of the most
respected theorists of the 20th
century.

NOTABLE NAMESAKES
Nathaniel Hone (1718-84)
artist, portrait painter and
co-founder of the Royal
Academy in 1768; Neil
Armstrong (b. 1930) US
astronaut. The first to walk
on the moon in 1969; Nelson
Mandela (b. 1918) anti-
apartheid activist who spent
27 years in prison but
became President of South
Africa in 1994; Noel Coward
(1899-1973) British actor,
playwright and composer of
light music; Norris McWhirter
(1925-2004) writer and
television presenter. He and
his identical twin brother,
Ross, created the *Guinness*
***Book of Records* in 1955.**

OBADIAH (pronounced 'oh
+bad + eye + ya') The shortest
book in the Bible bears the name
of *Obadiah*, a minor prophet.
Obadiah means 'servant of the
Lord'. It is similar in meaning to
Arabic *Abdullah*, 'servant of Allah'.
Thousands of children will know
the name, associating it with the
game:
Obadiah, light the fire; run, run, run.
In fact, the biblical Obadiah was
instructed not to light the fire,
but children's rhymes are often
more exciting than accurate!

OBERON (pronounced 'oh +
ber +on') When Shakespeare
was choosing the name for the
king of the fairies in *A Midsummer
Night's Dream*, he opted for
Oberon, although a French king of
the elves was *Auberon*. It seems
probable that *Oberon* and *Auberon*
are Germanic in origin and mean
'noble bear'. It is also just
possible that it is a form of
O'Brien, 'descendant of Brian'.
This is not as far-fetched as it

sounds. The Vikings carried the Irish surname to the north of England, where forms of it have been surnames for almost a thousand years.

OCTAVIUS is extremely well known but no longer popular as a given name. It means 'eighth child' and the movement towards smaller families means that it could rarely be used now with its original meaning.

ODHRAN (pronounced 'oh + ran') is a Gaelic name that means 'dark-haired'. SEE Oran

ODIN There has been renewed interest in Scandinavian names and folklore since the 19th century. In Scandinavian mythology, *Odin* was the creator god who was married to *Freya*. In a story that bears some resemblance to the death of Christ, *Odin* won the runes for humanity by hanging on the tree of the world for nine days. The runes were an ancient writing system that was thought to have secret powers. In Irish, *rún* still

means 'secret'. The meaning of *Odin* is uncertain but it suggests wisdom and power. *Odo* is occasionally used as a pet form.

ODO is a Germanic name derived from *od*, 'prosperity, good fortune'. Bishop Odo (c.1032-96) was a brother of William the Conqueror. He was made Bishop of Bayeux by his brother. Odo helped William in the Battle of Hastings and was rewarded with the town of Dover. Later, he wanted to be Archbishop of Canterbury but William gave that post to a holy priest. Unperturbed, Odo set his sights on the papacy. Eventually, William imprisoned his brother, but he was released on William's death and died on his way to the Holy Land. *Odo* gave the Bayeux Tapestry that depicts William's victory at the Battle of Hastings in 1066 to the Cathedral of Bayeux.

OGDEN is an English surname that comes from Oakden in Lancashire. The name means 'oak valley'. Many parents who select this name will be influenced by the American poet Ogden Nash (1902-71), who wrote such unforgettable lines as:

Candy is dandy
But liquor is quicker.
Or:
John Brown is stowed.
He watched the ads
And not the road.

OISÍN (pronounced 'o + sheen' or 'osh + een') is an ancient Irish name that has been re-adopted in the recent past. *Oisín*, 'little deer', was the son of Finn Mac Cool. His mother, *Saidhbh*, 'tranquillity', was transformed into a deer by the druids. She reared her son in the forest, but Finn found him when he was hunting and took his son home. There are many legends about *Oisín*, including the claim that he lived with *Niamh*, 'radiance', in Tír-na-n-Óg (Land of Youth) for 300 years and it seemed like a few weeks.

OLAF is a Scandinavian name that was used in the British Isles when the Vikings were at their most powerful in the 10th and 11th centuries. It comes from *ans*, 'ancestral' + *leifr*, 'relic'. It has been the name of a Norwegian king and a saint, and has given rise to the surname, *Oliff* and possibly also *Oliver*.

OLIVER is an English form of French *Olivier*, a name that has been used in France since the 9th century at least. It is likely that it comes from Latin *olivarius*, 'olive tree', and was probably first used for an olive grower or for a peacemaker. It is also possible that *Oliver* is a modified form of *Olaf*, 'ancestral relic'. *Ollie* is a well-liked pet form.

OMAR can be either Hebrew or Arabic. It means 'eloquent'. This is one of the names that can be given to Jew, Christian or Muslim. It was popularised in the 20th century by the Egyptian-born actor *Omar Sharif*. *Omar* comes from an Arabic word meaning 'life'. It occurs also as *Umar*. The name was popularised by the Persian poet, Omar Khayyam, who died around AD 1123. *The Rubaiyat of Omar Khayyam* was translated by

Edward Fitzgerald in 1859 and became one of the most popular poems of the time. Most people will know a few lines, including:

The moving finger writes and having writ
Moves on; nor all your piety nor wit
Shall lure it back to cancel half a line,
Nor all your tears wash out a word of it.

The word *omer* in Hebrew can mean a 'sheaf of corn' presented as an offering during the Passover.

ORAN/OREN/OREN is a Gaelic name that seems to be growing in popularity. It seems to be linked to *odhra*, 'dark-haired'. This name has a long spiritual history. It was the name of St Patrick's charioteer and it has been the name of at least seventeen saints.

ORLANDO is an Italian form of *Ronald*, 'strong rule'. The name was popularised in English by the hero of Shakespeare's play *As You Like It*, and by Virginia Woolf's novel, *Orlando* (1928). Woolf's character starts as a poetic Elizabethan nobleman and remains young for the next century. He escapes a massacre in Constantinople (now Istanbul) and falls into a deep sleep. When he wakes up, he is a woman and lives as one for the next 250 years. SEE Ronald

ORSON is a Norman name that comes ultimately from Latin *ursus*, 'bear'. It means 'bear cub' and is another indication of earlier societies taking names from the natural world, often giving the names of strong animals to boys. When we remember that many young men in the past were involved in wars, it made sense to hope that your son would be strong and intelligent. *Orson* came to the world's attention in the 20th century because of the fame of the actor Orson Welles (1915-85).

OSAMU is a Japanese name meaning 'law abiding'. Since being a good citizen is part of the Japanese ethos, this name is a wish that the son may lead a successful, harmonious life.

OSBERT is one of the many Germanic names to end in 'bert', meaning 'bright'. The *os* is Scandinavian and means 'divine'. *Osbert* gained publicity in the 20th century because of the poet Osbert Sitwell (1892-1969). The lives of the Sitwells, Edith, Sacheverell and Osbert, were as interesting to the public as anything they wrote.

OSCAR It is possible that *Oscar* is a Germanic name, coming from *os*, 'god, divine' + *gar*, 'spear' and it is certainly true that the name is popular in Scandinavia. It is equally possible, however, that *Oscar* is Gaelic in origin. In Irish mythology, *Oscar* was the son of *Oisín*, 'little deer', and the name would have meant 'lover of deer'. In addition, the Scottish poet James MacPherson (1736-96) used the name in *The Poems of Ossian*. Napoleon Bonaparte was such a fan of the Ossian poems that he insisted on calling his godson *Oscar* and he became Oscar I of Sweden.

OSMAN can be an English surname, a variant of *Osmond*, 'divine protector', but it is also a Turkish variant of the Arabic name *Uthman*, 'young bustard', and the basis of the term 'Ottoman', as in Ottoman Empire. This empire was established by Osman I at the end of the 13th century and expanded by his successors until it covered Asia Minor and a great deal of Europe.

OSMOND is a surname now, but in Anglo-Saxon times it was a given name *os*, 'god' + *mund*, protector. Versions of the name also occurred in Danish, Norwegian and Swedish, and it was in use by the Normans in the 11th century. Osmondiston is a town in Norfolk that may have been named after an 11th-century saint.

OSWALD is a Germanic name made up of *os*, 'god' + *weald*, 'rule'. It was popular in England prior to the Norman Conquest, being the name of a 7th-century English saint and a 10th-century

Archbishop of York. The earlier saint was converted to Christianity by the Scots and when he became king, he asked St Aidan to come to Northumbria to establish Christianity there. Oswald's name has been immortalised in the town of Oswestry, 'Oswald's tree'. When he was defeated in battle, he was nailed to a tree.

OTIS is an English surname that has become reasonably popular as a given name. It means 'Otto's son' and thus 'son of riches'. It was a common practice to use a final 's' to indicate 'son of'. We find it, for example, in Andrews and Roberts. *Otis* is most likely to occur in the United States, partly as a result of the fame of Elisha Graves Otis (1811-61). He produced the first professional elevator with a safety mechanism in 1852 and later installed the first public elevator in a New York department store.

OTTO is a Germanic name that comes from *od/ot*, 'riches, prosperity, wealth'. It is related to the 'Ed' in *Edgar*, 'prosperity + spear'. *Otto* has been popular in Germany for over 1000 years. King Otto the Great (912-73) was the Holy Roman Emperor.

OWAIN/OWEN is a Celtic name meaning 'well born' or 'yew born'. Variants of it are found in Wales, Scotland and Ireland. These particular spellings are most widely used in Wales. Owen Glendower (c.1354-c.1417) was a Welsh patriot who claimed Wales for the Welsh and led a national uprising against Henry IV. SEE Eoghan

OZYMANDIAS Few parents will opt for such an exotic name as *Ozymandias*, the name of an Egyptian king in Shelley's sonnet:

> *My name is Ozymandias, king of kings:*
> *Look on my works, ye Mighty, and despair!'*
> *Nothing beside remains. Round the decay*
> *Of that colossal wreck, boundless and bare*
> *The lone and level sands stretch far away.*

An unusual name can be an asset, however. It would be hard to ignore a child called *Ozymandias Brown* and he could always use *Oz* as a pet form. It is interesting to speculate if Orson Welles would have been so famous if he had used his given name *George* or if Piper Laurie would have achieved as much if she had remained Rosetta Jacobs.

BOYS

NOTABLE NAMESAKES
Oliver Hardy (1892-1957) American comedy actor, best known for his partnership with Stanley Laurel; Orlando Bloom (b. 1977) English actor whose career was enhanced by his roles in *The Lord of the Rings* and *Pirates of the Caribbean*; Oscar Wilde (1854-1900) Irish playwright, poet and short story writer. Author of *The Importance of Being Earnest* and the children's story *The Happy Prince*; Otis Redding (1941-67) African American soul singer who was killed in a plane crash; Otto Preminger (1906-86) Austrian-born actor and film director.

P

PABLO is a popular Spanish form of *Paul*, 'little one'. SEE Paul

PACO is found very widely in Spanish-speaking communities. It is a pet form of *Francisco*, 'the French man', and is very occasionally used as an abbreviation of the Latin name *Paschalis*, 'associated with Easter'. SEE Francis and Pascal

PADDY is an abbreviation of *Patrick* or *Padraig*, meaning 'nobly born'. SEE Padraig

PADMA is a much loved Indian name. In Sanskrit, the name means 'lotus'. In Indian mythology, this name was used by the god Rama and the goddess Lakshmi.

337

PADRAIG (pronounced 'paw + drig') This popular Irish name can be spelt in several acceptable ways, including *Padraic, Paidric, Paidrig, Padruig*. The name comes from Latin *Patricius*, 'noble', and it is the name of Ireland's patron saint. Indeed, the celebrations relating to his feast day on March 17th can be witnessed in all Irish communities worldwide and in several cities, including New York and Tokyo. SEE Patrick

PANCHO is a Spanish pet form of *Francisco*, 'the French man'. SEE Francis

PAOLO is an Italian form of *Paul*, 'little one'. It is also the name of an Italian silver coin that was called after Pope Paul V. SEE Paul

PARK is mainly taken from the surname, which owes its origin to Old French *parc*, 'enclosed space', and is found frequently from the 13th century onward. It is occasionally used as a form of *Padraic*. The link is clearer when we point out that, in some dialectal pronunciations of *Padraic* the 'd' is omitted. SEE Patrick

PARRY is a Welsh surname deriving from *ap*, 'son of' + *Harry*, 'home power'. SEE Henry

PASCAL The story of this name crosses religions and cultures. The English adopted it from the French, who used it as a form of Latin *Paschalis*, 'relating to Easter'. However, Latin *Pascha*, 'Easter', was a form of Hebrew *Pesah*, 'Passover'. The Passover celebrated the liberation of the Jews from their captivity in Egypt. This was linked to the Christian belief that Christ's resurrection on Easter Sunday liberated humanity from the slavery of sin.

PATRICIO This is an Italian form of *Patrick*, 'nobly born'. SEE Patrick

PATRICK Forms of *Patrick* are found in every European language and it has remained a popular personal name since the

338

time of Saint Patrick, who died around AD 463. He was born on the British mainland, possibly in Wales, possibly in Scotland, and his parents were probably Romanised Celts. *Patrick*, which comes from Latin *Patricius*, meaning 'nobly born', was captured by Irish mercenaries and taken to Ireland as a slave. For six or more years, he looked after pigs and sheep, and in the silence of his many nights on the hills he experienced a spiritual awakening. He escaped and went home, but felt that he was being called to convert the Irish to Christianity. Eventually he returned to Ireland, and is reputed to have converted the inhabitants by his piety and passion. It may also have helped that he is said to have performed numerous miracles, the most attractive of which was banishing all snakes from Ireland. Strangely, the personal name *Patrick* was more popular in Scotland than in Ireland until the early 17th century. The main pet forms are *Paddy*, *Pat*, *Patsy* and, more recently, *Rick*.

PATRYK is the Polish form of *Patrick*, 'nobly born'.

PAUL comes from a Roman family name *Paulus*, which means 'little'. The name is most intimately connected with the apostle who died around AD 64-67 and who is referred to as 'the Apostle of the Gentiles' and as 'Saul of Tarsus'. His original name means 'prayed for' and, to begin with, Paul opposed the teachings of Jesus. He experienced a visionary conversion on the way to Damascus and was sent to preach to the Gentiles. Paul was martyred in Rome during the rule of Nero (AD 37-68). Six popes have taken this name and it is also the name of several other saints, including the 4th-century St Paul the Hermit. Variants of *Paul* occur throughout the world. These include *Paavo* in Finland, *Pachjo* in Esperanto, *Paol* in Breton and *Pavlos* in Greek.

PAWEL/PAWL (pronounced 'pa + vell') is a Polish form of *Paul*, 'little one'. SEE Paul

PERCEVAL/ PERCIVAL

There are not many *Percivals* today but the name may well be in for a resurgence. *Perceval* was a mythological figure who was popular in the poetry of the Middle Ages throughout Europe. *Perceval* is the French form of the name of this knight, who epitomised the phrase *sans peur et sans reproche*, 'without fear and without any stain on his character that could be used to reproach him'. He was so pure that it was thought he would find the Holy Grail, the wine chalice used by Christ at the Last Supper.

The meaning of the name is uncertain. It may be from Old French *perce*, 'pierce' + *val*, 'valley', a name that would suggest speed and also, perhaps, an ability to hunt. More likely than this etymology is the suggestion that *Perceval* is a French approximation and reinterpretation of a Celtic name, probably *Peredur*, which is related to Welsh *peraidd*, 'pure'.

PERCY is a Norman surname, almost certainly derived from such settlements as *Percy-en-Auge* and in use in England from the 11th century. It is possible that the French places derive from *percer*, 'to pierce, penetrate, find a way through'. *Percy* is the family name of the Dukes of Northumberland and one member of the family, Harry Hotspur (1364-1403), was immortalised by Shakespeare in *Henry IV, Part 1*. *Percy* was the given name of the Romantic poet Percy Bysshe Shelley (1792-1822).

PEREGRINE For many people today, *Peregrine* is more closely associated with the falcon than with the pilgrims to whom the word was originally applied. It comes from Latin *peregrinus*, 'foreigner', and so this name has the same meaning as *Wallace* and *Welsh*. In early Christian times, the name was associated with our earthly pilgrimage and the saints called *Peregrine* would have interpreted their name in this way. The main pet form is *Perry*.

PERRY has two different sources. It can be a pet form of *Peregrine*, 'foreigner, pilgrim', or it can be from a surname that goes back to the 12th century. The surname *Perry* comes from Old English *pirige*, 'pear tree', and meant someone who lived near or tended pear trees. (In Old English, the 'g' of *pirige* was pronounced like a 'y'.)

PETER has been a popular boy's name for almost 2000 years. It was the name of the apostle who became the first Pope and who was martyred around AD 67. Peter's Hebrew name was *Simon*, 'listening to', and he was the son of Jonah. According to the Gospels of John and Matthew, Jesus changed Simon's name to *Cephas*, 'rock', because *Peter* was to be the rock on which his church was to be founded. The Greek equivalent of *Cephas* is *Petros*. There are many variants of *Peter* in world languages. There are also many pet forms, some of which, like *Piers*, are now regarded as names in their own right. SEE Piers

Forms of Peter

Variant	Language
Peadar	Irish
Peder	Danish
Pedr	Welsh
Pedro	Spanish/Portuguese
Peeter	Estonian
Peio	Basque
Petr	Czech
Petri	Finnish
Petros	Greek
Petur	Icelandic
Pietro	Italian
Pierre	French
Pieter	Dutch
Piotr	Polish

PHELAN/PHELIN

(pronounced 'feel +in'/'fail + in') This Irish name is related to *faol*, 'wolf'. The spelling is by analogy with *Philip*, to which it is not related.

PHILIP is a Greek name meaning 'lover of horses'. This has been the name of kings, including the father of Alexander the Great and Philip IV of France (1268-1314), also known as 'Philip the Fair'. It has been the name of many saints, including the first apostle that Jesus called. One of the saints after whom many boys have been called is St Philip Neri (1515-95). A very human story that is told about him is that he saw a man being taken to the gallows and said: 'There, but for the grace of God, go I.'

PIERCE/PIERSE These are variants of *Piers*, the medieval French form of *Peter*. Although some parents have taken the name from the surname that has been in use since the 13th century, the surname was a modified spelling of *Piers*. A less common variant is *Pearce*. SEE Peter

PIERO is an Italian pet form of *Pietro*. SEE Peter

PIERRE is the usual French form of *Peter*. SEE Peter

PIERS When the Normans invaded England in 1066, they took their favourite names with them and *Piers* was one of them. In the 14th century, William Langland (c. 1330-c.1400) wrote a

lengthy allegorical poem called *The Vision of Piers Plowman*. At one level, *Piers* represents an ordinary, hard-working, labouring man; at a second level, he represents a poor priest, trying to teach his congregation by example; at a third level, *Piers* represents St Peter, the rock on which the church was founded; and at a fourth level, he represents Christ who, like *Piers*, led the way to Truth. Usually, *Piers* is pronounced to rhyme with 'ears'.

PLACIDO/PLACIDUS Both forms come from Latin *placidus*, meaning 'gentle, calm, serene, pleasing, favourable'. *Placido* is used in Spanish-speaking communities and the Latin form, *Placidus* is rare outside monasteries.

POLYCARP was a bishop who was consecrated by St John the Evangelist, and who died around AD 155. The meaning of his name is uncertain but it seems to come from a Greek adjective meaning 'fruitful'. *Polycarp* was arrested and burnt to death because he refused to deny his faith. The name is popular among Christians in Africa.

PRESTON is a surname based on one of the many English towns and villages of this name. *Preston* comes from Old English *preosta*, 'priests' + *tun*, 'settlement'. It is most widely used in the United States but has some currency elsewhere.

NOTABLE NAMESAKES
Pablo Picasso (1881-1973)
Spanish painter and
sculptor, renowned for his
contribution to cubism;
Padraig Harrington (b. 1971)
Irish professional golfer ,
who won the *Open*
***Championship* in 2007; Paul**
McCartney (b. 1942) singer,
songwriter, composer and
member of *The Beatles*,
perhaps the pop world's
most iconic band; Pierce
Brosnan (b. 1953) Irish
actor and producer. He
played James Bond in four
films between 1995 and
2002); Placido Domingo
(b. 1941) born in Spain
but moved to Mexico as a
child. He is a world famous
operatic tenor.

Q

There are very few personal names that begin with 'Q' and those that occur in English-speaking communities are taken from other cultures and from surnames such as *Quinn* and *Quincy*. There is a tendency to use the 'q' spelling for exotic names such as *Quetzalcoatl*, the 'Plumed Serpent' of the Toltec and Aztec civilizations. He was regarded as the god of the morning and evening star, and as the symbol of death followed by resurrection. Occasionally, too, Arabic names are written with 'q' to indicate a particular glottal sound that does not occur in Celtic or Germanic languages. Since the Arabic

343

script is totally different from the scripts used in Western Europe, the use of 'q' or 'k' is only a rough approximation.

QABIL is from Arabic and suggests 'extremely able, gifted'. In English-speaking communities, it is pronounced like 'cab + eel'. This name is also spelt *Kabir*. When the 'q' is used for Arabic names, it is not followed by 'u'.

QADIR The form of this name immediately tells us that its inspiration is Arabic. It means 'powerful, influential' and is pronounced in English like 'cad + eer'. The first syllable is almost halfway between 'cud' and 'cad'.

QUENTIN is from Latin *Quintus*, 'fifth child' or 'fifth son'. The Romans used names such as *Secundus*, 'second', and *Septimus*, 'seventh', and these names were occasionally used in upper middle class English families. It is possible that some *Quentins* owe their name to the town of *Quinton* in Gloucestershire, which comes from Old English *cwen*, 'queen' + *tun*, 'manor, settlement'.

QUINCEY/QUINCY is a well-known Norman surname that has recently begun to be used as a given name. It was from one of several French place names, such as *Cuinchy* or *Quincy-Voisins*. The origin of these places is uncertain but it is likely that they were influenced by Latin *quinque*, 'five'.

QUINN is an Irish surname that is beginning to be used although, as yet, it is not as popular as *Kelly* or *Macauley*. The Irish name comes from 'son of Conn' and *Conn* is usually interpreted as 'wisdom' or 'counsel, good advice'.

QUINTIN/QUINTON

These are variants of the more popular *Quentin*, 'fifth child'. The spelling of the first syllable is a more accurate form of the Latin source *Quintus*.

NOTABLE NAMESAKES
Qabil Ambak Mahamad Fathil (b. 1980) Malaysian show jumper and winner of numerous equestrian prizes; Quentin Blake (b. 1932) English cartoonist and illustrator and author of children's books; Quentin Tarantino (b.1963) Oscar-winning American film director, screenwriter and actor. His films include *Reservoir Dogs* and *Pulp Fiction*; Quincy Jones (b. 1933) American musician, conductor and record producer; Quintin Brand (1893-1968) a highly-decorated pilot who achieved the rank of Air Vice Marshall during World War II.

R

RADI is an easy-to-pronounce Arabic name with the meaning of 'happy, content'.

RAFAEL is used occasionally for the more usual *Raphael*, 'healed by God'. *Rafe*, pronounced to rhyme with 'safe', is sometimes used as an abbreviation. SEE Raphael

RAFI/RAVI is a Hindi name meaning 'sun, fire' and suggesting that the child will be surrounded by warmth and light. *Ravi* is also the name of a river that rises in the Himalayas and feeds into the Indus. The Ravi is one of five tributaries that have contributed to the name 'Punjab'. In Hindi, *panj*, is 'five' and *ab* is 'waters'.

RAHEEM/RAHIM is an Arabic name meaning 'kind, benevolent'.

RAJA/RAJAN Both these names mean 'king, ruler'. *Raja* is from Hindi and *Rajan* is from

Sanskrit. Both come from *raj*, 'to rule'. Originally, the term was used only for princes and high-ranking dignitaries, but its meaning was extended during British rule of India. Indeed, the phrase 'the Raj' was used to refer to British sovereignty in India before Independence in 1947. *Raj* is used very widely as a given name by Indians throughout the world.

RAJENDRA is an Indian name meaning 'king of kings'. It comes from Hindi *raja*, 'king', and is comparable to Iran's *Shahanshah*, a title that was bestowed on Iranian rulers and meant 'king of kings'.

RALPH is a Norman variant of the Germanic name *Radulf*, from *rad*, 'counsel, advice' + *wulf*, 'wolf'. Most people pronounce this name like 'ralf' but some prefer an older pronunciation that rhymes with 'safe'.

RAMA is given as a name to Indian sons in honour of the god *Rama*, the husband of *Sita* and regarded as a model of an ideal man. He is seen as the seventh incarnation of the god *Vishnu* and worshipped by some as the supreme god.

RAMON is a Spanish form of *Raymond*, 'strength and protection'. SEE Raymond

RANDAL(L) is now used as a given name in its own right, having been adopted from the surname, which occurs as *Randal*, *Randall*, *Randel* and *Randle*. It is, historically, a shortened form of *Randolf*, meaning 'shield wolf'. The surname can be traced back to the 13th century. SEE Randolf

RANDOLF/RANDOLPH

The English language has been 'improved' many times over the last millennium. The 18th-century tendency was to replace 'f' by 'ph', largely because Greek had the equivalent of 'ph' for a similar sound. The 'improvement' included words that had no Greek connection, such as the Germanic names *Ralf* and *Randolf*. *Randolf* comes from *rand*, 'shield rim' + *wulf*, 'wolf'. It is one of the many 'wolf' names found in the Germanic languages, where the wolf symbolised courage, strength and co-operation.

RAOUL (pronounced 'ra + ool') is the French form of Germanic *Radulf*, 'counsel wolf'. SEE Ralph

RAPHAEL is a Hebrew name meaning 'healed by God'. *Raphael* appears as one of seven archangels in the apocryphal Book of Enoch. He is said to have 'healed' the earth after the sin of the Fallen Angels led by Lucifer. Today, most people associate the name with the Italian painter Raphael (1483-1520), who is admired as one of the most gifted painters of the Renaissance.

RASHID (pronounced 'ra + sheed') is a popular Arabic name meaning 'pious'. Its meaning ensures that it is given by many followers of Islam to their first son.

RAVI is a variant of *Rafi*, 'sun, fire'. SEE Rafi

RAY is often a shortened form of *Raymond*, 'strength and protection', but it is sometimes an adoption of the surname, *Ray*. This surname goes back to the 12th century. It began as a nickname from Old French *rei*, 'king', but was quickly established as a surname after the Norman Conquest.

RAYMOND was a popular Norman name that occurred in France as both *Raimond* and *Raimund*. It comes from the Germanic name *Raginmund*, meaning 'counsel, might, strength' + protection'.

REECE is an anglicised spelling of *Rhys*, 'ardour, enthusiasm, dedication'. This spelling, and its variant *Rees*, have been used as a surname since the 12th century. SEE Rhys

REGINALD is a Norman name that has been used as both a given name and as a surname for almost a thousand years. It comes from Old German *Raginald*, 'strength of counsel', and was latinised as *Reginaldus*. The pet forms *Reg* and *Reggie* are frequently used.

REMUS The Latin word for 'oar' is *remus*, and *Remus* was the name of the twin brother of *Romulus*, the boys who were suckled by a she-wolf, before being brought up by a shepherd, before going on to found Rome. The *Remus* that many parents know is *Uncle Remus*, the old slave who is the narrator of Joel Chandler Harris's *Brer Rabbit* stories. These stories, which are African in origin, are likely to have inspired the cartoon character, *Bugs Bunny*.

RENALDO is an Italian equivalent of *Reginald*, 'strength of advice'. SEE Reginald

RENÉ is a popular French name meaning 'reborn'. It has never been widely used outside France, where it continues to be liked.

REUBEN is a Hebrew name that probably means 'Behold, I have a son'. In the *Book of Genesis*, *Reuben* is the eldest of the twelve sons of Jacob and Leah. He agrees with his brothers that Jacob's affection for Joseph is unjust, but he persuades them not to kill Joseph but to sell him into virtual slavery in Egypt. *Reuben* is sometimes abbreviated to *Ben*.

REX is the Latin word for 'king'. Its history of use as a given name is short and dates back only to the 19th century. The surname *Rex/Recks* comes from an English word *rexe*, 'one who dwells near rushes'. It is always possible that, in choosing *Rex*, some parents have been using a surname. SEE Ray

RHYS (pronounced 'reece'). This comes from Old Welsh *ris* and means 'ardour, enthusiasm, dedication'. It has been used as a surname since the 11th century, when it was sometimes spelt *Hris*, a spelling that attempts to reproduce Welsh pronunciation.

RICHARD has been popular in the British Isles for almost 1000 years. It was introduced by the Normans and comes from a combination of the Germanic elements *ric*, 'power' + *hard*, 'brave'. The popularity of this name can be gauged by the number of its pet forms, which include *Dick, Dickie, Dickon, Dicky, Rick, Rickie, Ritch* and *Ritchie*, and by the fact that all of the pet forms listed have become surnames. There have been three English kings called *Richard*, the best known of which was *Richard the Lionheart* (1157-99), who led the Third Crusade to the Holy Land. Sometimes people wonder how *Richard* produced abbreviations like *Dick* and *Rick* which end with a 'k' sound. The answer is simple. *Richard* used to be pronounced like *Rick+(h)ard* but gradually the spelling influenced the pronunciation. An older pronunciation of this Germanic name is found in such forms as *Ricardo*.

RIDLEY is a place name in several English shires. It comes from Old English *rydde*, 'cleared' + *leah*, 'meadow, thin wood'. It has been used as a surname since the 13th century and recently adopted as a given name.

ROBERT Forms of this name found their way into all European languages. Like many popular names, it is Germanic in origin and was a favourite of the Normans. It comes from *hrod*, 'fame' + *berth*, 'bright'. Like another perennial favourite, *Richard*, it has given rise to a range of pet forms and surnames, including *Bob(b), Dob(b), Dobbin, Hob(b), Hopkins, Nob(b), Rob(b)* and *Robin*. William the Conqueror's father was called *Robert the Devil* because, according to his detractors, his mother had prayed to the devil for the gift of a son. Robert, Duke of Normandy was, in fact, a very devout man and died when he was on a pilgrimage.

ROBERTO is a popular Italian form of *Robert*, 'bright fame'.

ROBIN is now regarded as an independent name but it is a diminutive of *Robert*, meaning 'bright fame'. This name will always be associated with Robin Hood, a legendary English outlaw who lived, it is said, in Sherwood Forest in Nottinghamshire and fought the cruel sheriff to support the poor. SEE Robert

ROCK/ROCKY It is likely that these variants come from Old French *rocque*, 'large stone, crag'. It is possible that the name comes from the Worcestershire place name, Rock, which comes from an Old English phrase *pære ace*, 'at the oak tree'. The name was popularised by the actor Rock Hudson and by the boxer Rocky Marciano (1923-69), who was one of the few world champion boxers to retire while he was still at the top. Both forms are more likely to be given to a child as a nickname.

ROD is an abbreviation of Roderick, or, less frequently, Rodney. SEE Roderick

RODERICK can come from different sources. It can be a Germanic name composed of the elements *hrod*, 'fame' + *ric*, 'power'. It can also be an Anglicisation of Welsh *Rhydderch*, 'redhead'. *Rod* and *Roddy* are frequently used abbreviations. The link with the Welsh name is strengthened by the existence of the surname *Broderick*, which comes from *ap Rhydderch*, 'son of the redhead'.

RODNEY may come from an Old English place name *Roden*, 'fast flowing river' + *ieg*, 'island'. It has been used as a surname since the 14th century and as a given name for about 300 years. Many parents will associate the name with Rodney Trotter in the long-running BBC comedy series, *Only Fools and Horses*.

ROGAN is an Irish name containing the root *ruadh*, 'red (of hair)'. It has been used as a surname for several centuries and has occasionally been used by Polish families called *Roganski*. Many people will have heard of the Indian lamb curry dish called *rogan josh*. This *rogan* means 'oil' in Urdu.

ROGER is a popular Norman name of Germanic origin. It comes from *hrod*, 'fame' + *ger*, 'spear'. It was widely used in the Middle Ages and produced the rhyming abbreviations, *Dodge*,

Hodge and *Rodge*, all of which continue to exist as surnames. The word *roger* was used in radio communications to mean: 'Your message has been received and understood'. This is how the term was explained in the 1947 journal, *American Speech XXII*: 'In radio procedure the letter R, or roger, possesses the code designations 'received', or 'I have received your message', when signalled by the station addressed.' Nevertheless, since radio operators or pilots signalling 'roger' are acknowledging a message, it has also come to mean unofficially 'OK' or 'I understand'.

ROLAND is of Germanic origin, coming from *hrod*, 'fame' + *land*, 'land', and implying 'from the famous land'. It was introduced into the British Isles by the Norman Conquest. The name became popular throughout Europe because of the 12th-century medieval romance, *Chanson de Roland*, 'Roland's Song'. He was the most famous of Charlemagne's champions and resembles an Arthurian knight in terms of his courage and generosity.

ROLF is often considered to be an alternative form of *Ralph* but their origins are different. *Rolf* is a shortened version of *Rudolph* and comes from *hrod*, 'fame' + *wulf*, 'wolf'. It was popular in the Middle Ages and received a new lease of life in the 20th century. The name became familiar to television watchers because of Rolf Harris (b. 1930), the Australian painter, musician and entertainer. Harris was called *Rolf* because his mother admired the Australian writer Rolf Boldrewood.

ROMEO This name will forever be partnered with *Juliet* because of Shakespeare's play, *Romeo and Juliet*. *Romeo* probably means 'Roman man', but since the 18th century it has been used to mean 'passionate male lover', as in C. Anstey's 1766 verse:

May I oft my Romeo meet,
Oft enjoy his converse sweet.

RONALD is from the Scandinavian name *Roganvaldr*, combining 'might' + 'rule'. It is from the same root as *Reynard*, the fox in the *Roman de Renart* stories written in France between 1175 and 1250. The fox represents human beings who try to get as much as they can from life and who use their cunning to escape punishment. *Ronald* was also the name of Lord Cardigan's horse when he led the Charge of the Light Brigade in the Crimean War. *Ronald* Reagan (1911-2004) was the 40th President of the United States from 1981 to 1989, and Ronald McDonald is the advertising clown used by McDonald's fast food outlets. According to research, 96% of American children recognised Ronald McDonald. No president or politician came close to that and only Santa Claus proved to be recognised by more children! The usual pet forms are *Ron* and *Ronnie*. SEE Orlando

RONAN is an Irish name meaning 'little seal'. It became one of the most popular boys'

names in Ireland during the second half of the 20th century. It has been the name of several Irish saints, including a 5th-century missionary saint who lived among his fellow Celts in England and France in order to reinforce their Christianity.

RORY/RUARI is an Irish name meaning 'red-headed king' and it has traditionally been popular in Ireland and Scotland, although it is currently found throughout the world and is not necessarily used for a redhead. Rory O'More (c. 1620-55 AD) was the name of the Irish rebel and patriot who led the 1641 rebellion. It is possible that *Rory* is related to Welsh *Rhydderch*, which is often equated with *Roderick*.

ROSS is a surname that is found throughout the English-speaking world. It was recorded in England in the 11th century. Some of the Ross surnames come from the Germanic word *hrod*, 'fame'; others from Scandinavian *ros*, 'scrapings'; while others, including the Scottish county of Ross, come from Irish and Scots Gaelic *ros*, 'headland'. *Ross* occurred as a given name as in John Ross Ewing in the long-running soap opera, *Dallas*. There is a legend that the first Stars and Stripes flag was sewn by Betsy Ross (1752-1836).

ROY started life as Gaelic *ruadh*, 'red-head'. It followed the noun, as in *Peadar Ruadh*, 'red Peter', and was reinterpreted as a surname and a second given name. It has also been equated with French *roi*, 'king', a meaning that would link *Roy* with *Ray*. This meaning was given extra weight by the formula *le roy le vault*, by which a British king gives his assent to a parliamentary bill.

RUBEN is an alternative spelling of *Reuben*, 'Behold I have a son'. SEE Reuben

RUDOLF/RUDOLPH is a
form of *Rolf*. Its form is taken from Latin *Rudolphus*, which has given rise to Italian *Rodolpho*, the original given name of the film

star heart-throb, Rudolph Valentino (1895-1926). Valentino's film successes helped to familiarise the film-going audience with the name but its popularity may have been dented by the song, *Rudolph the Red-nosed Reindeer*, which is regularly heard in the run-up to Christmas every year.

RUFUS is a Latin nickname, meaning 'red-haired'. William the Conqueror's son William (c.1060-1100) was known as William Rufus, and the nickname occurs frequently in medieval manuscripts. It began to be used as a given name about 200 years ago.

RUPERT is a form of *Robert*, 'of bright fame'. It began to be used outside Germany in the 17th century when Prince Rupert of the Rhine (1619-82) came to England to help his uncle King Charles I in his war with the parliamentary forces. At first, Rupert had considerable success but he was badly defeated at Naseby in 1645. When his cousin Charles II became king in 1660,

BOYS

he settled in England and was instrumental in establishing the Royal Society. Many people will associate the name with Rupert Bear, the cartoon bear with a red jacket and a yellow and black plaid scarf. *Rupert* has often been regarded as an aristocratic-type name. SEE Robert

RUSSELL is one of the many names with the meaning of 'redheaded'. It comes from Old French *rousel*, 'little red one' and has been used as a surname, a nickname and a given name since the 11th century. The name is used in full and also in the abbreviated form of *Russ*.

RYAN has become a popular given name throughout the world. It comes from an Irish surname and probably means 'little king', a suitable title for a new son.

NOTABLE NAMESAKES
Ravi Shankar (b. 1920) Indian composer and sitar player; Ray Charles (1930-2002) African American singer, songwriter and jazz musician; Robert Kennedy (1925-1968) served as US Attorney General from 1961-4, during the Presidency of his brother, John F Kennedy . Robert was assassinated during his Presidential campaign; Roy Rogers (1911-98) singer and actor who featured in over 100 cowboy films mainly from the 1930s to the 1950s; Rex Harrison (1908-90) English actor who won the Academy Award for Best Actor for his role in *My Fair Lady* in 1964; Ryan O'Neal (b. 1941) American actor who achieved public recognition for his roles in the *Peyton Place* soap opera (1964-69) and the film, *Love Story* (1970).

S

SABEER/SABIR can be either
an Arabic or an Indian name. Its
meaning is debated but the
consensus of opinion links it to
'patient'. One person with the
name who has done very well in
business is Sabeer Bhatia,
President and Chief Executive
Officer of Hotmail.

SABURO is a Japanese name
meaning 'third son'. It implies
'good fortune' because, in the
past, it was fortunate for any
family to have three living sons.
The Romans had a similar
technique, using *Tertius* for a
third son.

SACHA is a frequent spelling
of Russian *Sasha*, a pet form of
Alexander, 'defender of men'.
There has been a growth in
popularity in Russian names
since the early 20th century.
Girls' names, in particular, have
been borrowed, *Tania* being a
typical example.

SADEEK/SADIK This Arabic

name means 'truthful' and
fits into a category of
calling children after virtues
or virtuous behaviour.
Truthfulness is a highly valued
quality in all cultures.

SALIM (pronounced 'sal +
eem') The modern Arabic word
Salaam, meaning 'peace', is a
greeting that is similar to
Hebrew *Shalom*. *Salim* is based on
the Arabic form and suggests
'peace and good fortune'.

SALVADOR is the Spanish
and Portuguese form of Latin
salvator, 'saviour'. It was
extremely popular for centuries
although it is slightly less so
now. It was, for example, the
name of the artist Salvador Dali
(1904-89), who was an
impressionist. His paintings are
a surrealistic combination of
photographic accuracy and
dream-inspired imagination.

SAM is usually an abbreviation
of the Hebrew name *Samuel*,
'God listened', but is has also
been used as a shortened form of
Samson, 'child of the sun', and

Samir. SEE Samuel and Samir

SAMEER/SAMIR is one of the most popular Hindi names for boys. It means 'gentle, refreshing breeze' and is associated with 'good fortune'. *Samru* is sometimes used as a pet form.

SAMPAT is a Hindi name meaning 'well to do, wealthy'. It is a given name that also carries a wish for the child's future well-being.

SAMSON was a leader of the Israelites. The story of his phenomenal strength is told in the *Book of Judges*. Samson's name will forever be linked to that of *Delilah*, the woman he loved and to whom he confided the secret that the source of his strength was in his uncut hair. His name seems to come from Hebrew *shemesh*, 'sun'. The variant *Sampson* occurs most frequently as a surname and the name has been used as a surname since the 11th century. It has been suggested that some *Samsons* owe their name not to the biblical hero but to a Celtic saint who went to Brittany in the 6th century and founded an abbey at Dol, where he is buried.

SAMUEL was a Hebrew prophet whose name means 'God listened'. He rallied the Israelites after they had been defeated by the Philistines. The Bible contains two books named after *Samuel*. He anointed *Saul* as king of Israel.

SANCHO is a Spanish form of *sancto*, 'holy'. The name is known in the English-speaking world partly because of the popularity of Don Quixote and his companion, Sancho Panza. *Sancho* is not educated like Quixote, but he has a store of proverbial wisdom which he shares with his master and the reader.

SANDY is a popular Scottish form of *Alexander*, 'defender of men'. It is also used occasionally as a nickname for a redhead. Records of its use in Scotland go back to the 15th century.

SANJAY is another name for

the god Shiva. It means 'victory' and implies victory not just in this life but over anything that would stand in the way of spiritual development.

SANZIO is an Italian form of Latin *sancto*, 'holy, saint'.

SASHA is a Russian pet form of *Alexander*, 'defender of men'. SEE Alexander and Sacha

SAUL was the first king of the Israelites. His name means 'prayed for'. At the beginning of his reign, he was close to God, but later he lost God's favour, in part because he resented David, who had been anointed as his successor. *Saul* is also the name of St Paul of Tarsus, the apostle who preached Christianity to the Gentiles and was executed in AD 67.

SAUNDERS is a Scottish form of *Alexander*, 'defender of men'. It is also taken from the surname which has been found in Scotland since the early 13th century. *Saunders* is found in an early Scottish ballad which contains the following verse:

'A bed, a bed,' Clerk Saunders said,
'A bed for you and me.'
'Nay now, nay now,' quod May Margret
'Until we married be.'

SAXON is a relatively modern choice. The Saxons were Germanic people who conquered England in the 5th century. The name probably comes from the root *seax*, 'knife' and the term 'Saxons' tends to imply 'English'.

SAYER is an example of a surname that is becoming popular as a given name. It may come from Old French *saier*, 'a maker or seller of silk' or it may come from Gaelic *soar*, 'carpenter'. The name is pronounced to rhyme with 'layer'. Unusually for a surname, this one began to be used as a given name from the 14th century.

SAYID is an Arabic name meaning 'lord, prince'. It is often applied to a Muslim who claims to be descended from Muhammad, through the prophet's grandson, *Hussein*. The spelling of the name varies and is often *Sayyid*. It is pronounced like 'sigh + yeed'.

SCOTT has been used as a given name for over 1000 years although many parents take it from the surname *Scott*. The term *scot* was originally applied to a person from Ireland, especially the north, and then by extension to the Irish settlers who went to live in what is now Scotland in the 5th century. The exact meaning of the name is uncertain but it may mean 'tatooed'. The novelist Sir Walter Scott (1771-1832) helped to popularise the name.

SEAMUS is an Irish form of *James*, which may mean 'heel' or 'supplanter'. It is extremely popular in Ireland and occurs occasionally in Scotland as *Seumas*. The popularity of the Nobel Prize winning poet, Seamus Heaney (b. 1939) has encouraged its use inside and outside Ireland. It is pronounced like 'shame + us'. SEE James

SEAN is an Irish form of *John*, 'God is gracious'. It is usually pronounced like *Shawn* (and is occasionally spelt this way). It can also be pronounced like 'shan' or 'shane'. It has always been a popular choice in Ireland, but the film actor Sean Connery (b. 1930), who played James Bond between 1962 and 1983, helped to make the name fashionable throughout the English-speaking world. SEE John

SEBASTIAN is a popular choice for a son's name in the 21st century and it has always been regarded as a fashionable option. The name means 'man from Sebasta' and *Sebasta* is derived from a Greek adjective meaning 'august, revered'. According to Christian tradition, St Sebastian was born in France in the 3rd century. He was a Christian but became an officer in the army of the Emperor and used his position to help persecuted Christians. He was denounced to the Emperor and condemned to be killed by arrows. A Christian woman went to bury him but found that he was still alive. She cared for him but when he recovered he refused to run away and hide. He found out where Diocletian would be and stood in front of him, urging that Christians were not enemies of the state. Diocletian ordered him to be beaten to death. He died in AD 303 and has always been regarded as a model of courage and perseverance. Shakespeare uses the name twice, once for the brother of the King of Naples in *The Tempest* and once for the brother of Viola in *Twelfth Night*.

SEBASTIANO is a popular Italian form of *Sebastian*. SEE Sebastian

SELWYN looks Welsh because of its spelling and it has been used as a given name in Wales. Its origins are debated. The Normans used it as early as 1170 and their usage seems to come from Latin *silva*, 'wood'. There was also an Old English given name *Selewine*, 'hall friend, companion', and, although the name is not recorded often, it may have reinforced the Norman variant.

SEOSAMH is an Irish form of *Joseph*, a Hebrew name meaning 'God shall add'. *Seosamh* is usually pronounced 'show + suv' or 'show + sue'.

SERGE(I) is a popular Russian form of an old Roman family name, *Sergius*. The meaning of the name is uncertain, but it may mean 'warrior'. There was a 14th-century Russian saint called *Sergius*, who was a mystic and reformer. He established many monasteries and is reputed to have saved Russia from being conquered by the Tartars in 1380. The strong Russian devotion to him helps to account for the status of the name in Russia. The Russian form rhymes with 'fair may'.

SERGIUSZ is a Polish equivalent of Russian *Sergei*. SEE Sergei

SETH is a Hebrew name that may mean 'God hath appointed' or 'substitute'. He was born to Adam and Eve after the death of Abel. The same name occurs in

Egyptian mythology, where *Seth* is a god who murdered his brother Osiris. The name also occurs in Hindi, where it means 'banker' or 'important merchant'.

SEUMAS is a Scots Gaelic form of *James*, 'heel, one who supplants'. It is less common than *Hamish*, which is a related form. SEE Hamish and James

SEYMOUR is a surname that has become a fashionable given name. The Normans brought a version of the name to England in the 11th century. It was *Saint-Maur*, a saint whose name meant 'Moor, African'. It is also possible that the surname was reinforced by the Old English trade name *seamere*, 'tailor', still found in *seamer*, 'a person who sews seams'.

SHAFIQ (pronounced 'shah + feek') is a popular Arabic name meaning 'compassionate', a word that means not just 'kind' but 'willing to share one's possessions but also the pain of others'.

SHAMUS is a variant spelling of *Seamus*, an Irish form of *James*. SEE Seamus

SHANE is an Irish form of *John*, 'God is gracious'. The pronunciation of Irish *Seán* depends on the dialect area. It can rhyme with 'dan', 'dawn' and 'dane'. SEE John

SHANNON This is the name of Ireland's longest river and its meaning is uncertain, although it is likely that it includes the adjective *sean*, 'pronounced like 'shan', meaning 'old'. *Shannon* has been used for both boys and girls.

SHAUN/SHAWN These are both attempts to represent the sound of Irish *Seán*, 'John', meaning 'God is gracious'. The *Shawn* form is most frequent in the United States.

SHAY can come from two different languages, so it has two possible meanings. English *Shay* comes from Old English *sceaga*, 'wood'. It can also be an anglicised spelling of the Irish surname *O'Shea*, meaning 'strong, keen-sighted like a hawk'. *Shea* is pronounced 'shay'.

SHEM is a Hebrew name meaning 'distinguished, renowned'. According to the *Book of Genesis*, *Shem* was the son of *Noah* and, as one of the few survivors of the Flood, the ancestor of the Israelites.

SHEPARD Although the spelling differs, this given name, which is popular especially in the United States, means 'shepherd, one who protects his flock'. In the Bible, a shepherd has a literal meaning, 'one who guards sheep', a metaphorical meaning, 'one who guards the chosen children of God' and an analogical meaning, 'God'.

SHERIDAN comes from the Irish surname *Ó Sirideáin*, 'descendant of the eternal treasure'. Richard Brinsley Sheridan (1751-1816) was an extremely successful playwright, best known, perhaps, for his plays *The Rivals*, written when he was 24, and *The School for Scandal*, written two years later in 1777. He became an MP in 1780.

SHERLOCK is an English surname derived from Old English *scir*, 'bright, shining' + *loc*, 'lock of hair'. (In Old English *scir* was pronounced 'sheer'.) This surname was first recorded over one thousand years ago, but it was Sherlock Holmes, the fictional detective, created by Sir Arthur Conan Doyle (1859-1930), who made the name universally well-known and popular.

SHERMAN is an Old English trade name made up of *scearra*, 'shear' + *mann*, 'man', and meaning not so much a sheep-shearer as a shearer of woollen cloth. *Sherman* was first chosen as a given name in the United States in honour of William Tecumseh Sherman (1820-91) who was a General and one of the chief Union commanders in the American Civil War.

SHERWYN would be an excellent name choice for a boy with athletic abilities because it implies 'very fast runner'. It is made up of two Old English

words, *sceran*, 'to cut' +
wind, 'wind', and thus
means literally 'wind-cutter'
but metaphorically 'one who
can run as fast as the wind'. It
has been a surname for 900 years
but a given name for less than a
century.

SHLOMO is a Hebrew name
derived from *shalom*, 'peace'. Its
English equivalent is *Solomon*.
SEE Solomon

SIDNEY was originally a place
name that became a surname but
is now more frequently used as a
given name. It may come from
Old English *sid*, 'broad, low-lying'
+ *ieg*, 'island in a river', or it may
be from *St Denis* in Normandy. St
Denis, who died about AD 273, is
the patron saint of France. His
name possibly means 'man of
God'. He was put to death at
Montmartre (martyr's mount).
The surname belonged to Sir
Philip Sidney (1554-86) who was
legendary for his courtesy and
gentlemanly behaviour. He was
mortally wounded at the battle of
Zutphen but, according to his
friend, Fulke Greville, he gave

his water bottle to another
soldier, saying: 'Your necessity is
greater than mine'.

SIEGFRID/SIEGFRIED is
the name of the hero of the first
part of the *Nibelungenlied*, a
13th-century German poem. The
name means 'victory' + 'peace'.
Siegfrid kills the dragon and
seizes the treasure that the
dragon was protecting. He then
marries Kriemheld and helps her
brother Gunther to win Brunhild.
Siegfrid is killed by Hagen but
Kriemheld has her revenge and
beheads Hagen herself.

SIGURD is a Norse name
derived from *sigr*, 'victory' + *orð*,
'word'. *Sigurd* is the Norse
equivalent of *Siegfried* in that he
kills a dragon and recovers
treasure. The poet William
Morris (1834-96) wrote about his
exploits in *The Story of Sigurd and
the Fall of the Nieblungs* (1876) and,
in this way, helped to popularise
the name in the Victorian age.
Morris believed that the story of
Sigurd was the north European
equivalent of the story of Troy.

SILAS is a shortened form of *Silvanus*, from Latin *silva*, 'wood', and suggesting 'wood dweller'. The name became popular with Puritans. It was selected by George Eliot (1819-80) for the hero of her novel *Silas Marner*.

SILVESTER/SYLVESTER

The form with 'y' is more usual now but *Silvester* was used more frequently in the past. The name comes from Latin *silvester*, 'dweller in the woods'. It was selected as the name for three popes and has been a surname in England since the early 13th century. Millions of cartoon fans came across the name in the Looney Tunes films about Sylvester J Pussycat, the anthropomorphic cat who had a lisp and suffered from the antics of Tweetie Pie.

SIMEON is a familiar biblical name. It means 'hearkening to' and it was the name of the patriarch who was the son of Jacob and Leah in the *Book of Genesis*. It is also the name of the prophet who saw the child Jesus in the Temple and recognised him as the Messiah. The Syrian monk St Simeon Stylites (c. AD 390-459) was the first Christian to practise an extreme form of asceticism that involved living at the top of a pillar.

SIMON is actually the same name as *Simeon*, but it has been used for so long that it has become a name in its own right. It was the original Hebrew name of St Peter and has been a popular Christian name ever since. *Simon* was also the name of the man from Cyrene who helped Christ carry his cross to Calvary in St Mark's Gospel.

SKIP has been used most frequently by people of Norwegian and Swedish origin living in America. It is the Scandinavian name for 'ship' and is the equivalent of calling a son 'captain of the ship'.

SOL/SOLLY are regular abbreviations of the Hebrew name Solomon, that is based on *Shalom*, 'peace'. SEE Solomon

SOLOMON is an English form of Hebrew *Shlomo*, the name of one of the best known characters in the Bible. King Solomon was the son of David and he lived from about 970 to 930 BC. His name was a form of *Shalom*, 'peace'. Solomon was renowned for his great wisdom and for building the first Temple in Jerusalem. Many people know the name from the nursery rhyme:

> *Solomon Grundy,*
> *Born on Monday,*
> *Christened on Tuesday,*
> *Married on Wednesday*
> *Took ill on Thursday,*
> *Worse on Friday,*
> *Died on Saturday,*
> *Buried on Sunday,*
> *This is the end*
> *Of Solomon Grundy.*

SOLON is not widely used outside the Greek community, where it is sometimes regarded as a form of *Solomon*, 'peace'. *Solon* (c. 630-c.560 BC) was an Athenian statesman. He is given credit for dividing citizens into four categories, based on wealth rather than birth and his divisions became the foundation of Greek democracy.

SPENCER is an abbreviated form of Old French *dispensier*, 'one who administers provisions, butler, steward'. It was a trade name that came to England with the Normans. It had become a surname by the 13th century and was popularised as a given name in the 20th century by the actor Spencer Tracy (1900-67). Earl Spencer (1758-1834) gave his name to a short, warm garment, known as a 'spencer'.

SPIRO is a popular Greek given name. It may be related to 'winding' or to 'breath, spirit'. The form occurs in the Latin proverb *Dum spiro spero*, 'while I breathe, I hope'.

SRIDHAR (pronounced 'sreed + ar'/'shreed +ar') is a popular Hindi given name and surname. It means 'wealthy person' and reflects the parents' wish that their son may have a good quality of life.

ST JOHN is usually pronounced 'sin + jin' and it has

been used quite frequently as a given name. It is selected in honour of St John the Evangelist, who was given the task of looking after the Blessed Virgin Mary when they both stood at the foot of the cross. In Christian art, he is symbolised by the eagle.

STACEY was originally a pet form of *Eustace*, coming originally from Greek and probably meaning 'fruitful'. It has, however, become a name in its own right and has recently been used for girls as well as boys. The variant *Stacy* also occurs.

STAN is an abbreviation of several names, such as *Stanley*, that begin with 'Stan'. In Old English, *stan* was the normal form of modern 'stone'. SEE Stanley

STANDISH is a place name in both Gloucestershire and Lancashire. It comes from Old English *stan*, 'stone' + *edisc*, 'pasture'. *Standish* was already in use as a surname in the late 12th century. Standish O'Grady (1842-1928) was an Irish writer. He wrote a *History of Ireland*

(published 1878-80) and then turned his attention to the myths and legends of Ireland.

STANISLAS/STANISLAUS

St Stanislaus(1030-79) is the patron saint of Poland and was the bishop of Cracow from 1072 until his death. He excommunicated King Boleslaus because he refused to live a Christian life and it has been alleged that Boleslaus instigated his murder. The name means 'government glory'.

STANLEY is the name of towns and villages in at least six English counties. It comes from *stan*, 'stone' + *leah*, 'wood, clearing'. It has been used as a surname since the 12th century and was very widely used as a given name, especially in the north of England. The name was given prominence in the Victorian period by the Welsh explorer Henry Morton Stanley (1841-1904). In 1868, when he was a newspaper correspondent, he set out to find David Livingstone, who had not been heard of for some time. Two years later, he found Livingstone.

STANTON/STAUNTON

is a place name in several northern shires of England. It comes from *stan*, 'stone' + *tun*, 'settlement, enclosure'. It has been a surname since the 11th century and has, like many surnames, become a given name usually by being passed on to a son via his mother's maiden name.

STAVROS is widely used in

Greek communities. It means 'crowned' and is related in Greek to *Stephen*.

STEFAN is a Polish form of

Stephen, meaning 'garland, crown'. It has become more widely used in non-Polish communities. SEE: Stephen

STEPHANUS is a form of

Stephen, 'garland, crown', used occasionally in Germany and the Netherlands. SEE: Stephen

STEPHEN comes from Greek

stephanos, 'garland, crown'. The name is a reference to the first Christian martyr. He was one of seven deacons appointed by the apostles to help distribute alms to the poor. He was taken before the Sanhedrin and accused of foretelling the destruction of the Temple and the victory of Christian values over the Mosaic Law. He was taken outside Jerusalem and stoned to death. Those who stoned him left their cloaks with Saul, who later became St Paul. Because he was the first to die after Jesus, his feast day is on the 26th December. His name refers to the fact that he won a martyr's crown by dying for his faith.

STEVEN is an early variant of

Stephen. The form with 'v' is recorded as a surname in the 13th century. SEE: Stephen

STEWARD is occasionally

found as a variant of *Stewart*. Interestingly, the spelling with 'd' is an accurate representation of the Old English *stig*, 'house, part of house' + *weard*, 'guardian', and it referred to a man who controlled the domestic affairs of a household. SEE Stewart

STEWART comes from Old English *stig*, 'house, part of house' + *weard*, 'guardian' and it referred to the person who looked after the day-to-day running of a house. By the 15ᵗʰ century, it usually referred to someone who ran the affairs of a royal household. In Scotland, the final 'd' was often changed to 't' so that, for example, 'forrit' was frequently used for 'forward' as in Robbie Burns's poem:

Come forrit, honest Allan.

(Pastoral Poetry vi)
The Lord High Steward of Scotland was the next in power to the king. He controlled the royal household and had the duty of leading the Scottish army into battle. When Robert the Steward became Robert II of Scotland (1316-90), the name *Stewart*, or its French equivalent *Stuart*, became the name of the royal house. Even today, one of the titles of the Prince of Wales is 'Great Steward of Scotland'. *Stewart* is a common surname that is

sometimes used as a given name.

STUART Mary Queen of Scots (1442-87) was the daughter of James V of Scotland and his French wife, Mary of Guise. She was sent to France as a child to be betrothed to the Dauphin. When she was in France, her surname was spelt *Stuart*, a form adopted by her descendants. Although *Stuart* occurs as a surname, it is more frequently found as a given name.

SULEYMAN is a Turkish form of *Solomon*. Suleyman the Magnificent (c. 1494-1566) ruled the Ottoman Empire for part of the 16ᵗʰ century. He extended the Empire, conquering Belgrade, Rhodes and Tripoli as well as parts of Iraq. He was a reformer and was responsible for completing many great building projects.

SUSUMU (pronounced 'sue + sue + moo') is a popular Japanese given name meaning 'advancement, improvement'. It symbolises the wish of the parents that their son will do well in life.

SVEN is a Scandinavian noun meaning 'young man'. It has the same origin as English *swain*, still found in words such as 'boatswain'. It has become popular throughout Europe, especially among people who are interested in Viking traditions.

SWEENEY is an Irish name, possibly meaning 'hero'. It has become a popular surname in Ireland and has recently been revived as a given name.

NOTABLE NAMESAKES
Sergei Bubka (b. 1963) Ukrainian pole-vaulter. Olympic gold medal winner and the first man ever to clear six metres; Simon Bolivar (1783-1830) born in Venezuela of Basque ancestry. He inspired the move for independence in several South American states; Spencer Tracy (1900-67) American actor named 'one of the greatest male stars of all time' by the American Film Institute in 1999; Stan Laurel (1890-1965) English-born actor who achieved fame as part of the 'Laurel and Hardy' double act; Steven Spielberg (b. 1946) American film producer and director, who has made more successful films than any other producer.

T

TAD is an abbreviation of *Thaddeus*, possibly meaning 'gift of God'. The use of *Tad* rather than *Thad* is explained, in part, by the fact that earlier forms of English often said 't' even though they wrote 'th'. The fact that we have 'Betty' from *Elizabeth* and *Tony* from *Anthony* lends support to the claim. SEE Thaddeus

TADDEO is an Italian form of *Thaddeus*. SEE Thaddeus

TAKASHI (pronounced 'ta + ka + she') is a Japanese name with the meaning of 'eminence, distinction, renown'.

TAKEHIKO (pronounced 'ta + kay + he + ko') can have two meanings in Japanese. It may mean 'soldier prince' or 'bamboo prince'. Either way, it implies status.

TAKUMI (pronounced 'tack + oo + me')is Japanese and means 'worker'.

TALIESEN (pronounced 'ta + lee + sen'/ 'tal + yessin') is a Welsh name that has gained in popularity over the last 50 years. It was the name of a 6th-century poet and the name means 'shining/radiant brow'. It is not absolutely certain how a 'brow' can 'shine' but it may be a metaphor for 'intelligent and handsome'.

TAMAR is a Hebrew name meaning 'palm tree'. It is now mainly used as a female name and is sometimes regarded as a shortened form of *Tamara*.

TAYLOR is one of the many surnames that have become given names. This one is derived from French *tailleur*, 'tailor'. Many of the trade names came to the British Isles with the Normans. To begin with, one might be described as 'Richard le Tailleur' and gradually the 'le' was dropped.

TEARLACH (pronounced 'char + lach' where the final 'ch' is like Scottish 'loch') is an Irish approximation to *Charles*, which is of Germanic origin and means 'man, ordinary person'. SEE Charles

TED/TEDDY is a popular abbreviation of both *Edward*, 'prosperity + guardian', and *Theodore*, 'gift of God'. Theodore Roosevelt (1858-1919) was the 26th President of the United States, from 1901 to 1909. He was known as Teddy Roosevelt and he gave his name to teddy bears. The form *Teddie* also

occurs. SEE Edward and
Theodore

TELFORD is, like *Taylor*, a
French trade name that became a
surname and then a given name.
The French form is *taillefer*, 'iron
cutter', and the change to 'ford'
happened because the trade of
iron cutting gradually
disappeared and people tried to
make sense of the name,
assuming that the second syllable
meant 'ford'. Thomas Telford
(1757-1834) was an engineer
who gave his name to a type of
road that was a great
improvement on earlier
thoroughfares.

TEODOR is a Polish form of
Theodore. SEE Theodore

TERENCE This is the most
usual spelling of the name but it
is also found as *Terrance* and
Terrence. It goes back to an
ancient Roman family name,
Terentius and, because of its
antiquity, its meaning is
uncertain. It may be related to
Latin *ter-*, meaning 'three times',
suggesting a three-times winner

or it may come from *teres*,
'rounded'. The name became
more widely known in the
Renaissance because of the
renewed interest in the comic
Roman dramatist *Terence*, or
Marcus Terentius Afer, to give
him his Latin name. The Roman
Terence was a freed slave and his
plays were praised for their
humour and their
well-constructed plots.

TERRY is an extremely popular
abbreviation of *Terence*. There is a
tendency for this spelling to be
used for men and *Teri* for
females, but this is not a hard
and fast rule. SEE Terence

THADDEUS is the name of
one of the twelve apostles. We
have to assume that he was
content to stay in the
background because the gospels
tell us very little about him. His
name seems to be a form of
Theodoros, a Greek name meaning
'gift of God'. His Hebrew name
was *Jude*, 'God be praised'. His
name may have been changed to
distinguish him from Judas
Iscariot. He is regarded as the

patron of hopeless cases. *Thaddeus* is abbreviated to *Tad*.

THEOBALD The first part of this name looks as if it comes from Greek *theos*, 'god', but *Theobald* is actually a Germanic name composed of two words meaning 'people' + 'brave'. It was popular with the Normans and seems to have been pronounced like 'Tibbalt'. Indeed, Shakespeare used the form *Tybalt* for one of Juliet's cousins in *Romeo and Juliet*.

THEODORE is a French form of Greek *Theodoros*, 'gift of God'. There are several saints called *Theodore* but one of the most interesting lived between 602 and 690 and was for a time the Archbishop of Canterbury. His appointment to the post came as a great surprise to everyone, himself included, because he was over sixty at the time and not an ordained priest! His appointment by Pope Vitalian proved to have been inspired because *Theodore* was a superb organiser. He created a scheme of sees and dioceses that continue to form the basis of the system still in use in the Church of England.

THEOPHILUS comes from the two Greek words, *theos*, 'god' and *philos*, 'friend'. The earliest Christian reference to the name comes from St Luke, who addressed his gospel and the Acts of the Apostles to him. There were several saints in the early church with this name, which is sometimes abbreviated to *Theo* and sometimes to *Phil*.

THOMAS has been popular for two thousand years and its popularity shows no sign of diminishing. The apostle *Thomas* appeals to most people because, although faith is an admirable quality, human doubt is totally understandable. In St John's Gospel, *Thomas* is called *Didymus* and both names mean 'twin'. *Thomas* is from Hebrew and *Didymus* from Greek. According to an early tradition, *Thomas* was sent to India and while he was there an Indian prince gave him a large sum of money to build him a palace. (According to this tradition, *Thomas* was a skilled carpenter.) *Thomas* gave the money to the poor and when the prince asked where his palace was, *Thomas* replied that he was building a palace for the prince in heaven. *Thomas* was once so popular in England that the abbreviation *Tommy* became the term for an Englishman in the same way that *Paddy* was selected to represent an Irishman.

TIERNAN is an Irish name meaning 'lord of the household'. It is pronounced to rhyme with 'near +nan'.

TIMON (pronounced 'time + on') is a Greek name, probably meaning 'honour, value'. Timon of Athens was so disillusioned by the ingratitude of human beings that he became a recluse, refusing to see anyone but his friend Alcibiades who was a general and a statesman.

TIMOTEO is an Italian form of *Timothy*, 'honour God'. SEE Timothy

TIMOTHY is the Greek name

of a disciple of St Paul. It comes from *time*, 'honour' + *theos*, 'god'. According to tradition, he was a disciple of St Paul, the first bishop of Ephesus and was martyred during the reign of Nerva (c. AD 30-98). *Timothy* has been especially popular in recent years, both in full and in its abbreviated form of *Tim*.

TITO is an Italian form of *Titus*, which is of unknown origin but may mean 'saved'. SEE Titus

TITUS has been the name of a saint and a Roman Emperor. Its origins are unclear, although it may mean 'saved'. One of St Paul's companions was called *Titus* and he is said to have become the first bishop of Crete. The Roman Emperor Titus (AD 39-81) attacked and sacked Jerusalem in AD 70, thus putting an end to an uprising. He fell in love with Herod Agrippa's daughter, Berenice, and took her back with him to Rome. The Romans did not approve of her, however, and so he gave her up.

TOBIAS is the Greek form of the Hebrew name, *Tobiah*, meaning 'God is good'. One story told about a *Tobias* is that he wanted to marry his cousin, Sara, but all her previous husbands had died on their wedding night. *Tobias* asked for – and got – the help of the archangel Raphael in overcoming the evil spirit who had been responsible for killing all Sara's previous husbands. This form of the name is popular in Germany, whereas its abbreviated form, *Toby*, is more widespread in the English-speaking world.

TOBY is a popular abbreviation of *Tobias*. It has been fashionable since the 18th century at least. The 'toby jug' is called after a Toby Philpot, who liked a drink. SEE Tobias

TOD(D) with either one or two 'd's, used to be limited to the United States but it is currently proving popular worldwide. The name comes from a dialect English word *tod*, meaning 'fox'. The nickname of 'fox' was given to people who were either as

clever as a fox; who had red hair like a fox; or who hunted foxes. The surname, *Todhunter*, was first recorded in 1332. The expression 'on your tod', 'to be alone', is rhyming slang from the famous American jockey Tod Sloan (1873-1933).

TOM is an abbreviated form of *Thomas*, 'the twin'. The popularity of this variant can be seen in such phrases as 'Tom, Dick and Harry' and in children's stories such as Tom Thumb. SEE Thomas

TOMÁS is a popular Irish form of *Thomas*. SEE Thomas

TOMMY is an abbreviation of *Thomas*. *Tommy Atkins* has been used as the name of the typical English soldier since the 19th century. SEE Thomas

TONY was originally an abbreviation of *Anthony* but it now occurs frequently as a name in its own right.

TREFOR is a variant of Trevor, 'large settlement'. SEE Trevor

TREMAYNE The Celtic word *tref*, meaning 'homestead, village, town', occurs in many place names throughout Wales and Cornwall and, to a lesser extent, in Herefordshire and Lancashire. The town of Tremaine in Cornwall comes from *tref*, 'village' + *maen*, 'stone'. It has given rise to the surname and first name *Tremayne*. The spelling of the name varies with *Tremeayne*, *Tremayn* and *Tremayne* all occurring in the 16th century.

TREVELYAN is another Cornish name that was inspired by a town in Cornwall. The town probably means 'Eliyan's homestead' but it may also be a combination of *tref*, 'homestead' + *melin* 'mill'. The word *melin* occurs as *felin* when it is used attributively.

TREVOR This Welsh name has travelled far beyond Wales. There are several places in Wales called *Trefor* from *tref*, 'village, homestead' + *for*, 'big'. (The word for 'big' is *mor* but the first consonant is modified in certain contexts.) The Welsh form *Trefor* is also used but *Trevor* occurs more widely.

TRISTAN/TRISTRAM

These variants were used by different writers of the medieval legend of *Tristan* and *Isolde*. According to the story, a young knight (*Tristan* or sometimes *Tristram*) is sent to Ireland by his uncle, the king of Cornwall, to accompany *Iseult* (also *Isolde*) a princess and Mark's future wife from Ireland to Cornwall. The young people accidentally drink a love potion and become lovers but, after various adventures, they both die, still utterly in love with each other. It is not easy to be certain what the name means, but it has come to be linked to *trist*, 'sad' and also to *tryst*, 'lover's meeting'.

TROY It is probable that the English surname *Troy*, which inspired some choices of this name, comes from the town of Troyes in France. Other parents have selected it because of the story of the Trojan War, the legendary ten-year siege of Troy that is described in Homer's *Iliad*. The Greeks were avenging the abduction of Helen by Paris, a prince of Troy. According to Virgil, some of the survivors of Troy founded Rome.

TRUMAN The meaning of this name is transparent. It has been used as a surname since 1215 and probably began as a nickname for a faithful, honest man. The name was given prominence by the American writer Truman Capote (1924-84) whose novels are regarded as literary classics. His best known book, *Breakfast at Tiffany's*, appeared in 1958.

TUDOR is a Welsh form of *Theodore*, 'gift of God', and has been used as a given name in Wales since the 12th century. It will always be associated with the House of Tudor, which lasted in England from 1485-1603. In purely chronological terms, this was a relatively short period, but it produced two of the most memorable monarchs in English history. Henry VIII dissolved the monasteries and changed the course of English social and religious history. He also had six wives, two of whom he executed. His daughter Elizabeth reigned from 1558 to 1603 and began the process of overseas acquisitions that laid the foundations of the British Empire.

TYBALT was the usual pronunciation of *Theobald*, 'brave people', in Elizabethan England. SEE Theobald

TYLER is an example of a trade name that becomes a surname and then a given name. The Normans not only conquered England, they 'conquered' architecture in that they brought their own tradesmen with them. As early as 1185, there is a reference to a Roger le Tuiler, Roger the Tiler. The noun that we spell 'tile' was regularly spelt 'tyle' from about 1375 until about 1700.

TYRONE is the name of an Irish county and it was popularised as a given name by Tyrone Power (1914-58), the film actor who made dozens of movies and who often played swashbuckling heroes. In the United States, the name is often pronounced like 'tie + rone', whereas, in Ireland, the first syllable rhymes with 'fir'. The county takes its name from *tír*, 'country' + *Eoghain*, 'of Owen'.

TYSON (pronounced 'tie + son') has been a surname since the 11th century. It comes from an old French word *tison*, 'a firebrand', and was used as a nickname for a quick-tempered individual.

NOTABLE NAMESAKES
Theodore Roosevelt (1858-1918) 26th president of the United States. He gave his name to the 'teddy bear'; Thomas Aquinas (c. 1225-74) Italian Dominican monk and the foremost theologian of his day; Tito Gobbi (1913-1984) noted Italian baritone and stage director. His operatic collaborations with Maria Callas are considered classics; Tom Hanks (b. 1956) American actor and producer. Won Academy Awards for best actor in 1993 and 1994; Trevor McDonald (b. 1939) Trinidadian-born television presenter and newscaster.

U

ULBRECHT (pronounced 'ool + brecht' where the 'ch' resembles the 'ch' in Scottish 'loch') is a Germanic name that combines *wulf* 'wolf' + *brecht*, 'shining, bright'. It is one of many 'wolf' names that are found in all of the Germanic languages. The Old Swedish form of 'wolf' was *Ulf*.

ULFRED (pronounced 'ool + fred') would make a possible change for parents who are attracted to *Fred* but who would also like to give their son a more distinctive variant. *Ulfred* means 'wolf peace' and its origins are Germanic.

ULRIC (pronounced 'ool + rick') This name can be either English or German in origin. The English name means 'wolf power' and the German name 'prosperity and power'.

ULYSSES (pronounced 'yool + iss + eez') is a Latin version of Greek Odysseus, who was one of the heroes of Homer's *Odyssey*, the epic that has recently been retold in poetry by the Nobel-winning poet, Derek Walcott. It is uncertain what the name means but it has the connotation of 'wanderer who eventually comes home'. Ulysses S Grant (1822-85) was President of the United States of America between 1869 and 1877.

UMBERTO is an Italian form of Germanic *Humbert*, a name meaning 'bright/famous warrior'. SEE Humbert

URBAN is from Latin *Urbanus*, 'from the city'. It was the name chosen by several popes, possibly because of the phrase *Urbi et*

Orbi, 'to the city [of Rome] and to the world'. This phrase is used in papal proclamations and blessings.

URI (pronounced 'you +ree') can be an abbreviated form of *Uriah* or *Uriel*. It is a Hebrew name and implies 'light'. It was popularised by Uri Geller, the entertainer who made spoon-bending fashionable television viewing in the 1970s.

URIAH is a Hebrew name meaning 'The Lord God is light'. It was the name of a Hittite officer in King David's army. Uriah had a beautiful wife called *Bathsheba*. David wanted to marry her but could only do so if Uriah were dead. He put Uriah at the head of his troops and Uriah was killed in battle.

URIEL is also a Hebrew name, possibly related to *Uriah*, meaning 'light' but also similar to *Ariel*, 'lion of the Lord God'. *Uriel* is the name of an archangel in John Milton's *Paradise Lost*, where he is described as 'regent of the sun'.

UZZIEL This name is only for connoisseurs of John Milton (1608-74). In *Paradise Lost*, *Uzziel* is described as next in power to the archangel *Gabriel*, who is especially honoured by Christians and Muslims.

NOTABLE NAMESAKES
Ulysses S Grant (1822-85) American general and the 18th president of the United States; Urban I was Pope between AD 222 and AD 230 when he was martyred for his beliefs; Umberto Eco (b. 1932) Italian philosopher and novelist; Uriah Heep is one of the most memorable characters in Charles Dickens' novel, *David Copperfield*.

V

VADIM (pronounced 'vad + eem') is often used as an abbreviated form of *Vladimir*, 'ruler'. SEE Vladimir

VAL is an abbreviated form of *Valentine*. SEE Valentine

VALENTINE is an English form of Latin *Valentinus*, which is based on Latin *valens*, 'strong, healthy'. According to tradition, St Valentine was a Christian priest in the 3rd century. He was executed by the Emperor Claudius for assisting other Christians. His name and his feast day of 14 February are associated with lovers. This tradition has almost certainly nothing to do with the saint. It was an old folk tradition that birds chose their mates on 14 February.

VALENTINO This is an Italian form of *Valentine* and a name that will always be linked to the Italian actor, Rudolph Valentino (1895-1926). He is often regarded as the quintessential screen lover and his sudden death at 31 almost ensured that his name would be immortalised.

VAN is used as a prefix in the Netherlands, more or less equivalent to 'de' in French. It means 'from' or 'of' and can be seen in such well-known names as Anthony van Dyck, Jan van Eyck or Vincent van Gogh. *Van* is now used as a given name. In addition to its Dutch origin, *Van* is widely used among the Vietnamese people. It means 'cloud' in Vietnamese.

VASILI(Y) (pronounced 'va + seal + ee') is a Russian form of *Basil*. It can also be spelt *Vassily*. SEE Basil

VASSILIOS (pronounced 'va + seal + ee + os') is a Greek form of *Basil*, meaning 'kingly'. SEE Basil

VAUGHAN is a widespread surname in Wales. It comes from *bychan*, 'small'. Occasionally it is spelt *Vaughn*.

VERNON can have two possible explanations. The first is that it was carried to the British Isles by people who came from one of the Norman towns called Vernon. These towns owe their names to alders and mean 'alder trees'. The second possibility is that it comes from Latin *vernus*, 'pertaining to spring'. It would be an acceptable choice for a spring baby.

VICTOR is a Latin word meaning 'conqueror, winner'. It has been popular as a given name for at least 2000 years and was chosen by early Christians to recognise the victory of Christ over sin and death. It occurs in most languages, the Italian form *Vittorio* being, perhaps, the most widely used.

VINCENT comes from Latin *vincens*, 'conquering, winning'. There are several saints of this name but the best known is St Vincent de Paul (1576-1660), who is renowned for his work among the poor and the underprivileged in Paris. According to one tradition, he was so moved by the plight of a convict that he took his place in the galley. The rowers in the galley ships of the time were either slaves or condemned criminals.

VIRGIL is the English form of the name of the Latin poet Publius Vergilius Maro (70–19 BC). The meaning of the poet's name is uncertain but it was linked to *virga*, 'a staff or rod'. Perhaps one of the most interesting bearers of the poet's name was an 8th-century Irish monk who became the Archbishop of Salzburg. In his case, *Virgil* was a latinised version of *Fergal*, 'man of valour'.

VITO (pronounced 'vee + toe') is from Latin *vita*, 'life', and is an Italian form of *Vitus*, the name of a child martyr who died about AD 300. St Vitus became the patron saint of people suffering from epilepsy, rabies or Sydenham's chorea, which used to be called St Vitus's Dance. It is also sometimes used as a shortened form of *Vittorio*.

VITTORIO is an Italian form of *Victor*, 'the conqueror'. SEE Victor

VIVIAN comes from an old Latin name, *Vivianus*, which is related to *vivus*, 'alive'. It was popular among the Normans. It began to be used for girls as early as the Middle Ages. In the Arthurian legend, the enchantress who trapped Merlin in a tower of air was called *Vivien*. The form ending in 'ian' is more likely to be used for boys, as is the form *Vyvyan*. There is no hard and fast rule, however. The final decision is with the parents.

VLADIMIR is very widely used in Eastern Europe and particularly in the Orthodox communities. It means 'peaceful rule/ruler'.

VYVYAN is a variant spelling of *Vivian*. SEE Vivian

NOTABLE NAMESAKES
Val Kilmer (b. 1959) American actor best-known, perhaps, for his role as Batman in *Batman Forever*, 1993; Van Morrison (b. 1945) Irish singer, musician and song writer; Vincent Van Gogh (1853-90) Dutch

post-Impressionist artist. His *Sunflowers* is one of the world's most easily recognised paintings.;Viv Richards (b. 1958) in Antigua is a retired cricketer. He is regarded as one of the best batsmen of all time; Vladimir Nabokov (1899-1972) Russian novelist and author of *Lolita* in 1955.

W

WADE is an example of a place name becoming a surname and then a given name. In Old English *wæd* meant 'ford' and many towns grew up around fords. It is possible, too, that *Wade* is a modern form of an Old English name, *Wadan*, which probably meant 'to travel with supernatural aid'.

WALDO is a Germanic name with the same root as *Walter*. It comes from *wald*, 'rule', and is

most popular in the United States.

WALLACE is one of many surnames based on the Old English word *wealh*, 'foreigner, Celt'. It is often thought of as an exclusively Scottish surname, partly because of William Wallace (c.1270-1305), who led a Scottish army to victory over the English at Stirling in 1297. The surname – or one of its many variants – is found in all parts of the British Isles. Variants of this name are *Wallis*, *Walsh*, *Welch* and *Welsh*. *Wally* used to be a popular abbreviation but it has lost ground since it developed the meaning of 'silly, stupid or incompetent person'.

WALLIS is a variant of *wealh*, 'foreigner, Welsh'. It has been less widely used as a boy's name since Wallis Simpson, the Duchess of Windsor (1896-1986) popularised it for girls. SEE Wallace

WALT is usually an abbreviation of *Walter*, but it began to be used as a name in its

381

own right because of the prominence of the poet Walt Whitman (1819-92) and the cartoon animator and film producer, Walt Disney (1902-66). His film *Snow White and the Seven Dwarfs* (1937) was the first full-length cartoon feature film with sound and colour and it is still a favourite.

WALTER has been a popular choice in the British Isles for a thousand years. It is a Germanic name involving the combination of *wald*, 'rule' + *here*, 'army, military group'. One of the most famous bearers of this name was Sir Walter Raleigh (c.1552-1618). He was a courtier, a poet and one of the greatest explorers of his time. He was eventually executed by James I, partly because James wanted to please the Spanish, whose New World possessions had been attacked by Raleigh, and partly because Raleigh's 1616 expedition to South America was a failure. Raleigh is given the credit for introducing both potatoes and tobacco to the people of the British Isles.

WARREN is a surname that has been used as a given name for several centuries. It has two possible origins. It may come from the Norman town *La Varenne*, meaning 'the game reserve', or it may be from a Germanic word *warin*, 'guard'. Indeed, the same surname could come from the different sources. Its recent popularity may owe something to the film actor Warren Beatty (b. 1937).

WARWICK is a place name that has become a surname and, more recently, a given name. There is a town in Cumberland called Warwick and it is the county capital of Warwickshire. The first syllable may come from Old English *waroþ*, 'bank of river' or *wering*, 'weir, dam', and the second is from *wic*, 'settlement'. In the 15th century, the Earl of Warwick (1428-71) was known as 'Warwick the Kingmaker' because, even when it meant changing sides, he unerringly backed the winner in the long-running War of the Roses. The form *Warrick* occurs in Australia.

WASHINGTON is a popular choice for boys in African American families. The choice is normally a mark of respect for George Washington (1732-99), the first president of the United States. The name comes from the town of Washington in Durham and this seems to mean 'the settlement of Wassa's people'.

WATSON For centuries, the pronunciation of *Walter* was identical with that of 'water'. The 'l' was not pronounced in a range of words, including 'walk' and 'talk'. The short form of *Walter* was thus *Wat*, as with Wat Tyler, who was murdered in 1381 after leading the successful 'Peasant's Revolt' against unfair taxes. *Watson* became a surname, meaning 'son of Walter', and, more recently, a given name. SEE Walter

WAYNE was originally a trade name for a 'carter' or 'cartwright'. It is the same word as 'wain' in 'haywain' and comes from Old English *wægen*, 'cart, waggon'. It is likely that the popularity of *Wayne* is due, in part at least, to the film actor, John Wayne (1907-82), whose name was actually Marion Michael Wayne. It is doubtful if John Wayne would have been as successful if he had insisted on being called Marion.

WESLEY was a surname based on one of the many English villages and towns called Westley, meaning 'western meadow'. The surname became prominent in the 18th century because of the charismatic preachers, John (1703-91) and Charles Wesley (1707-88). They are credited with spearheading the return-to-Christian-values movement that resulted in the foundation of Methodism. *Wesley* tends to be chosen by people of strong Christian beliefs but it is certainly not limited to Methodists. *Wes* is the usual abbreviation.

WILBERT It is probable that *Wilbert* and *Wilbur* were originally the same name but they have now become distinct. They both seem to have arisen from a

383

combination of *wilig*, 'willow' + *burh*, 'fortress town', implying 'fortress near willows'. The 'bert' ending is due to the influence of such popular names as *Albert* and *Robert*.

WILBUR is much more popular than *Wilbert*, but they have the same origin. SEE Wilbert

WILFRED/WILFRID

Some people argue that this name should end with 'frid', but the two spellings are equally widely used. A form of this name goes back at least fourteen centuries in England. It comes from *wil*, 'desire, longing' + *frið*, 'peace'. St Wilfrid (634-709) was a Northumbrian noble who was educated at Lindisfarne by Celtic Christians from Ireland and Iona. *Wilfrid* went to Rome to study and returned with a preference for Roman Christianity, which differed from the Celtic tradition in several ways, including the calculation of Easter. A synod was called at Whitby in 664 and the contingent led by *Wilfrid* won the debate and Roman practices

were installed in Whitby and, eventually, throughout England.

WILHELM (pronounced 'vill + helm') is the German equivalent of *William*. SEE William

WILLIAM has been one of the most popular names for boys for the last one thousand years. It was introduced to England by the Norman Conquest (1066), which was led by William, Duke of Normandy. It comes from a Germanic name which combines the elements of *wil*, 'desire, wish' + *helm*, 'helmet, protection' and implying 'protector'. It has generated the very popular abbreviations *Bill*, *Billy*, *Will* and *Willie*. It has been chosen as a name for kings, princes, dukes, barons, saints and ordinary men. It is also the given name of William Shakespeare (1564-1616), one of the greatest dramatists of all time.

WILSON is a surname meaning 'Will's son' and it has been extremely widely used as a given name, especially in the last 200 years.

WINDSOR was first adopted as a given name from a surname that was based on the town of Windsor in Berkshire. This town was originally *Windlesora* and may have meant 'landing place with a windlass'. 'Ora' is 'bank or landing place' and it is possible that a 'windlass' was built there to tie up boats. The name became more widely used when it was adopted as a surname by the British royal family in 1917 to replace the very German surname Saxe-Coburg-Gotha.

WINSTON has two possible origins. It may come from an Old English given name *Wynnstan*, which is made up of *wynn*, 'great joy' + *stan*, 'stone', or it may come from the surname that is derived from one of the towns called Winston. The towns are combinations of a given name, such as Wynn and *tun*, 'enclosure'. As early as the 17th century, *Winston* was used as a first name and it was given a boost in popularity by the British Prime Minister and war leader Winston Churchill (1874-1965).

WOLF(E) is occasionally used as a given name and it comes, as we can see, from 'wolf', the large canine, renowned for its strength, courage and willingness to hunt in packs. Many societies have named their children after animals that have admirable characteristics. This was the case, for example, of Native Americans. Anyone who knows about American history will have heard of the Sioux chief, Sitting Bull, who led his people in the fight to preserve their land and traditions. He defeated General Custer at the battle of Little Bighorn in Montana in 1876. The form with 'e' is generally taken from a surname that seems to have come to the British Isles with the Norman conquerors in the 11th century.

WOLFGANG is still found quite widely in German-speaking communities. It means 'wolf going' and suggests a wolf that will always move forward. It was the given name of Mozart (1756-91) and this link has contributed to its continued popularity.

WULFSTAN In Old English, *wulf* was the usual spelling for 'wolf' and this name meant 'wolf stone'. Bishop *Wulfstan* (1009-95) was the last of the Anglo-Saxon saints. He was a monk and later Bishop of Worcester. After the Norman Conquest of 1066, William I replaced most high-ranking Anglo-Saxon clerics with French ecclesiastics, but *Wulfstan* was an exception. It is not easy, even for a king, to replace a living saint!

WYNDHAM (pronounced 'wind + im') is a surname derived from the Leicestershire town of Wymondham, meaning 'Wigmund's farmstead'. The Normans who came from Wymondham referred to themselves as, for example, Robert de Wyndeham, but as they were anglicised the 'de' was dropped. The science fiction writer John Wyndham (1903-69), who wrote *The Day of the Triffids*, had *Wyndham* as one of his given names but he chose to use it as a surname as a writer.

WYNN There are several interpretations for this name. It may be from Old English *wine*, 'friend', or from Welsh *gwyn*, 'fair, handsome, holy'.

NOTABLE NAMESAKES
Walter Scott (1771-1832) Scottish novelist and poet. His historical novels, such as *Rob Roy* (1818) and *Ivanhoe* (1819) are still widely read and have been filmed many times; Wayne Rooney (b. 1985) English footballer who currently plays for Manchester United Football Club; Wilfred Owen (1893-1918) English poet who wrote about the futility of the war. He was killed in action one week before World War I ended; William III (1650-1702) Dutch prince who married the daughter of James II of England and took over the throne when James II's forces were defeated.

X

XAVIER has become a popular name largely because of St Francis Xavier (1506-52), the Spanish founder of the Jesuits. He was born in Xavier, Navarre, which had been an independent Basque kingdom. The Basque place name probably means 'new house'. St Francis Xavier was a missionary in several parts of Asia and is the patron saint of the missions. In English, the 'X' is usually pronounced like 'z' in 'zebra' and the 'av' rhymes with 'save'; but in Spanish, the 'X' is closer to 'h' and the 'av' rhymes with 'have'.

XENOS (pronounced 'zee + nos') is Greek and means 'stranger'. However, in traditional Greek culture, the stranger was honoured and the name continues to carry overtones of 'privileged stranger'.

XIMENES (pronounced 'zee + men + eyz') is a Greek form of *Simon*, meaning 'attentive, hearkening'. SEE Simon

XIMUN (pronounced 'he + moon') is a Basque form of *Simon*, meaning 'attentive, hearkening'. see Simon

NOTABLE NAMESAKES
Xavier Mertz (1883-1913) Swiss explorer who spent much of his time studying the Antarctic region; Ximenes was the pseudonym of Derrick Somerset Macnutt (1902-71) British crossword compiler; Ximenes De Cisneros (1436-1517) was a Spanish Cardinal and Statesman. He produced a polyglot version of the Bible.

YASIR/YASSER/YASSIR

is an Arabic name meaning 'soft'. Yasir Arafat (1929-2004) was the leader of the Palestinian people. He was awarded the Nobel

Peace prize in 1994. The name has a variety of spellings and the second syllable is pronounced either like the 'er' in 'father' or the 'eer' in 'engineer'.

YEHUDI is a Hebrew name meaning 'May the Lord be praised'. It is widely known because of the eminence of Yehudi Menuhin (1916-99), the violinist.

YESTIN is a Welsh name meaning 'fair, just'.

YEVGENI/YEVGENY (pronounced 'yev + gen + ee') is a Russian form of *Eugene*, meaning 'noble, well-born'. SEE Eugene

YIORGOS is a modern Greek form of *George* and means 'farmer, earth-worker'. SEE George

YORICK appears in *Hamlet*, not as a living character but as a dead jester who reminds Prince Hamlet of the transience of all life. The name is unusual. It may be that *Yorick* was Shakespeare's approximation to *Jorck*, the Danish form of *George*, which probably means 'farmer'. On the other hand, it may be a representation of *York*, which occurs as a surname and means either 'yew tree settlement' or 'place where boars are found.' SEE George

YORK is a surname that has begun to be employed as a given name. It comes from the city of York, which has a long history of occupation. Its meaning was originally linked to the yew tree but, as pronunciation changed at the time of the Viking occupation, it was thought to mean 'boar country'.

YUKI (pronounced 'yew + key') is a Japanese name with the two meanings of 'good luck' and 'snow'.

YUL This name was popularised by Yul Brynner (1915-85), the film star who played the lead role in *The King and I*. So many stories were told about him that it is not always easy to sort out the facts from the fiction. It seems probable, however, that he was born in Russia and was called *Yul* after a paternal grandfather with the name of *Jules*. This is a French form of *Julius*, which was an ancient Roman family name. SEE Julius

YURI This name became imprinted on the world in 1961 because a young Russian cosmonaut called Yuri Gagarin (1934-68) was the first human being to travel in space. *Yuri* is a pet Russian form of *George*, 'farmer, earth-worker'. Gagarin died on a flight-training exercise and was reputed to have stayed with his plane until it crashed so that the plane would avoid a school. SEE George

YUSUF is the Arabic and Turkish form of *Joseph*, a name of Hebrew origin meaning 'God shall add'. SEE Joseph

YVES (pronounced 'eve') The Bretons who accompanied the Normans introduced the name into Britain. Today, it is most frequently used by French speakers. It is said to be of Germanic origin, coming from

iwa, 'yew' although it may have been reinforced by Old English *ifig*, 'ivy'. In view of its occurrence in Ireland and Brittany, it is also possible that it is a modified Celtic name, related to Irish *iamh*, 'enclosure'. SEE Ives (GIRLS)

NOTABLE NAMESAKES
Yevgeny Yevtushenko (b. 1933) Russian poet who spoke out against the excesses of Stalinism; Yves Saint Laurent (b. 1936) Algerian-born fashion designer. His brand is now attached to a wide variety of items, including perfume and leather goods; Yusuf Islam (b. 1948) came to fame as Cat Stevens, musician, singer and songwriter. He converted to Islam in 1977.

ZACHAEUS Many of the 'Z'
names in English are Hebrew in
origin. *Zacchaeus*, sometimes
simplified to *Zacheus*, means
'pure'. It is usually pronounced
like 'zack + ee +us' and
shortened to *Zack* or *Zach*, also
pronounced to rhyme with 'Jack'.

**ZACHARIA(H)/
ZACHARIAS** Many Hebrew
names end in 'iah', including
Jeremiah and *Isaiah*. *Zachariah*
means 'The Lord God has
remembered'. This form is rarely
used in English, where *Zachary*
has been a favourite name for
centuries. The last king of Israel
was *Zachariah* and it was also the
name of John the Baptist's father.
He refused to believe that his
wife, Elizabeth, had conceived a
child in her old age and was struck
dumb as a consequence. He
regained his voice when his son
was born. *Zacharias* is an
alternative form that is
occasionally used. *Zechariah* also
appears, in the Old Testament, as

the name of a minor prophet. It
means 'God is renowned'.

ZACHARY is the most widely
used variant of this name. Just as
Jeremiah was simplified to *Jeremy*,
so *Zachariah* became *Zachary* in
English. SEE Zachariah

ZACK is a popular form of
Zachary. The spelling is based on
'Jack'. SEE Zachariah

ZAHIR is an Arabic name that
means 'resplendent'. It is
pronounced like 'Za + hear'.

ZANE is often said to be a form
of *John*, meaning 'God is
gracious', and this may well be
true, since *John* occurs in a wide
range of forms that include *Ivan*,
Johan and *Seán*. *Zane* does not
seem to occur before the 1920s
and that suggests that it may
have been inspired by Zane Grey
(1872-1939), the author of
extremely popular adventure
novels, mostly dealing with
cowboys. His name was actually
Pearl Zane Gray, Zane being his
mother's maiden name. One can
understand why he dropped
'Pearl' but it is less easy to

explain why he changed 'Gray' to 'Grey'. SEE John

ZEBEDEE is an anglicised form of Hebrew *Zebediah*. SEE Zebediah

ZEBEDIAH is a Hebrew name meaning 'gift of God'. In the Gospel of Matthew, it is the name of the fisherman father of the apostles James and John.

ZEKE is an extremely popular abbreviation of *Ezekiel*, meaning 'the strength of God'. It rhymes with 'peak'. SEE Ezekiel

NOTABLE NAMESAKES
Zachary Scott (1914-65) American film actor who chose to play the part of villains. He was a distant cousin of George Washington; Zebedee was the name of the Jack-in-the-box from the BBC children's programme, *The Magic Roundabout*; Zinedine Yazid Zidane (b. 1972) French footballer who captained the French national teams that won the 1998 FIFA World Cup and also Euro 2000; ZZ Hill (1935-84) African American blues singer.

NAMES FOR TWINS

Parents often feel a special need to indicate a close connection between twins. This is sometimes done by dressing them identically or by linking their names. The most frequent link is made by using alliteration:

BOYS	GIRLS	BOY and GIRL
Brandon and Brian	Caitlin and Chloe	Alex and Anna
Daniel and David	Ellie and Emily	Ethan and Elinor
James and Joshua	Jessica and Jordan	Jack and Jessica
Max and Michael	Madison and Mollie	Mason and Mia
Thomas and Tyler	Thomas and Tasmin	Ryan and Rebecca

Less often, the link may be the result of anagrams:

Adrian and Darian	Alice and Celia	Aidan and Diana
Brady and Darby	Carol and Coral	Dylan and Lynda
Leon and Noel	Marcel and Carmel	Jason and Sonja

Links of meaning also occur:

Brendan and Sara(h)	prince and princess
Colm and Jemima	both mean 'dove'
Dorothy and Theodora	both mean 'gift of God'
Kieran and Melanie	both suggest 'dark'
Thomas and Tamsin	both mean 'twin'

Links by historical or literary association:

Anthony and Cleo	*Anthony and Cleopatra*
Elizabeth and Darcy	*Pride and Prejudice*
Helen and Paris	*The Siege of Troy*

NAMES FOR TRIPLETS

The most frequent link is made by using alliteration:

Aaron, Ainsley and Erin
Hannah, Harvey and Harriet
Harry, Hayden and Hayley
Jack, Jacob and Jessica
Leo, Leah and Luke
Thomas, Toby and Tess

AVOID THE PITFALLS

When choosing the perfect name for your baby you should also give some thought as to how the name will sound when linked to your surname, or when initalised. Is it likely to lead to an unfortunate nickname?

The following checklist may help parents avoid some of the more common pitfalls:

➤ Check how the chosen name harmonises with the surname. Some people like rhyming names, such as Ronald McDonald or Sadie O'Grady. Others find them a source of amusement, and the bearer may suffer as a result.

➤ When the surname is a common one, such as Jones, it is worth considering an unusual given name. Inigo Jones (1573-1652), the architect, and his more modern namesake, Inigo Owen Jones (1872-1954), the Australian meteorologist, were given a first name that immediately individualised them. The same is true of Standish James O'Grady (1846-1928), the Irish writer and historian. But if you are choosing an unusual name, it is probably a good idea to give the child another one as well so that the child may, at a point in the future, choose the equivalent of James and Owen rather than Standish or Inigo.

➤ Check the initials and avoid those that make an unwanted word, for example:

➤ Brian Arthur Daly B.A.D.

➤ Olive Louise Dillon O.L.D.

➤ Wendy Edith Ellis W.E.E.

➤ Charles Arthur Dunne C.A.D.

➤ Occasionally a simple switch of names can help. Whereas: Robert

Alan Toner produces R.A.T., Alan Robert Toner gives the more attractive A.R.T.

➤ Check that the monosyllabic version of the given name goes well with the surname. Barry Teal sounds good but Baz Teal may be linked to 'Bastille'.

➤ Check that the children's names go well together, Sam and Ella are both popular but Sam 'n Ella sounds like 'salmonella'. Tom and Jerry are also attractive names, but the popularity of the cartoon characters means that parents might prefer to avoid them.

➤ Check that the initial sounds of the names cannot be switched to produce an unattractive alternative. Mary Helen could become Hairy Melon and Bertie Doyle would not want to become Dirty Boyle.

➤ Check that the given name will age well. A three-year-old Strawberry may seem attractive but will Strawberry like the name when she is eighteen or forty?

➤ Check that the names can be spoken easily. Judith Smith may be difficult for children to pronounce.

Also from Loreto Todd, the bestselling

CELTIC NAMES FOR CHILDREN

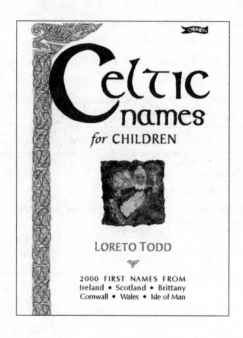

The definitive guide to Celtic Names – more than 2000
names from Ireland, Scotland, Brittany, Cornwall,
Wales and the Isle of Man.
Origins • meanings • Associated myths and stories